WEST BROM'S CULT HEROES

SIMON WRIGHT

Know The Score Books Limited

www.knowthescorebooks.com

KNOW THE SCORE BOOKS PUBLICATIONS

CULT HEROES	Author	ISBN
CHELSEA	Leo Moynihan	1-905449-00-3
NEWCASTLE	Dylan Younger	1-905449-03-8
SOUTHAMPTON	Jeremy Wilson	1-905449-01-1
WEST BROM	Simon Wright	1-905449-02-X

MATCH OF MY LIFE	Editor	ISBN
ENGLAND WORLD CUP	Massarella & Moynihan	1-905449-52-6
EUROPEAN CUP FINALS	Ben Lyttleton	1-905449-57-7
FA CUP FINALS (1953-1969)	David Saffer	1-905449-53-4
FULHAM	Michael Heatley	1-905449-51-8
LEEDS	David Saffer	1-905449-54-2
LIVERPOOL	Leo Moynihan	1-905449-50-X
SHEFFIELD UNITED	Nick Johnson	1-905449-62-3
STOKE CITY	Simon Lowe	1-905449-55-0
SUNDERLAND	Rob Mason	1-905449-60-7
SPURS	Allen & Massarella	1-905449-58-5
WOLVES	Simon Lowe	1-905449-56-9

HARRY HARRIS	Author	ISBN
WORLD CUP DIARY	Harry Harris	1-905449-90-9
HOLD THE BACK PAGE	Harry Harris	1-905449-91-7

AUTOBIOGRAPHY	Author	ISBN
TACKLES LIKE A FERRET (England Cover)	Paul Parker	1-905449-47-X
TACKLES LIKE A FERRET (Manchester United Cover)	Paul Parker	1-905449-46-1

FOOTBALL FICTION	Author	ISBN
BURKSEY The Autobiography of a Football God	Peter Morfoot	1-905449-49-6

CRICKET	Author	ISBN
MOML: THE ASHES	Pilger & Wightman	1-905449-63-1

FORTHCOMING PUBLICATIONS IN 2007

CULT HEROES	Author	ISBN
CELTIC	David Potter	978-1-905449-08-8
DERBY	David McVay	978-1-905449-06-4
MANCHESTER CITY	David Clayton	978-1-905449-05-7
RANGERS	Paul Smith	978-1-905449-07-1

MATCH OF MY LIFE	Editor	ISBN
BOLTON WANDERERS	David Saffer	978-1-905449-64-4
FA CUP FINALS (1970-1989)	David Saffer	978-1-905449-65-1
HULL	Grahame Lloyd	978-1-905449-66-8
MANCHESTER UNITED	Sam Pilger	978-1-905449-59-0

GENERAL FOOTBALL	Autor	ISBN
OUTCASTS The Lands FIFA Forgot	Steve Menary	978-1-905449-31-6
PARISH TO PLANET A History of Football	Dr Eric Midwinter	978-1-905449-30-9
MY PREMIERSHIP DIARY Reading's Season in the Premiership	Marcus Hahnemann	978-1-905449-33-0

PUB BORE: 1001 incredible facts to bore your mates with		ISBN
MANCHESTER UNITED		978-1-905449-80-4
NEWCASTLE UNITED		978-1-905449-81-1
SUNDERLAND		978-1-905449-82-8

CRICKET	Author	ISBN
THE 2006/7 ASHES IN PICTURES	Andrew Searle	978-1-905449-44-6
GROVEL! The 1976 West IndiesTour of England	David Tossell	978-1-905449-43-9
MY AUTOBIOGRAPHY	Shaun Udal	978-1-905449-42-2
SMILE LIKE U MEAN IT	Paul Smith	978-1-905449-45-3

WEST BROM'S

CULT HEROES

SIMON WRIGHT

Series Editor: Simon Lowe

www.knowthescorebooks.com

First published in the United Kingdom
by Know The Score Books Limited, 2006

First published in the United Kingdom
by Know The Score Books Limited, 2006

Know The Score Books Limited
118 Alcester Road
Studley, Warwickshire
B80 7NT
www.knowthescorebooks.com

A CIP catalogue record is available for this book from the British Library
ISBN-10: 1-905449-02-X
ISBN-13: 978-1-905449-02-6

Jacket and book design by Lisa David

Printed and bound in Great Britain by Cromwell Press, Trowbridge, Wiltshire

Photographs in this book are reproduced by kind permission of:
The Bache Foundation, EMPICS, Dave Hewitt, The Magee Family Archive, C. Edwin Vilade,
Barry Marsh, Laurie Rampling, Glynis Wright, Terry Wills

Jacket Photographs

Front cover

Left SuperBob Talyor is arguably the greatest Albion Cult heo of modern times

Centre All Hail The King! Jeff Astle celebrates yet another goal with his loyal subjects

Right Cyrille Regis won hearts and minds thanks to his legendary shooting on the run and
his charming smile whist attending numerous supporters' functions

Inset Inspirational goalscoring forwrd Ronnie Allen, whose vital penalty helped win the
1954 FA Cup Final for Albion

Rear cover

Left Darren 'Rig Dave' Moore celebrates clinching Albion's promotion to the Premiership in 2004

Right The Baggies' record goalscorer Tony Brown, as much a hero for his hairstyle as for
his goals

Author's Acknowledgements

Without the full-on help of so many of the extended Albion family, this book could not exist in such a detailed format. Albion historians Colin Mackenzie, Steve Carr and Kevin Powell were quite remarkable for their diligence and tolerance. Just how many times did you guys put me straight? There just weren't enough hours in the day for me to work for a living and live in a library, so coming to my aid were Steve Carr (again), my wife Glynis, Ian Thomas and Terry Wills, who never did quite master the microfiche. Making use of their specialist knowledge and pertinent memories were Steve Carr, Terry Wills (yes again!) and Norm Bartlam who wrote whole chapters and then endured the imposition of my writing style without (much) protest. Proofreading is a tedious, joyless process, so I'm indebted to wife Glynis (aka 'Queen Comma'), Steve Carr and Amanda Hume for their fortitude and endless corrections. Laurie Rampling, Barry Marsh, Dave Hewitt, Terry Wills and Glynis Wright were behind most of the illustrations used in this volume.

Literally thanks for the memories. So many kind people volunteered thoughts or rummaged amongst their records and yet hardly any of them needing his or her arms twisted. Among the gallant band were: Colin Simpson, Tim Joyner, Jon Aroussi, Merv Scobie, Chris Pascoe, Steve Sant, Gary Brookes, Mike Harrison, Peter Whitehouse, Ian Thomson, Dave Watkin, Alex Chapman, David Worton, Dave Morgan, Shay Dunne, David L. Paget, John Goddard, Keith Cotter, Tony Jones, Nell and Charlie Reynolds, Dennis Brennan, Rick Janowski, John Clegg, Josie and Des Garbett, Wendy and John Maxfield, Laraine Astle, Martin Lewis, Carly Lewis, John Woodward, Brian Maydew, Stuart Basson, Gerald Frost, The Royal Regiment of Fusiliers Museum, the South Wales Borderers Museum archivists, Chris Flanagan, Cyril Randle, Ian Thomson, Harold Salt, Richard Brentnall, Robert Plant, Peter George, Ray Matthews, Terry Box, Keith Cotter, Ben Payne, Frank Summers, (Super) Bobby Taylor, John Groarke, Mark Hitcox, Mark Pumphrey, Mick Brown, Andy Jenkins, Pete Smith, Ray Wilson, John Habberley, Ally Robertson, Ed Vilade, Janette Carlucci, James Vilade, Joe Mayo and Derek Kevan. Apologies and thanks to anyone who remains overlooked.

I mustn't forget Chris, Sam and their fellow patient librarians in Smethwick Local History section, who tolerated my fumbling efforts around their assorted microfiches. The cabaret was always interesting. I also made extensive use of the self-service facilities in Birmingham Central Library (the complete absence of staff was reason enough for my wife to believe I wasn't having an affair) and the personal archives of Terry Wills, Norman Bartlam and the Bache family.

And finally a big thank you to Adrian Goldberg for getting me the gig, publisher Simon Lowe for his support and my other half for just being there.

Simon Wright
August 2006

Contents

Introduction

> **"The crowd gives the leader new strength."**
>
> **Greek Philospher, Evenius**

"Give me twenty cult heroes, crowd favourites if you like, over the club's entire history", declared my Stoke-loving publisher, in itself a football supporting habit to put your teeth on edge. The Potters induce fist-waving memories of Mark Stein; and as for that wretched dirge 'Delilah'... But I digress. Note the two limiting factors in the request, particularly the time banding. For such a remarkable, ancient social organisation like WBA, boasting almost 130 years of existence, featuring every era signposts selections.

Then the second constriction, there can only be 20. A few were obvious – The King, SuperBob, Willie, Ossie, Big Cyrille, Bomber and Ronnie Allen. We can all agree on those names and isn't it significant that all bar Ossie were attackers? What does that say about our support? In addition, few could dispute the claims of Billy Bassett and Jesse 'Peerless' Pennington, legends passed down through generations of supporters. Beyond those names, another ten choices remained to fill in the remaining generation gaps.

I personally wanted my own favourites of Derek McInnes, Brian Jensen, Martyn Bennett and Gary Owen, but couldn't justify their inclusion even to myself, let alone anyone else. My original so-called short list bore a full 90 names, which meant I had to disappoint some of my would-be readers. The process of culling was painful. Bobby Hope was close to making the cut. So too Zoltan Gera. Jack Vernon and Jimmy Sanders were initially in and then out. Don Goodman was in and out four times. Remember for each hero in, someone was out.

As I canvassed opinion over a period of time I realised that Baggies fans really understood what I was getting at – Cult Heroes, those who excite us for so many more reasons other than simple footballing talent, not necessarily just great players. Interestingly there was no great enthusiasm to include Bryan Robson. Supporters old enough to remember his midfield pomp cannot completely get over his defection to Manchester United. Good for his career no doubt, but not for the football club that invested so much in him. Furthermore, his talents were somehow more taken for granted, rather than truly relished. That indefinable bond between player and supporter didn't exist.

The most unexpected inclusion is, of course, Harold Bache with only 14 games to his name. His nomination broke my self-imposed rule that all cult heroes must have played a significant number of games. World War One was hardly Harold's fault. I can only commend the reader to study the chapter to understand why this compelling character merits his place. As well as being unusual, it's also my favourite chapter. The endless slog of library microfiches becomes infinitely more tolerable when there is history to be rediscovered. Curiously, Harold's story never previously merited more than a few hundred words in any previous Albion publication. I'm convinced an imaginative film producer could make much of this potential script.

Other interesting characters from the past "dropped out" during the course of my research. I would love to feature Ted "Cock" Pheasant, Harry "Popeye" Jones, and the Reverend WC Jordan. Maybe next time?

My publisher championed the claims of John "Baldy" Reynolds, but anyone who played deliberately badly to engineer a move to Aston Villa cannot be allowed to rub pages with real Albion greatness.

Judging by all those who offered suggestions, pleas and criticisms, the most requested player who missed the cut was Laurie Cunningham. Great entertainer that he was, Laurie didn't, for me anyway, have the off-field charisma essential for all modern day cult heroes. Similarly, the inclusion of Lee Hughes will not please a section of potential readership. In response, I say, try to concentrate on the good times, when all our hopes were pinned on him, when he had virtually everything we ever hoped for – when he was us, out there banging in the goals for the Baggies. We'll never see his likes again.

No doubt there will be many other names tossed up by heated debate over who is the greatest Cult Hero of them all. That is a question I have not set out to answer, merely to explore the bond between these heroes and us, the supporters who help make them what they are. Each chapter seeks to understand why individuals became a favourite, set against the context of their career. These are warts and all features, freely covering disputes and off-field peccadilloes; aspects which saccharine-filled 'official' accounts either ignore or gloss over.

I've always said footballers are more than distant figures on a pitch; they're human, with human frailties and weaknesses. Within reason, I believe this more inclusive and honest approach, rather than diminishes, enhances the status of our favourites.

Simon Wright
August 2006

Foreword

I saw Albion for the first time at Leicester on 30th September 1964. I didn't know I was going until my Jeff signed his contract three hours before the match, and I didn't know anything then about West Bromwich, other than somebody said they are called 'the Throstles.

I went into that tall, tall stand at Filbert Street. I'd never seen anything like it. I thought I was going to fall off, but I reckoned I'd better get used to it, and do my bit, so I shouted, "Come on you Throstles" over and over. Then somebody told me that nobody ever uses that word! From then on, I thought, "Right, Laraine. You need to find out about West Bromwich." And I had to really quickly because me, Jeff and little Dorice were living there.

It didn't take me long to find out that Albion supporters really love their centre-forwards. My Jeff, Tony Brown, of course, and before him Ronnie Allen – they love their goalscorers, their heroes. Later years brought the talents of people like Cyrille Regis to the Hawthorns and supporters again appreciated their efforts, their goals. And always there was the rule that if players gave everything and didn't cheat them, the fans would always love them for it, and that applies to this very day. If one of them does something supporters like, even just by taking the time and trouble to talk with them before games, not coming the "Great I Am" all the time, like some do, suddenly, in their eyes, they're not just players any more, they're respected, treasured, cherished even, and for some, that love and respect lasts far longer than the time they finally hang up their boots. Whatever the occasion, whenever they're seen turning up at The Hawthorns for some important game or other, so respected are they, they're literally mobbed, just as my Jeff was when he was alive.

And that I suppose is hero worship.

And it's not just older supporters, either; the younger ones know all about the older players simply because their own dads and mums have wonderful memories and want to share them with their own children and grandchildren as well.

On top of looking at recent Albion men, this book is also a lovely way of making sure that the next generation of Albion supporters get to understand the past efforts of all those players long since gone, whose names, whose very souls, even, would otherwise remain buried in old newspapers.

After forty years, I reckon I know lots about the Baggies, but I know even more about their wonderful, loyal, respectful and friendly supporters, and this book is mostly aimed at them. I once heard Captain Graham Williams (he'll always be the Captain to me and my Jeff) say: "you're not supporters, you're friends." I couldn't have put it better myself.

Laraine Astle
July 2006

Dedication

This book is dedicated to Chris Hartle,
taken away for higher duties at the age of 43

He taught me about space

BOB ROBERTS

1879-1890
1891-1892

BAGGIES CAREER

Games	400+
Goals	2
Caps	3

MAGIC MOMENT

Flattening a Small Heath pitch-invading hooligan in the 1886 FA Cup semi-final

'THE PRINCE OF GOALKEEPERS'

IN the beginning, there was Long Bob. And a very young club called West Bromwich Albion, who rose spectacularly from being just another team playing on the wide-open spaces of Dartmouth Park to FA Cup winners in just seven years. Here was pure synergy, with man and club feeding off each other.

Most sources concur that Robert John Roberts was born in April 1859 in West Bromwich. Thus at 20, he was in the prime of his youth when a completely new football team needed players in 1879. Robert had previously played for West Bromwich Strollers as early as November 1878, and prior to that may also have played for his school – Christ Church. As well as players, the new team needed funds and sensibly enough would-be players were asked to pay a subscription of sixpence (around 3p) to get the club going. Bob Roberts is said to have been the first to hand his money over. Such is the stuff that legends are made of.

The Albion team was new, the game was really still in its infancy, and local newspapers took little notice of the sport. Despatching a reporter to a game was completely out of the question, and the only way a club might – and it was only 'might' – see any reference to their deeds in the local press was if a club official took the trouble to compile their own report and send it in.

Few players had a single position at that time, as not only team formations, but sometimes, even team numbers, varied. So it doesn't come as any great surprise that Bob played in different positions in different games – mainly full-back or half-back (midfield), or even up front, according to the reports that featured most of the twenty games that WBA participated in during that inaugural season. There's enough evidence to suggest he was probably not a regular performer. Neither is there any record of him playing in the famous friendly against Black Lake Victoria on 13th December 1879, a game, which for many years, was believed to be Albion's first ever game, but is now known to be their sixth.

Details are inevitably sketchy. Those match reports which did appear were limited to a very brief description of the play, a name drop for players who'd performed well, and occasionally, goal scorers might be listed. Roberts was never mentioned for any meritorious performances, but was noted as scoring for Albion in a 3-0 victory over Smethwick Holy Trinity on 28th February 1880.

Clumsy Big Bob just wasn't cutting the mustard. Someone summed up his outfield contribution thus: "As a forward he was useless, and as a half-back, or back, he could stop a man, but invariably missed the ball." It's entirely realistic to imagine him drifting away to try his luck elsewhere, had not persons unknown come up with the idea of giving him a go as a goalkeeper.

Curiously, this was the one position in the side that had a sitting tenant. Sam Biddleston always protected Albion's goal. And then one day he didn't. 18th December 1880, against a team from Wednesbury, sees an account of Bob Roberts appearing in goal for Albion for the first time. Quite what prompted the change for Biddleston is not completely clear. Certainly he never played for WBA again. At some point, Sam emigrated to North America, so perhaps the one factor prompted the other.

...yond the classic schoolboy reason of going between the bare posts (no goal nets until
...because he wasn't any good anywhere else, Bob's height and weight were distinct advan-
...s. Barging the goalkeeper, whether he had the ball or not, was a legitimate tactic of the time.
...o was a very big lad. Depending on which source is trusted, he was between 6' 1" & 6' 4" tall;
...r a variety of reasons, people in the 1880s were far smaller than today, and such height made
...im a comparative giant. The few team pictures that survive show Bob standing several inches
above his tallest team-mate. Even today, 6' 4" would make him one of the Baggies' tallest-ever
men. Add his weight (accounts vary between 12 and 14 stone) and you had a goalkeeper with the
solidity of the proverbial brick outhouse. Yet despite his physique, he was remarkably agile, had a
cool temperament, and a kindly good nature – all the attributes of a gentle giant.

His debut as a custodian was not a happy one. Albion suffered what may well have been
their only defeat that season, going down 0-2 to Wednesbury Royal George. However, despite
this setback, and possibly the odd mutter of, "Can he actually play anywhere?" the match
reports that are available suggest he retained his position right to the season's end.

Other than his build, Roberts was unusual in his choice of occupation. In its early days, the
team was comprised entirely of local men, many of them working for spring manufacturer
George Salter & Co, one of the town's largest employers. The strong links between club and
company were to be maintained for several decades to come, not just players, but stewards
and gatekeepers, too. Roberts, however, was a journeyman plasterer, a trade learned from his
widowed father James, with whom he lived at 31 Queen Street, virtually in West Bromwich's
town centre. With five children to support, life could not have been easy for Roberts Senior.

The rise of the fledgling club became noteworthy in their third season, when Albion battled
their way into the Birmingham Cup semi-final. At this time, the Birmingham Cup was the biggest
game in town. Reaching the last four equalled the achievement of West Bromwich Dartmouth,
previously the town's biggest club, who were already by this time on a downward slope. The
Dartmouth decided to concentrate on cricket, leaving the town's footballing baton with Albion.
Indeed, Dartmouth offered the newcomers the chance to use their enclosed ground during the
football season.

WBA's upward momentum continued. Twelve months later, they set their cap at two
competitions. In the Birmingham Cup, defeating Coseley and Wolves (4-2) gave them a semi-
final place against Wednesbury Old Athletic. Once again, they were bested in a closely-fought
2-1 defeat, "exceptionally brilliant" custodial work by Roberts keeping Albion in the fight. His
reputation was building, and there were suggestions that he was worth a trial to play for the
District. Most of all, he was noticed by his own supporters. The *West Bromwich Free Press*
recorded that, "Roberts received continued applause for the splendid defence he exhibited."
The Athlete was impressed with both custodians that day: "The feature was the excellence of
the keeping of the goalkeepers of both sides. They were both kept busy, and both warded off
some difficult shots, and both exhibited a skill, coolness and judgement rarely found."

Meanwhile, in the Staffordshire Cup, the Albion would not be denied their first trophy, and in
the second round, they knocked out Birmingham Cup holders Aston Villa. This was the first-ever
meeting between the two clubs, prompting both sets of supporters to greet each other cordially
with lumps of turf and stones. Once again, Roberts was catching the eye: "The play of Roberts in
goal was superb," commented *The Free Press*, following Albion's unexpected success in a
replay. Two more such victories gave them a place in the Staffordshire Cup Final, at Stoke.

The Albion team travelled to the Potteries on 21st April 1883 by train, with team and supporters mixed together. However, nobody had thought of how the players would get from station to ground, so presumably, they walked. Not ideal preparation, and so it was no great surprise that the weary visitors were pressed back by a rampant Potteries side; Bob was kept busy – too busy – trying to shut Stoke out. As one correspondent from *The Athlete* had it, "several rattling shots were sent spinning away by Roberts" before Stoke inevitably took the lead. Stung by the goal, Albion fought back bravely to score twice, only for the home side to equalise by the interval. With 15 minutes remaining, George Bell put the Albion ahead again, and although City pressed in the closing stages, West Bromwich held on for a famous 3-2 victory. *The Athlete's* correspondent chipped in: "Roberts may take a lot of credit for the win by his fine keeping," was his post-match verdict.

Long Bob was soon creating firsts of his own: come October 1883, he became the first Albion player to take part in a representative fixture, turning out for Probables v Improbables, a trial match to select a Birmingham FA team for the then popular inter-association games. "Roberts, in goal, was a veritable wonder, and I should think, at the present time, he is undoubtedly the best man for the position in the district," commented *The Athlete*.

Sure enough, Bob featured in Birmingham's 4-1 victory over Sheffield, in which "the feature of the match was the grand goal keeping of Roberts," according to *The Athlete*, whilst the *Birmingham Gazette* added, "had it not been for the magnificent form displayed by Roberts in goal, they (Sheffield) must have scored at least a couple more points." His performance was so good that he received special congratulations from the President of the association.

The following year, such was the goalkeeper's cult status that dozens, possibly even hundreds, of Albion followers deserted their side's match against Walsall Swifts to give the popular custodian backing at the Aston Lower Grounds, where he was playing for Birmingham v Glasgow. A few weeks earlier, Bob had really endeared himself to the club's followers by declining an offer from Preston Zingari to sign for them (at a time when professionalism had not yet been legalised). Indeed, this was just one of several attempts by other clubs to lure away 'The Prince Of Goalkeepers'. This was the downside of West Bromwich Albion playing clubs further and further afield, notably in embryonic footballing-hotbed Lancashire, following their Staffordshire Cup triumph. Roberts was hot property, but his loyalty endeared him further to Albion fans.

Bob was to represent Birmingham several times in the years to come, against Sheffield, Glasgow, Nottinghamshire and London. In the latter game, the *Gazette* commented "Roberts' services.....were called into requisition.....and by some judicious play, maintained his reputation as an accomplished goalkeeper......each time the ball eluded the vigilance of the backs, Roberts, with a coolness seldom seen between the posts, averted the shots."

He was also later selected for the annual Players v Gentlemen fixture, one of the top events of the social calendar, played at Kennington Oval in the presence of HRH The Prince Of Wales. Reputedly, HRH was so struck by the feats of the big goalkeeper, he repeatedly cried, "Well done, Bob." Such was his reputation locally and nationally that the goalkeeper was much in demand over the years. He played a part in least two international trials (and had to turn down others due to injury), and even once played for his county, Staffordshire, against Lancashire.

IN BOB'S DAY, goalkeepers occasionally wandered upfield when they were bored, generally when particularly hapless opponents were unable to mount any attacks worth mentioning. Not for Bob the rather mundane method of scoring via a freak long-range clearance (stories about him scoring from a long punt in the FA Cup v Derby Junction appear on close inspection to be incorrect). No, no – he wanted a real goal, and managed at least two, possibly three. The first came in a 15-0 Birmingham Cup victory over Bloxwich in November 1884, one source even suggesting he found the net twice.

His other 'proper' goal followed much later as part of a 23-0 massacre of Burton Wanderers in the Staffordshire Cup, Bob happily playing in midfield for much of the game. A Wanderers breakaway was highly unlikely because they only entered Albion's half to kick off after each goal. *The Free Press* reported, "Considerable amusement was caused by Roberts heading the ball and running up amongst the spectators, some of whom called out and invited him to have a drink." Just before he dribbled past a Burton player to register Albion's 19th goal, one shot from Bob hit a post. Burton clearly didn't heed the warning.

Content with his contribution, Bob then got back among the backs. Incidentally, an invitation to 'have a drink' was not such an outrageous one in that era: much like Victorian sailors with their daily rum issues, and Black Country chain-makers in nearby Netherton, Albion players had an official beer allowance. One newspaper described the scene: "There is something very amusing in the way in which the allowance of beer to each thirsty Throstle is doled out by the trainer, any attempt at further amounts being sternly put down."

Although club records for goalscoring are incomplete, it's likely that Bob remains the only WBA goalkeeper to score in open play. Penalty kicks were not introduced until Bob's day was nearly done, so there was little or no opportunity for the giant footballer to put his spectacular weight behind such a golden scoring opportunity.

Bob's club side continued to make progress, again putting Villa in their place in an FA Cup replay in 1885. During the course of their first meeting, " the first half was noticeable for the remarkable fine goal keeping of Roberts," as Albion escaped from enemy territory with a goalless draw. In the re-match, Bob had a rare rush of blood to the head. A Villa forward kicked him, so he kicked him back: the severity of the impact upon the opponent is not recorded, sadly. The visitors were given a free kick and the matter was forgotten. Cup holders Blackburn Rovers eventually ended Albion's run at the quarter-final stage: with home advantage, the Staffordshire side fancied their chances until Roberts cried off with rheumatics. Rovers scored twice, and the feeling abounded that Big Bob would have stopped both goals.

Villa took a measure of revenge by inflicting heavy defeat in the Birmingham Charity Cup, though, as *The Athlete* reported, "Roberts defended his charge in his best style, he saved many times in a most marvellous manner, and those shots that passed him were such that no (other) keeper could have stopped under the same circumstances."

For a young club to reach the last eight of the national FA competition was impressive enough, but, ever the pioneers, Albion wanted more and the following season, went all the way to the Cup Final, a first not just for them, but also for any Midlands side. Admittedly, five home draws and a bye aided their cause, but the path was not that straightforward. The Old Carthusians, for instance, were defeated by a single goal in Round Five, with no little thanks to West Brom's giant goalkeeper, as *The Athlete* noted: "Roberts had not a lot to do. He kept out several beauties, but two called for special mention, so smartly did he act when the goal seemed lost."

THE FA CUP run handed Roberts another opportunity to lay claim to being the first cult hero amongst Albion players. The Baggies beat Small Heath – latterly Birmingham City – 4-0 in the semi-final. During the game, a group of Birmingham youths invaded the pitch, surrounding and attacking the West Brom players. Unabashed, Long Bob laid out one hooligan caught sneaking up behind him, and presumably deterred anyone else from being so rash. As officials, supported by Police, tried to clear the pitch, the hooligan gang made for the exit, but as they did, by way of a 'leaving present', they hurled every available missile at parked vehicles. Hooliganism, apparently, is nothing new.

West Bromwich found themselves once more up against their conquerors from the previous year, powerful Blackburn Rovers, at the Oval. The Lancashire side had won the Cup in both the last two years, and were going for a hat trick, with a side largely unchanged in those three years. This was a stiff task for the Staffordshire rookies, but they were well supported, and actually came close to an upset: "Roberts had not a great deal to do in goal, but he played in his best style, and generally repelled all shots, and some were extremely difficult," wrote one correspondent as Albion's last line of defence gave them a secure base from which to attack. And attack they did, but their forwards froze in front of goal, and the game finished goalless, mighty Rovers subsequently feeling the need to make excuses about their players rushing their lunch in order to explain away their sudden, but perceptible lapse in form.

In the replay, at Derby: "Roberts defended his charge in capital style and repelled three or four shots that would have undoubtedly beaten a less trustworthy custodian'" But even with Bob giving everything, Rovers won 2-0. Albion's best chance had come and gone in London.

Albion at least lifted the Birmingham Cup for the first time, beating Walsall Swifts in a replay. In the re-match, a local correspondent enthused how Roberts: "was in his best form, and as he was kept pretty busy all through, he often saved shots and repelled attacks few goal keepers could have successfully met." Remarkably, big Bob turned provider, with a mighty long throw just before half time, from which George Woodhall scored. It was Albion's first shot on goal. Other than a short spell in the second half, the West Bromwich side needed to defend, often grimly, to hang onto their single goal lead.

Albion also went on to secure the Staffordshire Cup, but that was an old challenge. Albion now had bigger ambitions, they'd been so close to the FA Cup, and, having but briefly tasted the tempting fruit hanging on the vine, they wanted more.

And more they had next season. Four opponents were defeated before the Albion team travelled on a regular train service to Notts County in February 1887 for a quarter-final tie. Or rather most of the team did. Long Bob, not for the first time and, as befits such an outstanding man, was doing things somewhat differently. Being a keeper, and therefore eccentric in nature – even in those early days they enjoyed a certain 'reputation' – he elected to travel on the excursion train instead, which then arrived an hour late. Remarkably, the Notts County captain, Cursham, agreed to delay the kick-off until Long Bob finally arrived on foot, after sprinting from the station in his white jersey, full-length white trousers and a pair of hob-nail boots, an unusual sight which must have prompted at least some of the locals to wonder whether or not the local asylum had just lost one of its patients. Sadly, the reaction of passers-by to this giant man pounding the Nottingham streets in a tearing hurry is not recorded. More pertinently, neither are comments from his concerned team-mates. Cursham may well have bitterly regretted his generosity, Albion going 3-1 up before his side could build up any sort of attacking momentum. When they did, the tardy custodian blocked their way. "Notts improved and again and again attacked, giving Roberts no end of chances to sustain his reputation. This he nobly did."

If West Bromwich were to reach the Final, they needed to overcome the might of Preston North End, that era's answer to modern-day Chelsea, in the semi-final at Nottingham. But trains once again so nearly undid Bob. This time, he missed one completely, and was obliged to take a later one, so when the players took to the field, Roberts was nowhere to be seen. Then, with the game about to start, the crowd behind the goal dramatically parted, and there was the missing goalkeeper. Wearing his football gear, his modesty protected by a long overcoat, he leapt over the ropes and took his place in front of the goal as if his absence had never occurred. His dramatic late arrival didn't appear to disrupt his concentration unduly.

"Roberts' goal keeping was magnificent," enthused *The Athlete*, "and contributed largely to the victory of the Albion. Long Bob was kept busy, and did his work magnificently." Albion equalised an early Preston goal, then added two more of their own while the Lancashire club were unable to find any way past Roberts. It was a magnificent display from the custodian, one that made his name nationally.

Their Cup Final opponents at the Oval were fierce rivals Aston Villa. On the day, in front of 15,000 spectators, Albion looked the better side – until their opponents changed their tactics and made better use of the wings. From then on, the Birmingham side were on top. Then came disaster: believing winger Dennis Hodgetts to be well offside, Long Bob made no attempt to stop his goalbound shot, even though he could have done so easily. The goal stood, much to his embarrassment. *The Athlete* offered scant consolation: "No blame can be attached to Roberts, who had more to do than Warner (the Villa keeper) and did it right well – his reputation as a goal keeper was rather enhanced than damaged by his splendid goal keeping on Saturday."

Once ahead, Villa increased the pressure and "the goal-keeping of Roberts was now seen at its best; he saved several times miraculously." Villa captain Archie Hunter completed the scoring in the 88th minute when he ran at Roberts with the ball, the subsequent sickening collision leaving both men prostrate on the turf, but Hunter was just able (or conscious?) enough to poke the ball over the line with his foot. The defeat deeply shocked supporters far more used to winning: when the weary Albion party finally reached West Bromwich (admittedly at 4.00am on Sunday morning), there was absolutely no-one there to meet them.

BOB ROBERTS had thus far been denied the kudos of being a cup-winner, but by way of compensation, he quickly found himself able to proudly describe himself as Bob Roberts, England International. In January, he'd taken part in an international trial (North v South) at Kennington Oval, in itself a milestone for any West Bromwich Albion man. Thanks to his astonishing display in the FA Cup semi-final against Preston, widely regarded as the finest of his career, his England call-up was sealed. The 'Prince of Goal keepers' made his international debut against the Scots in March 1887, and was also reserve for the Wales game. Bob became the first Albion player to represent his country and was so proud of his achievement he wore his cap in every game he played thereafter. "Roberts kept goal well and fairly earned his cap – some of his saves were really brilliant – he was not the cause of losing, and he was awfully hampered by the backs" commented *The Athlete*, Two more caps were to follow in the next few years, both against Ireland.

In 1888, Albion reached the FA Cup final for the third season in succession, a 2-0 third round victory over Wolves achieved after Roberts had kept Albion on level terms at half-time. In the semi-final versus Derby Junction, Roberts, along with full-backs Aldridge and Green, kept Albion level before West Brom could bang in three goals. There was high praise from the *Free Press* "...two of the shots were the finest shots that ever a custodian had to manipulate, and few men but Roberts could have dealt with them as he did."

In the Final, Albion were predictably underdogs against proud Preston North End, as they had been when the two sides met in the semi-final a season earlier. But this was an Albion side victorious in over 80% of their games that term, a team now boasting talented newcomers like Billy Bassett in their ranks. The meeting of two such fine teams created much interest, and for the first time ever in the competition's history, the gates were closed before kick-off, with 17,000 crammed inside the Oval.

Preston pressed early and: "for twenty minutes or so, Roberts & co had no end of work to do." The Midlanders hit back strongly, though, and eventually took the lead. Stung, North End rallied, equalised, and then laid siege to the West Bromwich goal. The Midlanders defended stoutly: "shots from their forwards were returned by Roberts, whose goal keeping was most remarkable," wrote the correspondent for the *Times*. The man from the *Standard* added, "Roberts' goal keeping was brilliant all through the game." While Roberts was keeping Preston out at one end, Bassett was worrying the Lancastrians at the other end, his perfect cross setting up Woodhall to strike the decisive goal. Albion had won the FA Cup at last. Referee Major Marindin, who doubled up as trophy presenter, praised the "indomitable pluck and perseverance" of the Midlanders.

Albion also played in the Birmingham & Staffs Cup Finals, making it the third year running they'd featured in the finals of all three of the main cup competitions entered. In this final pre-League season, such progress maintained the club's income, and arguably more importantly, acted as a powerful homing beacon for talented local players. The Birmingham Cup was lost 3-2 to Villa, but that game was also notable for some rare criticism of Albion's ever popular keeper. Harsh words for such an outstanding player were almost unknown, and stemmed from the big custodian's habit of frequently appealing to the referee rather than listening for the whistle. It's likely that this lack of concentration may have contributed to Villa's first goal.

The Staffordshire Cup proved something of a marathon. Stoke were despatched 1-0 in the semi-final, with no little thanks to their last line of defence, who were "kept uncomfortably busy." The Final against Wolves needed three games. After a goalless first encounter, the *Free Press* reported: "Roberts defended his charge admirably," in a 1-1 draw after extra time in the second game, whilst, in the third and final game, "Roberts was not to be beaten, the spectators loudly applauding his brilliant and lightning-like save." However, Bob's efforts weren't enough, and the Wanderers eventually won the day.

1888/89 BROUGHT WITH IT the formation of the Football League: unsurprisingly, being such a powerful footballing force and current Cup holders, Albion were founder members. Although the League would quickly gain in importance, its initial impact was not great, with some clubs outside its auspices attracting larger attendances. Bob Roberts played in every League game that first season, despite some laments that his form was now deserting him and deputy Joe Reader deserved his chance to shine. The League was done and dusted by the end of February, with Preston the runaway champions, while West Bromwich finished in sixth spot. Come the draw for the last four of the FA Cup, the newly-crowned League Champions ended up facing Albion – the third such meeting of the two in the Cup in consecutive seasons. Despite Roberts "effecting brilliant saves", North End won by a single goal and went on to clinch the Double.

In October 1889, the goal keeper displayed his rebellious streak when he participated in an unofficial match at Walsall; not surprisingly, the FA were distinctly unamused. They suspended Roberts for four matches, three of which were the League fixtures against Villa, Bolton and Derby.

West Brom were now encountering something of a lean patch, a whole twelve months elapsing without winning any silverware. They came closest in the Staffordshire Senior Cup, reaching the Final, though they were fortunate to do so. It appears most likely that in April 1890, Bob had an accident at a hotel when he fell down a flight of stairs. His body was heavily bandaged into a rigid position that did not allow him to bend at all. This small handicap didn't prevent him playing against semi-final opponents Walsall Town Swifts, who were unaware of his difficulties until too late. With Long Bob displaying the kind of superhuman powers with which all Cult Heroes are blessed, Albion won 2-1.

TO WIN NOTHING was disappointing in itself, but nowhere near as shocking as the news that Bob Roberts was leaving! In May 1890, instead of accepting club terms for the new season, Bob told Councillor Heckis, Chairman of the Albion committee, that he'd had a better offer from Sunderland Albion.

Imitation Albion badly wanted to be top dog in the North-Eastern coastal town, and with rivals Sunderland freshly elected to the League elite, the other Sunderland side felt a need to push the boat out. Their formal offer to the big keeper was 50 shillings (£2.50) per match, plus a summer job that would guarantee him £2 per week. In addition, there was also the offer of a public house (Roberts was the licensee at The Three Horse Shoes Inn on High Street, West Bromwich, at the time). These terms, highly generous for the period, were far in excess of what Albion could offer. Naturally, the money was tempting, but moving from the Black Country and leaving behind the club that he'd done so much to build, was a wrench. The clinching factor, though, proved to be his sisters' relocation to the North East.

West Bromwich Albion were furious, and set up a sub-committee to "consider what action could be taken against Roberts for his infringement of contract". In practical terms, the answer was actually nothing at all. The keeper was out of contract, and had signed the deal with Sunderland before Councillor Heelis could even raise the matter with the full WBA Committee.

The *Free Press* newspaper summed up supporters' stunned reaction to the news: "The history of Bob Roberts is the history of the Albion club and vice-versa, and most people regard his severance from the club as about the least likely event that could happen. Whether he has taken a wise step only time can show, but it is about the most formidable blow the Albion could have received. It is no easy thing for Roberts to leave the club he put the first sixpence in to form, and possibly he wishes now he could undo what has been done."

No sooner had he signed the contract, Roberts was having doubts about the move. Once located in the North East, he quickly became homesick: worse, his wife was now unwell, and thus he was quickly exploring ways of getting back home. He tried to focus on his football instead, being an ever present in league fixtures, and his efforts helped Sunderland Albion finish runners-up in the Football Alliance, which later became adopted as the Second Division of the

Football League. Bob even collected more representative honours, appearing in the Football Alliance v Football League fixture at Sheffield. However, Sunderland Albion received virtually no support in its bid to follow Sunderland into the Football League, and within a year had folded.

IN THE MEANTIME, on 2nd March 1891, Roberts returned to Stoney Lane to play in a benefit match for Charlie Perry, and made it very clear then that he wanted to come back to West Bromwich. And indeed he did, returning to his native Black Country to play in the Final of the West Bromwich Charity Cup for WBA v Wednesbury Old Athletic in May 1891. Probably to the disgruntlement of keeper Joe Reader, Roberts was immediately given his place back in Albion's first team goal for the 1891/92 season. The new season started in fine style, Albion crushing the reigning champions, Everton, 4-0 at Stoney Lane, The *Free Press* commenting: "Roberts was always on the alert, playing a specially meritorious game.'"

Unfortunately, Albion's form then dipped, taking only two points from ten games in October and November, during a spell when Roberts and Reader shared the goalkeeping duties. Initially Bob's form was good, but he was playing under the strain of knowing his wife was seriously ill, and his form quickly deteriorated. She died in October 1891, after just three years of marriage. Bob understandably missed games following his wife's death; he was then suspended for a week after failing to follow committee instructions in a game at Sunderland, before finally being dropped because his form was just not good enough. Such was his loss of heart and form that he even played badly for the reserves.

Reader was restored to the side permanently in late November, and league form recovered to some extent, though not enough for Albion to avoid the ignominy of having to apply for re-election. Despite this, Albion went on to win the FA Cup again, beating the Villa 3-0 in what proved to be the last final played at Kennington Oval. Roberts missed this and only earned a recall to the side when Reader was absent, playing for the Football League against the Scottish League.

Even then, Bob wasn't himself in the 2-2 draw with Stoke City (April 1892), and *The Free Press* admitted "it was only due to the very poor display of Roberts between the uprights that The Throstles did not win, both the goals he let through being soft ones."

At 33, his skills apparently deserting him, the end was imminent. Bob had played around 400 senior games with WBA all-told, and this was a wretched way for a genuine West Brom original to end a fine career.

Even sadder was his decision to sign for Aston Villa the following term.

EVEN THOUGH surviving archives permit us no more than teasing hints about the personality of Albion's first significant goalkeeper, I like to perceive Bob as an 19th century Brian Jensen, a local version of the gentle Dane, though lacking the dehabilitating effects of the kind of 'condor' moments which so blighted Jensen's career. Roberts was a giant-sized inspiration to a generation of Black Country folk, a living embodiment of a superb Albion side, much in the way that would-be young black players were inspired by Cyrille almost a century later. After Bob, size mattered in West Bromwich and with so many subsequent crowd favourites standing over six feet tall, it still matters today.

BILLY BASSETT

1886-1937

BAGGIES CAREER

Games	500+
Goals	150+
Caps	16

MAGIC MOMENT

Bassett's wing play won Albion the FA Cup in 1888, the club's first national trophy

'THE FLYING WINGER'

"In his playing days, he was more than a wizard, he was a phenomenon. We shall not in our lifetime see such natural ability, such superb ball control and such fantastic and fascinating dribbling as that which was displayed by William Isaiah Bassett."

Reverend WC Jordan (ex-Albion player)

THE Dartmouth Park Band played *See the Conquering Heroes Come* over and over again. The famous West Bromwich Albion team and the FA Cup were home, driving through the town in a four-horse carriage. The band played on and on until the early hours as thousands of supporters cheered their team. It was March 1888, and 19-year-old Billy Bassett had just made himself rather famous.

The Baggies had been rank outsiders to lift the Cup, even though this was their third straight appearance in the Final. Their opponents were Preston, "Proud Preston", who just a season later would combine an FA Cup win with the first ever League Championship. The mighty Preston, who, even before that first ever 'double' triumph, were genuinely thought to be invincible after 43 straight wins, who took their pick of the best Scottish footballers, who'd scored 50 goals just reaching the Final... against 11 lads from in or around West Bromwich who each received ten shillings (50p) 'expenses' a week.

Legend has it the Preston players were so confident of success they asked for permission to be photographed with the Cup before the game. Referee Major Mandarin angrily denied the request. Mandarin was a traditionalist who had no truck with imported Scottish professionals.

Albion took a surprise lead in the Final, thanks to Bassett's approach play. He pounced on a poor clearance from the PNE keeper, sprinted down the right flank and crossed perfectly for Jem Bayliss to score from close range. Another effort hit a post shortly after the interval. His speed off the mark, and astuteness in spotting an opening, often bewildered his adversaries and, although Preston equalised soon after the interval, it was Billy who again made his mark, creating an opening for Woodhall, whose shot was turned onto a post by Bayliss.

Perhaps inevitably, it was Bassett who provided the match-winning pass for Woodhall to score the goal that brought the Cup to the Black Country for the first time. The *Free Press* reported "...the little one, after the first ten minutes, played with a confidence and skill which was perfectly astonishing. The way at which he went at his big opponents was most laughable. Go where they would be, he was ever dodging round their heels and repeatedly foiled them. Once, two of the giants went at him together and both he and they came to earth. With the nimbleness of a cricket, however, he was up and off with the ball before his big opponents could gather themselves together, much to the amusement of the spectators. He showed no vestige of fear, but went at his bulky opponents just as though they had been schoolboys and he a giant."

Had the young winger never played another game, his status and popularity would have been permanently guaranteed. He was selected to represent England against Ireland in Belfast a fortnight later. Accompanied by Albion team mates Bob Roberts and Albert Aldridge, England won 5-1.

And there were more trophies to chase. Having won the 'English' Cup, Albion were invited to meet the Scottish Cup winners, Renton, for the Championship of the United Kingdom in May. With football yet to become established outside of the British Isles, this was also a play off for the title of 'World Champions'. Bassett and Woodhall came closest to giving Albion the lead before Renton went ahead against the run of play. An early second half goal put Albion on level terms before a three goal burst on a bog of a pitch left the Scots clear winners. Never again would West Bromwich come so close to being the best team in the world!

FAR FROM BEING the meaningless competitions of today, the local Cups were the be-all and end-all for football clubs in pre-League days. Thus West Bromwich badly wanted to win the Staffordshire Cup to go with the FA Cup. Unfortunately, so did Wolves who eventually triumphed 2-1 in a second replay. In the first replay at Stoke, "Bassett and Woodhall only rarely did anything worthy of their reputation." In the first replay at Stoney Lane, Bassett and Woodhall "put in occasional good shots, but they did not play at all well together and were not nearly as conspicuous or as effective as usual. Indeed there was much quarrelling between this wing and the centre." Bassett had formed a formidable partnership with his inside-right, George "Spry" Woodhall, though not before Woodhall, in a 19th century example of dolly flying out of pram, refused to pass to Bassett because he resented the youngster being considered a better player than him.

Bassett, at just five foot six and weighing barely ten stone, depended entirely upon speed and skill to defeat burly opponents in what was a far more physical game than today; a game lacking bodily or financial protection against injury. Not only was he a fast runner, but also he could run with the ball, knew exactly when to centre and could place the ball in the goalmouth with uncanny accuracy. One of his favourite ploys, where space permitted, was to flick the ball past his marker, keeping the ball in play whilst he ran outside the pitch. Another trick was to cut in diagonally towards goal, rather than the traditional heading for the corner flag. He was also adept at stopping suddenly when in full flight, and back-heeling the ball to a colleague.

Thus Billy was Albion's first ever flying winger, an idyllic genre that has fascinated Baggies fans ever since. The nearest modern Albion counterparts are perhaps Willie Johnston and Laurie Cunningham, though neither really matched the role filled by Bassett. In that period, the sole job of the winger was to get past the opposing half-back. Few got the better of Bassett. He was at his best on the big occasion, which was great news for country, (for whom he supposedly never had a bad game), but not always so helpful for his club. Certainly the larger pitches at the Kennington Oval and Crystal Palace would have afforded him much more space than Albion's notoriously cramped Stoney Lane enclosure. In Billy's own words "I always disliked a narrow ground."

WILLIAM BASSETT, or Billy as he was universally known, was one of six children born to Charles and Rebecca Bassett. His father was a colliery agent and the family lived at 48 Overend Street, near West Bromwich town centre.

The first recorded mention of young Billy came when he represented Christ Church school at the age of just nine, amongst lads a couple of years older. As Bassett admitted much later "I had the reputation of being rather a slippery youth, and continued to play in these school games until I left school." The school adjoined the Four Acres ground used by the West Bromwich Dartmouth Cricket & Football Club (and later WBA), and Bassett would have been amongst the spectators at the games of the Dartmouth, then the town's top football club, a position usurped by the Albion as the 1880s progressed.

At the age of 14 "and a little wisp of a chap", Billy featured prominently for another local club, Oak Villa, where the average age was 18. "Finding enough pocket money to defray expenses for away matches" was a continual problem for him.

Conditions were basic, as the man himself explained. "I remember walking to Hamstead Hall, four miles from West Bromwich in a blinding snowstorm, and then finding no dressing room accommodation whatsoever. We had to get under the biggest tree we could find. There we undressed and got into our football attire, leaving one of our faithful camp followers to mind our clothes. When we went for them at the end of the match, we found them frozen stiff."

It was with another junior side, West Bromwich Strollers, that Bassett was spotted when playing in two local cup finals, and invited to join West Bromwich Albion, having appeared in a trial for the Albion earlier that season. Not that Billy needed much encouragement. "It is difficult for anyone accurately to convey the idea of reverence which every Black Country lad had for 'The Throstles' in those days." Bassett was just 17 when he joined the club in March 1886. Initially, he played in the 3rd XI, but by the start of the following campaign he had already progressed to the reserve team.

Once the 1887 FA Cup Final was out of the way, young Billy was given his chance in the first team challenge matches, making his debut against Third Lanark, one of the top Scottish clubs of those times. The crowd of 5,000 saw Albion win 3 1, Bassett featuring prominently with his crossing and shooting. A month later, he made the first of several appearances against Albion's biggest rivals, Aston Villa, whilst on 28th May he registered his first senior goal in a 2-0 win against Bolton Wanderers.

Billy began the 1887/88 season in the first XI. Even before the season started, he was described as "a clever and fast player, and is destined to become a conspicuous figure in the football world. His only drawback is his height, but for that his activity will more than make up." His early appearances for the first team were at inside-right (a support role to the centre-forward), as George Woodhall was already established on the wing, though these positions were ultimately reversed.

BACK THEN there were only Cups, no League. Success in the various local knockout competitions paved the way for meetings with successful clubs from other counties, as did the FA Cup that also became increasingly popular as the 1880s progressed. It was a risky existence, for just one defeat meant the end of the interest in that particular competition for another year, and paved the way for other clubs from within your town or neighbourhood to grab the public's attention. Consequently the success of West Bromwich Albion in reaching the Final of all three major cup competitions (Birmingham, Staffordshire and FA Cup) in the 1885/86 season was a major achievement.

Although winning the Birmingham and Staffs Cup competitions was a cause for much celebration, the FA Cup Final was lost to Blackburn Rovers, who thus won the trophy for the third consecutive season, a feat never since matched. A year later, Albion again reached all three cup finals, this time winning just the Staffs Cup. It was a grand achievement for young Billy Bassett to break into the team and keep his place in such a famous side.

Concern was expressed in some quarters that Billy lacked the physical strength considered necessary to compete at this level, but the doubters were to be proven wrong. This he did to such effect that Albion reached all three cup finals yet again, and at the third attempt, won the FA Cup at last. But prior to that, Bassett's first cup final appearance for the Albion came in the 1888 Birmingham Senior Cup against the Villa before 12,000 spectators at the Aston Lower Grounds. He exhibited some superb passing, the Albion coming from behind twice, with Bassett's pass leading to the second equaliser, before losing to a late goal.

WBA were about as successful as any club could wish to be. There was never any doubt that any new League of football clubs must include such a well-known progressive outfit. And so it came to pass – Albion became one of the invited dozen founder members.

Their League form was never great despite the little winger's best efforts. He was joint leading scorer for Albion, averaging a goal in every second league game, in that first season of league football. Bassett was a member of the historic team who played at Stoke in the first ever League fixture and indeed, his centre set up Woodhall for the clinching goal in a 2-0 win.

INEVITABLY, Bassett became a marked man in league, cup and friendlies that term. In the 1889 Staffs Cup Final against Leek, the *Leek Times* reported that "Smethurst stuck to little Bassett, whose international cap didn't frighten him, like a leech." Nevertheless, a Bassett shot was rushed through to give his side the lead, Albion eventually lifting the cup courtesy of a 2-0 victory.

The following season, with the League still just another competition, Albion were pleased to reach the Final of the Birmingham Senior Cup, but this time the enormous silver trophy eluded them as Villa won 2-0. The *Free Press* reporter claimed that "Bassett and Bayliss did not get on. Bassett made more effort than his colleague, but neither greatly exerted themselves." Albion put in a poor display. The *Birmingham Gazette* reporter saw things differently, claiming that "the feature of the match was the really grand exhibition of Clarkson (the Villa half-back) whose display was a revelation. He had both Bassett and Bayliss against him, but time after time beat them both. It must have been a new experience to Bassett to be so persistently taken down."

Bassett was Albion's highest paid player, albeit earning just £3 per week. Even that modest amount represented a spectacular increase compared to those 10 shillings expenses! Other clubs were always keen to sign him, as "Half Back", writing in the *Free Press* in March 1889 noted. "Rumour is busy concerning Bassett and quite a multitude of stories, some possessed of quite a grain of truth, but most of them surrounded with bushels of its opposite, one being told as to the fine opportunities which he has been offered."

There was more. "If I were in his place, it would require an offer surpassing fine to induce me to leave West Bromwich. To take a position elsewhere, purely for football, would be about the most absurd thing he could do, and he would not be the man I take him for if he did so. At present, he is among friends, and has a good berth with everything in his favour, and the wise course is to look very curiously before making any leap in the dark."

Despite the reporter's exhortations, some offers must have tempted the footballer such as the £200 per season proffered by Everton. When rejecting these temptations, it's easy to imagine Bassett expecting at least some appreciation back from his club. But from his perspective, he didn't always get it.

In October 1891, Bassett had a disagreement with club officials. The Albion team were staying in the Shaftesbury Hotel in London. Billy was chatting to several friends who had called in to see him. At 10.30pm, a club official told him to go to bed. The little winger reacted angrily, refusing to leave his friends and considered the order to be insulting. Bassett was summoned before the Board days later where he asked for a transfer. Rumours suggested Arsenal had made him a better offer. The Board declined to release Bassett and the wide player had no choice other than to accept their decision as final.

This was not the attacker's first transfer request, according to the *Birmingham Post*, who reported Bassett wanted to move to Molineux in the summer of 1891, but once again Albion's rulers gave him the thumbs down. Apparently, some sort of sweetener was offered to the player to ensure he remained, either a testimonial or a non-playing position at the club.

Two years later, the directors apparently needed a reminder, for Billy refused to sign his contract unless their promise was honoured. He was dissatisfied with the offer of a Monday afternoon match, because of the small attendance, holding out for a Saturday afternoon benefit fixture. He didn't get it and so reluctantly put pen to paper on the Tuesday before the season started. Fortunately, his benefit match against Sheffield Wednesday on Monday 27th November pulled in one of the highest gates of the season.

After falling at the semi-final stage two years out of the previous three, West Bromwich reached the 1892 FA Cup Final, after finally overcoming Nottingham Forest in a twice-replayed semi-final. Bassett scored in two of those ties. Their opposition in the last Cup Final at the Oval was once again Aston Villa, who were apparently as arrogant as Preston in their belief that they would triumph. According to their supporters, "it was a sheer waste of time and money for Albion to travel down to London. "

BUT ALBION HAD Billy Bassett. The winger again rose to the big occasion, setting up Albion's first two goals, the first after just four minutes when his speed took him beyond the Villa defence, and Geddes turned in his cross. Inside half an hour, another Bassett run finished with Nicholls doubling Albion's lead. Though the then chocolate and blues dominated in terms of possession, they had no answer to Bassett's speed, and the accuracy of his crosses.

Less than a fortnight after winning the Cup at the Oval, barely one thousand supporters turned up at Stoney Lane for the visit of hapless Darwen. With over 13 weeks since the last home League game, perhaps supporters might have forgotten about the competition. Albion were 5-0 up by half-time, with Bassett's goal the pick of the bunch as he dribbled past four opponents. So bad were Darwen that Albion's Captain urged his defenders to come forward too and the goals feast continued. Bassett completed his hat-trick, and Sam Nicholls scored his side's twelfth goal in the last minute, when he thumped both ball and goalkeeper in the net. The 12-0 win still stands as the highest margin of victory in the top flight of English League football. Barely three weeks later, the return match finished 1-1. This was not a good League season for WBA. By finishing in the bottom four, Albion should have been obliged to apply for re-election, but were excused the inconvenience because they'd won the FA Cup!

Hat-tricks were rare for the winger during his playing days, even with his cutting-in technique, although both he and Roddy McLeod obliged in a then league record 8-0 away victory at Molineux in December 1893. "It is doubtful whether he ever played a better game," reported the *Free Press*. Best of all was the six notched in one game a few years earlier, as Albion ran riot in a Staffordshire Cup game v Burton Wanderers, winning 23-0!

IN AN ERA long before the advent of blank weekends to accommodate international matches, cancellations to accommodate international call-ups, and international caps being handed out like sweeties, Albion fans could take great pride in Bassett's performances for England, even though these often deprived the club of his much needed services. Billy netted his first international goal in his first appearance against Scotland in 1889, opening the scoring from long range in the game at the Kennington Oval. However, despite leading 2-0 at one stage, England were beaten 3-2. There was some consolation as "Bassett was the brightest particular star of the forward division, and if each of the English representatives had performed as brilliantly as he, Scotland would not have been in the majority at the finish!"

In the 1891 game against Ireland at Molineux, Billy notched England's fifth goal in a 6-1 victory and "gave his best display of the season", whilst a month later against Scotland, Bassett did not disgrace himself, but was deprived of service on the right wing.

The legendary England centre-forward GO Smith said: "Though rather on the small side, Bassett was no easy man to move, and the way in which he could travel over the ground was marvellous. Taking rather short strides, he was down the wing like a flash, and it took a very fast back to even keep up with him. His merits as a player were by no means confined to his speed, as you see in so many cases, he could pass well, and neatly, and was a delightful partner, but almost every requirement of his was, to my mind, overshadowed by his power of middling. He could centre the ball from every position, sometimes seemingly over his head, and rarely did the ball go where it was not intended...as a player in his position, then, Bassett stands first. Scotland must have had enough of him, as he gained innumerable caps against that country."

A year later, he featured in a brilliant English display at Ibrox Park as England opened up a 4-0 lead inside 25 minutes; eventually winning 4-1, whilst in 1893 came probably his finest display in an England shirt. "Bassett's runs were pretty generally considered to be the feature of the match" said the *Chronicle*, reporting on Billy laying on a stream of accurate crosses as England won 5-2. Billy was one of three players to have featured in what was England's third consecutive victory over the Scots, and was awarded a special international cap in recognition of this. In the following year's fixture at Celtic Park before a crowd of 30,000, Bassett was England's saviour. Three minutes from time, Bassett went off on one of his well-known electric runs, and from his cross former Albion colleague Jack "Baldy" Reynolds equalised. "Bassett worthily upheld his reputation in this game."

In 1895/96, for the first time, Bassett appeared for England in all three of that season's internationals. These included a record 9-1 trouncing of Wales in Cardiff, with Bassett's partner, Derby County's Black Country-born Steve Bloomer, notching a record five goals. With football relatively unknown outside the British Isles, there were only three international games played each season, and with Ireland and Wales providing such weak opposition, it was not uncommon for fixtures against these two countries to be fulfilled on the same day, with two different XI's being selected. This would naturally reduce the total number of appearances Bassett could make for his country.

For the match against Ireland at Belfast, the England team sailed to Larne for a night's rest before the game, but Bassett had a particularly unpleasant trip and felt very ill on arrival in Ireland. A motherly old Irish woman took pity on him, saying: "And shure it's only the cold I'll have to be taking out of ye." She then put Billy's feet in hot mustard and hot water, gave him a mysterious concoction to drink, rolled him in blankets and vowed that if the cold had not gone by the morning she would "eat her ould grandfather that's been dead these forty years." In the morning Billy, as promised, was revitalised, and he played a full part in his country's 2-0 victory.

The true measure of his worth is that this was the eighth consecutive season that Bassett had appeared in the annual fixture against Scotland. His international career ended with a total of 16 appearances and 7 goals, but nowadays it is not unreasonable to suggest that he could have clocked anything in the region of 80 – 100 appearances for England.

What proved to be Bassett's final representative honours came when he played for the Football League against the Irish League in November 1896. He and his partner Steve Bloomer of Derby played, and the pair turned it on against the Irish. Once they ran half the length of the field, passing to each other, until an Irish full-back was heard to cry "oh, let the beggars have the ball." He was actually selected to represent England against Ireland the following February, but had to withdraw through injury, and lost his place to his great rival Charles Athersmith, whom Bassett had kept out of the England side for so long. With Villa on the verge of achieving the cup & league double, and Albion in decline, it was perhaps inevitable that Athersmith would get the chance to establish himself in the England team at Bassett's expense.

ALBION CONTINUED to chase silverware. Nothing less was expected from such a major club. There was a bizarre conclusion to the 1894 Birmingham Senior Cup Final against Wolves. On the pitch, Bassett was again prominent, breaking away down the wing and centring for Bastock to give Albion the lead after just eight minutes. Just before the interval, it was Bassett again, evading both Swift and Kinsey, carrying the ball half the length of the field, and scoring himself to give Albion a 2-0 half time lead. In between times, however, Albion had lost a player through injury and, in these days before the advent of substitutions, were consigned to play the rest of the game a man short. Wolves pulled a goal back, but with 15 minutes remaining Bassett again made his mark, sending Norman clear to set up a third goal scored by Geddes.

However, the extra man eventually told for the Wolves and the game finished 3-3. In the confusion that followed, the players left the field, despite the fact that extra time should have been played. Albion were naturally reluctant to play another half hour with such an obvious hand-icap, whilst Wolves were reluctant to take up the suggestion of no less an authority than Charles Crump, the President of the Birmingham Football Association, that the rules should be bent to allow Albion to field a substitute. In the meantime, the Albion team had got changed and one of the players had even gone home! Eventually, the cup was shared for six months each.

There were two personal firsts for the West Bromwich winger that year. On 28th April, during a friendly with Millwall, he became the first Albion player ever to be sent from the field of play for using 'unparliamentary' language to the referee. Presumably his ability and loyalty saved him from severe punishment. At the end of the same year, he underlined his national popularity by winning the Silver Cup offered by the *Answers* journal, having been voted by its readers as being the best player in the country – the equivalent of the modern Player of the Year award. He romped home with nearly 2,000 votes more than the runner-up, Jimmy Crabtree, of Burnley.

Albion met Villa in the FA Cup Final again in 1895 for the third time in nine seasons (not until Arsenal met Newcastle in 1998 did any two other clubs meet in the Final for a third time). Possibly the fastest goal in Cup Final history ultimately won the day for Villa, but Bassett played one of the greatest games of his life, taking advantage of the open spaces of the Crystal Palace ground. He seemed at times to be taking on the Villa defenders almost single-handedly, but all too often, he was lacking in support and was crowded off the ball. Nevertheless, he created a host of openings for his colleagues, and came closest to equalising himself with a shot against the bar. A then world record attendance at a football match of 42,652 was present at this game.

TWO DAYS LATER, the club's future was in the balance, with Albion looking set to take part in the 'Test Matches' that then determined promotion and relegation. Bottom of the table, and needing victory by five clear goals to avoid the lottery, Albion rose to the occasion to thump Sheffield Wednesday 6-0, with Bassett creating the first five goals. Cometh the hour, cometh the man.

The season then finished on a high note a week later, with victory at Villa's expense in the replayed Birmingham Cup Final, Bassett yet again proving to be a thorn in Villa's side by creating an opening early on for Hutchinson to score what proved to be the only goal of the game.

Little more success was to come Albion's way during Bassett's time as a player. The 1892 FA Cup winners were unable to add the Birmingham Cup to their list of honours, losing 2-5 to Wolves in the Final, as if to emphasise the fact that one man can never make a team. Likewise, a below-par Bassett was unable to stop Albion losing to Second Division Port Vale in the 1898 Staffs Cup Final. This proved to be his last cup final appearance for the club, for in 1899 he retired.

By now cup success was starting to elude Albion, and the club were struggling in the league also. Bassett was no longer enjoying his football and, not wanting to live on his reputation, announced his retirement at the end of the season at the relatively young age of 30. Sadly, his last league appearance was a quite awful defeat; 1-7 to the Villa.

BILLY BASSETT'S retirement as a player didn't bring to an end his association with the club. Indeed, this was just the beginning. Bassett, whose playing performances alone merited Cult Hero status, went on to serve the club for over 50 years.

In 1900, Albion moved to its new home at The Hawthorns, but, following Bassett's retirement as a player, the club's fortunes declined further. Relegation followed in 1901, and although the Second Division championship was won at the first attempt, a second relegation followed in 1904 and there was no easy way back. In late 1906, the *Sports Argus* lamented mournfully, "Since the days of Bassett, WBA have not had an outside-right whose occupation of the position has given complete satisfaction. A good many players have essayed to fill his shoes, but the fact has to be mournfully recorded that not a single one has succeeded to any memorable degree. The one and only William retains his unapproachable standard as far as the Albion are concerned. One is almost inclined to think that the International's wonderful wing play has, to some extent, rendered the followers of the club a little less appreciative of the merits of other outside-rights."

Meanwhile, Bassett followed the traditional retired footballers' route by joining the licensing trade. He then took over at The Dartmouth Hotel in 1906 and stayed there until retiring in 1920 (It was perhaps not surprising that another ex-Albion player, Harry Clements, replaced Bassett as licensee!) In addition, he became a director of three companies, which included the Imperial Picture Palace in West Bromwich. He also took up golf, becoming captain of Sandwell Park, and acted as a Football League linesman. He became a member of the Board Of Management of the West Bromwich & District General Hospital and in 1935 became a Justice of the Peace.

HIS BUSINESS ACUMEN came to the rescue of his former club when, in March 1905, with the club facing extinction, Bassett became part of a new board of directors and persuaded creditors to defer their claims for a period in two years. Being a particularly popular local figure, Bassett enjoyed huge credibility. In 1908, he became club chairman and rarely missed a board meeting between 1905 and 1932. In 1910, with Albion still in the Second Division, a directors meeting was called to decide whether or not the club should be wound up. These were difficult times. A bank official once felt it necessary to track the Chairman down to a local golf course in order to sign a guarantee for the players' wages that week. Only Bassett of all the directors attended the meeting, but dismissed closure immediately and enlisted the help of like-minded individuals who, along with himself, gave personal guarantees to ensure the club's survival, and paved the way for promotion a year later. At the time, the Chairman admitted he "had been connected with the club for 26 years, and this was one of the happiest days of his life."

Every morning of the week, he could be found keeping a watchful eye on the players training and on match days his advice was often invaluable. His popularity with succeeding generations of players was enormous, being particularly kind and helpful to the club's youngsters.

Albion's greatest ever achievement, the winning of the League Championship, came about in 1920, whilst the runners-up spot was attained in 1925, and, although another relegation followed in 1927, the unique double of being FA Cup winners and achieving promotion followed four years later. Indeed, Bassett led the team out at Wembley before the 1931 FA Cup Final victory, the club's first such success since Bassett's days as a player.

Bassett's health had not been good since August 1932 when, while travelling to Arsenal, he became so ill that he had to stop doing anything for six months. He recovered, but his heart was now much weaker. Since then he had recurrent attacks of increasing intensity. The players' well-meaning gesture at the post-match dinner after defeat in the1935 FA Cup Final to hoist their popular Chairman on their shoulders in the middle of the dance floor and sing "He's a jolly good fellow" probably wasn't a great idea. Billy had to resign from the committee of Sandwell Park golf club in early 1936 due to ill health, but was well enough to receive a silver casket and an illuminated scroll at West Brom's AGM in 1936, in recognition of his 50 years' service to the club.

However, on 8th April 1937, Billy had a heart attack in bed and, despite receiving oxygen, passed away. His death came just two days before Albion met Preston in the FA Cup semi-final at Highbury. Bassett was a member of the FA Council, who insisted on a two minute silence with accompaniment from a full military band. The Albion players were thus not in the right frame of mind for such a vital game. The match kicked off before the scheduled start, and Albion were a goal down before 3 o'clock, then three down inside half-an-hour, eventually losing 4-1.

Thousands lined the streets for Bassett's funeral the following Monday, along the three mile route from his home in Beeches Road, West Bromwich to the internment at All Saints church. Floral tributes, filling several cars and a lorry, were received from virtually every professional club in the land, whilst the list of mourners read like a Who's Who of past and present Albion players, football officials and other local organisations.

An obituary in the *Albion News* described Bassett as "guide, philosopher and friend to the club", whilst another in the *Midland Chronicle* described him as "the finest outside right the game had known." Fred Howarth, secretary of the Football League, described him as 'the most popular man in the game'.

No man did more for West Bromwich Albion than William Isaiah Bassett.

JESSE PENNINGTON

'PEERLESS'

1903-1922

BAGGIES CAREER

Games	495
Goals	0
Caps	25

MAGIC MOMENT

Refusing to bring down his opponent illegally in the 1912 FA Cup Final replay. Thus Albion conceded the winning goal, but kept their ethics, reputation and sportsmanship intact

AT the age of 38 years and 256 days, Jesse Pennington captained the Albion side against Liverpool on 6th May 1922. He was Albion's oldest ever player and the normal rules of ageing just didn't seem to apply to him.

Only three months earlier, "Linesman", writing in the *Sporting Mail* confessed "last week, writing of Jesse Pennington, who by the way has no greater admirer, I suggested he should be rested more often because Anno Domini could not be forever denied. Pennington must have anticipated this suggestion, for the very day these lines appeared, he played one of the greatest games of his life, and Anno Domini seemed as far off as, say, ten years ago. Though the writer still holds to his opinion, Pennington, however, refuses to be rested when he can play, though he often played under conditions that could hardly help but be harmful to him. In a great game against Huddersfield, he was the outstanding figure. His kicking, tackling, judgment, and above all, his marvellous anticipation of what his opponents would do were simply amazing and until the end he maintained a remarkable speed. After Saturday, comments on Pennington's age seem out of place."

Liverpool was Jesse's final competitive match. That evening, his doctor rang and asked him to visit. Although the medical man was an Albion supporter, he felt duty bound to tell Jesse that he believed he was now struggling. Jesse thought he had at least one more season. The club had retained his services and he'd even accepted the captaincy of the West Bromwich Dartmouth cricket club Second XI. Before re-commencing football training, he was "given a very stiff examination" by a doctor who also took x-rays. The results were depressing. "Jesse, you have an enlarged heart and a duodenal ulcer. No more football for you." A 19-year one-club career was at an end.

JESSE PENNINGTON was born at 45 Maria Street, West Bromwich on 23 August 1883, no more than a mile from Albion's eventual home. His father, William Henry Jesse, was a puddler, a heavy job in either the iron or steel industry. His mother was Mary Ann Pennington. In keeping with the fashion of the time, the family doctor delivered the new arrival at home. Jesse's practitioner in attendance was Dr Isaac Pitt. Next door lived Miss Clara Smith, sister of Albion Secretary Eph Smith, later to be the bride of Secretary Fred Everiss. As Jesse said himself, Albion was always going to be his destiny. Defending seemed to be the family's destiny with his brother also becoming a back, as an integral part of the all-conquering 4th Dragoon Guards football team in South Africa in 1907.

As a boy, Jesse supported Albion, walking the three miles from the now family residence in Pope Lane, Smethwick to the Baggie's home at Stoney Lane. A hole in the perimeter wall enabled him to get in without paying.

Playing, rather than watching, soon claimed the Black Country lad. At the age of 16, he was turning out for Smethwick Centaurs in the Birmingham Youth League. A year on, he represented the League against Small Heath (later Birmingham City), who were so impressed that they tried to sign him on the spot. But too late – he'd already signed amateur forms… for Aston Villa.

The history of both Albion and the Villains of Aston may have been so different had not the Birmingham club felt pressure to choose between Pennington and Aston lad Fred Miles, who effectively competed for the same position. The Villains chose Miles. "He was an Aston boy, so that was that" explained Pennington later in life with something of a sigh of relief. Jesse returned sadly to his native Black Country. He joined Dudley in the Birmingham and District League, the same League in which Albion reserves competed. At that time, Dudley had a fine side…or they did until Albion came a-knocking and "captured" four of their players, including Jesse, now 19. It was only later that the Baggies discovered that their new signing was already registered with Villa. Fortunately, the Aston outfit agreed to release him without fuss.

Albion paired Jesse with former Dudley full-back colleague Baverstock during their annual pre-season Whites v Stripes match on 15th August 1903. The defensive duo competed against their own club's first team forwards. Together, they were said to "exhibit a strong defence". The Hawthorns friendly was the teenagers' first appearance as an Albion professional. (Jesse had previously played as an Albion amateur at Molineux on 14th April 1903, in a benefit match for Wanderers centre-half Ted Pheasant.)

ALBION'S 1903/04 season started badly with a series of defeats. Full-back Kifford was sent from the field during a 3-1 defeat by Aston Villa. "He ran at Villa forward McLatchie, and kicked his legs from under him," explained the *Birmingham Gazette* in shocked tones. There was worse. "This completely spoiled the closing stages for the spectators. He laughed and clapped his hands in response to the cries of disappointment that met him from the stands." The dismissal was only the third in the club's history, with the fourth another 23 years distant. Kifford eventually received a six-week ban for his actions, during which he was not paid by the club as a mark of his shame.

Meanwhile, his obvious replacement was up against Burton United in the Staffs Senior Cup. "The Albion backs both made mistakes," wrote the correspondent. "but Jesse Pennington seemed to warm to his work as the game progressed, and looks like developing into a useful back."

Thus Jesse's full debut came at Liverpool on 26th September 1903. Up to then that season, neither side had won. "It will be a trying ordeal for Pennington, who makes his debut in the First Division, to figure in such a match away from home." Thus read the concerned tones of the local press reporter. With Albion regularly beaten by the opposition that season, it was hard to imagine that the 20-year-old debutant could make matters much worse. In the event, with the Baggies recording their first victory, the same correspondent wrote three days later, "Pennington played a very fine back game, being fearless and clever in tackling, while his kicking was vigorous enough for anything." Albion Director Doctor Pitt was thrilled. "Jesse, I am very proud. I brought you into the world. I have seen you play your first game for the Albion in the League, and we have won."

Following his sound debut, Jesse retained his first team shirt for two decades of dedicated service which was to write his name large into the history of West Bromwich Albion Football Club, becoming a legend who is still considered amongst the top five players to appear for the club even a hundred years later. That is the incredible impact he made, although the full story of Pennington's incredible career reveals there was far more to this Albion stalwart than usually first meets the eye.

IN 1903/04, Pennington played in every game until mid-January, before injury intervened as it would often throughout his Albion career. With limited medical and fitness training knowledge, serious injuries and illness were a regular occupational hazard, but one which spawned legends of Pennington's indestructibility. Consider these words from the man himself and read between the lines.

"Training was never a chore to me. I liked it, even though we only had a small shed where we did some skipping. Our main training was lapping, short sprints for the forwards, and practice matches." These factors, combined with international call-ups, meant that the full-back was to miss Albion games every season through finally submitting to a variety of serious injuries and ailments.

His worst injury and subsequent longest absence was due to a shoulder dislocation in a League match against Stockport in September 1909. Rain fell heavily in the second half, so much so that the players were briefly taken off the pitch. When they resumed, the turf was very greasy and a serious injury was always a possibility.

The *Sporting Mail* described his misfortune. "On Monday, Pennington fell heavily, and was compelled to retire from the contest. It was said at first that his collarbone had been broken, but a subsequent examination has shown that the injury is of a more serious nature. He has dislocated his left shoulder, and will be prevented from playing for at least two months. His services will be greatly missed, for his magnificent play at back has materially assisted the club in becoming prominent in the fight for promotion during the last 2 or 3 seasons. It is to be hoped that he will speedily recover from his injury, and will feel no after effects from it, for his clean and sound defence has endeared him to supporters of the club and football enthusiasts generally." Jesse didn't return to first team action until a fortnight before Christmas.

Not surprisingly for one so dedicated to Albion's cause, worrying head injuries were not uncommon, such as the concussion he suffered in a Cup match against Derby in 1907, and then again shortly afterwards in the annual England v Scotland battle. The defender "sustained slight concussion of the brain through putting his head in the way of one of George Wilson's powerful shots. While at the hotel, the West Bromwich man became seriously ill, and needed medical attention. He was not able to set out for home until Tuesday."

In the middle of the 1912/13 season, the full-back might be forgiven for thinking everyone was out to get him. At home to Derby on Boxing Day, "he was off the field for a considerable amount of time due to injury." Three days later at Notts County, he was "lame" for the last thirty minutes. His latest knock prevented him turning out at Middlesbrough on 4th January, but he returned three days later at Old Trafford. After 75 minutes of "fine work", the hapless defender was off the field once more after receiving a kick on the leg when diverting a shot. The kick was so severe that he was out of action until March.

Injuries to team-mates also impacted upon the defender, most notably against Derby in October 1910. Both Betteley and Timmins retired hurt in the first ten minutes. The latter bravely returned in the second half, but only as nuisance value. Derby were a goal up, but couldn't add to their tally, even against nine fit men marshalled into defensive security by Pennington. Albion played a one-back game (an offside trap) with Jesse as the solitary defender. Wrote the *Free Press* correspondent "Of Pennington's performance, it would be hard to speak too highly. He gave a really masterly display under most exceptionally difficult circumstances, and no back in England could have surpassed him." With minutes to go and Derby still leading, "Pennington was noticed to fall, and there was gloomy forebodings as to what was up but it fortunately proved but a trivial mishap and he was able to resume." In the 87th minute, Pailor equalised for the Baggies and "was almost overwhelmed by congratulations and hand-shaking from his comrades."

The football club did what they could to keep the players fit with regular trips to Rhyl "for sea airs" and to the Droitwich salt baths. Once, intriguingly, after a midweek Cup replay against Birmingham, the players were treated to a Turkish bath "to remove the stiffness and soreness residential in the strenuous midweek contest in which they were engaged."

Disease remained a constant worry in these unsophisticated times, even for the strongest. In February 1908, Jesse played poorly against Glossop. "Pennington was the only weak spot in the defence, the international having a very disappointing display." Within hours of the end of the game, he was diagnosed as suffering from influenza. The same month, he also endured land *mal de mer* (motion sickness) en route to Belfast to play for his country, a condition subsequently worsened by the vagaries of the Irish Channel. Thankfully, he recovered to play well in England's 3-1 victory.

In 1919, there were widely circulating rumours that JP was suffering from a fatal dose of influenza and pneumonia in the midst of the global epidemic that killed millions. The tales were not far from the truth. Indeed, Jesse was confined to bed. He did have the same illness that was literally killing dozens of people in West Bromwich each week and millions world wide. But Jesse was strong and made a full recovery. In early 1923, he fell seriously ill again. Such was his status, even in retirement; bulletins on his health were considered significant news in the local press. Once again, he battled through to win – as it seemed he had throughout his career.

JESSE'S DEBUT SEASON coincided with an Albion side en route for relegation. Still, for young would-be first team hopefuls, this was not necessarily such a disaster for their careers as such a downturn in club fortune always brings with it a need for fresh talent. Cynical supporters noted that, despite the drop to Division Two, and investing £16 in a horse to pull heavy rollers across the turf, Albion still managed to record a £419 profit.

Those were the theories going into the new season. Unfortunately, the Baggies were selling players, not buying, as the financial position was genuinely grim. Results regularly matched the balance sheets, leading to attendant team reshuffles. The thoughts of one local journalist made familiar reading "The difficulty Albion find is with the style of the Second Division. Scientific football in many instances is out of the question." Attendances were quite awful, starting with barely 4,000 and dropping as low as 2,072 for the visit of Gainsborough Trinity. Even those who turned up did so apparently when they felt like it, with claims in the *Chronicle* that only 500 were present to see the kick-off against Barnsley in December.

The club's existence was at stake. The players agreed to accept half-wages in December, but it wasn't enough. The following month, the directors appealed for money to keep going. Although Aston Villa, Everton, Stafford Rangers and even Northwich Victoria made donations; there was little local support. Fans didn't want to prop up a regime they didn't believe in. In desperation, the Directors declared that all donations would go to buy better players, and then sold another – Hadley to Aston Villa. The reaction was predictable. Even supportive local organs such as the *West Bromwich Free Press* bluntly declared, "The club is going to the dogs."

At a shareholders meeting in March, the Board resigned en-masse, and new men were voted in, to deal with the adverse balance sheet of £697. The new Board quickly brought in new players, and reduced admission prices. Attendances rose and the club were safe – in the short term.

Jesse slowly became a favourite of the Hawthorns crowd, as he accumulated dozens of fine appearances. In the unglamorous position of full back, there were only three ways to get noticed. Jesse's positive route of consistent top-notch performances was one way. Being dismissed from the field like his predecessor Kifford was another or finally to make numerous mistakes, which was ultimately self-defeating. Full-backs of the 1900s were the last line of defence, so bore far more resemblance to modern day central defenders than full-backs. There was no expectation of supporting the attack; their job was very simply to block out the opposition forwards, supported by the half-backs. They were expected to tackle forcibly and quickly, plus kick strongly. There didn't appear to be much expectation about finding a striped shirt, just kick that ball as hard and as quickly as possible in the direction of away. To do otherwise was to attract criticism. After defeat in Oldham Athletic's first ever home League match, Argus Junior commented "Jesse Pennington seems to be getting into the habit of delaying his clearance and I hope he will remember that the best back is he who gets the ball away with the least amount of delay." But his composure on the ball indicates the class of a player bound for greatness.

IN JESSE'S TIME, there was little merit in keeping clean sheets – not for them the Megson approach. Outscoring the opposition was the sole requirement. Thus defenders had much in common with defensive midfielders today – they were simply workhorses, whose labours were largely unseen and unappreciated. Reporters of that era would normally describe the defenders' contribution in one short sentence if at all, normally offering more expansive comments on the opposition forwards.

Despite the meagre reporting, and Albion's Second Division status, the defender built a reputation. His performances in a three-match marathon against First Division Stoke City in the FA Cup helped greatly, as W. McGregor noted in the *Sports Argus* ("A Journal of all manly pursuits") "Above all others, one man on the Albion side has enhanced his reputation during the club's recent encounters with the Potteries representatives. I refer to Pennington – he is the ideal footballer, and looks an athlete all over. He has been of splendid service to the West Bromwich team, and I question if he has ever played three better games in his life. Certainly the Selection Committee would do well to keep this dashing back under observation."

The England Selection Committee agreed, and chose Jesse to represent the English League against Scotland. Jesse gave a "cool and skilful" display. Chairman Harry Keys accompanied him to Glasgow, subsequently sending a telegram highlighting Jesse's "grand showing" to West Bromwich, where the Baggies were doing battle. The telegram was paraded around the pitch on a large board, and the spectators cheered enthusiastically. After such a showing, selection for England against Wales (becoming Albion's 13th England international in the process) wasn't a great surprise, though nonetheless enthusiastically received. Jesse received a special cheer from the Hawthorns crowd before the Blackpool game for his selection, and then earned " a round of cheers for the clever way he robbed the Blackpool left wing." Now he was getting noticed!

The entire Albion team travelled to Craven Cottage to see Jesse make his England debut (before immediately setting off for Rhyl for a training camp). Another cap followed quickly against Scotland, where once again "he distinguished himself". This was the start of a long international career; playing mainly as a defensive pair with the Blackburn Rovers legendary full-back Bob Crompton. The partnership was not without critics. In 1911, Bird's Eye, writing in the *Sports Argus* was quick to back the local man. "Since 1907/08, when the Albion back first represented his country, there has not been a better defender in England and he well deserves the latest honour conferred upon him. According to some of the critics, Crompton and Pennington have had their day, but while the Blackburn back may not be the power he was a few years ago, the West Bromwich man has never played better than he has done this season."

Even though England's results were impressive, Jesse was often more effective for club rather than country. "Not at his best" was an uncomfortably familiar comment on his international games. Criticism intensified by 1913 when the initials "PMG" were much bandied about as in 'Pennington Must Go'. Even the local press had doubts, with one *Free Press* reporter commenting "there seems too much of the "old firm" idea about the defence." The war diverted everyone's attention and Jesse continued to win more caps after the Armistice. Probably his most memorable England game was his last, the 1920 epic against Scotland at Hillsborough, Sheffield. Thirty-seven year-old Jesse captained his country in an epic 5-4 victory in wind and rain, which gave England the title of Home International Champions [a prestigious annual tournament played between the four home counties].

With all that practice early in his career, Pennington had little trouble kicking the ball firmly as required, accurately too. But his best asset was always his positioning, often described as "uncanny." Instinctively, he knew where the ball was heading, faster than any opponent.

It became his trademark. Such was the case in Albion's 1-0 away victory at Oldham in October 1908, where the *Argus* noted, "Pennington has never played with more brilliance. He always seemed able to divine the intentions of his opponents, and was as sharp and penetrating as a needle." Similarly in a Cup match at Bristol City two years later, 'Half Back' of the *Free Press* enthused "The man who shone above all others on the field was Pennington, who has rarely if ever made a greater display. His work was marked by superb judgement and excellent resource."

His consistency was remarkable. Even at 38, one reporter remarked on his contribution against Spurs, "Pennington saw three moves ahead, and intervened in time." JP rarely got physical, preferring to subtly nudge his opponent off the ball if he couldn't dispossess him with a fair tackle. This approach was quite unusual for its time and did much to suggest Jesse eschewed traditional values.

OPPOSITION SUPPORTERS were sometimes quicker to appreciate Albion's best player. 'Half Back', writing in January 1905, noted during a visit to Blundell Park, "Jesse Pennington was in quite exceptionally fine form, and the Grimsby spectators could not refrain from cheering the splendid clearances he made." Similarly, at Oldham, in what was the Latics first ever home League match in September 1907, Jesse was "deservedly applauded time after time for his fine work. He seemed almost infallible." The reporter noted a comment from one mill-hand "Yon Pennington is a stone-waller, not half." The *West Bromwich Chronicle* noted "among players, friends and opponents alike, he enjoyed a popularity which was almost unique, he was Jess to everybody, and when Albion were visiting the grounds of other clubs, there was always a succession of players and enthusiasts of other clubs eager to shake hands with one of the outstanding personalities of the game."

Often, only big FA Cup matches stirred Albion supporters into life. Such as the previously mentioned three match slog against Stoke, or a pair of Cup matches against Birmingham City in 1908. In the latter game, 'Peerless' was marking City's Eyre. The Blues man wasn't exactly the first player to be frustrated by Jesse, the forward was making no progress at all. The *Midland Chronicle* noted, "Pennington was repeatedly cheered for his magnificent returns" and such was the forwards' unease, "Pennington and Eyre almost came to loggerheads". In one incident, Eyre jumped wildly at Pennington, but missed and sprawled over on the turf. "The biter, thus bit, caused some laughter."

NOT ONCE did Jesse get his name on the Albion score sheet, despite his length of service. This wasn't seen as particularly noteworthy in that period. Unless they were penalty takers, full-backs literally didn't have a chance. Jesse had one go from the spot himself, in a seriously under strength side playing at Leicester Fosse in December 1904. The experience was not a positive one as the *Midland Chronicle* described, "Pennington missed a penalty, but it was not his fault. The ball was placed true enough, but Smith, the Leicester goalkeeper got at it in a marvellous fashion."

Jesse did find the net on several occasions, though it was inevitably his own. He managed a pair during 1909. Firstly, in the FA Cup against Bradford City when "O'Rourke and Pennington made for the ball, the former rushing in such a manner that Pennington could not help heading the ball through his own goal, thus equalling the score." The second came in a local derby against Birmingham City in December, after a misunderstanding with his goalkeeper Stringer. A third "oggie" followed in October 1910 at Burnley, when the defender, "who was facing his own goal, endeavoured to hook the ball over his head, but he merely planted it over Pearson's head into the net, the goalkeeper being taken by surprise."

OF COURSE no Cult Hero's story would be complete without tales of brushes with authority and Pennington's is no different. Jesse had an image of a gentleman, but he could only maintain such honourable intentions within the limitations of his social class. Having ideas "above his station", led swiftly to instant and painful reminders of his lowly status.

In February 1909, he was suspended "sine die" by the directors. Jesse fell out with the club's great and good over his benefit match against Leeds City the previous October. At that time, players were rewarded for long service, not with an additional match, but with part of the proceeds from a League match. The directors agreed that Jesse should have half the proceeds against the Yorkshire side, with a guaranteed minimum of £150. The player considered his five-year contribution to the club meant he was deserving of at least £250, a significant difference in an era of a £5 maximum weekly wage. Only a big attendance would resolve the matter. Mavis of the *Argus* did his best to talk up Jesse's benefit. "Albion has never had a better defender than Pennington, whose international distinctions are testimony to his playing abilities. He is scrupulously fair in his tactics, and always plays the game in the true spirit of sport, with the remit that there are few more popular footballers in the country today than Jesse Pennington."

Sadly, the crowd was only 13,554, the lowest of the season so far, and Jesse would only receive the lower of the two figures. As the *Free Press* delicately put it, "he made use of expressions that the directors found impossible to ignore. It is a great pity that a man who has done such excellent service and who has attained so excellent a reputation should have his career marred by such an incident."

This was dangerous territory for mere players to stray into. Two years earlier, Bruce Rankin, one of the Albion's best attackers at the time, had been sent home in disgrace from a training break in Rhyl for "insubordination." Within days, he was ignominiously transferred to Manchester City.

The *Argus* steamed in on Jesse's insolence, "Public opinion supports the attitude of the directors. Players are only the servants of the club, not the masters." Canvassing the opinion of mere spectators was not in the mandate of journalists in that era. Thus 'public opinion' and the party line were probably identical. But in a more conciliatory tone, the reporter added, "Pennington probably recognises that he let his feelings get the better of him."

After backing down by "expressing his regret" to the Board, Pennington was restored to the first team, after missing only one game. But the ill-feeling persisted and in the summer of 1910, the full back refused to sign his new contract. "Has Jesse signed yet?" was heard repeatedly throughout the Black Country during the close season. The dispute centred on money. Although Chairman Billy Bassett claimed the club had offered the player the maximum wage, this was disingenuous, for additional under-the-counter payments were rife in the game. Jesse wouldn't be the only Albion player to represent his country and discover that his fellow stars were paid far better than he. If this was so, then Jesse's timing was unusually poor, because club finances were very tight. Rumours abounded, and separating fact from fallacy is always difficult. One shareholder, a Mr Bastable, asked the club board to comment on reports that Pennington had been badly treated, but Bassett would not be drawn. Perhaps he was mindful that Jesse was an influential member of the fledgling Players' Union.

Alternatively, there was talk at the end of the previous season that Albion players were unhappy with their weak side, and considered reinforcements were urgently needed. The Baggies had picked up only one point in their last five games, including a 5-1 thrashing by Hull City.

EITHER WAY, to not sign his contract was once more dangerous ground for the player. The club owned his registration, and Jesse could not choose to move to another English professional club without their consent. The contract rebel considered a move to Belfast Distillery, but he had much to lose – his international career, possibly most of his wages, his business, friends and family – so, instead, in the same week that Florence Nightingale was buried, he signed for Kidderminster Harriers of the Birmingham League, outside the influence of the Football League. The move was a massive drop in status. Was this just a protest or a general disillusionment with the slave-like status of the full-time footballer? His friends asserted that he was determined not to again figure in the Albion ranks.

In addition to playing for Harriers, there was mention of him managing a "well-known" Kidderminster hotel. Furthermore, as a result of the defender's signature, "many members had offered to pay weekly contributions towards the cost of running the team," according to the club secretary, thus implying that perhaps Jesse would not be financially worse off in the lower League.

Albion were unimpressed. Pennington was their asset. Understandably, there were several enquiries from other clubs. In public at least, Chairman Bassett maintained, "We wanted to sign him. Many clubs have asked our price. We have got no prices. We wanted to sign him." However, one local newspaper claimed Albion sought a transfer fee of £1,500, a massive amount for the period.

FA committee member Mr W. McGregor sided with the club and quickly pronounced, "Pennington must satisfy the Council of the FA that he has special grounds for his proposed change. If the Association are not satisfied with his reason for a change, he must not come to terms, or Ireland will be the only "open port" for him. But wherever he may go, unless transferred with the Albion's consent, he will remain an Albion player." Within days, Harriers were informed that the England International could not sign for them. The FA's influence was far wider than that of the League. George Moulder, described as a secretary at Kidderminster, said the letter "was a great disappointment", adding that he thought the actions of Pennington was "entirely justifiable."

In modern parlance, Jesse was stuffed. For a time, he remained defiant, turning out at left-back for the Harriers in a charity practice match on 27th August where "there was a great crowd which gave him a very enthusiastic greeting as he appeared in Harriers colours". His options were to leave the game altogether, go to Belfast Distillery (much the same thing!) or sign a contract with WBA. He signed.

DESPITE THE SENSE of injustice, Jesse was very quickly back to top form. Barely a week after his reluctant signature, the *West Bromwich Free Press* commended his play against Fulham. "Pennington played a hard and persevering game, affecting many smart clearances and delighting the crowd by one particularly fine return as he lay upon the ground."

Jesse stuck with his principles of fair play. To quote the *Midland Chronicle*, "he set an example of personal conduct and dignity which left its impression upon the whole team." His most famous example of being true to his beliefs came in the 1912 FA Cup Final replay against Barnsley. Two minutes from the end of extra time, there was no score. Then Barnsley's Tufnell ran onto a long ball with Pennington virtually alongside him for ten yards. Jesse could have brought the striker down well outside the penalty box, but chose not to, unlike their opponents who'd been kicking wildly all night. Tufnell continued his run and scored off the post. The Free Press offered a consolation. "It ought to be mentioned that Pennington has rarely played a greater game. He hardly made a slip or a mistake during the whole match."

Jesse was never to get that close to the FA Cup again. His previous best was reaching the semi-final in 1907. Albion faced an all-star Everton outfit. Sadly, Jesse's own mistake let Sharp of Everton in for the winner in a close 2-1 defeat. The FA Cup was a huge competition in this era, yet the international refused to take advantage of his status. In later life, he revealed, "I have been offered money many times for FA Cup tickets. But not once in my life have I accepted a penny more than the price on the ticket. I don't believe in it."

Ample compensation came in the form of a League Championship medal. The Baggies were unstoppable in the 1919/20 season, racking up over 100 goals.

In their crucial home game in March against eventual runners up Burnley, the *Midland Chronicle* highlighted the midfield and defence's mastery of the Lancashire club. They commented, "Pennington's display fully justified the assumption that he is England's greatest full-back today. He was invincible." The Baggies won 4-1.

Albion made certain of the title with four games still remaining, by beating Bradford Park Avenue 3-1 at the Hawthorns, in front of 30,000. There was even a poem celebrating the event, but the writer shouldn't have bothered going after the Poet Laureate's job – it was awful.

The Albion team were presented with their trophy after the last home match against Chelsea. The main interest in the game was the contest between Pennington and Chelsea's forward, Jack Cock. Although the Londoners' best player, Cock repeatedly came off second-best to "Peerless", prompting ironic cries of "Let Cock have a kick" from the jubilant faithful. By special request of the Chairman, League President John McKenna presented Albion's only Championship trophy, not to Bassett as per the custom of the day, but to club captain Jesse. McKenna claimed, "Never has the Championship been won by a more brilliant team."

Said Chairman Bassett of the triumphant team, "They were good, clean, honest-living men and there was never any trouble with them." The Captain agreed: "I've been pleased to have played for West Bromwich Albion for seventeen years, and in that time, I cannot think of an instance when the referee has been justified in speaking to any Albion player for having done anything against the rules of the Football Association."

The late Bill "Popeye" Martin was a legendary Albion supporter. Born in 1913, Bill saw his first game just seven years later. Even by the early 1980s, Bill's claim to have seen Jesse in action as part of the Baggies' Championship team was probably unique. Pennington later became a family friend, initially through his sports and cycle shop in Smethwick, which the footballer first opened in 1908. "He an' me Dad were great mates. The first time I ever met him was when I was five. Me Dad went in the shop with me and got talkin' to him. Me Dad said "it's my lad's birthday today." And Jesse said "'ave a look in the winder, see if you like anything." He'd got all these little Hornby railway carriages in the winda. I had my eye on a little mini one in red, green and black. So I says "Yes, that little carriage." "Great!" he says, patting me on the head. "I'll wrap it up and you can have it as your birthday present. And then you must come to tea.' I was chufftest."

FOR MUCH OF Jesse's career, just playing in the top Division seemed elusive, never mind any pipe dreams of actually winning the League Championship. Year after year in the Second Division passed, most with hard luck stories of coming so close to promotion. With the maximum wage firmly in place, Albion's Captain wasn't losing out financially by not being in the top flight, more the experience of regularly competing against the best in the country. The full-back had seven years of the second tier before Albion finally lifted the "coffin lid" (as the Second Division Championship was nicknamed due to its odd shape) in 1911.

Defeating Huddersfield 1-0 in the final match was just sufficient to secure the Championship. Jesse even had a shot on the opposition goal during this game, but presumably with his nose streaming blood, he missed the target. The *Argus* described the after-match scenes of the tumult of promotion celebration. "Like a wave, the crowd swept round the grandstand, and, amid an almost indescribable scene of enthusiasm and hilarious joy, the Albion players were fetched from the dressing room to mount the stand and face volley after volley of cheers. It was a scene the like of which had never been witnessed at the ground before." To loud cheers, Captain Jesse said it was the proudest day of his life.

With Jesse being such an upright citizen, he made an unlikely target for bribery; yet one foolish individual did try in 1913. A well-dressed gentleman visited his shop, claiming to be a Mr Johnstone, an Everton director (Albion were at home to the Merseyside club the following day). He offered £5 (just over a week's wages at that time) to each of the Albion players if they failed to win. JP invited the visitor to make the offer on one of his business memos and later, he reported the incident to Chairman Billy Bassett. Bassett called the Police. The game was, by coincidence, drawn 1-1. Afterwards Pennington stood under the Hawthorns stand wearing a coat over his strip. Johnstone met him and handed over the cash. The defender gave the money to his Chairman, while Johnstone was arrested. The "Everton director" was later revealed as one Frederick Pater from Birmingham. He received six months in jail and the cash was divided between local charities.

SUCH WAS HIS standing in society Jesse once ran for election to the Council, standing as an independent against Councillor George Betts in the Spon Lane ward. In 1919, Labour man Betts was a clothier and draper, living in Oldbury Road and with an impressive Council record. Jesse was described as an "athletic outfitter." On Polling day, he travelled with the team to Notts County rather than be at the polling station. He emphasised throughout his battle that he didn't wish to take advantage of his football status; he merely sought to stand as a citizen.

A local cartoonist sought to link the Baggies' rout of Notts County with the election campaign. A Throstle was pictured; telephone in hand, with the message "Eight nothing." "M'yes, not a bad majority, but Pennington says it's nothing to what he'll have at Smethwick." In the event, Betts was re-elected, securing 1,436 votes to the Albion man's 760 (50% turnout). Jesse was gracious in defeat, acknowledging the strengths of his opponent. He made such a positive impression that he was invited to stand again, though he declined. The Spon Lane residents put on a public dinner the following month, and Jesse was invited as their special guest.

In fact in an era sixty years before the advent of the sporting dinner and after-dinner speaking circuit, Pennington was regularly asked to attend dinners or speaking engagements. For instance, in early 1922, he was spoke at West Brom Town Hall on the snappy subject of "The value of outdoor recreation in its relation to the education of the child." A medical expert was the other main guest before a small but enthusiastic audience. All the first team players were present to take a collection on behalf of the Mayor's Boot Fund. Jesse did his best, and in between eulogising on the benefits of an outdoor life, he revealed, "at the extreme end of a football career, I enjoy the game as much as I did in my younger days."

Presumably the international didn't manage to work into his speech the full details of his epic trips to Bradford in 1920, but on other occasions, it was surely too fine a story to resist. The Baggies side travelled to Bradford City by train on a very foggy day. They were disappointed, if not surprised to find the game postponed. Hastily, the two sides agreed a re-match on Monday night with the visitors spending the weekend in the woollen city. Due to a family bereavement, Jesse was obliged to return home that night. On Monday morning, he travelled north once again; arriving just in time for the referee to decide that play was impossible. The Albion party took the 3.20pm train to Stockport. The service was scheduled to arrive just five minutes before a connection from Manchester, which would take them speedily home. Due to foggy weather, the four-hour journey to Stockport took seven hours. The weary party managed to catch a later connection, arriving back at Dudley Port in the Black Country at 1.00am. Then there was just the small matter of walking home...

Poor Jesse spent 16 hours travelling that day. The match was re-arranged for December. Once more the team travelled, and once more the match was postponed. It eventually took place in February.

AFTER SETTING A new appearance record for an Albion player only broken by Tony Brown's extraordinary devotion and longevity over 50 years later, Jesse Pennington's legacy still reverberates around the Hawthorns. His sense of fair play and solid stoicism in defence are the stuff of legend.

Fan Chris Flanagan recalled meeting the great man whilst still a whipper-snapper in Halfords Lane in 1952.

"I was standing with my Dad and Uncle and Dad had just nubbed out a fag when Uncle nudged him.

'Jesse!' said Uncle Bert to a man in a belted mac and grey hat who had just stepped up onto the pavement.

They exchanged words and then Jesse looked down at me. Jesse Pennington smiled and touched my shoulder. Jesse Pennington! I had him in my scrapbook... a photo clipped from the *Argus*... captained Albion and England... played way back when full backs had centre-partings and lump hammers in their boots. But he didn't look like any of them then. He was upright, alert, old world. And here years later – in 1952 – he still was.

I'm not sure what he said to me, but that matters little now. I'd met him."

For this is one legend that has great and interesting substance. One of his most important pieces of defending came in the 1912 FA Cup Semi Final against Blackburn. The *Chronicle* reported, "Just before the finish, Chapman shot from a crowd of players, Pearson appeared to be beaten, but Pennington who had fallen back into the goal, got to the ball with his head and amid considerable excitement, saved the situation." Jesse had taken Albion to Wembley with a typical piece of defending, popping up just when he was needed. The Baggies were safe in Jesse's hands.

HAROLD BACHE

1914-1915

BAGGIES CAREER

Games	14
Goals	4
Caps	0

MAGIC MOMENT

What might have been – the Duncan Edwards of his generation?

'HG'

> "Harold Bache was the best ever, capable of doing the most unexpected thing, unorthodoxy being his strong point; the flashing shot, the mazy dribble, the accurately placed pass, it all came so easily to him."
>
> **Fred Everiss, Albion Secretary**

THERE'S a small village in Worcestershire called Churchill. It's not far from Kidderminster; just turn right off the A456 to Kiddy when you see the signpost for the village – go right through the place, keeping to the main drag, and about a mile beyond that, you'll see a war memorial on the left-hand side, set some way back from Stakenbridge Lane. This commemorates that village's war dead, and those who served. On it are the names of four members of the Bache family, including one Lieutenant Harold Bache of the Lancashire Fusiliers, and West Bromwich Albion FC.

HAROLD GODFREY BACHE was born in Churchill, near Kidderminster, on 20th August 1889, probably within the confines of the family home, Stakenbridge House. He was the youngest of eight sons born to William Bache. The legal profession and sport were always prominent in the well-to-do Bache household. Dad was well known in West Bromwich legal circles (he founded Bache Solicitors, which still exists today, though without any resident Baches). "Legal Bache" (as he was commonly known) was a fine cricketer with both West Bromwich Dartmouth and Salters. He also turned out for West Bromwich (Dartmouth) FC during the mid-1870s to early 1880s. So occasionally did six other members of the family, including several of Harold's older brothers.

In 1891, when Harold was just two, William became a Director of West Bromwich Albion, although commitments elsewhere meant he only served for a year. Sadly, William died in 1899, aged 54, when Harold was only ten. He would not lack for male guidance though, with seven older brothers, and numerous uncles.

Significantly, since John Salter married Ann Bache (William's Great Aunt) in 1827, the fortunes of the Salters and the Baches became intertwined. William's second son Ernest (commonly known as Bill), became an engineer at Salters, where he came into daily contact with his relative, the famous George Salter, who played such a prominent role in the fledgling years of the Baggies.

Harold was educated privately in West Bromwich, and then at King Edward's Grammar School, Birmingham, where his remarkable all-round sporting talents first came to the fore. He then became Captain of the first cricket eleven, for whom he'd already played for four years. In his final season of 13 matches, he averaged over 41 per innings as a left–hander and took 31 wickets. His remarkable haul of three fifties in one week, including one against the Masters, even made the pages of the *Sports Argus*. At 16, he'd captained the Rugby Second XI through an unbeaten season, before moving on to the first team. There was still time to play outside-left for West Bromwich Hockey Club. The *Argus* observed, "He has not yet found time for Association football."

From King Edward's, he was accepted by Caius College, Cambridge in 1908. In addition to studying for what appears to be a teaching degree with history elements, Harold played rugby union, tennis at University level, and in the Wimbledon singles, hockey at county level, and first class cricket for Worcestershire and his University, some twenty matches in all between 1907 and 1910. Running was fun, too, for Harold, who excelled at 440 yards and half-mile events.

HAROLD FINALLY found time for the Beautiful Game, typically rising to the challenge so well that he became Captain of the University football team. He was the first ever from the rugby-loving King Edward's School to hold that honour. The *Athletic News* featured Bache in October 1910, describing him in terms that were to become familiar. "He is a magnificent dribbler, and for a man of his small avoirdupois [weight], possesses abnormal pluck and dash". At the time, Harold stood 5ft 8 inches high and weighed 10 stone.

In addition, he played for England amateurs seven times (remarkably scoring seven goals in a 20-0 rout of France in 1910) while regularly turning out for famous amateur side Corinthians over a five-year period. The vast majority of this club's players came from Oxford or Cambridge, and regularly beat the best professional sides in the land. He averaged two goals per game for the Corinthians. *The Times* in 1911 compared him to the great G.O. Smith, who played for England twenty-one times in the 1880s and 1890s. "Like G.O., he possessed that wonderful faculty of slipping his opponent, and to the wonderful dribbling ability, he added the priceless gift of being a most dangerous shot in any position."

Bache joined the unpaid side's tours to Spain, France and Canada. One Canadian newspaper admitted "Bache was in his most dangerous scoring mood, and one knows what that means," while another one ran with, "Bache was the shining star of the field, being prominent in attack and defence... he was known to shoot and break the crossbar." The latter claim was later refuted as an exaggeration, but with the Cambridge striker scoring 19 goals in five games, it was easy to get carried away. The happy amateur team returned home on the liner Lusitania.

THE FIRST LINKS between WBA and the Caius man date back to 1910, with the *County Express* noting, "Last season, there was some talk of him turning out with the Albion." Such a link-up wasn't possible at the time; as the feature went on to explain, although the tone remained hopeful. " Someday, we may see him leading the Albion attack." In the short-term, Bache's goals were benefiting the University team. In 17 matches between the start of the season and February 1911, Cambridge scored 85 goals. Of that number, 42 were in Bache's name. The *Standard* described H.G. as simply "the finest amateur forward playing today."

Harold relocated to Cumbria in early 1911, probably to conclude his teaching degree with hands-on experience. Both Kendal Rugby Club and Kendal Cricket Club were very pleased with both his arrival and his prowess. In the school holidays, Harold "occasionally assisted" the short-lived West Bromwich Springfield Football Club, or West Bromwich Dartmouth Cricket Club, depending on the time of year. A *Midland Chronicle* reporter was on hand for one such match for Springfield. "We recollect during a game versus Hagley, what a delightful exhibition he gave on the extreme left wing. He was that day faced with a rough, heavy and somewhat clumsy full-back, but he waltzed merrily around him, and although being on the small side. The easy and clever way he can beat opponents is oftentimes very tantalising to them."

Once his degree was secured in August 1912, the all-rounder moved again to St. Andrews College "to engage in scholastic coaching in Eastbourne." This time, the lucky beneficiaries were the ailing Eastbourne FC. Harold missed the kick-off against Addiscombe Park, but didn't miss the net, scoring the first seven goals in a 10-0 slaughter.

Meanwhile in West Bromwich, WBA couldn't manage ten goals in a month, let alone one game. Although the Baggies were more than holding their own in the top Division in 1913, they relied overly on Jesse Pennington and his defensive colleagues shutting out the opposition. Their current forward line was goal-shy, West Bromwich amassed only 46 goals in 38 matches, six and nine goals less respectively than the bottom two sides, Preston and Derby. Only two clubs in the First Division scored fewer goals, yet Albion did finish in an impressive looking fifth spot, just a point shy of Villa in the runners-up position. If only the Hawthorns outfit could acquire a goalscorer, then who could stop them?

It's easy to imagine that with so many of Harold's relatives based in West Bromwich, at least three of his brothers Foley, Charles Sidney, and Eric all being articled in the family legal firm, plus Bill Bache and the now ageing George Salter at the scale manufacturers, the subject of "little brother being just right for the Albion" was a familiar topic. Previously, a dispute between the Football Association and the Amateur Football Association made such a move impossible, but by 1913, reconciliation cleared the way.

By now, Harold was teaching English at the Ecole de l'Isle de France in Liamcourt, near Amiens, Northern France. Physically getting to him would not be easy. Inevitably Secretary-cum-jack-of-all-trades Fred Everiss was dispatched. This was a difficult and arduous journey in this period, made even more difficult for Fred as he had only just returned from Ireland. The weary official managed to travel as far as Amiens before darkness beat him. Unable to secure accommodation overnight, possibly because of the language barrier, he spent an uncomfortable, and no doubt cold, night at the railway station. The following morning, Fred continued his epic journey on foot for eight miles before getting a lift on a passing farm wagon. Harold Bache was in class but an enthusiastic colleague Mr King (enthusiastic after initially cursing loudly having been got out of bed) agreed to take his class. Bache himself was a strange sight, with two black eyes the result of playing hockey the previous day. Despite his surprise and dishevelled state, Bache needed very little persuasion to join his local club for the big Cup match against Villa and "as often as possible afterwards," signing on the dotted line in just ten minutes. On his long way back home, Everiss was obliged to divert to the FA offices in London to hand in the completed registration document.

HAROLD RETAINED his amateur status; a great curiosity in what was now an all-professional game. The only other amateur to turn out for the Baggies during that era was the Reverend W.C. Jordan, also a centre-forward. To play, purely for the love of the game, must have fascinated the hard-working Black Country audience.

The *Midland Chronicle* was mightily impressed with the signing. "Bache is a regular box of tricks on the football field. He has heaps of pluck, yet he is a brainy player and he knows how to avoid the bumps." The *Free Press* were a little more restrained: "As from past records, it would seem that Mr Bache will supply a need long felt, namely that of a first-class goal getter" while as the *Daily News* pointed out "good Corinthian forwards know how to pass: in fact, you cannot teach him very much about football."

The new signing was pencilled in for his first game against Middlesbrough – but a late dose of influenza meant that Fred Everiss had an apologetic telegram rather than a new striker – "much to the regret of the crowd" according to the *Sports Argus*.

Harold made his Albion debut in a rather important match a week later – in the FA Cup at Villa Park in February 1914. The "slim, black-haired, slightly stooping youth" was completely undaunted by the occasion or by the 58,000 in attendance, according to the correspondent at the *Midland Chronicle*.

"By his clever cool and plucky exhibition, H.G. Bache left a great impression. He was a marked man throughout, and the attentions (of several Villa players) were closely bestowed upon the amateur, who was watched as a cat watches a mouse. But despite this, he shone, and was, in my opinion, the cleverest footballer on the field. He was nippy and fast, and his touches to his colleagues were beautiful, and should have been utilised, only there seemed a lack of understanding between them which lost many good chances. But the way he eluded his opponents who showed him no consideration, was marvellous, and he was as slippery as an eel, as most of the Villa defenders... found out to their sorrow. Once, one of the Villa men sent the amateur yards, and it was thought he was hurt, but he got up smiling and being such a fine athlete, it got him a big advantage, and the philosophical way he took things made him a big favourite with the crowd." However, a physical Villa team battered their way to a 2-1 win. *The Argus* added "Bache went straight through and beat the goalkeeper with a delightful shot" but the reporter was alluding to Villa's Joe Bache (no relation) rather than Harold Bache.

So tough was the Cup-tie that even normally mild-mannered Jesse Pennington got "stuck in" with a vicious tackle that winded his opponent for several minutes. Days later, rumour spread quickly around the Black Country that Albion forward Sheerman had been fatally injured in a collision with Villa's Lyons, and subsequently died. Albion moved quickly to deny the stories, admitting he was staying at Jesse Pennington's house in Smethwick and confined to bed. Sheerman was alive – if not very well.

The Albion directors were criticised for choosing an amateur. Wrote 'Brum' in the *Birmingham Gazette*, "I see that some contemporaries have suggested that Harold Bache was a complete failure. I cannot conform to that opinion, but I do think, on reflection that it was a mistake to put him into the team for the first time in a match in which science was likely to be at a big discount." Other journalists disagreed, such as Argus Junior. "The faults Harold Bache displayed were those of one not accustomed to the work of the men alongside him. He kept the ball on the floor, was smart in his passes, nippy in his movements, and quick to seize his chances. The cause of the defeat did not rest upon his shoulders."

For reasons that are not totally clear, Harold didn't play again that season. He was said, "to be unavailable" for the next League fixture against Derby. Most likely, he returned to his French teaching duties for in April 1914 he led a party of Liamcourt boys to England to play football against his old school from Folkestone. Harold couldn't resist turning out himself – at centre-half – with the Eastbourne press describing him "as a towering presence." Subsequently, the French party played in a hockey tournament in nearby Folkestone.

In May, the Baggies entertained Corinthians with H.G. lining up for the visitors. The amateurs beat the professionals 4-0 (not uncommon at the time for the Corinthians were a brilliant side) with

Harold setting up the first goal with "one of the most brilliant forward passes it is possible to conceive." Harold added the second goal himself in an exhibition fixture that didn't have a single foul in 90 minutes, implying Albion, sans Pennington due to a family bereavement, weren't exactly pushing themselves.

THE CHURCHILL MAN stood out in Hawthorns pre-season training for the 1914/15 season. "He created such a great impression" exulted one writer. In the traditional final warm-up match (Stripes v Whites – basically the Albion squad forming two teams, with all proceeds to local charity), there was no doubt who attracted the attention of the near 7,000 crowd. "The most prominent figure was H.G. Bache, whose cleverness in dribbling and placing often brought him the highest appreciation of the crowd. He had hard lines twice before he was successful in putting a goal to his credit after some pretty play." Another correspondent added, "The crowd often applauded his brilliant work."

The new season opened on a Tuesday afternoon with a 2-1 victory at Newcastle. Bache lined up as an inside-forward. At five and a half foot high and weighing less than 11 stone, he was never going to outmuscle the opposition. Harold was a man of many talents, however. As the *Sports Argus* had it "he is undoubtedly a clever player, and the best tactician among all the Albion forwards." The Geordie victory was followed by a bashing at 'Boro. Still, the commentators again singled out the Albion amateur as "far and away the best forward on display."

Bache's home debut followed a week later. In normal times, the first opportunity to see such an exciting (and unpaid) attacker in the Albion ranks guaranteed a healthy gate. These were not normal times. Would-be attendees were learning to fight or indeed were already on their way overseas. In addition, the September weather was particularly unkind, with heavy rain throughout the day. Thus only 6,481 turned up for Sheffield United (1-1), 10,000 below the final home game of last season. Many of those attending felt guilty that they were indulging in such frivolous pursuits, even though everyone believed the war would be over by Christmas. A common newspaper quote of the times described supporters as "loitering louts who have neither love nor loyalty for their country." As a further reminder of their duty, a military band paraded during the interval with attendant loud appeals for more recruits. In such an atmosphere, no-one present could fairly appreciate the dash and élan of Harold Bache. Time after time, his probing passes set up his rather lumbering centre forward Poulton. "Bache was wonderful," exclaimed the local press, despite him having to accurately move a greasy ball on slippery turf.

Chairman Billy Bassett and his Albion board offered their help to form a new battalion – the 10th South Staffs, presumably along the lines of a Pals battalion (where men from a single town or industry enlisted and served together). The Army were given unfettered access to club offices while Albion players would attempt to persuade their counterparts from other clubs to sign up. The Baggies were understood to be supplying a company of footballers (as companies consisted of 200+ men in those days, the players must have come from other clubs also). The plan met with the approval of the Mayor of West Bromwich, Councillor Charles Sidney Bache, Harold's older brother number 3.

The recruiters were never far away. A small army of them moved among supporters during the derby match at Villa Park. Bache was again at inside-forward, backing up Swift as the main striker. Although Swift did score, generally he was no improvement on Poulton. Once more, the amateur stole the show with his drive, vision and shooting ability, even though the home side won 2-1. "The star artist of the Albion attack." "The brainiest forward on display" were just two out of numerous accolades.

The recruitment drive bought results. Harold was the first Albion player to volunteer for the war. With his income secure, and no dependents requiring his attentions being other considerations, it was no doubt instilled into Harold from an early age that with his privileged position, came a responsibility to respond when his country needed him. Several of the younger Bache clan had already joined up. Eric and Kenneth received their enlistment instructions on September 24th. (His two oldest brothers were above the recruitment limit). Most likely, he considered Army life to be just another adventure, or to use the vernacular of the day, "a gay lark." Initially, he enlisted as a private in the new 10th Battalion. In the short term, he was able to continue playing.

AS A SERVING SOLDIER "doing his bit", Bache could be fairly exempted from criticism aimed at football players and supporters. His name and his deeds could be mentioned in the pub or the workplace without rebuttal. 18,000 left their troubles in their old kit bag and travelled to the Hawthorns to see Albion demolish Liverpool 4-0. Harold was now a centre-forward and loving the role, and using his speed and eye for a pass to fine effect. He might have scored, but passed unselfishly to Morris, who was better placed and duly netted the Baggies' third goal. The correspondent from the *Midland Chronicle* wrote, "Bache was repeatedly applauded for his brilliance. This is probably Bache's last game with the Albion for a time, and it is a pity when he is doing so splendidly, he should have to say goodbye to the football field to commence a course of training for the battlefield." The *Birmingham Gazette* was quick to add their approval. "Bache has the innate talent for grasping the possibilities of a situation before they have began to dawn upon his opponents, and largely accounts for his effectiveness."

Harold had secured the no. 9 shirt… as long as the army would let him have it.

There was one other lasting memory of this splendid victory. In a very rare example of impromptu collective voices, sections of the Hawthorns crowd bellowed "FIVE" (modern day chanting, as we know it, can trace its roots no earlier than the 1960s). Harold had played a very full role in creating such unity. A recruitment rally was staged in the main stand immediately after the game, and 14 men volunteered to join the Comrades Battalion (part of the new 10th Battalion).

Harold missed the Baggies' next game (lost 2-0 against Spurs), as he was obliged to travel to Lichfield with two of his brothers for military duties that day. Fortunately, he was granted leave the next weekend to travel to Bradford PA. With his leading of the line in his usual unselfish manner, the Baggies were unstoppable. The 4-1 win included Harold's first Albion goal, as described by Mavis. "Like a flash, Bache slipped behind Blackburn, and on the instant made a great drive and beat Drabble all the way. It was such a goal as drew a roar of appreciation from the [Bradford] supporters." In the last minute, he and Morris broke through the PA ranks, and once again Bache stood back for Morris to score. Mavis again: "H.G. Bache worked a revolution in the efficiency of the forward line." The *Albion News* was equally enthusiastic: "the home defenders could do nothing with him. He continually sent them running one way, while he passed the ball in the other. His artistry was superb, and roused the admiration even of the home supporters. "Another critic opined: "Bradford were, in popular parlance, big enough to eat them, but when it comes to playing football there was no comparison possible."

Even the Football League had noted Bache's impact, and selected him for the Football League v Irish League fixture in October at the Hawthorns after just a remarkable seven appearances.

The West Bromwich press approved. "He thoroughly deserves the honour bestowed upon him. His selection was significant as he was the first amateur to receive this honour since professional football became the norm, and was perceived as an encouragement to other amateurs, hopeful of joining the 'big League'". Sad to say for the League's ambitions, Harold was "all at sea" that afternoon, with a rare poor game, according to Birmingham newspapers. The *Free Press* chose to dwell on the positives: "His pretty footwork was admired by all." The Football League triumphed 2-1 in front of 10,000 spectators.

Three days later, he was "unexpectedly delayed at his military quarters" and shorn of his services, the Baggies forwards were like sheep without a shepherd. After the 0-0 with Oldham came a 0-0 with Manchester United with Bache all at sea. Literally. He'd transferred from the South Staffs to the Lincolnshire Regiment, then in training with the Chums Battalion at Grimsby, an obscure location in the 21st century, but the back of beyond in 1914. His leadership qualities were quickly identified as he was promoted to Corporal. Typically, he set up a charity football match between the Chums and the 5th Lincolnshires, with the £34 profit donated to Grimsby and District Hospital.

AFTER THIS POINT, his army postings become confusing. Local reports were clear that Harold had been offered a commission with the South Staffs. This was an easy assumption to make as Harold had undergone Officer Cadet training at University (how he found time for this additional activity on top of all his sporting activities and tuition isn't clear). In fact, one of Harold's brothers, Eric, had been offered a commission. Harold had also applied for officer status, but was awaiting a response. Nevertheless, Harold was apparently returning home to assist in recruiting for a new West Bromwich company. Argus Junior was impressed. "This is the best bit of news heard for many a day in Throstledom." But these reports may also have been incorrect for other sources have him still in Grimsby in early November.

With their number one striker available again, WBA's forward line went from ridiculous to sublime. Bolton were brushed aside 3-0 with brilliant skill from Bache. Keepers dived, opponents tackled… all to no avail. Two minutes from time, Sheerman raced away and centred for Bache to score at close range.

Bache was clearly the difference between below par and effervescence, mediocrity and goals. "What a wonderful difference the appearance of H.G. Bache makes to the Albion attack" enthused the *Midland Chronicle*. "Apart from his own individual work, which is always par excellence, the amateur's inclusion seems to give confidence to the rest of his colleagues, and his beautiful dribbling and accurate passes are indeed a great help to the side. When he came onto the field, he received quite an ovation from the Hawthorns crowd." With an attendance of 7,817, 'crowd' seems almost an exaggeration. Admittedly, the weather again played a part in the small attendance. The press, located in the Smethwick End, were unable to see who scored Albion's second and third goal, such was the gloom. The Football League remained under great pressure from the national press to abandon their competition. It was considered both unseemly and an unnecessary distraction. Indeed, Bache himself, with his upright Cambridge upbringing, would feel the dilemma acutely. Who really needed him most?

Both the Birmingham and West Bromwich press were unanimous. With Bache at centre-forward, the Baggies would inevitably win and win well. Without him, they were really not very good. Unfortunately, nobody had told Blackburn Rovers. They beat the Baggies 2-1 despite the presence of the Albion's talisman, Morris netting the visitors' solitary goal. In a re-run of the Bradford PA match, he and Bache were clear on goal and H.G. stood aside for his fellow forward. In the very last minute, the Blackburn keeper made a brilliant save from Bache to preserve the points for his team. The crowd included a number of injured Belgian soldiers.

The status quo was restored against the 'Pies' from Nottingham. Bache's clever footwork, in the best traditions of the Albion passing game, raised the enthusiasm of the 10,000 crowd. Fresh from a "few days leave", the Baggies centre-forward was rampant. His two successive shots at the County goal set up Morris for an easy strike. H.G. set up the second goal before adding the finale, dancing his way around three defenders before defeating Albert Iremonger with a side-footed shot. The supporters were "unbounded in their enthusiasm" as they metaphorically saluted their favourite. Harold was a one-man reason to escape from the devilment of the war for a few hours, the entertainer, the source of excitement, the reason to be at the Hawthorns, a breath of normality in an abnormal world. This, more than ever, was the forward's time. Revered although defender Jesse Pennington remained, Bache was the player to provide memories to take to France or Belgium – which was where inevitably many of the spectators were headed.

This same theme was picked up by Harold's niece, Mary Bache, who wrote in the 1960s: "Harold's neat stylish action and clever dribbling is still recalled with enthusiasm by all who saw him play." Mary went on to boldly claim, "it was due to Harold's influence that WBA developed a style closely resembling the Corinthians, with low short kicking and short quick passing." There is precious little evidence to support this assertion, and it appears unlikely given Harold's few games with their attendant erratic pattern. More likely is that his team-mates would give him ample possession, and fit in around him because they quickly realised his was the best route to winning matches.

Bache even made the leader column in the *Sports Argus*, traditionally a Villa preserve. Argus Junior felt a need to damp down the excitement. "Generally the notion is that Harold G. Bache, with his sinuous and Corinthian ways, has brought about the wonderful improvement [in Albion's form]. Well, I am not going to deny it and belittle the Cantab's enormous influence, but as one soldier does not make an army, one man, even a Bache, cannot make a team. Bache has improved the forwards, but in addition to getting goals, you have to stop goals to win."

HAROLD'S COMMISSION finally came through in early November, and with it, another transfer. He was now part of the 11th Battalion of the Kings Royal Rifles at Aldershot. On the 14th, West Brom completed their trio of North East slogs with a journey to Roker Park. They returned with all the points too, the Mackems unable to cope with Bache's "brilliant dribbles" and his usual unselfish nature. If Sunderland couldn't cope, the Baggies' next opponents Sheffield Wednesday certainly could. Wednesday detailed both Parkes and Spoors to take care of Bache, and take care of him they did. The "running fire of adverse comment" from the Baggie faithful didn't detract from the marking job. The West Bromwich cult hero's opportunities were severely limited "but when he did get in a shot, it was always on the mark, and he certainly deserved to score on at least one occasion." The match finished without goals.

The Wednesday match was almost the end of Bache's Albion career. The ever-mobile demands of the army (he was now with the 10th Lancashire Fusiliers, stationed in Dorset) prevented him from playing any matches in December. The Baggies just had to get along as best they could. Harold played his final League match, at home to Middlesbrough on

2nd January 1915. That he was available for selection was excitedly noted in a prominent sub-heading in the major Birmingham paper. "H.G. Bache may play."

The following Monday, "Brum" in the *Athletic News* described how "the occupants of the stand literally sprang from their seats and gave the military footballer an ovation" after Harold scored the only goal. "It was indeed a startling effort. The Corinthian had been baulked time after time. Once he hit the post with a very fine shot, and he had several other accurately delivered volleys charged down. It was late in the second half when he pounced on the ball, and tried, apparently in vain, to shake off his wasteful opponents. Then, while running at right angles to the posts, he suddenly checked the ball, and although apparently the opening he sought was as remote as ever, he shot with electrifying vigour and the ball flashed in the net, far out of Williamson's reach. It was one of the most brilliant goals the writer has ever seen."

The fervour with which supporters greeted Bache's play was very rare in those days both because it was not a common occurrence anyway, but also as, with the war settling in for a long winter the country was in the grip of a huge depression. Bache's footballing genius allowed that gloom to be lifted for those lucky few at the Hawthorns for a brief hour and a half on a Saturday afternoon. He inspired through what Pelé would later call the Beautiful Game at a time when the public needed him most. But in those uncertain times, Bache's last visit to the Hawthorns went unheralded. There was a war on, and everyone had his or her own worries.

A week later, Albion lost 1-0 in the FA Cup at Hull, despite Bache's presence. City had realised the Albion threat and "marked Bache with particular keenness." 'Stop Bache and you stop WBA' seemed to be the familiar message. But Harold was never to threaten an opposing defence again. Qualifying as a Bombing Officer took priority, him being pretty handy with a cricket-ball – bombs were thrown in similar fashion – Bache would have stuck out a mile as an obvious candidate for the job. Incidentally, despite the name, Harold's role involved the use of what would be called hand-grenades these days; versions approximating those in use today had only just been invented in 1915. More likely, Harold was initially trained on the variety whose fuse had to be ignited before throwing, and which were deemed pretty unreliable at best and downright dangerous at worst! The colloquial name for bomb-throwers at the time was "The Suicide Club."

BEFORE LEAVING the country, Harold lined up twice for a 'Corinthian Under Arms' side against an Aldershot Command XI at Aldershot. In the first game on February 27, Harold predictably found the net as he "beat the backs, and steadying himself, scored with a smashing right footer." In the return fixture on March 20th, he scored four times. But such footballing heroism paled into total insignificance for us when we uncovered the bravery of this talented man in the face of enemy action as he brought the ethos with which he played the game for the Baggies onto the fields of France.

According to the Official History of the 10th Battalion, when it embarked at Folkestone for France, Harold, then a Second Lieutenant, was with 'A' Company, as Bombing Officer. Harold, his 80 bomb throwers, and the rest of the Fusiliers were in for long and hard times on the front line.

By September, the Regiment were based at an undisclosed location, presumably near Ypres. Half the company were billeted in an empty barn, and the others at a little cow house at the end. A working party on the road gave away the location, and quickly drew shellfire. One shell came through the barn roof, killing 20 soldiers and wounding 27 more. The officers rushed out to help. Captain Roberts spotted Harold dashing forward, with two sergeants, as even more shells landed around them. Roberts ordered his fellow soldiers to take cover behind a building but Bache refused, shouting back "I can't leave the wounded in danger!"

In another incident, there was a breach in the parapets (front defensive wall of trench) and with enemy machine guns pouring bullets into the gaps, Lieutenant Bache was "walking about the trenches, pulling the wounded out of danger, encouraging his men and binding up wounds, every moment in peril of his life." Added Captain Roberts with considerable understatement "it is difficult to explain to those who have not been in the trenches, what this means..."

On the 6th February 1916, the Flanders-based Fusiliers moved into a piece of Ypres real estate called "The Bluff", which was partially bisected by a canal. After a major attack, the Germans seized The Bluff and also took around 600 yards of front-line as well. Because he realised that he must attack before dawn if he was to have any chance of recapturing the position, Major G.L. Torrens did precisely that at 4.15 am on February 15th. The attacking force was in three parts; the York And Lancaster troops on the right, Harold Bache's Lancashire Fusiliers in the middle, and a bombing party on the left. The right party met with stiff resistance, which held them up, Torrens leading forwards any reinforcements he could find, while the remainder worked their way on; the Regimental Diary refers to this as 'fighting hard', presumably a mastery of understatement. The three parties eventually reached the top of The Bluff and bombed the enemy in New Year Trench. Some even succeeded in getting into the trench proper, and hand-to-hand fighting continued for at least 45 minutes. Sadly, the numbers were insufficient to carry the day, and the attackers were compelled to fall back, pursued by bombs and machine-gun fire, and it was around this time that Harold Bache was killed.

HOW HAROLD DIED is not recorded. His commanding officer Major Torrens claimed in a letter to Harold's mother that her son was shot by a sniper and "died very happily and instantaneously"). Given that the claim is not duplicated in Regimental records, it is quite likely that this "kinder" version was aimed at ameliorating his mother's grief a little. Partial confirmation can be found in a separate letter to Mrs Bache from Lieutenant Geoffrey Barratt, who repeated the soothing "death was instantaneous", but added "I will not worry you with the details of his last doings." Significantly, the regimental journal made reference to 'hand to hand fighting' and it was pretty common for both British and German solders to have what might be termed 'blunt instruments' to hand for such an eventuality. Whatever did happen, the end must have come pretty suddenly; just as well, really, as medical assistance for a severely wounded man was pretty rudimentary at that time. Harold's body was never recovered. His name is recorded on the 1927 memorial to those who have no marked grave at Menin Gate, Ypres.

It's also interesting to note that the severity of the action in which Harold was killed was later recognised by the powers-that-be; for gallantry shown during that operation, Major Torrens was awarded the Distinguished Service Order, two captains were mentioned in dispatches, and Military Medals were awarded to four of the NCOs and men taking part. Harold's name wasn't included in that list, but as the award of gallantry medals during that war was largely down to luck, or being in the right place at the right time – cynical squaddies used to refer to such decorations as 'coming up with the rations' – it's quite possible that Harold, too, laid down his life for his country in equally inspiring circumstances without official recognition for his bravery.

Back in West Bromwich, the local press were fulsome in their tributes. "One of the cleverest footballers of his day, an ideal centre forward and his brilliant exhibitions with the Albion at the Hawthorns will not be easily forgotten by Midlands sportsmen."

Councillor Kendrick, at the West Bromwich Council meeting in March proposed a condolence motion. During his lengthy tributes, he described Harold as "a worker, a hard worker and a good man when the time for play came, too. He was a gentleman in the largest sense, an English gentleman, and a sportsman."

Billy Bassett added his own tribute. "Bache is the greatest forward I have seen since the old days when the game produced men of individual skill. "

Harold Bache was just one death among millions during the supposed 'war to end all wars'. Yet his loss particularly stands out because of the waste of talent, the unrealised potential lost forever. He was the only senior WBA player to lose his life while contracted to the club. We'll never know just how much further his Albion adventure could have gone. The addition of his skills to the Baggies' already devastating attack in their post-war Championship winning side might have pushed their success beyond a single season. Bache played for the Football League just prior to the conflict, and commentators of the period were convinced that an England cap was inevitable. And from there? New club records and a dynasty of success? Who can say with certainty? It's perfectly possibly that had he survived, the Worcestershire Wonder may have chosen another path, another sport or another go at teaching.

HAROLD'S PREMATURE DEMISE bears comparison with another footballer born close to the Hawthorns. Another young man with Black Country roots. Unlike Harold, he'd already played and scored for his country, but there was so much to come, so many new audiences to enthuse, records to break, Cups to win. Until the day a plane crashed on take off in Munich… and Manchester United's Duncan Edwards was fatally injured. Edwards' death is marked by a grave in Dudley Cemetery.

Although Harold had gone, his contribution is remembered in several local places. His name, together will all the other Churchill men who did not return home, are remembered in a memorial window in the local Church. The new window was marked by a dedication service on Christmas Day 1919. H.G. Bache is also among the 115 West Bromwich casualties immortalised in new reredos (panelling) and a mural tablet in Holy Trinity Church. Brother Eric Bache gave the dedication address in late January 1920. Further afield, he's mentioned on the Gonville and Caius College war memorial.

In February 1922, Colonel JV Campbell VC of the Staffordshire Regiment unveiled a mural to all the Albion people (players, and deputy secretary) who had served or given their life during the war. (Lieutenant W.H. Jackson of the West Yorkshire Regiment was the other fatality). Each name was engraved on a brass tablet, surmounted by a portrait of Harold Bache in his football attire. The picture and the metal scroll remain on display at the Hawthorns to this day, located near to the Boardroom. The impression he made in those 14 brief appearances in a blue and white shirt should never be forgotten.

Years later, Albion players paid their own rather less permanent tribute to Harold and others who didn't return. The day before the 1931 Cup Final, the 'team of boys', as they became known, placed a wreath adorned with club colours on the Cenotaph in London in memory of their counterparts who fell during the war. The inscription read: "From the West Bromwich Albion Football Club to those great sportsmen who never returned."

TOMMY MAGEE

1919-1934

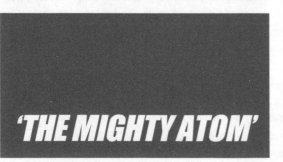

BAGGIES CAREER

Games	434
Goals	18
Caps	5

MAGIC MOMENT

Magee's snapping tiger role was the perfect platform from which to beat Villa 3-0 in November 1931

'THE MIGHTY ATOM'

FOR little Tommy, this was the best afternoon in his best season in his long Albion career. The *Birmingham Gazette* correspondent opined "when considering the man of the match award, nearly everybody plumped for Magee – a sterling tribute to a man in his thirteenth season, and facetiously called the veteran, because in a team of twenties, "thirty plus" ranks as an old man.

"Where is Curtis?" a Birmingham supporter pondered; he was in Magee's pocket. The way in which Magee positioned himself for the pass, intercepted it, pivoted and despatched the ball to a well-positioned colleague was beyond reproach, and, in the early stages, he had the temerity to introduce the ball to goalkeeper Hibbs by dropping it on top of the bar."

Two goals from W.G. Richardson added to an ever-increasing volume of rain and the Baggies' defensive strength was too much for the Blues to match. "The team of boys" – the WBA side had the lowest average age of any team to play in the Final – had won the FA Cup. City did score, though Tommy considered the goal unfair. "Gregg was a yard offside – he was in front of me and I was the last Albion defender, apart from the goalkeeper."

As the soggy Albion team climbed the steps to the Royal Box to collect the FA Cup from the Duke of Gloucester, the blackest of black footballers was heard to ask, "Has it been raining?"

AS A GENERAL RULE, Albion supporters don't do defensive midfielders. Destructive spoiling players sit uncomfortably with the club's pure football traditions. That every team needs one is accepted, but collectively, we don't have to like it. And generally we don't!

Tommy "Mighty Atom" Magee was a rare exception. He was the best of his genre – a genre which fulfils an unglamorous, functional and often dull role. In this job, participants run themselves into the ground and are then subsequently dropped. Modern day supporters will immediately make mental comparisons with Andy "AJ" Johnson, an inevitable though unfortunate link, given the amount of ridicule hurled in the nominal Welshman's direction in recent seasons.

Johnson is no more than a superficial cipher. Magee blocked out the best strikers in the country. He also had pace, could play as a winger if required, passed accurately, and served the club for 15 years.

Other than Johnson, in the modern era Derek McInnes was a real captain, but his inability to pass the ball accurately was a constant source of irritation. Carlton Palmer is a slightly closer match, though a perverse one, as Carlton is as tall as Tommy is short. Palmer didn't stick around to really show what he could do. Furthermore, his immature off the field activities made shipping him out a social as well as a financial necessity. Further back in time, Maurice Setters had a similar team role, but his uncompromising style, otherwise known as "kick everything that moves", caught the attention of so many referees that no-one was overly concerned when he was sold to Manchester United. Over the decades, only a handful of Albion men have fulfilled similar roles to Magee, and none so effectively.

Club Secretary and de facto manager Everiss was fulsome in his praise of his right half. "He knew that football was a manly game, calling for qualities of pluck, grit and endurance. When he got hurt – as all men do – he never whined or grumbled. Tommy played football for the sheer love of the sport. He was fain to measure his strength and skill against the best pros in the game. Like his pals, Jimmy Edwards and Teddy Sandford, he dearly loved to rough it in a manly charge with the best and cleverest exponents of that period. Tommy was one of the midgets of the association game, and it was never known for him to play really badly for Albion or England."

Harold Salt, one of Albion's oldest active supporters, saw his first game in 1929. "Little Tommy was the darling of the Brummie Road End, and indeed, of all the crowd. 'The little bantam cock' my Dad called him and every youngster identified with him; they all wanted to play like Tommy Magee. What a character."

Harold is adamant that the first Baggies middle section he saw are still the best he'd ever seen. "Magee, together with Billy Richardson and Jimmy "Iron" Edwards comprised what I consider to be the most dependable, strong and capable half back line I ever saw in what I call 'logical' team arrangements."

When the trio properly came together in September 1930, they meshed perfectly. They were able to build on the confidence that winning the first four games of the season brings. Tommy was no longer simply a hard working and highly popular individual, he was part of a powerful threesome who knew each other's game and instinctively covered for each other. The three men first made the same teamsheet for the final eight games of 1929/30, though "Iron" Edwards was turning out as a forward. In a remarkable surge of form, the Baggies won their last seven games. Using the adage of never changing a winning team, Tommy retained his No. 4 shirt, much to his relief after a long exile with the stiffs. The Baggies rattled in 23 goals in those final eight fixtures. The new improved midfield set-up was the driving force behind the Baggies' 1930/31 season, one of the best in the club's history.

BY THE END of September, WBA were top of the Second Division and sniffing promotion. The Baggies were full of confidence and full of goals, partly due to the introduction of a young and exciting talent in the form of a certain W.G. Richardson. Cardiff were beaten 6-3, Forest 6-1, Barnsley 5-0 and Stoke 4-0. The Widnes man was supporting the attack more often, in addition to his famed defensive qualities. Tommy scored during the aforementioned demolition of Stoke in December, in what turned out to be his last-ever goal.

Despite all the distractions of a Cup run, Albion kept on track for promotion – just about. The team were wobbling with mistakes creeping in, such as during a 2-1 home defeat by Southampton in February when Tommy gave away the first goal. "Instead of kicking into touch when he had the opportunity, the Albion half-back indulged in fancy deceptive work with the ball near to the corner flag and left winger Arnold refused to 'take the bait,' with the result that the winger sent across a disconcerting square service, which eventually went into the net off an Albion defender." Thankfully, promotion rivals Spurs had their own serious attack of jitters.

By May, Everton had won the Second Division Championship comfortably, but if Albion could win their remaining two games, they'd join the Scousers in the First Division. With Albion travelling from their Buxton base (to escape the wake of their FA Cup success), Stoke were beaten 1-0 at the Victoria Ground. Magee charged out of the back line to set up W.G. Richardson for the vital winning goal.

And so on to Charlton. Over 52,000 packed into the Hawthorns to see Albion do battle with the Londoners for the fifth time that season. Athletic would not go quietly. Twice Horton beat Magee and twice Charlton scored. Twice Albion came back to level before snatching the lead twenty minutes from the end. They would not give anything away again. Finally, Charlton were beaten, and Albion were promoted. The final whistle was greeted with a massive pitch invasion. No-one would leave until proper homage had been paid to a remarkable side.

To properly mark their achievements, the players each received a replica FA Cup – about 18 inches high. For many years, Tommy's replica took pride of place in the Cross Keys pub in West Bromwich. The Keys was run by Tommy's youngest daughter June and her husband Ken. It was one of Ken's weekly jobs to polish the trophy every Sunday. Indeed, the whole pub became a shrine to Tommy with around 50 pictures adorning the walls.

In 12 years, Tommy had moved on from his debut as a raw 20 year-old to the very top of his professional tree. The name of T. Magee, "a dashing young inside-forward who shows such promise" featured for the first time on an Albion team list for the home match against Oldham Athletic on 30th August 1919. The day was special, for it marked the resumption of League football after the horrors of the First World War. The Baggies won 3-1 in front of 19,084 spectators. Magee turned out at inside-forward, one of the usual quintet of forwards in a standard 2-3-5 formation. The *Midland Chronicle* commented "he was by no means prominent and acquitted himself with no outstanding display, but nevertheless he is a promising addition to the team." In his first appearance, Tommy, at five foot three inches, set a new record as the smallest ever Albion first teamer, a feat that held until the early 1990s, when the one-inch smaller Stewart Bowen played a handful of matches.

That Tommy was able to start his football days with such a big name club is quite remarkable. His story is unique in Albion history.

THOMAS PATRICK MAGEE was born in Widnes on 12th May 1899, to James and Agnes, their first child. 23-year-old James worked as a chemical labourer in the town. Like most Magees in that area, their family had Irish ancestry.

As a child, Tommy attended St Mary's School. He quickly became interested in sport, playing football for Widnes Athletic and rugby league for Appleton Hornets and St. Helen's Recreation. He actually signed pro forms for St. Helen's, but was injured in his second match and decided rugby was not for him.

Following so many other starry-eyed teenagers, young Magee lied about his age to enlist and was accepted as a drummer boy in a labour battalion. This was a nominal title, offering no concessions for his age. He may or may not have had a drum to lug about – either way he was just as exposed to German shells as any adult.

Despite his lack of height, Tommy was picked to play as a centre-forward for inter-unit matches. He was a natural, despite his rugger background. By happy coincidence, one of the many onlookers for these service battles was Tom Brewer, an Albion supporter.

Quickly, Brewer wrote to Albion Secretary Fred Everiss recommending, "the wizard playing for us out here. I think he could do great things for your club." The story goes that Everiss wrote to Magee's commanding officer, one Lieutenant Hill – whose home just happened to be in Smethwick – enclosing amateur forms, which Tommy duly signed in the trenches. It's a common myth that the youngster effectively joined the Baggies during active service, with attendant images of a brave young soldier crouching in a trench with shells raining down, attempting to keep the precious paper dry. The reality is much more mundane. Tommy's autograph is dated 27th January 1919; two months after a ceasefire had been agreed. The conflict existed only in a technical sense until the Treaty of Versailles was agreed.

The Widnes teenager was highly fortunate to be released from his army duties a few weeks later. Little thought had been given to demobilisation. The whole process was frankly botched, creating much bitterness in the ranks and back in England. Many soldiers waited as long as a year to return home.

Signing a contract to play for First Division West Bromwich quickly brought a reward. Magee ran out at centre-forward against Aston Villa in a Colts (third team) match on 22nd March. This was his first appearance in an Albion jersey, indeed his first properly organised football match of any kind. A most successful introduction it was, too, with the ex-drummer boy troubling the opposition from Birmingham B6. He scored twice in a 5-0 victory.

Five weeks later, after scoring regularly in the Midlands Victory League (a four club match practice exercise set up by WBA), Magee signed professional forms. "I had no option, he was brilliant" explained Albion Secretary Fred Everiss.

YOUNG TOMMY was excited as he turned up for his first day at work with one of the country's biggest football clubs, alongside some of the most famous players in the country like Jesse Pennington. He stood out immediately, with observers convinced that Magee, along with Howard Gregory, were the pick of the seniors' team.

These were troubled times for the area and indeed, a frustrated and war weary nation. In the dark days of mud and bullets in France, Black Country men mentally built up West Bromwich as a peaceful utopia. The reality fell well short of their dreams. Work was hard to find, with over 4,500 unemployed men in Oldbury, Wednesbury, and West Bromwich combined. Dozens died every week across West Bromwich from a new fatal strain of flu, which swept across the globe. Four other Albion men – Bentley, Reid, Sterman and Vardy returned home from active service at the end of January 1919. A month on, Crisp and S. Hatton, who'd won a Military Medal during his service, rejoined their team mates.

The gloomy picture was reflected nationwide. Rationing remained in force. Coal, the sole source of heating, was desperately short. Coal theft was a thriving industry. The continued absence of loved ones was a burden for everyone. Worse, over 800,000 males were maimed by the war. Most were found work of a kind, but by the autumn of 1919, 50,000 still sought employ-ment, while a similar number remained in hospital. Football as a panacea was an unrecognised concept in that era, unlike it proved after the 1939-45 war. Few could put into words the beneficial effects of such a distraction. They just went to the match and felt better for doing so.

Following a decent debut against the Latics, Tommy retained his first team place and his first goal came at Newcastle just days later. Crisp set him up from a corner, and Tommy's powerful shot beat the keeper. He missed a good chance to double his tally "because of an indiscriminate kick which went wide." More accolades were slow to follow for the newcomer. In fairness, the Baggies were not short of goalscorers or headline grabbers. During Albion's 5-2 September win at Goodison Park, a victory appreciated by the home crowd; a correspondent noted, "only the impulsiveness of Magee prevented a larger score."

In February, Magee dropped out of the first team, and did not play again that season. Thus he was a mere spectator, as the Baggies became comfortable League Champions by nine points. However, as the baby of the team at 21 years old in his first season, 24 games with seven goals was a grand start. He remains, to this day, the youngest Albion player ever to win a Championship medal. The directors employed only 18 players in the first team, and with 3 of those only making four appearances between them, the remaining fifteen showed remarkable resilience and stamina. Players turned out while injured, either through ignorance, or through fear of losing their place. Furthermore, any trip outside the Midlands took on epic proportions, travelling overnight and arriving home in the wee small hours.

As well as a medal, Tommy also had a wife, marrying Elizabeth Fanny Yates in West Bromwich. His new wife also originally hailed from Cheshire and, highly significantly for the time, was pregnant with their first child. The pressure was on to "do the decent thing" and do it quickly. So, an April Sunday would suffice. A summer wedding was out of the question. Among the witnesses was Tommy's team mate Sammy Richardson. Presumably too, Elizabeth subsequently moved out of her accommodation in Mitchell Road to join her new husband at 119 Burlington Road, West Bromwich (near to the Vine pub). Such proximity to the Hawthorns was commonplace, and perfectly normal at the time. In those pre-car times, players and their families all lived locally.

With a wife and child to support, Magee needed all the appearance money he could get. Unfortunately for family finances, he didn't return regularly to the Baggies first XI until October 1921, by which time he was a proud Dad to daughter Irene. Tommy was now considered to be a right-winger. This was not a good period to be overly concerned about preferred playing position, or, frankly, even being in the first team. Having a job at all in a recession was important – having a job receiving decent and guaranteed money was as good it got. Unemployment was mounting by the week, virtually doubling in West Bromwich in just three months.

Tommy couldn't even claim to be a regular reserve player in these difficult social times. Reports were rarely positive about his contribution, with frequent mentions of "weak shooting" or "sent outside". Magee had most of the assets needed to be a professional footballer, but perhaps inside or centre-forward was not his best position. So the next logical choice would be to play on the wing. Speed was more important than size out wide, and he began to get noticed, notably at Villa Park, where his contribution was described as "exceptional."

A COMBINATION of illness, FA call-ups and lack of form from his team-mates (the Baggies' first home goal of the season didn't arrive until late October) gave Magee his big break in the number 7 shirt. England international Claude Jephcott came a cropper at Middlesbrough in September with an injury which put him out of action until the following April. Magee did his best to impress the Board of Directors, who then selected the team. Finding the net at Bolton helped his cause, scoring from "a very oblique" angle after another new face, Blagden, set him up. Albion's form slowly picked up with Magee frequently combining cleverly with Blagden. He even scored a few goals himself, though one Cup effort at Liverpool was ruled illegal when he knocked both keeper and ball into the net. Tommy may have been vertically challenged, but he was a tough cookie. An example of just how tough came at Goodison; Tommy was "...laid out. Despite shouts of the spectators, neither the referee, linesman or players took any notice, and a spectator jumped over the barrier, took off his overcoat, and laid it over the prone half-back until the arrival of the trainer. He soon resumed and was again in the thick of the fray."

Crosses from Tommy set up goals at Preston, both at home and away at Chelsea, at home against Barnsley, and at Burnley, as the Widnes man built a name for himself. He positively starred at Bradford: "Magee was alone in approaching the usual brilliance of the line. His centres were always at the psychologically correct moment, and were characterised with neatness and precision. His good sense, however, only served to show the frequent ineptitude of the front men."

Rarely in peacetime has football been so irrelevant to the Black Country. Local miners were striking, destitution was rife, while at West Bromwich Law court in early 1922, 300 Police baton-charged an unhappy crowd of several thousands. Potentially deadly flu was everywhere with West Bromwich doctors now seeing over 20,000 cases in just one month. Perversely, rarely have Albion's remaining supporters needed the beautiful game more and, as they flocked to the Hawthorns, they took to the determined little bloke on the wing. He was like them, up against the odds all the time, but getting through by trickery, strength and perseverance. Perhaps they saw a reflection of their own lives in "wee Tummy" as he was sometimes known.

And yet still the football club were not satisfied. Jephcott was the preferred choice on the right wing, and the Widnes man considered no more than a reserve. "Not a finished player, but a useful man in an emergency."

To underline these sentiments, Jephcott had a run-out against Newcastle in April, a move announced weeks in advance. Tommy didn't play that day, but returned the following match – away to just-crowned Champions Liverpool. Regular right half-back (the midfield of the time whose role was to "get the ball and part with it.") Sammy Richardson was hurt in a collision with a Liverpool player, and had to leave the field. A bad cut over his left eye required four stitches. In a career-changing move, Magee was asked to fill in for the stricken destroyer. He made an immediate impact in a marvellous personal triumph. Enthused the *West Bromwich Free Press* "He effectively blocked the way of [Liverpool forwards] Hopkin and Beadles, and kicked strongly in defence." Buoyed up by their inspirational right-half, ten man WBA went on to beat the new champions 2-1 on their own ground.

Liverpool had immediate opportunity for revenge in the return fixture a week later, the final League game of the season. Albion selected a young reserve, Watson, at right-half in what transpired to be his only first team game. Watson was unable to prevent his Red opponent from charging past him and the game was virtually up by half time. Captain Jesse Pennington, remembering Anfield, swapped Watson and Magee during the break, and once more Tommy made an impact. "Magee certainly shaped better than Watson against the clever Liverpool left wing," opined the Chronicle's reporter.

Albion had a new option at right-half, and Tommy had a new career in front of him.

With Claude Jephcott available once more on the right wing, Tommy started the 1922/23 season in his second new position. At first, being the link between defence and attack didn't come easy, and enthusiasm alone wouldn't get him through 90 minutes. Being "an animated bundle of concentrated energy and industry with unlimited pluck," according to the Argus, wasn't sufficient in itself. After a few matches, doubts arose that he was the man for the job. In the fifth fixture, a 2-0 defeat at Villa Park, Claude Jephcott broke his leg and was carted off to a nursing home, never to play again. The right wing berth was thus available, but Magee retained his No. 4 shirt for the re-match.

Before a 40,000 crowd at the Hawthorns in September, Tommy made his name and his reputation. Villa's forwards found a diminutive snapping tiger in front of them who would not let them pass. His hustle and energy, his "unfaltering stability" and being "a terror for his size", provided a platform for a glorious 3-0 victory. The *Midland Chronicle* gleefully outlined "giving the Villa the severest trouncing they have had in these local derbies for eleven years." A sound piece of advice for any aspiring Baggies Cult Hero, if you want to get noticed, do it before the biggest gate of the season against your local rivals.

IN AN ERA when all players had the same coloured skin, wore the same boots and sported identical, short haircuts, any distinguishing features were sub-consciously well received. Good visibility in the 1920s heavily industrialised Black Country was a bonus, not a guarantee. Pollution was a normal social hazard. Smoke poured out of factory and colliery chimneys, and all too often knitted together to block out the sun. Fog or the potential for fog was often blamed for low attendances in winter.

The infamous pea-souper could prove fatal. For instance, Sarah Barnsley of Tipton drowned when she fell into the local canal, having lost her way. "As usual, it bought tragedy," reported the local press wearily. The absence of a roof for many spectators at the Hawthorns also hampered identification, as did poor eyesight, two decades before the start of the NHS. Size really did matter for Albion supporters. Particularly tall players (six foot was about as big as they came then) or rather small ones literally stood out. Add skill and dash to a non-standard sized body, and crowd favourite status was always a strong possibility.

Post-Villa, the diminutive right-half was suddenly a name, a player worthy of watching in action. All Albion's subsequent opposition such as Everton, Bolton and Sunderland found the "animated bundle" a great obstacle. He was here, there and everywhere, and heartily cheered by the Albion support. In the Baggies' 5-1 rout of Spurs, Tommy was even mentioned favourably in the London press (traditionally considered to be ignorant of the Midlands), a news story in its own right in the Black Country. The only concern for supporters was the inclusion of Magee meant no place for the fine Sammy Richardson. It was a dilemma: Sammy did get a chance at Blackburn, but did his cause no good at all with a limp performance in a 5-1 defeat. This was awkward for Tommy too because he and Sammy were great pals.

THE ARRIVAL OF Sunderland for an FA Cup match broke the Hawthorns attendance record. Over 56,000 crammed in, with numerous journalists also in attendance for the big "English Cup" match. Tommy and his fellow half-backs dominated in an Albion victory, and once again, his name shone from national titles. The FA Cup, enjoyed remarkable status and prestige in that era: supporters from the away team would be in attendance, a novelty otherwise reserved only for local derbies. This was the season which would result in the first ever Wembley final, white horse and overcrowded pitch, beginning a legend which prevails to this day. That around 200,000 people would wish to watch a mere football match gave as good an indication as anything that this game had taken a grip of the nation's imagination and passion in these grim times.

Albion home supporters were generally a laid back bunch. Though they would prefer their side to win, applauding or even cheering opposition players or moves was commonplace. If Tommy could "turn it on" away from home, the opposition supporters would willingly show their appreciation – and it made his name all the more. For instance, at Burnley, "Magee, who is Lancashire born, always has a fine reception, and on Saturday, the Burnley crowd fully appreciated the wonderful play of this little half-back. He bottled up Cross and Waterfield, and the spectators recognised it by giving him rounds of applause. On his form this year, Magee stands an excellent chance of earning a much sought after international cap."

SUCH WAS Tommy's rising reputation, he was selected for England trial matches against the South. Once more, the London press were impressed. "Magee was a distinct success," admitted a *Daily Mail* reporter. His battles against the two opposition forwards made the whole match interesting. Tommy had another trial, this time against the North. His contribution to that match at Leeds was far more modest, however he was subsequently picked to represent his country against Wales in the Home Internationals (a popular annual League competition between the four home nations).

Tommy, according to the *Birmingham Mail,* was "one of the most popular of all the Albion players, both among his colleagues and the club's supporters." More recognition followed when the midfielder played in the second of two matches against Sweden in Stockholm in May. Three more caps eventually arrived – against Belgium at the Hawthorns, Scotland at Hampden, and France in Paris. Being a local resident made good served to deepen Tommy's popularity according to the *Chronicle.* "He received a capital reception when it was made known he had received another cap."

Much was made of Tommy's small frame, but in his era, he was probably just below average weight at 10 and a half stone. Nine of Albion's registered players were lighter, with a few below ten stone. Neither was his lack of inches quite so distinctive at that time. Goalkeeper Pearson stood just over six foot tall, but none of the other double winners were over five foot ten. Eight inches difference was certainly enough to be noticeable, but not an impossible shortfall to overcome.

His two most often used nicknames of 'Mighty Atom' and 'Pocket Hercules' were not original titles. It is likely that they were 'borrowed' from other great players in much the same way, in later decades, that any player called Robson was automatically dubbed "Pop", after the West Ham man who bore the original sobriquet. Patsy Gallacher of Celtic was known as the 'Mighty Atom', while Everton's Jack Sharp was dubbed 'Pocket Hercules' as far back as 1899.

Tommy was invited to join the FA XI on their epic voyage to Canada in 1926. For invited, read, "you're going". What the FA said, the FA got. For a man with such a modest background, this was a glorious extended opportunity to travel abroad without anyone shelling him – to visit such exotic locations like Toronto, Vancouver and Calgary, and other places he'd never heard of. The tour was a wearisome 18 game slog. The games stretched through May, June and July, involving numerous uncomfortable days rattling across the vast acreage of Canada by train. Tommy played in 15 of the 18 fixtures, all of which were won. His young wife Elisabeth gave birth to their second daughter, June, during his absence.

This tour was literally not the trip of a lifetime because five years later, Tommy went again. Magee, together with double-winning colleagues Cookson and Shaw were all selected to represent the FA. There were only 11 games this time, over two months. Fortunately, someone made the sensible decision that the players would not train between matches. The party travelled out on the Canadian Pacific liner "Duchess of Atholl" on the 15th May 1931, and didn't return until late July, just in time for pre-season training. Once more, every game was won with some ease, Cookson alone amassing 26 goals. The FA expressed their contentment with the efforts of the touring party, awarding each player an international cap and £10 additional personal expenses, a decent boost to Tommy's £7 weekly wage. Every player was also invited to a banquet in London.

Tommy's hopes of more international fayre were damaged between these two trips by the not insignificant problem of relegation. A deadly combination of leaky defence and the forwards' inability to find the net led to the drop in 1927. Only 15 goals each for top scorers Carter and Davies was not good enough for such a big club. "Singularly unimpressive" as one irate fan described their contribution. To quote the nursery rhyme, when they were bad, they were horrid. At West Ham, for instance, the correspondent for the *Birmingham Gazette* noted, "when Albion caught the infection, and emulated the example of the United in a display of wild and aimless kicking, the crowd indulged in a form of communal hilarity which one has never heard equalled."

IN GRIM TIMES, supporters feel a need to grasp what positives they can. In 1986, Steve Hunt, seemingly taking on the opposition by himself, caught the eye. In 1991, Don Goodman's pace and goals offered ultimately false hope. In 1927, it was little Tommy, refusing to let his opponent get past him and supporting his front men where possible, which captured the attention of supporters and reporters alike. The *Gazette* reported typically on a defeat at Old Trafford. "The magnificent display given by Magee. He smothered Thomas out of the picture altogether and repeatedly made forward thrusts that ended in a perfect pass to Davies or Carter. The crowd were highly appreciative of the little man's performance." Filling in for injuries, Tommy made a few effective appearances on the wing, though without his defensive skills, the defence sagged. Albion needed two Tommy Magees – at least. However, even Tommy's enthusiasm and form waned as relegation became inevitable.

Like many other top-line players, Magee found adjusting to the different style of the Second Division most difficult. He was below his best for months on end, chided for making forward runs at the wrong moment, or not tackling his opponent quickly enough. Lamented the Post correspondent following a home defeat against Nottingham Forest "Magee certainly played a long way below the form which in the past has won him international fame." After this low point, his timing and all round game improved somewhat, if still rather up and down. The consistency of another Richardson (Bill) at half-back only served to highlight the contrast. Returning from whence he came, though, remained elusive. As Albion have traditionally found throughout their history, returning to the top Division after relegation is both difficult and highly frustrating.

Still, there were the occasional high points, such as a victory at Clapton Orient, as the *Chronicle* correspondent recorded. "One saw admirable work from Magee, who took a new leave of skill from the occasion and proved himself a very able defender and a half-back, who, when the opportunity presented itself, was not only aggressive, but skilfully aggressive. That is to say he made of his right wing a smartly working trio in which Glidden, Carter and he were conspicuously useful."

Tommy managed only to score two goals in four seasons in the lower Division, curiously both against the same opposition – Stoke City. The first was a fluke, when his long punt so startled the City keeper (albeit he did have Albion striker Cookson "in attendance"), that the ball skidded off his hand into the net. The second, in December 1930, surprisingly was his last ever goal.

Poor health didn't help. Wee Tummy turned out for a crucial Cup quarter-final replay at Huddersfield, "Magee took a resolute hand in the spoiling process, considering that he had just left bed after an attack of influenza, he summoned up his strength to equal his zeal with rare pluck, and in the first half, particularly kept Smith establishing anything like a perfect liaison with the centre and right wing."

After such an effort, he presumably suffered a relapse and was rested for the next League game at Vale. Or that was the idea, until Carter was taken ill en-route. A wire was sent to 'Get Magee'. Arriving by "special car", he was asked to play on the right wing. Sadly, he wasn't fully fit, and could do no more than lay the ball off when it came to him. Albion were wretched, losing 8-1 and Tommy felt wretched too. He played very little part in the rest of the season, even after he was restored to full health. Neither did he make much of an impression on the next as the trio of Richardson, Evans and Darnall were playing so well together. The Mighty Atom was a second team regular, and still not in the best of form.

He made one of his most public appearances of this time in August 1931, not on the football pitch, but as a pallbearer at the funeral of Albion Director Harry Keys, the six most senior players carrying the coffin. The future looked grim until a happy coming together of a dynamic midfield and a goalscoring machine were united, and a promotion charge was suddenly on.

MANY ALBION supporters thought that the 1931/32 season would prove to be a farewell one for the diminutive midfielder. He'd given them good service, they'd loved him, but now he was obviously coming to the end. Not so, the directors including the name of Tommy Magee on the Retained List. (At that time, players were either Retained – effectively a one-year contract – or released or transfer listed). The local press were taken aback, but quickly rallied. "It is a great tribute to Tommy Magee, the veteran of the side, that he should be retained after 13 years service with the club. That there is 'life in the old dog yet' has been amply demonstrated by his wonderful performances during the latter half of the season. His experience of First Division football as a member of the Albion side before relegation should be an asset to the younger members next season." However, despite his extra time, football life again became more problematic for Tommy. Following on from such triumphs would be admittedly difficult for anybody.

Still, the first season back in the top flight began superbly for the club's senior professional. Tommy's tackling was an integral part of an excellent team, who had the temerity, as a promoted side, to challenge strongly for the title. The Baggies had the toughest opener possible – at Highbury, against League Champions Arsenal. Remarkably, Albion won 1-0 with the Widnes man highly prominent. One commentator said, "it was gratifying to see how well Magee acquitted himself against the James-Bastin wing. His Canadian tour has given him new vigour." By this point, the England international had played football continually for twelve months, without any substantial rest, due to his inclusion on that FA tour. Eric Brook, the famous Manchester City and England forward said Magee, together with Edwards of Leeds, were the hardest right-halves he had ever played against. "They play so much on top of you that it is difficult to go ahead, and I usually have to make a back pass."

At Christmas, life became much tougher for the right-half. He injured his knee in the Christmas Day battle with Birmingham City, and couldn't play in the return fixture the following day. It was the end of his run of 61 successive first team games. At first, doctors feared a dis-placed cartilage, for which an operation was required. Thankfully, the final diagnosis was a torn ligament and (long overdue) rest was the only cure. Without him and other key personnel, the Baggies slipped from second position in the League to finish sixth. "Magee's absence has been severely felt" lamented the *Albion News*.

Tommy was a day short of his comeback game against Wolves reserves in late February when domestic tragedy struck at their new home at 34 Westbourne Road, West Bromwich. His wife went to the bathroom on Friday night to take a bath. Tommy heard a noise, and hastened to the bathroom, where he found his wife dying, struck down by a brain haemorrhage. It's impossible to comprehend the anguish he must have endured at that moment, and since. His other half was just 33 years-old, and they had two young daughters to care for. Elizabeth Magee was buried at St. Peter's Church, Whitehall Road, West Bromwich. It is at such times of crisis when personal popularity is tested. Tommy didn't want in this respect. People lined the streets the entire distance (around one and a half miles) between the family home and the church and St. Peter's was full to capacity with family, friends, supporters, players plus two club directors.

His parents made the trip down, and a saddened Tommy returned with them to spend a few days back in his hometown of Widnes. He returned to piles of sympathetic letters from his team-mates and supporters, to which he responded with a "thank you" small ad in the local press. By mid-March, he was playing football again, cheered heartily on and off the pitch against Manchester United's second string. After all, he knew nothing else, and had to provide. But life would be difficult for a widower with two children, even with support from his in-laws. Fortunately, Elizabeth's grandparents ran the nearby Dunkirk Inn at nearby Greets Green and Tommy and his children moved in with them. The arrangement was ideal in several ways. Tommy always loved a drink, even on a matchday. His idea of relaxation was simply to have a good time with team mates like WG Richardson and Harold Pearson, friends or later on his son in law. Attending race meetings or the dogs were both particular favourites (later in his life, he ran a chain of bookmakers in Widnes). Another regular haunt was Ted Sandford's café. He was naturally outgoing with always a joke or two to share. Tommy regularly referred to the Black Country as "crow country" as in "caw do this" or "caw do that".

Some kind of temporary relief from Tommy's loss came in April, when the Baggies ven-tured northwards to turn out for a benefit match against a Widnes Select XI in order to raise funds for the local Widnes rugby club to buy their ground. As a Widnes lad, Tommy was named captain for the night. It was an uplifting return home. The West Bromwich side was met by a jazz band, which escorted them through crowded streets to meet the Mayor at the town hall. The visitors won their match 4-1 (£200 raised) and then were welcome guests at a banquet.

Tommy returned to the first team for the opening games of the new 1932/33 season, reunited with Bill Richardson and "Iron" Edwards. Then, after a run of four matches without a win, changes were made. Jimmy 'Spud' Murphy seized his chance, performing so well in the No. 4 shirt; he eventually played for his country. Tommy was to play only five more games at the top level in the following eighteen months. His regular absence from the second team further emphasised the writing on the wall.

His first team farewell came at the Hawthorns against Huddersfield in March 1934 in a 3-2 defeat, and a brief farewell it was, a leg injury causing him to retire hurt after just half an hour. His low-key departure (no benefit game) from the club he'd served for a decade and a half, followed on the 5th May, marked only by small sub-headings in the local press. The only Baggies player to win both a Cup winners and a Championship medal was never seen again in League football.

CONSIDER TOMMY as a miniature midfield Jeff Astle, a man who contributed as much off the field as on it. He broke a mould that was hastily re-pieced together after his departure, by breaking up opposition attacks and being genuinely appreciated by supporters and England selectors for doing so. No other Albion man since enjoyed such positive feedback. Of course, there was more to him than endless running and tackling. Thanks to his son in law Ken Taylor, we can now also appreciate Tommy the man – down to earth, modest; always ready to share a pint (or pull one in the Dunkirk). His gregarious nature was so well received in such a basic hard working area like the Black Country. Despite those Cheshire tones, he was one of us.

WG RICHARDSON

1929-1945

BAGGIES CAREER

Games	444
Goals	328
Caps	1

MAGIC MOMENT

His goals won
the 1931 FA Cup,
and promotion...
in eight days!

'GINGER'

ON 29 March 1959, an unremarkable charity match was staged at the BSA Recreation Ground in Small Heath, Birmingham. The Midland All-Stars were doing leisurely battle with the combined might of the TV All Stars XI. Before kick-off, the captain of the Midland All-Star side was photographed next to the TV Stars' captain, one Bernie Winters.

After 20 minutes of the second half, the captain of the Midland All-Stars chased the ball down the right wing, but collapsed near the corner flag. He was carried from the pitch, but was dead on arrival at Birmingham Accident Hospital. William Richardson, West Bromwich Albion's most prolific goalscorer was gone. "I'm sure this is the way he would have wanted it – wearing a number 9 shirt," offered his widow bravely. W.G., as he will be forever known, was two months short of his 50th birthday.

YOUNG WILLIAM was born in 1909 in Framwellgate Moor, a mining village in close proximity to Durham. Not surprisingly, his father supported his family by working underground in a pit. His favourite pastime was supporting Sunderland. His son was carefully taught that there was really only one football club worthy of his time. And, as he was making a name for himself as both Durham County schoolboy and England Schools international triallist, Richardson Senior went right to the top to get advice about his son's talent, seeking out the Mackems' best-known player, Charlie Buchan. The footballer was precise with his thoughts. "Don't let him play for three years when he leaves school. His muscles will adjust themselves to his physical growth by then, and he will be all the better." Charlie's advice was sound: in those days, boys literally played against men because there were no age-limit matches.

So William left school at 14, and joined the United Bus Company in West Hartlepool working shifts on Saturday afternoons: football was well and truly off the agenda until he reached 17. His frame now suitably broadened by that time, he joined a local club, quickly turning a famine into a feast by scoring regularly. Hartlepool spotted him before too long, and signed the then-bus conductor as a part-time professional.

In the summer of 1929, Jesse Pennington happened to be holidaying in Hartlepool with former Albion team-mate Bob Pailor. Noting his host was particularly enthusiastic about a young footballer with 19 goals to his name, Jesse was quick to contact the Albion. As a result, Fred Everiss and Director Lou Nurse travelled, and persuaded Hartlepool manager Will Norman to sell William Richardson for £1,250. As Bill recalled "The three of them were waiting for me when I got off the bus to go home for my dinner; I was a bus inspector then. We all trooped into my house where Mother was getting my meal out of the oven, and I signed on in the front parlour, aspidistra and all."

The Framwellgate forward made an instant impact at his new Midlands club, as noted in the *West Bromwich Chronicle*. The "most successful in the first practice game included

Richardson. In the second half [of the traditional Whites v Stripes public match] W.G. gave a rousing display which changed the whole aspect of the game and enabled the Whites to win. Scoring one goal himself, and providing Short with the chance to add another, Richardson proved himself to a capable leader and a force to be reckoned with."

There was an obvious difficulty. Albion already had a William or Billy Richardson in their squad. The other Richardson was a local-born centre-half, one of a host of intelligent signings in 1929, including Ted Sandford, Jimmy Edwards, and Bert Trentham, all of whom would play a part in Albion's renaissance. To distinguish between the two Richardsons, the North-East newcomer was called Ginger, because of the colour of his hair, or more commonly by his initials, W.G. In the official football documents of the club, however, the centre-half was always W. Richardson No.1 and the centre-forward W. Richardson No. 2.

Naturally, the newly dubbed W.G. started in the Central League, making his debut against Huddersfield. According to the *Albion News*: "Richardson gave an impressive display – confirming the high opinion formed of him in the practice games." He didn't score that day, but his first goal wasn't all that far away, nor his second and third... Two in a game were common-place, such as the brace against Derby in a 12-2 win; there were several hat-tricks, too, even the odd four or five, over 50 goals in all. Such prowess could not be ignored. W.G. made his first team debut against Millwall on Boxing Day in 1929, replacing the injured Cookson. He scored in a 6-2 win, and went on to play in five out of the next six matches, finding the net against Barnsley, before Cookson returned. The Baggies were not short of goalscorers at the time, with their main three forwards managing 72 between them that season.

A series of injuries put young W.G. back in the first team in November 1930. Playing at inside-forward, rather than as the main striker didn't help his cause, but once switched to No. 9, he found the net eight times in eight games, meaning he was now in the team to stay, missing only a handful of games between then and September 1937 and every year he was the club's top league scorer.

Goals always make for popularity among the supporting hordes, but W.G. was so enthusiastic and wholehearted that even without his goals, he was destined to be popular. For instance, in a match against Burnley in December 1930, he'd needed the magic sponge after colliding with the Clarets goalkeeper. Within 15 seconds of re-entering the pitch, he'd made the most of a pass from Carter to score the winning goal. Curiously, for such an instinctive goalscorer, he proved to be wonderfully unselfish, dutifully passing to better-placed colleagues rather than shoot himself. Sometimes too unselfish, as in one game against Man City, when he effectively had a one-on-one with the City goalkeeper "but to the amazement of the crowd, he flicked the ball in the direction of Robbins, who had little hope of using it."

BUT ALL THAT was in the future, in the short-term there was a little grumbling among the Hawthorns faithful: bringing in a youngster was all very well, but why at the expense of Jimmy Cookson? Cookson was himself highly regarded with over 100 goals to his name. He did have one final chance to redeem himself in February 1931, though, when W.G. moved to inside-forward to allow Cookson the No. 9 shirt. In two games, Cookson didn't score, but Richardson bagged three. With promotion to chase, this was not a time for further experiments: the old King was dethroned, his Albion playing days virtually finished. A new King of the Hawthorns was to be crowned.

And just not promotion: West Bromwich also fancied the FA Cup, despite their Second Division status. W.G.'s goal knocked out Charlton in a Third round second replay, and Spurs bit the dust in Round 4. In the next tie at Fratton Park W.G.'s solitary effort knocked out First Division Pompey. Not that he knew too much about it, mind: as W.G. made contact with a loose ball in the goalmouth, he fell flat on his face. "No-one was more amazed than me when I realised it had gone in."

There was more to come. The ginger-haired striker found the net in the quarter-final at home to Wolves, where he was described as being "Albion's most virile and dangerous forward." No doubt bucked by such a description, W.G. scored the winner in the Molineux replay. Nothing like crucial goals in Cup matches against local opposition to raise your popularity! *The Chronicle* reported on the replay: "W.G's leadership was inspiring enough to make his colleagues feel he was worth supporting." When asked what he remembered best about the victory, W.G. modestly overlooked his own contribution. "My abiding memory of that game was Harold Pearson saving a lob from Jimmy Deacon, who was clean through in the second minute. It was the sort of shot you don't expect a goalkeeper to save."

The semi-final was against Everton, runaway Second Division leaders, at Old Trafford. Hardly a balanced location for such an important match, but nevertheless, special trains transported 3,000 Albion supporters, with more travelling by coach, Evertonians heavily outnumbering them.

On the pitch, the Midlanders probably felt outnumbered as well, as the Scousers battered away at the West Bromwich defence, missing chance after chance. As W.G. himself remembered: "From the first minute, every Albion supporter must have had his heart in his mouth, and there it must have stayed for the first half an hour. Every Everton forward missed more easy chances than you could count. I was at centre-forward – the spectator with the best view, for I couldn't have touched the ball more than half a dozen times in that half hour."

The Baggies hung on, hoping desperately for a break. In the second half, they got one. Glidden crossed into the Everton goalmouth, hoping that W.G. might get a piece of it. The Everton custodian, Coggins, was so disconcerted by the sight of the onrushing W.G. that he hadn't noticed the ball's trajectory had been diverted by the wind. By the time he did, it was past him and in the net. W.G. again: "The goal was like a whole season's luck rolled into one... Coggins had his eye on me, and before he knew what was happening, the ball had bounced over his head into the net." The Baggies hung on to their slender lead to the end when: "hundreds swarmed across the playing surface," according to the *Chronicle*, "and before the players had time to get to the dressing room, they were caught and slapped and patted in a most affectionate, if somewhat brusque, manner."

ALBION WERE AT Wembley for the first time in their history, and so too were neighbours Birmingham City. All West Midlands trains would leave for London that day, pouring into Paddington station every 12 minutes over a seven-hour period. The Argus claimed 48 special trains left Snow Hill and New Street stations alone by 11.00am, this on top of the scheduled service. Albion received 80,000 applications for a meagre 7,500 tickets. A radio "beam-back" to Dartmouth Park, West Bromwich, was offered as a consolation to the tens of thousands of disappointed spectators – there being no big TV screens back then.

Cup Final Saturday was wet and miserable. On a soggy pitch in the rain, the two sides slogged away manfully. In the first half, Carter spotted W.G. making a run, and found him with an accurate pass. Richardson's shot wasn't the best, but it was sufficient to deceive the Blues keeper. W.G. had now added scoring at Wembley in the Cup Final to his list of achievements.

No Cup Final side, up to then, had ever recovered from being a goal down, but Birmingham hadn't read the script and hit back, equalising in the 59th minute. From the kick-off, a trio of Albion forwards charged forward against still-celebrating opponents. Supporter W.J. O'Reilly will never forget that moment. "To see the Albion players passing and re-passing the ball, drawing nearer and nearer, bigger and bigger until Hibbs dashed out to dive at Richardson's feet, only for Billy to trick him and walk the ball into goal, was my greatest thrill in watching football for 65 years."

City were bereft. Their heads went down and, bar a panic in the last five minutes; it was a comparatively easy task for the soggy Baggies to see out the rest of the game. Less than two years after turning professional, W.G. had scored two goals in an FA Cup Final – immortality guaranteed!

The *Birmingham Gazette* summed up the achievement. "It is safe to say there is no prouder man in the whole of England than W.G., West Brom's centre-forward. To score one goal in a Cup Final is an achievement of note: to get two, each time giving your side the lead, is an achievement. Fame has come early to Richardson comparatively early in his career, for he is only in his second season with Albion."

The leg-weary Baggies accepted the trophy from the Duke of Gloucester, who offered his own appreciation: "Your boys have been wonderful". The Cup winners rested overnight at Eastbourne before taking the silver pot home to West Bromwich the following day. Over 200,000 people turned out to greet both victorious team and trophy, its first appearance in the town for nearly four decades.

BUT TIME FOR celebrations was limited, as the Baggies were still chasing promotion. Truth to tell, the FA Cup had badly affected their league form, with only one win recorded in both February and March. Luck was with them – their nearest rivals Spurs had caught a crab of their own. Five precious strikes from W.G. in mid-April secured four points out of six. A nervous 1-1 draw at home to Bradford, though, meant West Brom had to put their Cup triumph aside, and win both their last two games to go up.

On a tense Thursday night at the Victoria Ground in Stoke, Albion did just enough to get the result they needed. Inevitably, it was that man again, W.G. Richardson, putting away a half-chance, just enough so that a missed penalty by West Brom's George Shaw didn't matter.

One game left… Charlton Athletic at the Hawthorns, in front of 52,000 people. Albion officials might fairly inquire where all these supporters came from: with the predictable exception of the derby with Wolves (40,000), the final match drew a gate double that of the previous highest League attendance that season.

The match itself was a dramatic one, with Athletic seemingly determined to spoil the party. Twice they led, and twice the weary Baggies determinedly drew level – then, with only 20 minutes left, Glidden's cross was headed home by… it just had to be W.G., didn't it? The Londoners finally got the message, and didn't trouble Albion's defence any more. After the last whistle, the crowd poured onto the pitch until a sea of flat caps, mufflers, and dark coats replaced every bit of green. It must have been much like our own flooding of the Hawthorns turf on 'Survival Sunday' in 2005, except with silverware to cheer instead of mere survival.

Just like us, Albion's new-found 1931 army of supporters weren't going anywhere until the players made an appearance.

With irritating understatement, when responding to a question about his favourite time at the club, W.G. would only modestly say: "The best week for both myself and the club was the last week of the 30/31 season, when I scored two goals on the Saturday at Wembley to win the FA Cup from Birmingham; the only goal of the match at Stoke on the Thursday afternoon; and the winning goal against Charlton Athletic at the Hawthorns on the following Saturday."

A civic banquet was subsequently held to mark the achievement of the "double winners." Which included a new song, specially written for the footballers of West Bromwich.

> "Welcome the victors
> Youthful, faithful, true.
> Who at Wembley conquered
> As they meant to do.
> Football so inspiring
> Won the Cup and fame
> Sing the Albion's praises
> Join in this refrain"

Secretary Eph Smith worked at the Hawthorns for 54 years. When asked about his favourite goal, he didn't hesitate – for him it was W.G.'s winner in the '31 Cup Final. "Whether it was that Birmingham had just scored, and had not got over it, we shall never know, but not one of their side touched the ball until Harry Hibbs picked it out of the net. To see a goal like that at any time is a thrill – but to see it in a Cup Final, scored by one of our own side, is something that will remain with me to my dying day."

FOR WEST BROMWICH ALBION, traditionally more of a Cup team, a good run in the FA Cup was an expectation. In the following three years, the team only managed to win a single Cup match, so by 1935, a certain cynicism was creeping in. Add frustration to cynicism in Round Three against Port Vale, as only a very late goal from W.G. secured a 2-1 win. Sheffield United came and were conquered 7-1 with remarkable ease, a classic W.G. hat-trick blunting the Blades. Said the Chronicle correspondent: "It did me good to see W.G. make a comeback as marksman." This was more like it – a Cup run. Nearly 25,000 packed into Stockport's ground to see the First Division side put the locals in their place, 5-0. The match was played in "appalling conditions", with two more goals from the ace marksman. "W.G. Richardson proved a good leader, and the others backed him up enthusiastically."

In excess of 56,000 were present at the quarter-final at home to Preston, to see those old Cup foes defeated by a single goal, set up by a W.G. free kick. Excitement was mounting. With eight of the 1931 Cup Final team still in the current line-up, could the Baggies win the Cup again? Second Division Bolton were eventually defeated in the semi-final, which went to a replay; inevitably, that man again, W.G. Richardson, was on the scoresheet in both matches, including the key first goal (a "rising shot") in a 2-0 victory in the re-match. Wembley again! And again on the back of Richardson's goals.

It may be fairly said that Albion's Cup Final team selection proved crucial. Should they go with established players Carter and Glidden, who were not fit, or should they stick with their less experienced – but fit – understudies? Carter and Glidden got the nod. The gamble failed: Carter got a knock on his injured knee after 33 minutes, and became a hobbling passenger, leaving a mighty big ask against a Sheffield Wednesday side rated among the best in the country. The ten men battled bravely, and somehow scored twice against the Yorkshiremen.

At 2-2, and with only five minutes remaining, W.G. was put clear through Sheffield's defence. This was such a familiar scenario, with normally only one ending, that Secretary Fred Everiss whispered to Chairman Bassett: "Here comes the Cup again".

Richardson ran forward into the penalty box, against a goalkeeper John Brown, who looked like a rabbit caught in headlights, yet he was a full England international. He froze and didn't move off his line: W.G. could have dribbled the ball right into the goal past the immobile Brown, but tried to place the ball – and missed the goal completely. The hero of 1931 had just cost his club the Cup: Wednesday then scored two late goals to win 4-2.

W.G. would never visit the twin towers again as a player, although he was to accompany the 1954 team in the capacity of trainer. His best hope came two years later, when straightforward victories against three lower-Division opponents (and five goals for the striker), presented Albion with a home quarter-final tie against the mighty Arsenal, the team of the thirties. A new (and still unbeaten) club record attendance of 64,815 crammed into the Hawthorns. W.G. set the Baggies on the way in the 10th minute, when he pounced on a goalkeeping error. So strong was his shot that the ball rebounded off the taut netting, and landed outside the penalty area. When Mahon added a second, it was all too much for the Londoners, who eventually lost 3-1. Cheering crowds invaded the pitch at the end, and wouldn't go home until Secretary Fred Everiss had made a 'thank you' speech.

Preston were the semi-final opponents, but it was not to be West Brom's year. Albion's hugely popular chairman, Billy Bassett, died just two days before the big game. No-one felt like taking the field, a feeling heightened by the FA's insistence on a two-minute silence. West Bromwich were a goal down in minutes, three behind in half an hour, but it just didn't seem important any more.

W.G. RICHARDSON was an all-round talent. He could head, pass both accurately and cleverly, shoot, and was exceptionally fast in a short dash. Such was his ball control that later on in his career, he took all the corner kicks for the team. As the *Albion News* said: "the facility and accuracy with which W.G. takes corner kicks with either foot is a valuable asset." There were long-range goals (a 25 yarder against Stoke in December 1930), not to mention bursts of skill, such as against Sheffield Wednesday, when he beat two opponents, then ran between the Sheffield backs before defeating the keeper. Charging goalkeepers was an accepted part of the game at that time: Gilfinnan of Portsmouth, and Turner of Huddersfield were amongst those made to look very silly by W.G. knocking the ball out of their hands and tapping it over the line.

Sometimes, he could be lucky and unlucky in the same match, as the club programme illustrated. "In March 1932, Albion beat West Ham 3-1 in a fine demonstration of how good fortune can swing in just one match. All Richardson needed to do was to tap the ball over the line.

Somehow with the side of his foot, he managed to scoop the ball over the crossbar. By contrast, when the opposition keeper attempted to clear the ball, it struck W.G.'s head, then hit the post before rebounding to the grateful forward. This time, the ball crossed the line in perfect safety."

It's hard to know how anybody can top scoring five goals to secure two honours in barely a week, but W.G. tried his best. Getting one over Albion's oldest rivals was always one of his best routes. In November 1931, Albion played Villa for the first time in five years. There were almost 60,000 in attendance, Albion's biggest gate of the season by a whopping 20,000 margin. As the game wore on, the visitors from Birmingham were almost literally run off their feet by opponents who were yards faster and more thrustful. W.G.'s rare header was the middle of three goals without any reply. "Richardson was invariably too good for Villa defender Talbot, and was a veritable thorn in the flesh for the Villa defence," wrote the *Chronicle* correspondent.

Several thousand happy Baggies invaded the pitch at the end of the game. But those who live by the boot... A month later, at home to Birmingham City, the striker was guilty of missing an easy chance from two yards out (City won 1-0) and a fortnight after that, in a painful 2-1 home defeat in the FA Cup by Villa, W.G. shot wide from three yards out. The popular marksman was a sure bet to find the net against local opposition, scoring against Wolves and Blues in five consecutive seasons, and in four straight against Aston Villa, who presumably then chose relegation to avoid any more punishment. Their last Villa Park derby ended in a 7-0 rout for the Baggies, with W.G. scoring four times, as well as missing two further excellent chances near the end. The victory was a triumph for speed, method and accuracy from the Albion men as they kept the ball on the ground, even managing four first half goals against a howling gale. At the time, it was Villa's worst ever defeat at home, and manager McMullan resigned shortly afterwards. Now that's the kind of thing that makes you a hero in these parts!

Perhaps there was just something about claret and blue that galvanised William "G" into a higher gear. In November 1931, the Baggies were playing at Upton Park. After five minutes, W.G. collected a long clearance and scored at the second attempt. On seven minutes, an inviting centre fell nicely for W.G. – 2-0. With the Londoners having just kicked off, the excited striker burst between two defenders to net his hat-trick. Less than sixty seconds later, W.G. did it again, knocking in a cross from Woods. He'd scored four goals in five minutes. "During 30 years experience of football reporting, I have never seen anything so wonderful as the way in which West Ham were swept off their feet by the Albion" wrote 'Wanderer' in the *Sunday Express*. To their credit, the home supporters rose as a man to their executioner, cheering W.G. every time he touched the ball.

The *Albion News* added: "W.G. Richardson deserves every credit for the brilliant way in which he took his chances, but he was the spearhead of an attack which for a time operated like clockwork." Meanwhile, back at the Hawthorns, the reserves were putting ten past Liverpool, with Cookson netting seven of them. Both first and second teams led 4-0 at half time. The news from London was greeted "with tumultuous cheering" by supporters at the Hawthorns.

IF GOALS make your heroes then W.G. was your man. Other feats of scoring included a five-minute hat trick and four goals in total against Derby at the Hawthorns in September 1933. The foursome included a rare penalty. As the Free Press had it: "there can be no two opinions about the value of W.G. Richardson. Without him occupying the berth, the team is never the same potent force."

Barely three months later, W.G. netted a hat-trick at Everton in a 7-2 spectacular on New Year's Day. He'd amassed 17 goals in total, but clearly that was deemed insufficient, as he was dropped three weeks later! Without a win in four fixtures, losing 0-1 to Blackburn at the Hawthorns was the final straw, as the *Chronicle* explained. "Throughout the game, they [Albion] did most of the attacking, but they missed opportunities with exasperating frequency, and their finishing generally was nothing less than wretched... As though to crown everything, W.G. Richardson failed with a penalty kick... His shot went straight to the goalkeeper and rebounded off his knees... What blame there is to be attached lies with the forwards. Constructive methods seem to be unknown to them." W.G. missed two matches before being recalled against Derby.

Clearly Albion standards were very high in this era, as the striker had been dropped the season before due to "loss of form", according to the Free Press. The centre-forward hadn't scored for three whole games. Would that the 2006 vintage were to set such high standards. His absence didn't help, West Bromwich lost 3-1 at home to Sheffield Wednesday, so back came W.G. against the Wolves – and promptly scored twice. Two months later, there were back-to-back hat tricks against Leicester and Portsmouth, and later that same season; "Ginger" found the net in nine consecutive league games. Only three men in Albion's history have equalled or bettered that feat.

In the 1935/36 season, W.G. scored 39 League goals – a club record that remains unbeaten to this day. The Albion News commented on the Boxing Day 5-2 win over Middlesbrough that featured four goals for W.G. in the second half:

"A brilliant individual achievement. The first of the four rewarded a magnificent dash between the backs, and a lightning shot. The second followed a tussle with Brown in which the latter had his knickers torn, and while he was on the sidelines donning another pair, our centre-forward was completing his quartet of goals. His low swift shots were completed with such precision, that Gibson had no chance to save." W.G. was quite unstoppable in the next six weeks, regardless of the state of his opponents' knickers.

Two more followed in the next match against Manchester City (won 5-1), singles against Middlesbrough in the return fixture and Stoke, followed immediately by back-to-back hat-tricks in an 8-1 slaughter of Blackburn, and 6-1 demolition of Liverpool. Sad to relate that although the Baggies scored 89 goals that season, they also conceded 88. Their 39-point tally gave them safety by a 3-point margin.

And being the goalscoring legend that he now was, W.G. benefited from the odd lucky goal. In a friendly against the Corinthians in January 1932, W.G. accidentally scored. Carter's hopeful cross was heading well wide of the goal until it hit the centre-forward on his head and the rebound flew into the net. As they say, you have to be in the right place to be a goalscorer. So regularly did his name appear on the Albion scoresheet that W.G. was also credited with some goals which he clearly didn't score. In December 1939, he was reported as a goalscorer for the Albion, but this came as something as a shock to the striker who was laid up in bed that day with a heavy cold.

BEING THE First Division top scorer would normally lead to international recognition. Richardson was hopeful of adding to his solitary cap, earned against Holland in 1935, when England's regular centre forward, Ted Drake of Arsenal, was unavailable. Albion's top striker was thrilled to wear the heavy, woollen cream shirt of his country.

In May 1936, in recognition of his leading scorer status, W.G. was selected for Probables against the Possibles in an international trial match, which included several Second Division players, and even two from the Third Division. Richardson did everything possible asked of him by scoring all the goals in a three nil win: "He became a great menace every time he touched the ball" said one spectator. And yet W.G. wasn't picked for the England v Scotland match, Arsenal's Drake being preferred again. As ever, playing for Albion was a big drawback for international hopefuls. A year on, he was relegated to the Possibles team, and predictably, scoring didn't bring any reward.

In 1937, Albion agreed a fee of £7,000 to sell W.G. to Manchester United [the then transfer record was the £11,000 paid by Aston Villa for J. Allen in 1934], but the two clubs had overlooked something – W.G. refused to go. Albion didn't force the issue, so their top goalscorer stayed. The old stager – he was now all of 28 – was playing fewer matches now, as injury caught up with him. His goals, too, were fewer in number, with only 15 recorded in 1937/38. He had a rival too in raw-boned Harry Jones, who was sometimes preferred as centre-forward. An unfortunate set of circumstances, including a highly leaky defence, saw Albion relegated that season.

As war in Europe approached, W.G. was now Albion's shortest forward at just 5 foot 7 inches tall; indeed he was almost the smallest player at the club. He spent much of the 1938/39 season with the second team. Meanwhile, four young players all made debuts in September. At 29, did W.G. already feel old and past it? Maybe he was best out of first team action, as the fixtures didn't always consider the strains on the players.

Early on, there was a Thursday afternoon fixture at Norwich, the team staying overnight and then catching a train the following morning... for Plymouth! After that Saturday afternoon affair, there was no train back until 8pm, meaning a 3.00am return to West Bromwich. One of the new men, Harry "Popeye" Jones, now had W.G.'s No. 9 shirt full time, and continued to find the net rapidly. His goals continued after war was declared, and indeed he missed only one game up to March 1940, before injury and war service ended his career.

After a number of decent showings with the "seconds", W.G. reclaimed his first team shirt. A remarkable display at Old Trafford in a Third Round Cup replay cemented his status with one goal scored, and three more set up in a 5-1 win, subsequently receiving more compliments for his football prowess.

In February 1939, with the Baggies reduced to ten men through injury, they still managed to beat Southampton 2-0 in some style. "W.G. dashed down the left with Affleck in pursuit. His pursuer overbalanced and slipped. Richardson ran to the touchline, and slipped across a head-height centre, which Elliott turned into the net."

Albion's hopes of a return to the top flight were dashed in April when dramatically, their goals dried up completely. One goal in seven matches was out of character for a forward line who regularly found the net three or more times per match. The goals returned in the final fixture, a 4-2 win over Norwich, in what turned out to be the last full League game until 1947. Thus, Richardson scored his last real League goals for Albion in this game. One might have hoped for a spectacular ending, but it was not to be. The second of his brace was a header which the Norwich keeper dropped, and the ball apologetically rolled over the line. Only 3,000 turned up to watch. War was horribly imminent.

Set in context, the wartime Leagues were a brave, defiant morale-raiser, an attempt at preserving an oasis of normality in desperate times. But with an often-unrecognisable team, playing in an unrecognisable strip, and sometimes in unfamiliar locations, hostilities footie was hardly momma's home cooking. Locally, Aston Villa sat out some of the competitions, while bomb damage-improvements to St. Andrew's had the Bluenoses playing away from home, often at Villa Park. Games were regularly cancelled because of travel difficulties; both teams were sometimes stuffed with guests, or needed to borrow opposition players to make up their numbers. Notts County once turned up without a goalkeeper, while a weary Swansea team arrived three hours late (and predictably were 5-0 down after 25 minutes, losing 8-2 with W.G. scoring five). Even when playing at home, Secretary Fred Everiss once went into the crowd to recruit two hopefuls to make up Albion's team against Walsall.

Little wonder that historians normally list W.G.'s 100 wartime League goals separately, lending them the afterthought nature of the Zenith Data Cup. Frankly, W.G. was past his best (a few months past his 30th birthday when war was declared), sometimes playing in the absence of younger men.

That said, scoring all six in a 6-1 victory over the RAF, five against Swansea and Villa, six past Luton and several hat-tricks must merit at least a nod of acknowledgement. Who can ever ignore an Albion man putting five in Villa's net? The *Midland Chronicle* and *Free Press* in May 1943 could not. "The shining star of this 6-2 victory was centre-forward Billy Richardson. After 14 seasons with the club, he is still a power as leader of Albion's attack. His five goals were all opportunist: that gave the 6,000 crowd something to remember in the close season. Had it not been for the hard defensive grist of Callaghan, and smart saves by Waterman, he might have had two or three more." This was a purple patch for W.G. with hat-tricks in three of his previous four games.

Albion were more fortunate than most, with access to their own players in the early years of the war. In March 1940, Minister Ernest Brown was questioned in the House of Commons by MP William Robinson if he would enquire into the circumstances in which 12-18 players of West Bromwich Albion, with no previous knowledge of the work, had been given jobs with a firm of munitions manufacturers, where experienced staff had to meet their military obligations. The Baggies felt horribly exposed, and subsequently didn't miss any opportunity to point out their players' contribution to the war effort: "We now have 15 members of our squad in the Forces" was a not untypical early justification, and the numbers mounted throughout the conflict. Initially, W.G. "did his bit" with the local Police Reserve, a commitment which varied enormously from season to season, at his lowest point he was able to play only twice in 1939/40.

Youngster Peter George described some of the sights and sounds of a home match during the war. "Before joining the queue for the "boys" entrance in Halfords Lane (admission 6d) it was my solemn duty to walk to the players' entrance, clutching our autograph books. Nearly every player arriving wore some sort of services uniform – Army, RAF, Royal Navy, Merchant Navy, Police, Fire Service – and although we didn't see any Land Army girls (more's the pity) we often did see Italian prisoners-of-war in their brown uniforms, and a huge orange disc sewn into the back of their tunics. The P.O.W. camp was just opposite, behind the Co-Op laundry in Camp Lane. Conversations between us teenagers tended to be like this: –

"Who's that RAF Sergeant?"

"Who's the army bloke?"

"That's Stan Cullis. He's England's centre-half!"

"He looks as if he's going bald!"

"Watch out, here comes a copper!"

"That's W.G. Richardson of the Albion, he's a Special."

"There's another one up there on traffic duty!" "Who's that then?"

"That's Don Dearson of Birmingham and Wales."

"Think he'd sign?" "We could try!"

"That's Jim Sanders – he's a fighter pilot. He's with Charlton, but he's playing as a guest today for us."

"Is he a real fighter pilot?"

"Oh yes, they say he's shot down 10 Jerries!"

Post war, the Albion veteran refused to hang up his boots. At the age of 36, West Bromwich asked for – and got – a fee of £250 from Shrewsbury Town, a fifth of the original cheque that they'd given Hartlepool all those years ago. Any grumbles from the Shropshire folk were quickly stifled as their new signing scored 55 goals in just one season. But time was running out, even for W.G., as a footballer. He needed a new career, something longer-term.

The Albion goal record-holder took advantage of the FA Coaching scheme to qualify as an instructor or coach. By happy coincidence, Albion needed a coach, and were delighted to recruit a man with both pedigree and qualifications: "This is just the sort of job I wanted." rejoiced W.G. The prolific forward was a popular coach, and was perfectly capable of practising what he preached.

Pete George was briefly an Albion footballer after the war: "My father took me to my first Albion match in 1937 to see W.G. From that day, he was my hero, so I followed him throughout the war. When I reported back to the Hawthorns in 1949 after my National Service, I was delighted to see W.G. had been taken on the training staff, coaching the Central League and Midland Midweek teams. Bill was a practical joker of the highest standard, but as my own father had died in 1937, shortly after that first game, I looked upon W.G. as a second father."

Derek Kevan, who knew a little about shooting himself, admired his coach. "Billy used to like a joke, and was a nice chap. Even in those days, when he used to hit a ball in training – along with Ronnie Allen, who was on a par, Billy was one of the finest players for hitting a moving ball that I've ever seen."

Midfielder Ray Barlow agreed: "W.G. joined in our forwards' shooting practice, and he really showed them how it should be done. He still packed a tremendous shot, and he was so consistent. The lads were rolling the balls to him, and he was cracking them home like a machine." W.G. loved the involvement, and continued to play whenever he had the chance. And then one day, he played his last game.

W.G.'s funeral was held at Holy Trinity Church, West Bromwich, before cremation at Perry Barr. Six members of the 1930-31 Cup-winning side carried the coffin. He was also remembered with a minute's silence at a home match against Manchester City.

The last word goes to another Albion crowd favourite, Ray Barlow: "Always ready with a grin and a leg-pull, Bill was a real "player's man", a likeable figure who had hundreds of friends."

RAY BARLOW

1944-1960

BAGGIES CAREER

Games	482
Goals	48
Caps	1

MAGIC MOMENT

His surging run at Wembley led to the crucial penalty that turned the 1954 FA Cup Final

'DADDY LONG LEGS'

> **"Ray Barlow was my hero, a great left half. So calm, played it easy, just knocked it about."**
>
> **Bobby Moore**

DURING World War II, Albion played in all blue shirts. Indeed, they were grateful to get those because of the strictures of rationing. Replacements were hard to come by with the football club appealing regularly and hopefully to their supporters to donate clothing coupons. The temporary Regional League structure was rather a hit and miss effort, with each club attempting to fulfil as many scheduled fixtures as possible, with their final position based on average points per game. The ball, for which a permit was required, was made out of stitched panels of leather with a huge lace-up opening into which was placed an inflatable rubber bladder. Heading said ball when it was wet risked injury. All this fun was available for a flat match fee of 30 shillings (£1.50) each.

The entire West Bromwich squad either served His Majesty in the forces or were employed in factory work, normally munitions. Naturally, the team members varied from match to match, with guest players or triallists regularly called upon to make up the numbers.

Into this strange scenario within an even stranger world came a young player from Swindon. Raymond John Barlow made his debut for Albion's first team versus Walsall in a War League Cup match on 3rd February 1945, which Albion lost 2-0. By contrast, another cult hero, WG Richardson, was playing in his final fixture. Little did anyone present know that the banner of cult status was passing so neatly between these two Albion legends, nor how it would transfer from a goalscoring legend to an imperiously vital half-back.

RAY WAS BORN in that well-known railway town on 17th August 1926, the only child of Thomas and May Barlow. "Just ordinary" was Ray's simple description of his childhood. He didn't begin to grow until he was 16 and then couldn't stop, something of a problem for his mother with rationing in force.

He was spotted playing for the Garrard's works side in Swindon by former Albion centre-forward, Jimmy Cookson. Apprentice toolmaker Ray was completely two-footed and was comfortable either at inside-left or inside-right (best compared to a modern day striker's role). Cookson put together a Select side, made up from all the club sides around Swindon. Garrard's managed a 3-3 draw with this elite team, with Ray scoring all three. By happy coincidence, Ray's father was an occasional drinker in Cookson's pub and Jimmy asked him one day: "Do you think Ray would like to go for a trial?" Subsequently, Ray was happy to sign amateur forms for Albion on 20th June 1944.

Months passed without any news. Only in October, when the local Villa scout was sniffing, did the Baggies formally invite him for a trial at the Hawthorns. Just one game with the reserves was sufficient for secretary Eph Smith to say, "Bring your Dad next week. We'll want you to sign as a professional."

Despite a decent showing against the Saddlers, inside-forward Barlow did not play for the firsts again until the following season, when he scored 12 goals in 32 Football League South games, most noticeably, his first goal (at Newport in a 7-2 thrashing) and his first hat-trick against Spurs. Ray already boasted his first nickname – "Boy Barlow" – and comparisons were already being made with the great Charlie Buchan.

Many more alternative names followed, such was his popularity, mainly connected with his height. "Lofty", "Tiny", "Legs", "Daddy Long Legs" or "Skyscraper" were the most commonly used. Conversely, "Sugar Ray" Barlow was an obvious link to famous boxer Sugar Ray Robinson, though what gentle Ray Barlow had in common with an aggressive pugilist, other than his first name, isn't easy to define. Probably the title was ironic.

One less flattering monicker was "First-Half" Barlow, a sarcastic reference to his inability to pace himself through the whole game. The accusation stuck, with a degree of justification, throughout his entire career. "He had a good first half, with through passes constantly spelling danger. Then he slowed up," wrote local reporter Dick Knight about a match at Fratton Park in January 1951. Over eight years later, during a home defeat by Spurs, the Birmingham Mail correspondent noted, "Barlow started off like a bomb, but faded a little towards the end. If he was to conserve his energy a little more…"

Supporter Colin Simpson recalled Barlow's post-war debut in the new transitional League. He had, for those days, particularly among professional footballers, very long hair, which kept falling over his eyes, causing much sardonic Black Country humour. When he appeared at the next home fixture, his hair was appreciably trimmed, and more in line with the short back and sides style of the era.

Team-mate Peter George remembered the new arrival. "We trained with him and he was a smashing chap. A few of us nicknamed him 'Zummerzet Zider' because of his lovely West Country accent, although I believe he hailed from Wiltshire." One of Ray's party tricks was already evident. "With his long legs, he could bring a ball down from 7 feet, and then execute a perfect pass." Talk to any supporter of a certain vintage about Ray Barlow, and sooner rather than later, they'll mention how he was famed for not getting his shorts dirty. Ray thought nothing of trapping a heavy leather ball at shoulder height and directing it accurately to a colleague, all in one sweet movement. Think of John Cleese ('Boy' Barlow was just over six foot tall) with football skills for a crude approximation.

BEING BORN IN 1926 meant that the Swindonian was too young to fight in the war, but the army were determined to see him in uniform, and he was duly summoned for national service. He did his best to continue his football career, slipping out of camp whenever he could. Sadly, he chanced his arm once too often in March 1947 and the army exacted retribution on Private Barlow by posting him to the Tank Regiment in Palestine as a Gunner. Playing for the Palestine Army team wasn't quite the same, particularly for a teetotal non-smoker.

Overseas service unsettled Ray (Charles Matheson of the *Argus* claimed "he looked something like a scraggy end" upon his return) and he was painfully out of form at the Hawthorns. He even missed games due to "sore feet", a condition thought to be a legacy of ill-fitting army boots. (In the early fifties, he was unimpressed to be called for his Z-reserve training, basically a two-week refresher event. Resisting the urge to scrawl "Bollocks" all over the form and return it as so many national servicemen did especially around the rise of Suez, he spent two weeks in a tank during the summer of 1951).

Much had changed at the Hawthorns in his absence. For the first time ever, the stars in stripes had a manager, Jack Smith, who took over from retiring jack-of-all-trades Fred Everiss. The new man added 13 new players to the club, much needed for once again, West Bromwich were attempting to get back into the top tier of the League, having been relegated in 1938 in painful circumstances. The Baggies had lost their last three matches and finished two points short of survival, despite having registered 14 wins.

THE LONG-LEGGED RECRUIT did score some excellent goals as a forward, notably a spectacular 30-yard drive at Bury in August 1948. But his passing ability was more akin to that of a midfielder, or wing-half, to use the jargon of the period. Jack Smith chose to use his skills in the midfield and turned him into a half-back. Such a switch was curiously part of Albion traditions – it was a well-trodden path including two members of the 1931 Double team in Teddy Sandford and Tommy Magee. After an eye-catching spell with the Albion reserves playing in the middle of the pitch, Barlow made the first team in the same position, and was just as impressive.

Argus Junior was among his admirers. "Ray Barlow, at half-back, is addressing the ball differently. One day, maybe, this long-legged Swindonian of skyscraper altitude will develop a spring in his heels. When that happens he will be able to get up for high balls which others might require stilts. Barlow does not use his head a lot in the strictly heading sense. Does not have to with such strength of body and leg. Ray seems to have glue on the end of his boots as he fetches the ball down from shoulder height by sending either foot on an airborne mission. His control is exceptional and, oh boy, how he uses that long pass."

Supporter Paul Collins was typical of Ray's admirers. "Strong in the tackle and after getting the ball, Ray always had or made time to do what he wanted. He would ease past an opponent or two and then that ground-eating stride took him clear. A further strength was the weight and direction of his passes, particularly the one inside the full-back for the winger."

But injuries elsewhere meant another stint at inside-forward supporting big forward Dave Walsh as West Bromwich chased another promotion and FA Cup double. Fulham, Spurs and Southampton provided the competition in a four-way scrap for two promotion places.

IN MARCH, Ray plus goalkeeper Sanders and full back Kinsall missed the train to an away game at Cardiff City. Hasty arrangements had to be made to drive them to the Principality and much to the relief of the manager; the trio reached Ninian Park half an hour before kick-off. Not that Ray was perturbed as he set up both goals in a 2-2 draw. Albion's second goal is worthy of particular mention: Barlow hooked the ball over his head to Williams, the striker repeated the feat and it fell beautifully for Walsh to score.

Progress in the FA Cup was halted by a single goal defeat by eventual winners Wolves in the quarter-final stage, but promotion was still on. Barlow's efforts were to prove crucial in the run-in, thanks to his vision and accurate passes. With four games to go, a 1-1 draw at Southampton, where the "long legged Swindonian" battled on despite a leg injury, was just enough for Albion to keep their noses in front. Ultimately, the Baggies needed two wins from the last three – Ray scored in a 2-0 victory over Barnsley, and not just any goal, according to the Argus. "Albion's outstanding personality was Barlow. His craft and accurate passing were a treat to see, and he scored a grand goal following a solo run from 30 yards out"

And so victory at Filbert Street would suffice. Although Leicester were good enough to reach the Cup Final, they still needed a point to avoid relegation to the Third Division. The official gate was just under 35,000, although many more scrambled in over the walls, and estimates suggested another 30,000 outside. The home side had all the play, but the visitors had all the goals – three of them with the last one from Barlow, hooking home from an acute angle. At the end, the 5,000 travelling Albion supporters invaded the pitch, and carried the entire promotion-winning team around the pitch on their shoulders.

A "mild form of polio" put Ray out of action for most of the next season back in the top flight. He'd lost weight, and so the football club asked the Dyce family, who ran the Hawthorns Hotel, to take the player in and feed him as lavishly as restrictions allowed. Meat was still rationed, as were petrol and sweets. Houses were in short supply and new-fangled TV only accessible to the wealthy. These were difficult times.

It wasn't until November when Ray returned to first team football – playing up front again. Ray could simply play anywhere, and was initially happy to do so without complaint, a trait that endeared him to management and supporters alike, although he probably wasn't expecting his next opportunity to shine in an unusual position. In March 1954, goalkeeper Norman Heath was injured at Roker Park. Barlow volunteered to stand in, not such a surprise, as local reporter Charles Matheson explained. "Ray really can keep. I've seen him do quite spectacular things between the sticks in training. He has the build and the reach and the grip to be a success there." Ray won a standing ovation from the Roker faithful for his makeshift performance in the Albion goal, finally beaten only four minutes from time. Sad to say, the unfortunate Heath, with 169 games behind him, never played again. Ray's versatility did indeed seem endless, his long throw-ins becoming an Albion staple. He'd take penalties, too but with only a moderate degree of success.

One of Barlow's most endearing qualities for Albion fans was his surging desire. It's normal manifestation came merely in his zest, vigour and playing style, but Ray wasn't above taking advantage of weather conditions in order to improve his team's chances, as supporter Ben Payne remembers: "We were playing Aston Villa on a very foggy day, so foggy that a modern game would be abandoned. Suddenly, Billy Goffin, a nippy Villa left-winger came sprinting out of the gloom with an Albion player on his tail. The lanky figure of Ray Barlow could just be seen over in the centre. As clear as a bell, I heard him shout "here, Bill". Without lifting his head, Goffin whipped the ball over whereupon Ray Barlow lifted his leg, bought the ball under control and went trotting up the field with it. We were left with the amusing sight of an exasperated Goffin standing with hands on hips."

THE PROMOTED TEAM did enough to maintain their top division status for a couple of seasons. Goalscoring was a problem, a source of frustration for Barlow, who, now a fixture in the starting line-up, match after match would set up opportunities for his front men only to see them wasted. The West Bromwich Chronicle and Free Press noted in a 1-2 defeat at home to Spurs, "when promising moves initiated by Barlow and Kennedy broke down, they must have had a feeling akin to despair. So much so that towards the end, both were taking the ball upfield themselves in an effort to achieve something their forwards could not. Barlow's conso-lation goal two minutes from time was just reward for a grand wholehearted game." One supporter, R Williams, summed up the universal frustration in rhyme:

"Half-backs, full-backs, goalie too are seldom slacking…"

"But in this forward line, there must be something lacking."

Manager Smith admitted he'd attempted to purchase twenty different centre-forwards. Each time, he had either been refused outright or the other manager would counter with "Give us Barlow or Kennedy in an exchange deal and we'll talk." In the absence of new talent, existing squad members were tried up front, including Barlow again. Requests from Albion managers became quite frequent enough for Ray to be regularly quoted as saying, "I know what you're going to ask me, and the answer is Yes. I'll play anywhere for you, Boss." The team came first in that era, and Ray gallantly played the role of the loyal club man. While it worked in his favour in terms of his dedication and adaptability being appreciated, supporters and press alike were unimpressed that such a great midfield talent should be misused in this way.

Fortunately, the arrival of new talented attacking players such as Ronnie Allen (who would eventually fill the troublesome central striking role), winger George Lee, and innovative managers like Jesse Carver and Vic Buckingham, eventually saw the team blossom into one of the most attractive sides in the country. Good times to be a Baggie, but these pleasures were typically celebrated in a mute manner as veteran supporter Terry Wills recalled.

"At five to three, the players would run out for the first time to loud cheers. This being very much the era of the 'stiff upper lip', it was perfectly reasonable for them to expect to cheer when scoring a goal, AND for good play, of course. Otherwise, the crowd spent the rest of the game being quietly appreciative of the fare served up for them on the playing surface. Swearing was frowned upon. If anyone temporarily forgot their manners, terrace etiquette demanded somebody yelled, "hey, there's a lady here" and the reply was invariably the standard apologetic Black Country response, " Sorry, chap." Nevertheless, the match was always the big pressure relief-valve for what was for many, a dull and dreary working week consisting of nothing but unstinting manual labour."

THE FAMOUS Dudley – Kennedy – Barlow classic half-back line played as a trio for the first time in April 1952 at Maine Road, where they were described as "the mainstay of the side". Once together, they were formidable, providing a stable platform to build an exciting Albion team around. That season finished with 13 points gathered out of the last available 16.

Jimmy Dudley was a former goalkeeper and winger (versatility seemed essential in that era!) who amassed over 300 games for the Albion. Joe Kennedy was a giant of a centre-half. Although the pair were jointly the tallest members of the side, Barlow broke up attacks with his feet at any height, leaving Kennedy to deal with aerial balls.

But sad to relate, the much-quoted trio were more often myth than reality. After their initial spell together up to February the following year, injuries and filling in gaps elsewhere meant the threesome averaged barely 10 games per season together right to the end of the decade.

As is common with such players who can play anywhere, Barlow's versatility often meant his personal good was subjugated to the needs of the team. As he became older, Ray considered himself solely a half-back. He was not best pleased when injuries to the regular strikers saw him again pressed into service up front midway through the 1955/56 season. After 13 reluctant games, he made his position very clear to the local press. "I am not a centre-forward. And, try as they might, West Bromwich Albion will never make me one. That is why I am unhappy at the moment" opened his 500-word plea. "If things start to go wrong and we start to slide backwards, I hope the fans will not blame me." Such a breast-beating statement must have been difficult for this most gentle and modest man. The return to fitness of striker Johnny Nicholls a fortnight later spared his discomfort.

In February 1953, the Baggies chose another manager in Vic Buckingham, who replaced the short-lived Jesse Carver, unable to resist a lucrative offer from Italy, "a fee no English club could pay." Buckingham was a man with a plan. He wanted Albion to emulate Spurs' "push and run" tactics (Buckingham was a former Tottenham man) utilising long passes rather than short ones. Barlow would provide the passes, 40 yarders were, after all, his speciality, while the forward pairing of Ronnie Allen and regular scorer Johnny "on the spot" Nicholls would do the rest. The whole team, from back to front, were encouraged to pass the ball and then defend when they didn't have possession. The plan was radical for its time, but worked because Albion had the right blend of players. After finishing fourth in 1953, they just missed out on the double twelve months later.

THE BAGGIES started 1953/54 in magnificent style. Newcastle were defeated 7-3 on their own ground ("the crowd simply rose to us... and we were 3-0 up" gaped defender Stan Rickaby) as the stars in stripes lost only one of their first fifteen games. The first six away games were all straight wins. Chelsea were crushed 5-2, Manchester United beaten home and away, all unable to cope with the Baggies' first time, quick-passing game. WBA now stood for "We'll Beat Anybody. "

Providing the bullets for the deadly forwards was Ray Barlow, although sometimes he cut out the middle man. For instance, against Sunderland, he let fly from fully 40 yards and his wind-assisted shot found the gap below the crossbar and above the goalkeeper's fingers. Later, he hit the bar before setting up George Lee for the second and final goal. Just a normal day at the office...

A small squad, combined with injuries and international call-ups at the wrong moment, cost Albion the title, their season turning on a crucial match against Championship rivals Wolves in April. With ace goalmen Allen and Nicholls (55 goals between them) both selected for their country, good ol' Ray was asked to fill in up front. As Ray explained, their absence was crucial. "I got injured early on in the match. Bill Shorthouse clogged me after ten minutes, but I had to carry on because there were no substitutes then. We lost a silly goal and ended up losing 1-0 and the league pretty much went with it, because the confidence went out of the side. We knew we could have finished them off and we hadn't done it." The Baggies painfully slipped out of top spot after that local derby. With Albion recording only one win and one draw in the last five games, the Championship went instead to Wolverhampton by the margin of two victories.

BUT THERE WAS still the '54 Cup Final looming. Cup holders Newcastle were beaten in a classic fifth round match. Barlow scored one of the three goals as Spurs were dismissed in a rather comfortable quarter-final before Third Division Port Vale made life very awkward in the semi-final, having the temerity to take the lead before the Baggies just squeaked home 2-1 to meet old Cup foes Preston at the Twin Towers.

Many years later, Ray revealed his Wembley memories to the *Albion News*: "It was a big thrill to walk out in front of 100,000 people. You have butterflies for an hour before the game, and then it's nice to get out on the pitch and get on with it, but there was a real tingle from walking out in front of all those people and then walking up the steps to collect the medal after the game… It was a typical cup final really, a lot of nerves, a lot of mistakes, and it was one of those matches where it didn't really get going, which sounds funny if you think there were five goals in it."

Barlow gave his usual 'laid back' display. An outrageously offside goal by Preston's Wayman was partly responsible for Albion trailing 2-1 with only 25 minutes left. Could West Bromwich miss out on both prizes? Ray got his infamously long legs moving. He dodged one tackle, and then evaded another before Tommy Docherty bought him down and the referee gave a penalty. "It was obstruction at most," said Ray, honestly. "Just an indirect free-kick, but the ref had made such a boob with Wayman…" Ronnie Allen scored amid incredible tension with Albion keeper Jimmy Sanders unable to watch. The momentum was now with the Midlanders. Frank Griffin completed the job three minutes from the end.

ALBION'S CHANCES of returning to Wembley again that decade were thwarted, by defeat in the 1957 FA Cup semi-final replay to Villa in wretched circumstances. Albion supporters of mature years still rage about this Cup exit. The first game finished 2-2, with Villa equalising through Peter McParland five minutes from the end. As John Thompson wrote in the Express, "So often it would seem Villa would be outclassed. So often the tall commanding figure of Ray Barlow broke their attacks and their hearts. Barlow was uncanny in his positional movements." Ray was understandably a little peeved. "I thought we should have had the game won in the first half. But we faded after that."

In the replay, Albion were again the better side, but a cynical foul by former Albion man Dugdale on Ronnie Allen took out the ace goalscorer. Albion's ten men, with Barlow outstanding all over the pitch, hit everything but the net, while the Villains pinched the game 1-0. Ray Barlow was never to get that close to Wembley again.

Testimony to the character of our 'Leggy' hero was confirmed when he was the first Albion player to walk into the Villa dressing room and say to Johnnie Dixon, Villa captain, "Well Done! We have had our turn at Wembley. Now it's yours – and we hope you bring the cup back" That was probably the only occasion that a large majority of Albion fans were prepared to argue to the contrary with their hero!

Dick Knight in the Evening Mail was one among many to offer what succour they could. "No team has ever been so great in defeat. A giant above all players rose to stamp his class and personality, upon this never to be forgotten game. Ray Barlow spurred his depleted team on with his burning enthusiasm, and his own classic play. When they were reduced to ten men, he was a forward and a defender in one, and came within inches of launching Albion into the lead."

A year later, the Albion side battled against the odds to defeat both Nottingham Forest and Sheffield United in the Cup, with just ten men. Yet the emotion of the post-Munich nation was just too much to compete with against Manchester United in the FA Cup quarter-final. The Albion skipper explained: "The crowd was fantastic for the replay at Old Trafford. I've never seen anything like it. The coach was completely blocked in by supporters, who mostly couldn't even get into the ground. It took us ages to get into the dressing rooms. I can remember in the last minute, Bobby Charlton picking the ball up on the right wing, ghosting down, a young lad, jinking past two or three, coming up to the line, pulling it over, a perfect ball for Colin Webster to put it in. And curtains for us." The Baggies, good though they were, could not take on seemingly the whole world and a referee intimidated by the 60,000 inside the stadium and half as many outside.

The two sides met at the same venue in a League match just three days later and, in the absence of the Cup hysteria, the Baggies showed their real class by winning 4-0. But this was scant consolation.

BARLOW HAD CLASS, but was also prepared to put his body on the line. On top of a black eye at Sunderland in August 1954, in 1955 Barlow broke his jaw against Cardiff. Despite having his jaw wired up, to allow just the minimum chin movement which permitted a liquid-only diet, Ray missed only three games before returning to the Baggies line-up.

In terms of footballing ability in midfield the nearest modern day counterparts for Ray can only be England stars Stephen Gerrard or Frank Lampard. The Albion man really was that good. Consider this glowing review from a correspondent in the *Liverpool Echo*, who witnessed League leaders Everton being outplayed by the Baggies at Goodison. "One man stood out. Ray Barlow, the tall West Bromwich left-half, strode through this game as like a professor of the Soccer arts. He was terrific. At times, I thought his legs were telescopic as he snipped off the intended through pass, and surged though the fluid Albion front line into devastating action. What a man and a half Barlow proved himself in defence as in his majestic first-half attacking role." Like "Legs" Barlow, Gerrard and Lampard make the game look easy, wherever they are on the pitch. They can score, pass, tackle – attack or defend. The most lamented Duncan Edwards bears comparison, too. All, like Ray, are great favourites.

Albion supporter Peter Whitehouse, had his own thoughts: "What made him stand out was his outstanding ability to bring the ball from the penalty area to the opponent's defence and lay off a pass that was a scoring opportunity. He had long legs that with his long stride made him appear to be strolling between the two penalty areas. It was only when you saw opposing players running hard trying to stop him that he realised how fast he was moving. He was a player before his time, most wing halves then were expected to be good tacklers and then hoof the ball hopefully up to their forwards."

Despite his numerous admirers, Ray was called up to appear for his country only once. Invariably, Portsmouth's more defensively-minded Jimmy Dickinson was preferred. Ray was regularly the team reserve; in those pre-substitute days, it was a highly frustrating position. His first non-appearance as spare was as early as 1951 against Portugal. One journalist came up with yet another nickname for the Albion star – Ray "Bench" Barlow. Still the £50 he received, equivalent to a month's wage, must have eased his irritation. His solitary cap was earned against Northern Ireland in October 1954. As Ray himself said: "I was surprised when I got my cap because I thought I'd missed the boat, I'd been consistent and never got in, so to finally get a call up was one of the highlights of my career, there's nothing like playing for your country."

STILL, RAY DIDN'T completely miss out on foreign travel just because he was an Albion player and therefore not worthy. He was part of the FA party that toured "the Americas" in 1953. Furthermore in June 1957, the Baggies were the first British professional club to tour Russia, playing three games over fifteen days. The players needed to make a rather large cultural adjustment, such as feigning interest in a full day's tour of the 16 halls of Moscow's Agricultural and Industrial Exhibition.

"We had a good tour," said Ray, recalling the visit many years later. "We were the first team to beat a Russian side, but foodwise – it was a bit of a disaster! I lost half a stone. The first meal we had there was this macaroni soup at Riga airport, with all grease on the top, with a boiled egg floating in there somewhere. It wasn't all bad, but it wasn't to our liking. Certainly, half a dozen were trotting to the toilet all the time!"

More foreign travel followed when Albion were invited to Spain to play in a special benefit match against Athletico Bilbao to recognise the achievements of one of their great stars, outside left, Agustin Gainza, who had served Bilbao for 18 years. 35,000 people turned out expecting the home side to win in temperatures close to 90 degrees. But a weakened Albion side shocked them by winning 1-0. The Spaniards were quick to appreciate the visitors, and one man in particular, as reporter Charles Harrold described, "Barlow gave the crowd everything. That was why he was the hero. Whenever he had the ball, murmurs of anticipation swept round the ground."

A year later, the squad were breaking new ground again, with a four-week visit to the USA and Canada. There's an often seen tour picture, taken in Halfords Lane, with the squad resplendent in suits and ties. Ray is on the extreme right of the picture, holding the hand of his two year old daughter Lesley, busily stealing the entire scene.

AS WITH ANY player in the era of the maximum wage, Barlow had to make the most of any other talents to earn some extra pennies and plan for his future after football. Ray went into business with team-mate Stan Rickaby, setting up the Albion Cabinet Company in 1953, with offices in Pitt Street, West Bromwich. The pair designed a compact gramophone record cabinet with a built-in storage system and their plan was to sell them by mail order at six guineas each (£6.30p). But, as if to illustrate the fragility of a footballer's career, Rickaby was injured the following year and never played for Albion again. With his partner departed for Poole Town, Ray needed to re-think his plans, not least because his days as a single man were no more, having married Beryl Austin in late summer 1955. Around the same time, Barlow received £750 benefit money, equivalent to a year's salary. Benefit money was a kind of bonus for loyalty – £500 after five years service or £750 after ten years. The money was taxable and was an alternative to a benefit game. In practice, many smaller clubs ignored the rules and paid the player what they could afford or what they could get away with. West Bromwich Albion were a big club and could easily afford these sums.

Ray and his new wife opened a newsagency in Bull Street, West Bromwich and moved into the flat above, thus finally tearing himself away from the Hawthorns Hotel, where he'd lived for over six years! Ray was particularly known for his sweet tooth, so a newsagency held certain dangers. An expanding waistline would not help him on the pitch.

IN 1957, Len Millard asked the manager to transfer his club captaincy to Ray Barlow. Ray had deputised while veteran Millard was injured and felt the new man should carry on. "I'm good at winning the toss, if that's any help!" responded Ray in his usual modest way when asked about his new responsibility. Another change was to quickly follow. Stalwart centre-half Joe Kennedy was injured, so Ray filled in and played so well he now became a fixture in the No. 5 shirt. Bolton manager Bill Ridding was among his admirers. "He's fantastic, incredible, brilliant, the best in the game. There can't be a finer centre-half in the country" he gushed after Albion, who played with ten men for 85 minutes, earned a 1-1 draw in August 1958 against the Wanderers, then a power in the land. Barlow was cleverly marking Nat Lofthouse.

But did Albion need Barlow's passing skills to support the front men more than they needed him to bolster the defence? The debate raged for months in the local press. But age was a factor for the 32 year-old Captain and the less mobile defensive position could prolong his playing career. In theory.

During the opening fixtures of the 1959/60 season, the debate arose again – was Barlow or the fit again Kennedy a better choice as centre-half? The decision initially at least, was that Barlow, ever versatile, should try out at left-half (midfield) once more. But as journalist Charles Harrold warned "Barlow cannot cope with 90 minutes of going backwards and forwards all the time from wing half." In the end, the question was academic. "Tiny" got injured.

BARLOW HAD RARELY been injured or unavailable throughout his career. Admittedly he'd been obliged to sit out five fixtures around Easter 1959 for a most unusual reason. The Birmingham and England full-back Jeff Hall stood next to Ray during a five-a-side match, but the following day was rushed to hospital with polio. The killer disease was much feared at that time, as it was highly contagious. Ray himself had suffered mildly from it as we have already seen. Anyone who had been in contact with a sufferer was obliged to wait for 12 nervous days before doctors could be sure one way or the other. During that period, exercise was not recommended because it could potentially make the disease worse. Ray didn't catch polio, but tragically, Jeff Hall did not recover, and died shortly afterwards.

Fast forward to late 1959 when Ray was enduring fluid on the knee. Hopes of recovery were dashed in his comeback game at St. James' Park, when stretching for a ball damaged his knee once more. "Now, it looks as though I will have to have a good rest," observed Ray. Little did he know just how long that rest would last. Or that his next appearance seven weeks later at home to Manchester City would be his final one of his Albion career, typically filling in at centre-half for the absent Kennedy.

He looked slow, although ironically for "First Half Barlow", he improved as the game went on. His knee remained a problem. One specialist considered he had arthritis. Concerned supporters from all over the country wrote to Ray, suggesting their favourite cure for arthritis. Ray read all the letters and was so impressed with one suggestion that he even met the writer. A second expert opinion made the picture less clear, suggesting that the Swindonian needed a cartilage operation.

Meanwhile, the Baggies were managing perfectly well without him. Record signing Bobby Robson took over at left-half and made a splendid job of the unfamiliar position. Full international Bobby also took over as captain and worse... took over Barlow's column in the *Sports Argus*. A string of youngsters had made their debut, such as 16-year-old Bobby Hope. It was clear that the club was evolving. It was time to go. The latest medical opinion advised him to retire, but Ray wasn't ready. "My heart is in football and I have been a first team man for 14 years and I don' intend to give up easily." In the summer of 1960, he moved to that well-known rest home for Albion veterans – St. Andrew's.

The last word goes to modest Ray. "I enjoyed playing football and all that went with it. I had a happy life in the game. What more could you ask for?"

JOE KENNEDY

1948-1961

BAGGIES CAREER

Games	397
Goals	4
Caps	0

MAGIC MOMENT

Scoring the clinching third goal at Leicester in May 1949 to secure promotion

'SPRING-HEELED JOE'

"**JOE** Kennedy is the highest paid footballer in the country." So deduced the *Birmingham Mail* in 1952. Their logic was simple – Joe received maximum club wages and regular win bonuses. Those, added to an involvement in every representative game (England, Football League and FA XI), meant top earner status. Joe was reserve for three full internationals that year, plus reserve for the Football League, finally seeing action as Captain of the FA XI. Reserves received the same pay as participants: second-string, left out, hard luck story, this was a typical cameo of one of Albion's most effective defenders of all time. Still, at least his 12th man status for his country meant he could visit Wembley for the first time ever. Joe certainly made sure of securing a souvenir – "I've got a piece!" – he brightly announced in the dressing room afterwards, as he waved around a section of Wembley turf. "It cannot be long until he gets his full cap" opined the Albion News hopefully.

CUMBERLAND-BORN Joe had come a long way in three years, as indeed had Albion. He'd had something of a difficult baptism – but then Joe's career and legendary status was based on battling against the odds. That's why Albion folk loved him. Like them Joe suffered adversity and came through it, more often than not on top. He was an inspiration to them in prosaic times and his hero status began to develop from his very first appearance in a striped shirt.

In April 1949, the Baggies were chasing promotion to the old First Division, and needed a hole filled in the right side of their midfield at Kenilworth Road. 23 year-old Kennedy was chosen for his first match, a notable step up for a novice who'd only made his reserve team debut less than two months earlier. But he didn't let anyone down. "Kennedy showed up well in his unaccustomed role," commented the *Sports Argus* afterwards.

Joe kept his place in the next game – a spectacular 7-1 thrashing of Bradford, and also at promotion rivals Southampton, where "he worked like a Trojan". The Albion had been eight points behind the Saints at the end of March, but the South Coast team had imploded. The Baggies caught them up; with just three games remaining, they had their nose in front, and rather liked the notion of keeping it there. The Saints battered frantically at Albion's door for the first 45 minutes with Kennedy playing his part in the rearguard action, then the visitors caught them on the break and Southampton only managed an equaliser in the last minute of the game. It was a major result. Promotion was in Albion's hands, and two wins from their trio of remaining fixtures would do nicely.

Manager Jack Smith then made a brave decision. Young Kennedy would remain in the first team, but up front, at the expense of a woefully out of form Jack Haines. Joe was a big lad, quite superb in the air, but so inexperienced for such a big occasion.

Barnsley were defeated 2-0 easily enough, and with Southampton having completed their fixtures already, a win at Leicester would mean promotion. Joe didn't let his manager down.

While City battered away gamely, it was his intervention that gave Albion the lead. Argus Junior described the moment in the *Sports Argus:* "The tall, dark young man has a striking gift of making himself airborne. There's a spring in his heel, apparently. At Leicester, Joe was so quick in going up for a free-kick that he beat goalkeeper Major in the air and nodded down for Dave Walsh to score the first goal." Joe followed that up with a goal of his own, his first for the club, when he finished off an Albion corner. Two goals to the good after 25 minutes, the visitors could sit on their lead, and eventually win 3-0. The Baggies had their promotion, and young Joe had his nickname – "Spring-heeled Joe" (or Jack – supporters memories vary on this point).

The newcomer had permanently made his mark on club history. Supporters never forget the men who secure promotion: think Bomber Brown in 1976, "Big Dave" Darren Moore, plus "Super Bob" in 2002, not forgetting Jason Koumas's "all but wrapped up" finish at Sunderland, back in 2004. It prefers hero status on these men and Joe Kennedy stands equal with any of them.

JOSEPH PETER KENNEDY was born in Cleator Moor in November 1925; a small town in Cumberland, known locally as "Little Ireland". The community owed its origins to mass-immigration from the Emerald Isle during the early 19th century potato famine.

Football and defending in particular was in young Joe's blood. Centre-half was his father's preferred position, resulting in more than one offer to turn professional, but he steadfastly refused them all. Sadly, he died while Joe was still studying and playing football at St. Patrick's school, the Kennedy family subsequently moving to Manchester at the outbreak of war, when Joe was 14. The youngster had a troublesome appendix, which required an operation; for 3 years, he played no football at all, instead working on the railways as a fireman.

When he was 16, young Kennedy returned to his Cumberland roots, where his interest in football revived. His first club was Cleator Moor Celtic, a long established amateur side of Irish ancestry, who play in green and white hoops. To this day, Celtic maintains their tradition of developing young players, the most recent of which is Liverpool's goalkeeper Scott Carson, who travelled to the World Cup in Germany in the summer of 2006 as England's third choice. Joe progressed to Workington before moving back to Manchester, and two years in the South of England followed, serving as a gunner in the Royal Artillery, while turning out for the army football side as well. Then back to Manchester again, working in a local factory as a turner, playing football for their works side.

Joe played regularly for Altrincham reserves at centre-half, and could boast of a solitary outing with their first team. Many clubs watched him but were concerned that he appeared one-footed; something at that time not acceptable for a defender, apparently. What his critics didn't know was that he was having intense training to improve his kicking; Arthur Gale, a former Albion man, who resumed his teaching career after his footballing days was, in1948, head-teacher of a school in Altrincham. While happy to give his time as an honorary trainer-coach at his local football club, then in the obscurity of the mid-Cheshire League, naturally, Arthur recommended the young defender to the Albion.

A month after he came of age (21, in those days), Joe was allowed to choose from his suitors, and without hesitation chose West Bromwich, although he'd probably never been there in his entire life. As he advised his mother only to pack a few clothes for him, his destination was to him irrelevant, as he feared wherever he was heading; he'd be home within a week. Not so, it would seem: Albion's original £500 bid was matched by Manchester City, Preston, Bury, Crewe, Everton and Manchester United, who had collectively thought they had him lined up before the Baggies pinched him from (literally) their own backyard. Kennedy was eventually Hawthorns-bound in December 1948, in exchange for a measly £750.

PHYSICALLY, Joe was very lean, with a pale face, but blessed with heavy eyebrows and dark, curly hair. His interests were fishing, racing pigeons, table tennis and bowls. (He once won a pork pie in a fishing competition, and was unwise enough to tell his team-mates. Cue endless mickey-taking, of course). Joe was sometimes described as 'taciturn', or in more kindly terms, as 'quiet and modest'. Certainly, he didn't go in for smiling as a hobby, but then what centre-half of mean reputation does? As one reporter had it: "Kennedy's facial expression would surely remain the same even if an earthquake split the Hawthorns turf beneath him."

In this era, such a personality was no barrier to genuine crowd-favourite status. New-fangled 'television' had yet to gain mass appeal, radio coverage was very limited, and unlike today, the press were both polite and deferential. Joe had to communicate only at the odd supporters club function, or more normally, on a one-to-one basis in the street on the bus to and from games. Occasionally, a pressman would painfully extract a sentence from him. Quite who at the *Birmingham Mail* came up with the idea of firing twenty questions at Joe for a sports feature clearly didn't know him very well. Perhaps they were happy with a series of minimal responses, as it superficially covered a lot of ground. Hopefully, they were, because that was all they got!

Only in his later days did the Cumberland man open up somewhat. Perhaps being a senior professional made a difference. Or becoming a husband or father: whatever was behind his later mellowing, his comparative outburst after his 10 men side had held out for a replay against the might of Blackpool in the Cup came as a distinct surprise. Joe described his feelings as the Seasiders had a chance in the last few seconds. "In the few seconds it took, I thought 'this is it. We'll be beaten. There were 15 players in the goal area, and the ball was tee-ed up for a shot. Jim Sanders'll never see it, I thought. It looked a winner. I turned to watch Jim, and suddenly he dived to his right. He had the ball. I thought ' He'll never hold it.' But he did. He hung on that slippery ball as though it was as dry as on a summer day. It was a great save."

Joe always wanted to play as a central defender; initially though, with Irish international Jack Vernon resident as the club's first choice stopper, he had to be content with playing slightly further forward and wider. But this wasn't easy for him, as the Argus noted: "When he should be on the flank, Joe finds it hard to keep away from the middle. And it's such a waste of effort and good material with Jack Vernon already covering." A year later, when 'Spring-heeled Joe' was pressed into service up front; once more he was "prone to lie too far back." Still, when together, the trio of Vernon, Kennedy and Barlow were a formidable midfield line, and Joe was quick to learn. For instance, after a 4-1 win over Fulham, journalist Jack Littlewood declared Kennedy as man of the match because: "On Saturday he had the hallmark of the class wing-half, and despite two injuries carried on unswervingly in making the ball do the work."

Through most of the 1950/51 season, Joe continued to make his name in midfield. With the Baggies unable to find the right blend up front, the two wing halves, Barlow and Kennedy, tried to be everywhere at once. Every single game, they both defended and supported the attack. Sometimes they were the attack… But the pair couldn't always do everything for their moribund colleagues. Even former Villa manager Alex Massie had sympathy for the job the duo were trying to do: "I say Kennedy and Barlow are over-worked owing to the fact they are very often facing three forwards when the centre forward plays deep…" The following season was only a little better, with one *Argus* reporter lamenting: "Albion matches are stereotyped. Their strong defence controls the game, and their attack hammers away, hoping that enthusiasm and bursts of wing skill will produce a goal."

Joe made his debut in his favoured central defensive role at the Baseball Ground in October 1950, deputising for Vernon. He took to it as naturally as a salmon leaps a weir. The *Birmingham Mail* correspondent was suitably impressed: "Kennedy so effectively dominated the field wherever he was operating that neither Parry nor Stamps had any hope of exploiting a central spearhead policy. There was just never a gap or a loophole through which they could get more than a sight of goal."

Despite this fine showing, Irish international Vernon understandably remained the main man at centre-half. Eleven months passed before Joe had another go in what is still largely known as the 'No.5 shirt'. Talk about last minute! With all the apparent organisation of a Sunday League team, he'd been told he would play at centre-forward (another unfamiliar position), but at the last minute, Vernon was unable to play, so he was now playing centre-half instead. Joe was rusty, not having played for the first team that season, and needed time to adjust.

Unfortunately, Newcastle didn't give him that time. As the defender later admitted: "I was lost for the first fifteen minutes." The game finished 3-3 with Kennedy enjoying a wonderful second half. Former Albion man Sandy McNab was impressed, declaring, "We've seen England's centre-half here tonight." Handily, England supreme Walter Winterbottom was at the Hawthorns that day.

Veteran Vernon's days were numbered: extended injury problems were followed by news of his father's ill-health back in his native Belfast. The big defender felt obliged to end his footballing days there and then, and return to take over the family butchers. This was Joe's chance.

JOE QUICKLY BECAME popular both at home, where "his cleverness in attack and defence had the crowd cheering", and in these less-partisan times on the road as well, such as at Roker Park in October 1952. "Several times Kennedy won the praise of the crowd" for subduing the Mackem's star striker, Welsh international Trevor Ford.

Talking to the *Albion News*, Ray Barlow recalled how he left the high balls to Joe. "I never used to head the ball if it was coming in, I'd just shout "Your ball, Joe," and he would come and get it. He was pretty near unbeatable in the air – if he ever missed one, you'd stop for a split second and think, "What happened there?" I don't think Joe liked kicking the ball very much! He'd just roll the ball out to the wing-halves, and let us get on with it. Great reader of the game, timing was perfect. He used the ball well; it all came naturally to him. "

But veteran fan Peter Whitehouse believes Barlow's assessment doesn't do Kennedy justice. "What made him such a crowd favourite was his sheer artistry on the ball. Jackie Vernon, who played before him, and Jimmy Dugdale were stoppers; in other words they won the ball and got rid of it – anywhere. Joe had all the skills of an attacking midfielder. He could win the ball in a crowded penalty area right off the toes of a forward. He'd then quite calmly push it round said opponent and give it to an unmarked team-mate. Many were the choruses of "Good ol' Joe" as he converted defence into attack."

Of course, every player has a bad game. One of Joe's came in a 6-1 drubbing at Turf Moor. A misunderstanding between Kennedy and goalkeeper Sanders handed the Clarets their first goal – but worse followed, Kennedy and Sanders literally banging heads in classic Keystone Kops style. A heavy defeat and a headache! In fact pain and discomfort were to dog Joe all through his Albion years.

In his Albion youth, he once injured his ankle at Chelsea, but continued as a hobbling passenger on the wing. Once, he forgot his disability, picking up a loose ball then running into the middle, but shooting over. After that Kennedy was out for nearly a month, and typical of Joe's ill-fortune, he suffered a head injury in his comeback game.

In a 2-0 defeat at Sheffield Wednesday years later, Joe played despite suffering from flu. As a role-model in a struggling team, he must have felt pressure to continue playing. He somehow mustered an outstanding performance, even in his enfeebled state. With Maurice Setters sent off, and Ronnie Allen carried off, losing by only two goals seemed a decent trade-off. Don Howe remembered the post-match dressing room scene. "We couldn't step into the bath because it was too hot. Joe went straight in and sat there – still shivering, and covered in goose pimples."

There was something about the Hillsborough club, as Joe was also rendered hors de combat in the return fixture. During the second half, he collided with Wednesdayite Keith Ellis. Suffering concussion and double vision, Joe wandered up and down the right wing like a punch-drunk boxer, with team-mates encouraging him by shouting "the pigeons are coming in, Joe!" (racing pigeons were his passion). After Albion scored their third and clinching goal, the trainer helped the stricken defender off the pitch. The sympathetic cheers ringing all around the Hawthorns barely registered. Neither had Albion's third goal. And yet there was even tougher to come. The following season, Don Howe thought he'd help out his team-mate in a dif-ficult defensive situation, but only succeeded in elbowing Kennedy in the face. Joe was knocked unconscious, completely oblivious to the stimulant effect of the trainer's ammonia capsule.

In one week in September 1956 – Joe had a cyst removed on Monday, Thursday he gashed his leg after falling off a low wall and on Friday he had an unpleasant visit to the Dentist.

But whatever the ailment Joe simply soldiered on. In 1957, at Wolverhampton, second-placed Albion visited the League leaders. Following a collision, Kennedy's eye swelled to the size of a duck egg, but Joe played on bravely, with that eye completely closed, albeit accepting a stop-gap role as emergency striker. "Even with one eye, Kennedy made an astonishingly effective forward," penned one reporter from the nationals. Even with their main stopper out of position, the Baggies continued to play the better football, but a really harsh penalty, given against his deputy, Ray Barlow, meant Albion settled for one point instead.

Joe always seemed to be battling back from one kind of injury or another. He endured a painful and worrying double-cartilage-removal operation in February 1953. Would he recover? Many others had not. Although initial signs were good, he broke down in training two months later. Inevitably, the hacks failed to get much comment from Joe. They settled for his economical "tough, but it's the luck of the game." Then, so characteristic of his ill-fortune, Joe broke his nose playing for the reserves, very early into the following term. He finally returned to the team in November against Sunderland; as the Argus observed, it was if he'd never been away. "The ease with which he went through the game was the hallmark of a class player." But quickly, his form deserted him, and he was dropped, Jimmy Dugdale getting the nod as stopper instead.

ALBION WERE pursuing the elusive 'double' at that time, so watching from the sidelines must have been painful. Big Joe was recalled for three games in the crucial run-in to the 1953/54 season, firstly at right-back, and then in midfield; sadly, Albion lost all three games. Even worse, the League Championship was heading straight to Wolverhampton, and Joe was heading straight back to the reserves.

But injuries continued to plague the under-sized squad. Albion's first choice 'keeper, Norman Heath, was out of action, and so too was regular right-back Stan Rickaby. Who would fill this shirt at Wembley for the Cup Final? Joe Kennedy, of course. It was his first Cup match for 15 months, but the unlikely full-back grew into the role magnificently as the match unfolded. Famously, Albion came from behind with Ronnie Allen's second goal, this one from the penalty spot, levelling the game. Joe's through ball put the Albion striker in for a hat-trick chance, but the shot just eluded the post. Joe would not be denied, though; his pass to Reg Ryan allowed the winger to set up Frank Griffin for the 87th minute decider.

Albion had won the Cup, their first trophy since 1931. Even the upright figure of Chairman Major Keys temporarily forgot his military dignity; he was spotted standing, up, cheering with the rest.

Joe had finally got one over Tom Finney, a regular opponent over the years, who, contrary to popular belief, didn't always play by the rules. In later times, Joe recalled being pushed and barged by the forward while waiting for a corner to be taken. Despite his appealing to the referee, it was obvious that no-one believed that Gentleman Tom could do things like that.

By the mid 50s, the man from Cleator Moor was once again master of the middle. His rival for the shirt, Jimmy Dugdale, gave up the fight and left saying: "I could never hope to replace Joe Kennedy, so I put my future first." Joe was a hardened professional by then, playing his 200th match at Bloomfield Road, Blackpool. Not only could he defend, he was additionally supplementing the forward line. There was even a rare goal (against Charlton), one of only four for the Baggies in his entire career. With five forwards, it was rarely considered necessary in this era for centre-halves to go up the field for corners and free kicks, their priority being to mark at least one of the players the opposition would leave up front.

SEASON 1955/56 drew parallels with those at the start of the decade. Goalscoring was a constant problem, particularly away (Albion lost seven straight on the road), and the contributions of Kennedy and Barlow were vital to keep the Baggies in the game. The pressure was on – being only mid-table in the top League just wasn't good enough. This was West Bromwich Albion, after all.

Albion broke the losing run with a 1-0 win at Preston in October. Wrote one correspondent "Joe Kennedy was in England form in anticipation and interception. One lost count of the number of attacks that broke down through his intervention."

A win at Championship-chasing Wolves in the FA Cup gave an adrenalin rush, a moment to be treasured, and Joe was at the heart of the 2-1 victory. Reporter Edwin Buckley: "Kennedy stood out against this mass Molineux attack. He coolly headed away centres and took control of the penalty box to such an extent that Wolves attack was blunted." On such signal victories are reputations secured.

Joe's talents were now being recognised at a higher level. In October 1955, he played for the FA XI at Bristol, Albion at Sunderland and England 'B' in Manchester, before travelling to join training with the full England side at Porthcawl. In 12 days, he'd covered 1,000 miles, all by train. Months later, he was in top form for England 'B' against Scotland 'B'. A full cap was surely imminent... and then he broke his collarbone. Albion's No. 5 collided with Bolton's Nat Lofthouse, and came off worse. For five weeks, Joe wore his left arm in a sling, struggling to do even basic tasks like tie his own shoelaces. He would not play again until mid-September. Meanwhile, Ray Barlow was picking up rave reviews as his deputy, a situation that would return to haunt Joe later in his career.

Joe's injuries, illnesses (such as shingles – out for a month), the occasional being left out of the side after disputes with the manager, plus being an Albion man, all conspired to ensure he never won that elusive full England cap. Joe didn't always help himself: not making the most of playing for the FA XI at Stamford Bridge in late 1952 (effectively an England B game) for example. Even the benevolent local press considered his contribution as "only average" adding, "he didn't seem comfortable." Sheer bad timing, such as captaining an FA XI thrashed 7-1 by France, also played a leading role. However valid his personal contribution, certain fingers would always point at the team captain in that particular situation.

Then there was Billy Wright. The man from Wolverhampton always barred his way to a full England cap. Joe regularly drew praise for his games at 'B' level, but it was never quite suffi-cient to satisfy the full team selectors, even at his mid-fifties peak. The nearest he would get was as 12th man in the famous thrashing by Hungary in 1953. He did make an appearance for 60 seconds, though – helping the trainer carry his magic sponges onto the pitch. And yet Charles Matheson of the Argus, a regular watcher of both men, considered Joe to be stronger than Billy Wright. "There's so little on which Joe can be faulted, even by the purists. He has the mobility to venture forward now and again. His tackling is Grade One, he is tops in the air, and although he has skill in ball play, he does not fiddle needlessly." There were suggestions that Billy Wright could fill in as a defensive midfielder to give the Cleator Moor man a game, but this never happened. Joe's angst was greatly increased with so many of his team-mates getting the nod instead: just think Allen, Kevan, Howe, Robson and Barlow.

Joe became great friends with Albion winger Billy Elliott, who also originated from an obscure part of Cumberland. When Elliott retired from full-time football, he took over the Great Western Arms in West Bromwich town centre, a hostelry where there was ample living accommodation included with the pub. By coincidence, Kennedy and fellow Baggie Frank Griffin needed to find somewhere new to live, as the current landlords wished to end their arrangement, and so Billy invited them to become his tenants. There were obvious temptations involved, but officially at least, Joe's interest in the pub was no greater than politely helping out mine host to move the empties. He preferred table tennis in the local club than supping in his "own" house, so we're led to believe. Joe lived with the Elliotts for three years, then married West Bromwich girl Angela Thomas, and set up home together.

Joe didn't always have a smooth relationship with Albion managers. Early in his career, he wanted a wage level guarantee. When the club turned him down, he didn't sign his new one-year contract, the season kicking off with the Cumberland man literally refusing to play ball. He didn't get back in the first team until mid-September as a result.

When Joe read a newspaper story in January 1956 claiming he would be swapped for Fulham's Bobby Robson, he probably felt another disagreement coming on. Nothing whatsoever had been said to him about a move. His wife Angela was expecting baby Michael, so any potential upheaval was terribly unwelcome: even in these comparatively modern times, mere players didn't have much say in transfers. Fortunately, Chairman Major Keys himself hastened to seek out big Joe on the training ground to assure him that the story was quite untrue. Albion did eventually sign Robson, but in exchange for a cheque, not a defender.

And good that Kennedy stayed as he was in the form of his life. In November 1956, a 1-1 draw with Manchester City moved one *Birmingham Post* correspondent to comment, "Albion's dominating figure was again Joe Kennedy – rarely at fault with head or feet and revealing an uncanny power of anticipation. His wonderful consistency has been a big factor in wielding together Albion's defence into one of the most dependable in the country."

Against Forest at home in the FA Cup in February 1958 which finished 3-3, Kennedy marked his 300th game with another domineering performance. Yet, although "he ruled the centre of the field like a miniature John Charles," his mistake led to a goal for the visitors. Kennedy left the ball to Sanders who didn't come out and Simcoe scored.

LATER THAT YEAR, Joe endured a stomach problem. Having had a medical during pre-season, he wanted to wait for the results before playing again. Manager Vic Buckingham didn't agree, so, highly reluctantly, the centre-half turned out in a practice match. His disinclination was obvious, quickly leading to an argument where Joe was told to leave the field, and was dropped from the first team. The player accepted his fate: "I'm not going to ask for a transfer or do anything silly. My roots are in the Midlands now. I'm happy here."

The concern for Joe was that Ray Barlow was now playing in his centre-half position. The manager considered Ray his first choice, feeling that the leaky defence from the previous season needed improving. It was certainly a dilemma. The Albion front men were missing Barlow's craft from midfield, and similarly, Barlow couldn't hope to match 'Spring-heeled Joe's' remarkable aerial ability. Neither did Joe give away penalties (only one on record), whereas Ray gave four to the opposition the previous season (and would go on to allow four more by December). But Ray was getting on a bit, and the argument went that the stresses and strains of midfield were a bit much for him. Albion started the term in modest fashion but... four wins in the next five matches eased the unrest, as did briefly going top of the League that December, despite Joe's long-term confinement to the stiffs.

At the time, the supporters' view was clear. They wanted "one of the best and cleanest players Albion have ever had" back in the No. 5 shirt, and Barlow back in midfield. "We Want Joe" chanted supporters during a 3-2 home defeat by Everton in October, rebellious stuff indeed for the time. They also made use of the only channel of protest open to them by writing to the local newspaper. A letter from Yvonne Hill neatly summed up the views of several corre-spondents. "Kennedy's skill in the air and his distributional play are unrivalled by anyone West Bromwich could hope to play at centre-half."

Joe's chance eventually came in January 1959, at Deepdale, as Barlow was injured. Albion won 4-2; their eighth away win of the season. Naturally, he spent the first half adjusting, but the second 45 was a glimpse of the old Joe. But it wasn't enough for him to keep his place as he battled with his fellow cult hero, Barlow, for a place in the side.

When 'Spring-heeled Joe' returned to the first team a month later for a decent run of matches in Division One, his coolness under pressure enabled the Baggies to end a run of eight games without a win. As one player confessed at the time: "we were almost afraid to touch the ball." Albion came from behind to beat Blackpool, Joe holding the back line together largely single-handledly, allowing Bobby Robson to play as a sixth forward as the Baggies won 3-1. Only now did Kennedy feel able to talk, as expansively as he ever managed, about his period in the cold. "I was a bit upset when I was left out of the League team, but after a bit I began to enjoy my football with the youngsters."

Joe was back, and back to stay, as Barlow's knee troubles would eventually finish his career. It is debatable whether Kennedy's imperious form in this period, which truly secured his cult status at the Hawthorns, would have ended Barlow's career at West Brom anyway. Reporter Jeff Hollinshurst observed at Preston: "Ambling Joe Kennedy was the complete master in the middle, leaving not even the eye of a needle through which Tom Finney could find a way." This, for a player basically overlooked the previous season. He was in exceptional form at the time, arguably the side's best player in what was perceived then as difficult times – being mid-table at the top level of the game.

As usual, not everything went to plan. Joe Kennedy ran onto the turf at Craven Cottage with kick-off imminent – then the bottom eyelet on his right boot burst. The first kick sent his boot flying, so Joe hastened to the touchline to get his boot repaired. Fulham kicked off while he was on the sidelines, and some 45 seconds later, they were a goal up, the Londoners going on to win 4-2. Inevitably, another injury took yet another month out of his career – six stitches in a cut scalp after being carried off against Newcastle. Just the half dozen, only a month? Small beer! Reserve midfielder Archie Styles recalled the bruising nature of the era. "When they went into the tackle, I could hear the bones crunching. It was not for me. I got out."

As the fifties became the sixties, Joe continued his majestic form, with a posse of national and local journalists seeking weekly alternatives to their stock phrases. Still he looked international class, and frequent were the suggestions that he deserved a cap – even at the age of 34, and with 350 games behind him. Tom Finney, Manchester United's Dennis Violett, nor any of the big name forwards of the day for that matter, could defeat him. So positive was the feedback on his contribution to a FA Cup fourth round victory over Bolton, it could have glowed in the dark. A rare goal followed in the fifth round at Leicester, Joe's first for over four years. It was a scrambled effort late in the game from a corner, but came too late to save the Baggies from unexpected elimination. Yet, every month or so, there was speculation that Player A or player B "was to be Kennedy's successor". Most notable of these was defender Stan Jones, who signed in the summer of 1960 from Walsall.

Albion started the next term in dreadful style, and after three straight defeats, changes were deemed necessary. So in came Stan, fresh out of the Fourth Division. Although he did well enough, the defeats continued and so Joe returned. But 'Spring heeled Joe' had lost his bounce and was distinctly human. (Say it ain't so!) There were still fixtures, mainly at home, where he stood as an unbeatable rock, Bolton's Nat Lofthouse among the frustrated centre-forwards who simply weren't permitted to do anything with the ball. Too often, though, by his immense standards, Joe was caught out of position, and an own goal at Everton (the fourth of his career) didn't help either. To compound his thoroughly miserable afternoon, he was knocked out in a collision. Fortunately, he recovered, and played on.

IN A HUGELY embarrassing episode, the Baggies were beaten 3-1 in the Third Round of the FA Cup by Lincoln City, bottom of the Second Division. City hadn't won a Cup match for seven years. By sharp contrast, this was the first time in 29 years that West Brom had played just one FA Cup match in a season. Kennedy was moved to protest: "their first goal was well offside. We have had far too many like this given against us this season. " Or was it just that Joe's powers were on the wane? He was now 35. After a run of four defeats with 12 goals conceded, Joe was taken out of the firing line. Explained manager Gordon Clark. "Joe tells me he has been feeling the strain in the last few games. He agrees that every injury now takes twice as long to heal than it used to, and he needs a rest. So I told him to go away and forget all about football. I believe he has gone to stay with his parents for a few days."

With a new centre-half, the Baggies won seven matches in a row, their best run for 30 years. Joe would not be adding to his 397 games. In May 1961, he was given a free transfer. So too was Ronnie Allen. The last two remaining members of the '54 Cup winning side shut the door behind them.

Supporter, DJ Hill, penned a tribute in the local press. "It is hard to believe that we shall not see Joe grace the Albion colours again. His value to the team can hardly be measured and he deserved more honours than he got."

RONNIE ALLEN

1950-1961 1977 AND 1981-1982

BAGGIES CAREER

Games	458
Goals	234
Caps	5

MAGIC MOMENT

His 88th minute goal relegated Aston Villa in 1959

'BLACK-HAIRED IDOL'

CULT hero status at the Hawthorns tends to be earned over a period of time, or conferred on an already well admired player for the act of scoring a vital winning goal in a promotion campaign or in a vital FA Cup tie or even the final. But for one of our heroes his legendary status began the very first day he set foot inside West Bromwich Albion Football Club.

RONNIE ALLEN was born in Fenton, Stoke-on-Trent on 15th January 1929, the first born of George Henry Allen and his wife Elsie. A younger sister, Barbara, was to follow six years later. Ronnie's Dad was a builder and had dreams for his son. Ronnie had dreams too.

"Even during my schoolboy days, I dreamed of football fame, since I lived in Stan Matthews' home town. But never once was I fortunate enough to attend a school which had an association football team. At Hanley High school in the Potteries, Rugby Union was the only game played, and although I enjoyed handling the ball at scrum-half, soccer and a round ball was what I wanted" explained Ronnie, through the medium of his 1955 autobiography "It's Goals that Count." Rather like the player himself, the publication was breaking new ground. "Goals…" was one of the first autobiographies written by a footballer.

Alan Lowndes also attended Hanley High school. "I met Ronnie at school after passing my 11 plus. He saw me playing football one dinnertime, and took me under his wing. He taught me to shoot with both feet. I recall one particular match I was playing in. The score was 0-0, when their keeper came out to the edge of the penalty area, and he booted the ball upfield. It came to me and as I trapped the ball, I heard Ronnie's voice from the touchline shouting, "Lob it, Alan." With the keeper stranded on the edge of the area, I duly obliged and scored the first goal in an eventual 2-0 win."

Ronnie also played for a local junior side Northwood Mission, widely known as the strongest team in the area. Apart from Master Allen, others in the side included Reg Potts (later to enjoy a notable career at Vale), Basil Hayward (Vale and Portsmouth), plus one Bill

McGarry (Wolves and England). Ronnie generally played wide in attack. Lining up in a hapless opposition team thumped 8-1 by Northwood (Ronnie scored "once or twice") was 17 year-old Roy Matthews, who remembers how Reg Potts's father trained both his son and young Ronnie in a discreet manner, so that Ronnie's Dad wouldn't find out.

After all, Ronnie Allen studied at the high school and must have a "proper job", not play silly games. Ronnie disobeyed his father by signing for Port Vale and persuaded Reg Potts to do the same.

THE THIRD DIVISION NORTH outfit signed Ronnie on amateur forms in March 1944 at the age of 15. He made his first team debut in the wartime league at 16. In addition to football, he worked as a laboratory assistant for a porcelain company owned by one of the Vale directors.

Within a year, the lad from Fenton was holding down a regular first Port Vale team place on the wing. Even better, two hat-tricks enabled him to finish top scorer with 13 goals to his name. However, playing for a Potteries football club wasn't sufficient reason to escape National Service, so the Fenton teenager reluctantly began "doing his bit" in January 1947. Fortunately, footballers had an easy life in the forces. Indeed, many were still able to turn out for their club most Saturdays.

Supporter Stephen Gabb recalls, "my late father served in the RAF at the same time as Ronnie Allen. They played together in a game in which Ronnie scored ten before half-time. He was banned from entering the opposition half during the second period, yet he still managed to score from within his own!" Turning out for the RAF representative team put the Vale teenager in the shop window for several First Division clubs. All were sniffing, but none were biting, so Ronnie continued to find the net in the Third Division North.

Even the best players make mistakes. During one match, Vale were awarded a corner, and Ronnie went to take the kick. He moved away from the corner flag, preparing for his kick, and fell backwards over the dog-track fence surrounding the ground. Fortunately Ronnie was uninjured by his fall and climbed back to join in the laughter.

Shortly after his 21st birthday, the Vale hotshot had a busy Saturday. He married 19-year-old Constance Brewer in the morning (the Stoke press didn't consider the new Mrs Allen worthy of naming, she was described only as an "Etruria resident" – Etruria being one of the small towns that make up the Potteries). Most of his team-mates were present, though none managed any more than a sip of champagne because Vale had a match that afternoon against Watford. Ronnie went straight from reception to ground to lead his team (he was named Captain for the day) and scored the first goal in a 2-0 win. The goal was one of 40 he managed for the Potteries' less famous club. Port Vale remained a modest side. Even with the Fenton teenager contributing mightily from the flank, during his spell, their highest finishing League position in the basement Division was eighth.

Allen's all round talent deserved a bigger stage, and it was the Albion who gave the newly-wed his chance two months later. A Vale club record £20,000 transfer was negotiated in 30 minutes. With a maximum wage in force and players basically owned by clubs, Ronnie didn't have any say in the deal.

REPORTING TO HIS new workplace was not a straightforward business for a young man unfamiliar with geography outside Stoke-on-Trent. He travelled by train from Stoke to

Birmingham as instructed, alighted at Dudley Port and caught a number 74 bus to the Hawthorns, where he was to meet up with his team-mates. Ronnie was fearful of missing his stop, and nervously asked the driver several times not to forget to tell him where to get off.

In March 1950, Pete George was a young forward at the Hawthorns. His chances of playing in the senior side were suddenly boosted by first team forward Billy Elliott tearing a tendon and Cyril Williams breaking his leg.

"This meant I was first choice for the first- team. Imagine my frustration when I dashed into the dressing room to see the team sheet had AN Other at number 7. 'Who on earth was he?' I asked Bill Richardson, our trainer, what was going on, and he replied, "there's a transfer on". I asked him who, he couldn't tell me. We all went to Ted Sandford's café, had tea and toast, and played the one armed tic-tac bandit (a fruit machine] with the odd sixpence. At 5pm, I bought my *Evening Despatch*, "Albion sign ALLEN from Port Vale" was the headline. Allen was the AN Other."

The new signing went straight into the WBA first team on the wing. Albion were then a newly promoted side struggling for goals. Propitiously the opposition on 4th March 1950 just happened to be Wolves.

His first day at the office started badly. The Potteries young man knocked on the door of the Players' Entrance upon which the doorman asked him whom or what he wanted.

"I want to come in, please"

"Have you got a ticket?"

"No, I haven't got a ticket."

"Then bugger off!"

In high dudgeon, the new boy approached a policeman.

"Excuse me, officer, I'm trying to get into the ground"

Again, "have you got a ticket?"

"No, I'm a player."

"Now come on sunshine, you're not a player, you're not big enough."

"Well do me a favour, will you go the secretary's office, and ask him to come out, and tell him who I am?"

Off went the obliging constable to track down Secretary Eph Smith.

"There's a young man outside who claims to be Ronnie Allen."

"Never seen him before in my life" came the discouraging reply.

Eventually, and thankfully, Jack Smith the manager popped his head round the door saying, "Where have you been? Come on in."

It was five to three, and with the a 3 o'clock kick-off looming, the new boy said later "I've never changed so quick in my life!"

Not surprisingly after such an unsettling introduction, the Fenton forward found getting into the game very difficult. Furthermore, playing in front of the Hawthorns' biggest ever League crowd (60,945 – with an estimated 10,000 more locked outside) probably needed much mental adjustment for one used to Vale-sized crowds of 5,000 or less.

Wolves went one up. With only a single goal to the Baggies' name in the previous six matches, just where would an equaliser come from? And then… A cross from George Lee soared over the heads of the old gold and black defenders, and there, at the far post, was the debutant, meeting the ball on the volley with his left foot to crash it home. Note the left foot – Allen was a right winger. Spectacular debut goal, against Wolves, with his wrong foot... cult hero status started right here.

"GOT TO GET the ball in the old onion bag" was Ronnie's regularly used expression, and he did. He became club top scorer six years in a row, a remarkable record of consistency topped only by W.G. Richardson in the club's history to date. His 27 strikes in 1954/55 made him the top marksman in the First Division, and in three other seasons, he ran the top scorer very close indeed.

All these goals despite the keenest attentions of numerous defenders, as this typical match report illustrates:

"One, two, three.... one, two, three.... Ronnie Allen flickered through the Wolves defence with the verge of a Bolshoi ballerina. Then whump! For the third time, Allen hit the turf after describing a not-so-graceful, but very spectacular arc. And once again, the Allen worshippers called on the referee to denounce [Wolves defender] Stuart".

Despite his remarkable consistency, Ronnie was to win only five England caps. Partly because of the usual Midlands backwater prejudice (Astle, Bomber Brown, Barlow, Kennedy, Regis and many others could feel equally hard done by) and partly, as astute commentators of the time considered, he was so far ahead of his time that the tramline-tracked selectors simply didn't understand him. Ronnie himself provided an example. He was paired with Sunderland's Len Shackleton for a trial match – England against Charlton at the Valley. Both "Shack" and Allen scored hat-tricks in a 7-1 win yet England manager Winterbottom berated them after the game for not passing the ball as he'd instructed.

An England side played Albion in a trial game at the Hawthorns before tackling World Champions Germany at Wembley in 1954. England won 6-3, with Ronnie enhancing his chances of winning another cap by netting a hat-trick against his own club defence. Prior to the Wembley clash, German manager Sepp Herberger admitted he was perturbed about the speed and mobility of Allen and demonstrated on a diagram, the vast area in which he expected the West Bromwich player to operate. His fears were realised. The 'Genie' scored in a comfortable 4-2 victory.

Still, in an era when internationals were staged at the same time as League matches, his country's loss was his club's gain – and Baggies fans knew Allen's worth. The only debate about his inclusion in the line-up was which position he should play in? Ideally they'd like Allen to cross from the wing for Allen to convert in the centre.

Stratton Smith in the Daily Sketch agreed; "Soccerwise, Albion manager Vic Buckingham has a stick of gold in England cast off Ronnie Allen. The skimpy, devastating little man with the looks of a Latin lover, and the eternal motion of a whole–hearted soccer brilliant. Where to play him? "Oh brother!" sighs Mr Buckingham. If they (being the lumped mass of supporters and press) had their way, Ronnie would be played in all five forward positions at once! Accept first that Allen IS the Albion attack. That no other player has his sense of positioning; nor his gift of pulling a ball out of trouble; nor his split-second decisiveness in knowing when to stop and when to go. Frankly, he's 80 percent of Albion's fund of ideas – and I deplore deeply that he should ever have escaped the England set."

Ronnie Allen and penalties seemed to go hand in hand. Whenever a referee pointed to the spot, the Baggies top scorer was quite deadly. His team-mate Frank Griffin in later years described the maestro's technique. "He was fantastic – truly fantastic. He hit the ball so hard once he burst the ball. Left foot or right foot, it didn't matter to him. He'd keep a mental note of which keeper he'd sent the wrong way, and next time he faced them, he'd use the other foot and put it in the opposite corner." Even Ronnie missed occasionally, but so occasionally that it made big news. After missing one against of all teams, Aston Villa, he was surrounded by a posse of reporters at the end of the game, asking what had gone wrong.

IN ALL, Allen found the net 234 times for the Baggies. This in itself is full justification for cult hero status. Albion supporters instinctively love a goalscorer, but then who doesn't? Almost every consistent finisher for the Baggies has had appreciation showered upon them, but Ronnie was more than just a goalscorer. He could use both feet, giving the advantage of being able to pass a ball instantly. Albion goalkeeper Jimmy Sanders was quite clear. The Potteries man was "the best two footed player I've ever seen. At Bolton, he hit the bar with his right foot and smacked the rebound in with his left."

Allen's shooting power couldn't be bettered, while his mental agility to envisage a potential goal-scoring situation was a joy to behold. And he was versatile too, able to perform in any of the five forward positions – and did so regularly. Weaknesses were hard to identify. There was the physical one of not being very tall, but height is nature's doing. He scored only a few goals with his head. Numerous publications feature a photograph of Ronnie throwing himself full length to get on the end of a cross in a 1950s game at the Hawthorns. It looks spectacular and one imagines that the ball flew into the bottom corner of the opponent's net with bullet-like accuracy. Not so, as fan Terry Wills recalls, "The fact is that Ronnie completely missed that cross. I had a perfect view of the action and he was at least a yard away from making contact." But that photo is now used as something of an iconic image with which Allen is remembered for his goalscoring feats – an example of how rose-tinted spectacles can be applied when a player's status is unimpeachable.

Writing for the *FA Book for Boys*, Ronnie concluded that "being on the short side, I came to the conclusion that I must make the utmost of my ability to move more quickly than the big fellows and devise my own special methods of getting within shooting range of that goal."

Ronnie always played with a smile on his face, illustrated in a match at Filbert Street against Leicester City. It was one of those days. Albion as a team weren't playing well, Ronnie's shooting followed suit. A cross from the right, his marker eluded and the fans were already celebrating. Ronnie somehow managed to not only miss the target, but the stadium as well, ballooning the ball briefly into orbit. Ronnie simply grinned and joked with his colleagues.

EVEN WITH THE exciting new forward on board, scoring goals continued to be a problem at the Hawthorns. So too was the League position by October 1951, after only a solitary win was recorded in the first eight matches. Various players had been tried at centre-forward without a great deal of success. Manager Smith asked Ronnie if he fancied a shot at the job. He didn't. "My first reaction to the idea was that it was a stupid one. Insofar as I could not expect to out-jump those big centre-halves, or bore my way through the middle on my own. I told Mr Smith, although I didn't fancy my chances, I would have a go, and do as he told me".

The first two attempts weren't particularly encouraging, but on the journey to London to meet Chelsea, Albion's centre-half and captain, Jack Vernon, suggested to Ronnie that it might be useful to know the tactics he most disliked centre-forwards using against him, and offered a few tricks he could try out. Ronnie was immediately inspired and encouraged. The 'Pensioners' (as Chelsea were unflatteringly nicknamed at the time) were beaten 3-1, with Ronnie scoring twice and from then on, 'Mr Versatile' decided he'd adopt a pioneering new role. A roving commission, his strategy being that whenever possible, he'd position himself to always be available for a pass. This was tactically groundbreaking stuff in an era of rigid formations. Centre-forwards were always the central pivot on which all attacks were based. They kept basically to one small area of the pitch, where they would be marked by a centre-half. Centre-forwards did not wander off doing their own thing!

So add in the phrase "tactical intelligence" to the Allen CV. In the following games, the roving striker took full advantage of a succession of confused centre-halves, scoring in nine of the ten matches. And Ronnie carried on finding the net, finishing the season with 35 goals from League and Cup, and in the following season, another 21 goals saw Albion finish fourth, their highest league position since 1933. He was also selected to represent England against Switzerland. The later but more famous 'Revie Plan' from Manchester City, which relied on forwards dropping deeper to pick up the ball, thereby confusing their one-dimensional markers, owed a debt of gratitude to Allen. Laughably, the Revie Plan was later described as "revolutionary."

The Baggies' main man described the centre-forward's position as the "hardest role, but I love it." Playing as a static target man wasn't the only point on which he disagreed with the thinking of the time. "Let me answer those who criticise me for not charging and chasing goal-keepers. Ninety-nine times out of a hundred, these tactics prove futile and a waste of energy. They often cause unnecessary trouble. I'm in favour of the continental style, which gives the keeper the freedom of the penalty area once he has gained possession. That takes time and allows the opposition to cover in any case. Of course, if I have the challenge to beat the keeper to the ball, I take it. But I see no reason for charging him on the six-yard line, and as usually happens, give the opposition even more time to regain their balance."

Even the best forwards can end up frustrated as reporter Bill David described, "Little Ronnie Allen versus big Ron Reynolds in the Spurs goal, that was the vital duel. The giant in the green jersey came out on top. But magnificent as Reynolds was, my heart went out to the non-stop Allen. If ever a man did enough, and some more, the wee Albion centre-forward did in this match. Allen shot from all angles and often from only half chances. When it wasn't Reynolds pushing aside his power drives, some other Spurs defender was in the way. All this one-man bad luck for Allen seemed to take the steam out of Albion for a time. But back again came Albion and it was the spring-heeled Reynolds who kept them at bay. On eighty-four minutes, Allen hit a low volley only to see Reynolds stretch his full length. This time Allen could not restrain from beating his hands into the mud in disappointment." Those final words were a fair summary of the man. He focussed completely on success, and if it wasn't forthcoming, he felt even more downtrodden than the supporters – another connection which intrinsically linked Ronnie to his fans.

MANAGER JACK SMITH abruptly left the club in April 1952, replaced by coach Jesse Carver. Training had meant dressing in a grey polo-necked jumper, grey shorts and pumps (lightweight rubber soled shoes). Directed typically by Fred Reed and W.G. Richardson, training invariably started with two laps jogging around the Hawthorns running track followed by one lap walking, then the same again until Fred and Bill decided sprints were in order. This consisted of racing along the Halfords Lane track from the Brummie Road End to the Smethwick End. After a few of these, training transferred to the grandly named gymnasium – in reality a bare room under the Halfords Lane/Smethwick Corner stand. It was "equipped" with one heavy medicine ball plus another hanging from the ceiling about eight feet from the ground. W.G. would use a snooker cue to get the ceiling ball moving, and then invite each player to jump to make contact with it. There was no contact between footballs and feet, on the rather spurious basis that absence would make the players all the keener on Saturday.

Carver rejected this thinking. He allowed the players to wear their football boots and train with a ball as opposed to endless running. Carver's stay was short – just eight months – before Lazio made him an offer he couldn't refuse, but he left an exciting legacy. Allen's imaginative tactical theories on the beautiful game could only have been stimulated by these new methods. Fortunately, Carver's replacement, Vic Buckingham, was of similar progressive mind.

IT WASN'T ONLY Ronnie's goals and imaginative tactical play that led to him securing a permanent place in the fans' hearts. He was a genuine 'nice guy', who always appreciated the support the Black Country worshippers bestowed upon him and the team, and he was ever considerate of supporters. The "Nice Guy" test remains a prerequisite for any Albion crowd favourite in the last half century, though less important for successful forwards. Fortunately, all the best Baggies goalscorers possess off-field charm (or perhaps more allowances are made, it being hard to make fine judgements during star struck moments).

Ronnie wasn't a sole crowd favourite. In a successful era of so many stars in stripes, he was one of several. Nicholls, Barlow, Kennedy and others were all magnificent players and all deserved cult hero status.

Quite why this 'pleasant personality' criterion only appears to apply from the 1950s is hard to easily quantify. Significantly, the cult hero as an entity hit new heights as a result of the propaganda era of the Second World War and its cult of celebrity associated with the RAF and film stars of the time. Post-war, newspapers gradually deepened their sporting coverage, and so did radio. Sporting heroes took over from military ones. Gradually, footballers escaped from their one-dimensional confines to become individuals who could speak, think, and even write for themselves. Another factor is footballers' wages. An insignificant issue in the 1950s, but certainly after the maximum wage was scrapped in the following decade, top line sportsmen slowly pulled ahead of average wages, with the "Nice Guy" factor becoming both an accolade and a justification.

It was commonplace in the fifties for team and supporters to meet on the train travelling to away matches. Hundreds of Albion followers would gather at New Street Station in Birmingham, resplendent in an array of blue and white scarves and outsize rosettes. The Baggies were playing at Blackpool one day and to reach Bloomfield Road, passengers had to disembark at South Shore Station and then walk a goodly distance. Fan Terry Wills recalls, "together with all the rest of our support, we started down the road whirring rattles (heavy, unwieldy wooden noise-making devices) above our heads bellowing 'Albion, Albion'. To my astonishment, Ronnie joined in. He took my rattle and whirled it around his head and ran down the road joining in a chorus of 'Albion, Albion.' The respect and admiration he gained from that one moment couldn't be measured."

But there was more. Albion had played badly at St. James' Park in August 1954, losing 3-0. At that time, a one-way trip from Newcastle to Birmingham took seven hours and the glum, silent supporters knew they wouldn't arrive back at New Street until 2am on Sunday morning. Fan Terry Wills again, "The door of our compartment slid open, and Ronnie Allen said, 'I'd just like to apologise for our performance today lads. We know we let you down. Sorry about that, but thanks for your support. We'll try and do better next time.'" Ronnie had recognised the travelling faithful and made a conscious effort to offer those consoling sentiments. On such a platform is a hero constructed.

Indeed Ronnie always found time to chat to fans, whether at Supporters Club meetings, outside the ground, on a train to an away ground, or as recalled by supporter Gary Brookes, on a golf course. "On return to the club house one evening, we enjoyed a few drinks and a meal, with Ronnie recounting a host of entertaining footballing memories. We were the last people to leave the club in the early hours after what was for me a truly memorable day". Allen was a fine raconteur, and once in story telling mode was fascinating company. Supporters Club Secretary Alan Cleverley remembers chauffeuring the striker to and from a supporters club meeting in Kidderminster, "Ronnie was telling so many tales on the way back that I wanted to make the evening last as long as possible. I was driving more and more slowly 'til literally we were moving only at five miles an hour."

THE EXTENT OF Ronnie's contribution to dressing room harmony was sizable too. In September 1958, he saw Randolph Turpin lose his World Middle-weight boxing title. On his return, he gave his team-mates a demonstration of Turpin struggling to avoid the count. Like a puppet being jerked on strings, Ronnie rolled frantically around the dressing room. Explained Ray Barlow, "every time someone came in, we whispered to them, "ask Ronnie about the fight" and each time Ronnie went through his antics again. It was good fun until Ronnie tumbled we were pulling his leg".

Golf was always important to Ronnie. He was awfully good at the sport, regularly beating the professional at his local course. Indeed at his peak, he played off a handicap of four, twice winning the Professional Footballers' Golfing Championship and twice finishing second. Graham Williams, the captain of the 1968 Albion Cup-winning team recalled his early days at the Hawthorns. "We youngsters had so much respect for the '54 team that we used to call them Mr Allen, Mr Barlow and Mr Dugdale. I used to caddy for Ronnie when he played golf at Sandwell Park or Handsworth on a day-off and I hated it. I took up squash instead."

Ronnie had film star looks, and immaculate dress sense. In a reference to the golden age of the cinema, local reporter Charles Harold once described him as "the black haired idol of the Hawthorns crowd". Most of Hollywood's leading lights were 'blessed' with black hair including the swarthy, handsome legends Clark Gable, Robert Taylor, Errol Flynn, Howard Keel, Victor Mature, and numerous others. Add together the goals, the clever play, the off-field charm and good looks and Stanley Matthews' often repeated observation about Ronnie Allen – "he was the complete footballer" – makes perfect sense. Think Michael Owen with a telepathic partner to get something close to the Baggies roving centre-forward.

GOALSCORERS ARE always at their most effective as a partnership. Ronnie's record was decent without being outstanding, until he found his on-field partner. When Allen received an eye injury before a FA Cup match at Blackburn in February 1952, young Johnny Nicholls played instead, and did remarkably well, even though he lacked Allen's ball skills. On Allen's return, Nicholls kept his place and that was the start of a fine and lucrative partnership. Johnny shared the same attitude to the game as his forward partner. In just two seasons, the partnership netted 111 goals.

The understanding between Ronnie and Johnny really was something to behold. If Ronnie had the ball, he knew instinctively where his poaching partner would be to receive a pass likely to cause most damage. Conversely, if it was the 'poacher' in possession, he instinctively knew where Ronnie would prefer the ball to be played to him. The pair bore topical comparison to Lesley and Sydney Piddington, a 'second sight' radio act that astounded the nation courtesy of their amazing radio broadcasts. Once Lesley was ensconced in the Tower of London, while her husband sat inside Broadcasting House. The challenge was to pass on a paragraph from a book chosen by a third party, by telepathy. And they did it! Albion's deadly pairing used their own understanding to take the Baggies to new heights in the 1953/54 season.

For the first time ever, the two top teams in the land were the Black Country's finest – West Bromwich and Wolverhampton Wanderers. As a result, a new, keener rivalry built up which exists to this day. Albion made a flying start ahead of their rivals, with a series of outstanding results taking them storming to the top of the table, and it was inevitably the 'terrible twins' of Allen and Nicholls who plundered the goals. It was as if they'd heard they were going out of fashion and wanted to stock up before the shelves were cleared. So, as the New Year came in, hopes were rising that Vic Buckingham's team could become the first team since Aston Villa in 1897 to achieve the Holy Grail status of double winners – League Champions and FA Cup Winners.

Allen believed the narrow FA Cup Fifth Round win over Cup giants Newcastle was the best game he'd ever played in. Two first half strikes from the little maestro rocked the Geordies back, but a battling show of defiance led by Jackie Milburn reduced the arrears.

In Ronnie's own words "Then came the turning point of the match. We forced a corner-kick on our left wing. As our winger George Lee came to take the kick, I started to run along the eighteen- yard line towards him. He drove the ball towards me at a great pace, and I timed the run-in just right to volley the ball goalwards with my left foot on the half-turn. This was a shot I had practised many, many, times in training, and now my efforts were rewarded. The ball rocketed into the top left hand corner of the net. I can't describe my personal joy over this goal, and I didn't have time to think about it before my colleagues were shaking my hand."

The Baggies went on to reach Wembley for the first time since 1935 by despatching Port Vale in an uncomfortable semi-final. The late winner came from a contentious penalty, scored by Ronnie against his old side. It was an agonising moment all round. Many Albion supporters turned their heads away. Others shut their eyes. But for the rest, they had to see the outcome, and as his ferocious shot hit the net, unrestrained joy was the order of the day. Naturally Vale fans were far from happy. One wrote to Ronnie asking "why didn't you shoot wide, as you know only too well it wasn't a penalty? After all, the Vale gave you your chance and it was your duty to miss this in return."

INJURIES AND international call-ups eventually did for the Baggies' League hopes. The England selectors had barely shown interest in Albion's top scorer to this point, yet selected both Allen and Nicholls to play for England versus Scotland on the same day Albion met Wolves. The "Terrible Twins" sunk the "auld enemy" between them, but meanwhile, in their absence, West Bromwich were losing to theirs. Albion's league form slumped. The final straw was a particularly painful 6-1 defeat at Villa Park. The great man felt "slightly down in the dumps. We had let the League Championship slip through our fingers, having managed only half a dozen points out of the last twenty."

The Cup Final provided much compensation. Albion beat Preston 3-2, with the peerless Allen notching twice. He scored the opening goal, and then after Preston had taken a 2-1 lead, Albion's fate depended on their top striker's ability to score from the penalty spot.

But there was a problem to overcome. As Ronnie put the ball on the spot, it rolled away.

"Referee, can I put the ball behind the spot"?

"No" came the reply "Put it on the spot."

Ronnie did as he was told. Consequently the spot-kick lacked his usual panâche.

In what is probably the best known of all FA Cup Final illustrations. Albion goalkeeper Jimmy Sanders is in the foreground, holding onto his goalpost, his back deliberately turned. He just couldn't bear to watch Ronnie Allen hurtling towards the penalty spot. Time was running away, and this spot-kick had to go in... It did, squeezing under the goalkeeper.

Yet, as Allen turned to go back to the halfway line, the referee wanted the final word.

"If he'd saved that shot, I'd have made you take it again, because the 'keeper wasn't standing on his line."

"Well if you had" responded Ronnie, "you could have taken it!"

Scoring a late penalty in an FA Cup semi-final and finding the net twice in the Final are the Allen goals that remain most cherished in supporters' memories. But there was one more at least on a par with those history-making strikes. On 29 April 1959, Villa visited the Hawthorns. The Villains had to win to stay up. With just two minutes remaining, a solitary one-goal lead gave them a top Division future – until Ronnie Allen intervened. He picked up the ball just inside the 'D' with his back to goal; a typical swivel to lose his marker, a thunderbolt strike and the ball was in the net. Villa were down. Joy unconfined!

As the striker explained much later, on a club history video: "these things happen in football, and someone has to go down. Unfortunately, a late goal scored in the rain flew into the back of the net and poor old Villa were in the Second Division. I did feel bad in a way. Joe Mercer, their manager, was a good friend of mine. He was the first person to come for a chat and say, well done Ronnie. I was more sorry for Joe than the Villa."

But there was more, words to be shared only with close friends. "I didn't really mean to score. I just swung my boot and it flew into the net. I always felt that having as many Midland teams in the First Division was best for the area. We always had enjoyed great games and full houses, and I wanted them to continue. But as it turned out, it was a perfect strike, and no-one was more surprised than me when it flew into the net."

Even almost half a century ago, these were dangerous sentiments, public thoughts not to be shared with the Albion faithful, still hurting from an unjust Cup semi-final exit at Villa's hand two years earlier. Privately, the directors, with an eye on club finances, agreed with their top striker. A 50-50 receipt split of huge home and away gates, plus no travelling expenses to be paid for Villa Park, were lost to the bank account.

HOWEVER MUCH Ronnie Allen achieved, his wage packet continued to reflect the strictures of the maximum wage. £12 was the limit at the end of the 1940s, an amount that rose slowly through the fifties to £20 at decade's end, with deductions in the close season. Many players, if not all, chose to take a second job, partly to boost their income and partly to ensure they had alternative skills to earn a living after their sporting career came to an end. Ronnie acted as a representative for Repton Engineering, selling small fasteners. Frequently, Bobby Robson joined him. Baggies fan Steve Gregory remembered the excitement in his father's voice when he "would tell of the times Ronnie called at the factory where he worked, promoting screws and bolts."

In the end, Allen never needed to seek work outside the game. His Albion farewell came in a 3-2 win on 25 February 1961 at home against Bolton Wanderers. Appropriately he found the net. With Derek Kevan now in charge of scoring goals, it was time to move on. Ronnie re-located to London where he added 37 more to his overall tally from the wing for Crystal Palace before hanging up his boots. Subsequently he managed Wolves, Athletico Bilbao, Sporting Lisbon and Walsall. He also married again, to Cynthia Mary Henn in Birmingham Registry Office. And then? Back to the Hawthorns.

Initially in 1977, he became a scouting adviser, and famously not only found Cyrille Regis at Hayes, but also overcame the Board's reluctance to pay all of £5,000 for his signature by threatening to buy him with his own money. Albion's decision makers were not particularly adept at crucial decision-making in this period. Huge favourite player-manager Johnny Giles was allowed to leave rather than concede power to him. The job went to Ronnie Allen, but without a contract. Result? They lost him as well!

Ronnie himself: "The first time I became manager, it went very well. I joined Albion in August, and on Christmas Day 1977, West Bromwich Albion were top of the First Division. And the then directors did not believe in giving me a contract so I said, "I'm sorry, I can't go any higher. It's either now or never for a contract. Then they said, "Wait till the end of the season" – which I didn't agree with. I left and that was that"

Winger Willie Johnston remembered the manager's abrupt departure, "We had this game fixed in Saudi. We didn't want to go unless we got paid. Management said we'd get £200. Fair enough. So we flew in to Dubai and Ronnie said he had to go and see Prince 'so and so' to get the money. So we waited. One hour went by, then 2, 3, 4 and five hours. Still no money and then Ronnie comes bursting in to apologise for taking so long. He hands out the money, and tells the players to take the money to the nearby gold shop to convert it into gold. Then he told us he's just signed a two-year contract in Saudi, and he wouldn't be coming back with us."

RONNIE ALLEN did return through the Albion manager's revolving door in the early eighties. It wasn't a particularly happy time for him, and he was diplomatically moved upstairs the following term. Now in his fifties, he found the modern game difficult. Bryan Robson had left the club in one of the first examples of transfer by newspaper, and Allen had not invested the club record transfer fee wisely.

Popular player Martyn Bennett didn't consider his manager as inspirational. "One team talk consisted solely of the gaffer saying we need to win today because I need the bonus to buy new curtains." Neither did team-mate Derek Monaghan, who remembered team-talks consisting of the manager describing the goals he'd scored against that particular opposition. And yet, although supporters look upon those nine months ending in May '82 with much frustration, a limited, unbalanced team did reach the semi-finals of both the League Cup and the FA Cup. A quarter of a century later, Baggie people still dream of reaching one semi-final, never mind two!

Bobby Gould invited Allen back as an unpaid adviser and he stayed with the club under the next three managers until 1996. Forwards in particular benefited from his skills. "Everything Ronnie said made sense," said Bob Taylor "and he was always there for me if I wanted to practice to improve my technique." In addition, the immense respect from older supporters remained.

Long-standing fan Cyril Randle relives a moment when Ronnie was a coach under Ardiles, "One day, I was up at the ground to buy away tickets, and ended chatting with two oldish traffic wardens about yesteryear. Just then, Ronnie came shuffling down towards us, concerned he might be nicked for parking and, thinking I was their well-dressed boss, he asked if he was OK to park. I said to Ron, "If it was left to me, you could park on the centre circle of the pitch, mate." Both wardens added "too bloody true, mate" He was amazed and delighted that we remembered him."

In May 1995, Allen played the last seven minutes of a friendly at Cheltenham. This was a pointless end of season affair with both manager Alan Buckley and his assistant Arthur Mann starting the game. The pitch was bone hard and no place for a frail looking 66 year-old. Thankfully, the opposition kept a respectful distance allowing left-winger Ronnie to find an Albion player with each of his three touches during his final appearance.

Ronnie didn't enjoy good health during his later years when both Alzheimer's and Parkinson's gripped him. In August 1997, he had a benefit match against Aston Villa. Older supporters had tears in their eyes to see Ronnie being wheeled around the pitch on a golf trolley, wearing his 1954 Cup Final winning shirt. Supporter Colin Simpson, "I cried to see so great a sportsman bought low by the cruel twist of fate. This is the only time I've shed tears at the Hawthorns." Younger fans couldn't be expected to understand the poignancy of this moment. Some just sat in their seats. Others stood, clapping politely. The old codgers, including some Villa fans among the crowd of 16,855, joined in to show their appreciation.

Ronnie now required 24-hour nursing home care. He could talk lucidly to numerous visitors about his glory times on his good days. He even chalked a number 9 on the door of his room. Friends took him to the Hawthorns for matches, but his memory was failing badly. After one home match, he asked, "What time is the kick-off?" On his bad days? No, it's best not to dwell on his bad days. Best to remember him in his prime, a goalscorer supreme.

A POISONOUS front-page exposé by a regional Sunday newspaper painted a terribly negative picture of Ronnie's condition. Furthermore, they claimed the football club were doing nothing to help. The accusations created unnecessary additional distress, re-opening old wounds in a very public arena. The conveniently overlooked Testimonial match had garnered a six-figure sum, which covered nursing fees. There was nothing more to be done, but wait for the end.

Ronnie Allen died on 2nd June 2001. Included among the many tributes was one from a sportsman who had no involvement in the beautiful game – golfer Seve Ballesteros. "Ronnie was a wonderful person. I am lucky to have shared his friendship. When I first played for the Ryder Cup team at the Belfry, the place I headed for at the end of the day was Ronnie's home. He had a unique passion for golf, football, and sport in general. When I heard of his death, it was very upsetting. I count myself lucky to have shared the friendship of such a wonderful person."

West Brom's winning 1888 FA Cup team with goalkeeper 'Long Bob'
(back row third from right) and Billy Bassett (sitting, second from right)

Roberts was so proud of his England cap
that he wore it on every imaginable
occasion, including during matches

Billy Bassett was without question Albion's
most complete wide player of all time,
ahead of the likes of Willie Johnston and
Laurie Cunningham

The England team to play Scotland in Glasgow in 1912, with Pennington back row on right. Jesse's full-back partner, legendary England captain Bob Crompton, is the esteemed gentleman with the handlebar moustache with the ball between his legs.

Albion's most capped Englishman, Jesse Pennington, boasts 25 caps to his name. He served Albion for nigh on 20 years and rightly earned the nickname 'Peerless'

The man who would have been a great, but was cut down at the Somme. Harold Bache's name adorns the War memorial in Churchill, leaving us to wonder at what might have been.

Bache's Royal Lancashire Fusiliers commission. HG became the first Albion player to sign up, following in the footsteps of his brothers and making a mockery of accusations that footballers hid behind the game to avoid service.

The only Albion man to hold both League Championship and FA Cup medals, Mighty Atom Tommy Magee poses in his England shirt in a never before published photograph

Magee's lack of inches can clearly be seen (third right) as the 1931 FA Cup winning side parade their hard won trophy around Wembley led by goalscorer WG Richardson (second left) and captain Tommy Glidden (with FA Cup)

WEST BROMWICH ALBION F.C., 1930-31.
ENGLISH CUP WINNERS.

| Mr. F. EVERISS. Secretary | | RICHARDSON, W. | CARTER | PEARSON | | TRENTHAM | | SANFORD | F. REED. Trainer |
| SHAW | MAGEE | RICHARDSON, W. G. | Mr. W. I. BASSETT. Chairman | | EDWARDS | | WOOD | | GLIDDON Capt. |

Three Cult Heroes in a row in one photograph. (Front row second from left)
Tommy Magee, 'Ginger' Richardson and Chairman Billy Bassett, with the Baggies'
1931 FA Cup and promotion winning team

A never before published pre-season
photograph of midfield dynamo
Tommy Magee

WG 'Ginger' Richardson bagged 328 goals
in 444 games in his entire Albion career,
including hotly debated wartime matches

'Ginger' is all smiles and getting used to being the centre of attention after scoring both goals to bring home the 1931 FA Cup

The ultimate midfield player, Ray Barlow was famous for his 30 yard passes. His party trick was to control the ball with his foot at head height and bring it down perfectly

Always popular when returning to the Albion, three Albion legends of the 50s and 60s.
Ray Barlow (centre), Graham Williams (second right) and Derek Kevan (far right),
milk the longevity of their popularity alongside Kevin Kilbane (far left) and Alan Miller

Ray Barlow (left) and Ronnie Allen with long term fan Terry Wills at a meeting in 1993, showing off Terry's 1954/55 scrapbook. which heavily features both players

Perhaps the most iconic image in Albion history. Goalkeeper Jimmy Sanders cannot bear to watch as Allen slots the equalising spot-kick to make it West Brom 2 Preston 2 in the 1954 FA Cup Final. Of such moments are Cult Heroes made

Most of the 1954 FA Cup winning side show off their spoils at Euston station before boarding the train. Of our Cult Heroes, Ronnie Allen stands behind captain Len Millard with the Cup and Joe Kennedy is behind Allen to the right

The rugged Joe Kennedy was a consummate defender, who starred in Albion's Golden post-war era. Arguably the Baggies' best uncapped defender

The quiet and often dour Kennedy trained hard and played hard, never showing the innumerable injuries that eventually forced him to retire

The unstoppable 'Tank'. Derek Kevan scores West Brom's equaliser at
Craven Cottage, Fulham in a 2-1 win in December 1960

Derek Kevan is always a welcome visitor to supporters functions.
As one of few Albion men to play at a World Cup, here he shows off an
England cap from the 1958 Finals to veteran supporter Terry Wills

Tony Brown, complete with the bubble perm which made him a 1970s fashion, as well as football, icon, in typically tongue-wagging action...

...And more recently signing autographs. Tony has attended more supporters functions than any other player. Another record!

Even megastars like Frank Skinner need heroes. Tony Brown obliges

A rarely seen photograph of 'The King',
Jeff Astle, in 1964

The King nets again and sparks the regular
tumult of celebrating young supporters on
the Brummie Road in awe of their talisman

Jeff couldn't resist any temptation to
grab a mic. Invited to sing Blades song
'Greasy Chip Butty' at Bramall Lane before
a match, he refused unless he could sing
a song for Albion fans too!

Laraine Astle with grandchildren Matthew
(left) and Tayler (right) at the opening of
the Astle Gates at the entrance to the
East Stand from the Birmingham Road

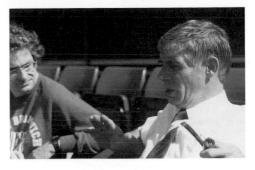

The suicidally brave John Osborne makes a flying save from Fulham's Johnny Haynes

Osborne in conversation with the author at Worcestershire County Cricket Club during his time there as Commercial manager. One of the most entertaining footballers the author has ever met, Ossie relived his golden days with a dry humour

Willie Johnston hands back the runners up trophy of the Rangers pre-season tournament with a look of typical cheek after he was wrongly presented with it, following his Albion team's victory

Johnston picks himself up off the turf after yet another kicking at the hands of a bewildered opponent. The crowd clearly don't like their Willie being kicked

Willie Johnston shows off his ball skills streaking down the Hawthorns touchline!

Exuding charm as always, Cyrille Regis. He exploded onto the scene, making an instant impact with his goal against Middlesbrough thanks to Ronnie Allen's judgment

Regis displays his awesome power as he shoots against Spurs in December 1982 despite the attentions of Gary Mabbutt (left), Gary O'Reilly and Graham Roberts (No. 6)

Super smooth Cyrille always seems to be surrounded by admirers – on or off the pitch!
On this occasion at the 2001 PFA Player of the Year Award dinner

Don Goodman and Bob Taylor were the only reason for Baggies fans to smile during the
late 1980s and early 1990s. Their goals lit up the club's most dismal era

Taylor, like any modern Cult Hero, knew how to celebrate a goal – and stir up the passion of the fans

THAT goal from THAT game. An iconic image for a whole generation of Baggie people. SuperBob's clincher against Palace and Premier League here we come.

Lee Hughes was that rare animal, an instinctive goalscorer, who had come off the Hawthorns terraces to be lauded by his own kind

Hughes celebrates scoring against Bristol City with Fabian De Freitas in a 3-1 win in September 1998

Richard Sneekes was a truly modern Cult Hero, a dissenter from the team ethic, a player who divided fans over his commitment, whilst exciting them and playing to the crowd and the camera…

…earning him mythical status, which, combined with his regular change of hair style á la David Beckham, meant Sneekes wigs were de rigeur for devotees

'Big Dave' scores the crunch, promotion-clinching goal in the first half of the vital last game of the 2001/02 season against Crystal Palace...

...and then celebrates like only a central defender with a record of 6 goals in 93 games can! The celebrations were all the better for knowing that Wolves would be denied promotion at the last!!

DEREK KEVAN

1953-1963

'THE TANK'

BAGGIES CAREER

Games	291
Goals	173
Caps	14

MAGIC MOMENT

A typical barnstorming hat-trick in a spectacular 6-5 victory over the Central Soviet Army touring team in a highly prestigious 'international' friendly

> **"Kevan is an excellent player. He has much heart, a good technique, good distribution, good tempo and he goes straight for his objective"**
>
> **Ravenko, manager of the Central Soviet Army team**

BORN in 1935 of working class stock in Ripon, Derek Kevan enjoyed a normal disciplined childhood. Any mischief such as throwing stones, or scrumping apples saw father Albert, a pipe-layer by trade, and an ex-Royal Marine officer, doling out his own justice.

Derek's introduction to the beautiful game was an unconvential one. At the age of eleven, he discovered a talent for heading a ball. On spotting his ability, his sports master told him "you're in the school team at left-back." Derek was two years below the average age of the team, but he didn't look out of place due to his bulky frame.

Eventually, he graduated to his natural position up front. His first big break came when a scout from Bradford Park Avenue saw him playing for Harrogate and District in the West Riding County Cup. They beat Burley and Wharfdale 4-2 and his two goals impressed the watching scrutiniser. Three weeks later, he had his first PA outing in a local derby against Bradford City's juniors. He scored five in a 6-5 victory.

The following season he signed professional forms for Park Avenue. Manager Vic Buckingham gave him his debut against Mansfield in October 1952. Buckingham departed for pastures new in January, but by then Derek had done enough to be regularly considered. In his 15 League games for PA, he found the net eight times – an excellent ratio for a complete novice.

In less than a full season, his name was being mentioned in some very high circles. On 29 July 1953, this six foot, aggressive but raw 18 year-old forward moved from his local Fourth Division side to one of the biggest clubs in the country – WBA. Albion gave Park Avenue £3,000 for his signature, safe in the knowledge that few knew more about Kevan than their new gaffer Buckingham. Even so, it was a brave move as Kevan acknowledged many years later. "I think Vic was taking a bit of a gamble with me, for I was a big awkward devil. He told me I would have to work hard if I wanted to make the grade ...and that is just what I did."

At the time, Kevan did what every teenager did in that era. He sought parental guidance. "I asked my Dad if he thought I should sign for them and my Dad said "you get yourself down there. Listen to the advice and act on it. And remember do your best. ALWAYS do your best."

Dutifully, Kevan followed his Dad's advice and that of the Albion management. Not that he had much choice in the matter. "W.G. [Richardson, club trainer] would give you the biggest bawling out you could imagine, and that were only during practice! I never had a bad word for him because he pushed you to the limit." Derek's learning curve was flattened by the interference of National Service. During his square-bashing days he found permission to play for his unit was difficult enough, never mind his club.

Anyway, there was no chance of forcing a way into Albion's first team. The country's best club – so close to achieving the mythical Cup and League double in 1954 – already had the country's best strike force in Ronnie Allen and Johnny Nicholls. There was no room for novice raw-boned teenagers. So went the theory. Problem was, the first team strikers lacked experienced cover. The normal stand-in was half-back Ray Barlow, but moving him forward would be at the expense of his midfield talents. Furthermore Ray wasn't keen on playing up front. So when Ronnie Allen picked up an injury, big Kevan got his chance, making his top Division debut against Everton on 24th August 1955. The Baggies won 2-0 in blazing heat and the debutant scored both of them.

Such a start sounded remarkable and yet somehow it wasn't. Derek Kevan didn't look the part. He was clumsy, awkward, lacked finesse and of course being compared to Ronnie Allen didn't help. The *Birmingham Mail* was cautious. "A story-book debut for the well-built Kevan inasmuch as he weighed in with both goals, but as usual too much publicity from the national press for a quite ordinary performance. I hope Derek is wise enough not to let it go to his head. Strange to see a six-footer leading the Albion line, but this lad will no doubt learn that only 100% ball control is good enough for the First Division. Let that ball wander too far from your foot and it's a 'gonner' against these quick-tackling defenders. Still he showed promise and I shall look forward to seeing what he can do when the weather has really broken."

The following week, Kevan played at Old Trafford and scored again. A fortnight later, his fourth goal flew into Sheffield United's net. He was club top scorer – but after six games in the big time, Ronnie Allen regained his fitness and the newcomer was relegated to the stiffs.

Kevan was to play only one more game that season (a 4-0 defeat by Manchester City in March) as, when Allen was absent, Ray Barlow was reluctantly pressed into service again. In public at least, the teenager was philosophical, "All I could do was carry on and wait for another chance."

THE FOLLOWING SEASON (1956/57) spawned his 'marauding' reputation. A solitary win from the first five matches persuaded Buckingham to give the Ripon forward a second chance against Portsmouth. Scoring in a 2–1 win gave the manager the confidence to keep the big man in the team and once in, he was in to stay, missing no more than twenty games over the next seven years. And yet there were always people ready to criticise.

Albion supporters had notoriously little patience in the mid-fifties. They expected the 1954 all-conquering side to continue ad infinitum, but football isn't like that. There have been only three true dynasties in post-war British football history. Spurs' early sixties double winners collected silverware by the bucketful throughout the next ten years. Liverpool won almost everything in sight from the mid-1970s for 15 years and then Alex Ferguson's Manchester United swept all before them in the 1990s. The introduction of the Premiership has changed all that, of course, with the cash concentrated in so few clubs that there are now four concurrent dynasties which seem to the modern fan to be destined to share all the silverware between them for decades to come.

Back in the mid-fifties, most of Albion's players of what now must be recognized as one of the club's two golden eras, incredibly became targets. Even walk-on-water Ronnie Allen got the bird once against Bolton for a series of poor passes. In early 1957, Bobby Robson was being booed every week. Derek Kevan got the most stick of all because of his inelegant style of play. The difficulty lay in making the most of his strengths and minimising his weak areas. Kevan needed the ball in front of him. That's how he worried the opposition. Playing with his back to goal was not his game because frankly, he didn't have the ball skills or the vision.

Provided he was finding the net, Kevan could ride the criticism. But between the Portsmouth game in September and late January 1957, he had just eight goals to his name. At that time, such a total was considered paltry. Far worse was the manager playing Ronnie Allen on the wing so he could accommodate the big man in the No. 9 shirt. Even those who were pro-Kevan expressed their concern at his lack of goals. Derek himself ruefully admitted, "It seems incredible I can't turn out the sort of shots in a match that I hit in practice games."

As ever, the local press reporters were stuck in the middle, trying to keep everybody happy. The *Birmingham Mail* again, "Particularly on the receiving end is 22 year-old Derek Kevan, the up and at 'em Ripon man who stepped into Albion's centre-forward spot. The fans want a Ronnie Allen replica. Who doesn't? They should be satisfied with one Allen in the line-up and give more encouragement to the lad who has the unenviable job of stepping into their idol's shoes. In all fairness, of course, big Derek has not been an outstanding success. There has been room for criticism. But for him alone, I don't think so. Particularly when the service was anything but generous."

Even the normally mild-mannered Ray Barlow had a strong view. "It made a big difference to Derek Kevan's career when he moved to number 10, he was bloody awful at centre-forward." And yet in September 1955, the *Argus* reporter wrote, "Kevan is just not First Division class as inside-forward". They particularly noted his inability to trap a ball. These opposite viewpoints from knowledgeable people say much about the mixed reception that The Tank endured in his leaner times.

After a run of poor results at the turn of the year, Ronnie Allen was restored to his preferred centre-forward role while Derek Kevan was switched permanently to inside-forward – a close supporting position for Allen. In his new role, he had slightly more room and space and as a result found the net more often. Gradually opinions on The Tank's capabilities became more enlightened. He still had his critics, but others were now appreciating his strengths such as tabloid journalist, Bob Morley, describing a 4-2 victory at Stamford Bridge "In inside-left Derek Kevan, they had the game's finest forward. Kevan had the ability to open an opposing defence with a well-judged pass and is a dangerous marksman. Certainly an England prospect."

To force his way into the national side, he'd have to displace the then current favourites – Newcastle's 'Wor' Jackie Milburn, Middlesbrough's Brian Clough, and Bolton's Nat Lofthouse. All were similar in style, particularly Lofthouse, who had no qualms when it came to putting himself about at the expense of opposing defenders. But the England selectors picked the Albion man over them all for the side to play Scotland in March 1957. England's latest international was unaware of his call-up. Having spent the afternoon in the Tower cinema, he was astonished to be surrounded by a bevy of eager reporters when the film finished. "I thought they were taking the mickey," he told me recently from the comfort of his own armchair. When prompted for his memories of his international debut, his eyes twinkled, "I could feel the hair rising on the back of the neck. When they played the National Anthem, it was a wonderful feeling. I wanted to prove my worth. It was a marvellous day."

England won 2-1. *Argus* reporter Eric Woodward noted Kevan's contribution. "Albion's 22 year-old blond giant, playing his first representative game, scored England's equalising goal before Duncan Edwards roared through to hit a great winner a few minutes from the end... On this show Derek is well worth his place. Not that Derek gave a five star display and was competent in everything he did. He must surely get another chance. The crying shame was the poor use his colleagues made of him. He ran into the open spaces intelligently. Was ever ready to have a crack at goal, yet hardly had a pass worth sprinting for. So he looked little better than the rest. It was a wrong impression. Kevan in fact looked the only England man likely to score." Maybe the most significant words of all were those that made up the headlines. "KUDOS FOR KEVAN – AND HIS CRITICS." The great dilemma – could Kevan play or not? – was yet to be fully resolved.

ALBION'S DOMESTIC season that had promised so much petered out. But the FA Cup was looking highly promising. Doncaster Rovers, Sunderland, Blackpool and Arsenal had all bitten the dust with Big Kev scoring four times. Aston Villa were the semi-final opponents. The first match was drawn with the Birmingham side scraping a fortunate equaliser near the end. That frustration was minor compared to the replay.

Even though the Baggies had ten men for most of the game after an injury to Allen, they hammered Villa all over the pitch. Except where it mattered. Villa scored once and successfully hung onto it.

Derek was inconsolable. "I don't mind admitting tears came at the end. I missed several chances and I think I hit the woodwork twice. Once I was clean through and hit the ball quite hard. It beat Nigel Sims in goal, but it then struck Stan Lynn on his heel and flicked over the bar. I can't think of many printable comments aimed in my direction after the game. Most were in jest, but some people still haven't forgiven me." It was perhaps fortunate that he didn't know then that he would never come that close to a domestic honour again.

Over the nine months of the 1956/57 season, the big forward had amassed 20 League and Cup goals, including a purple patch of 7 goals in 7 League games. The total made him club top goalscorer, five ahead of Ronnie Allen. Clearly, the international had something about him and there was more, much more to come. But first, there was a tour of Russia, awkwardly timed exactly a month after the season finished.

If not all his own supporters appreciated the Tank, the Russians certainly did. Kevan's all-out, aggressive style earned him five of the Baggies eight goals in their trio of games. The Soviet press gave him a new name, 'Lion of Moscow'. Almost a half century later Derek wistfully reminisced, "I really enjoyed the Russian tour. It was very noticeable how they treated their people. Mind, there were soldiers all over Moscow. We thought it would be very wise to be on our best behaviour."

Buoyed by his success on foreign soil, the big man steamed into opponents in the new First Division season. In a 50/50 challenge, there would invariably be one winner. Shay Dunne recalled coming up against The Tank at the Hawthorns at a time when there was a red running track around the pitch. Derek hit him so hard that he flew through the air, landing on the cinder track. That tackle, and the landing, really hurt and it took Shay about five minutes to get back on to the field of play with his shorts and legs covered in the red cinders from the running track. "Only a tap" scoffed Derek, when the Luton man challenged him later. "I'll get you back," threatened the sore opponent. Indeed he did in the return match, completely flattening The Tank when the referee wasn't looking. "I thought you were kidding!" lamented Derek.

The Tank regularly received knocks – in fact he became as legendary for them as for his goals. After one particular assault, he retired hurt to the dentist to have 11 teeth removed. Despite his discomfort, he still kept his promise to attend Maurice Setters' wedding. The following year, he had another kick in the mouth at Newcastle, forcing his dentist to take his top front teeth out. His team-mates called him "Gummy", fully utilising the sadistic humour of footballers. When fellow forward Johnny Nicholls heard The Tank was doing a TV interview, he hid his false teeth and only confessed to their whereabouts after much panicking by Derek.

Kevan was regularly on the receiving end. After a match at Goodison Park, in which he was booed throughout following an accidental collision, the Albion team found themselves surrounded by a hostile mob of several hundred teenagers as they attempted to reach their coach. Blows and kicks were aimed at several Albion men. Derek recalled "As I tried to get into the coach, some of the fans tried to close the sliding door with me outside. I managed to get in, but as I was doing so, someone kicked me on my right leg." Even when they were safely on board, the mob repeatedly spat at the windows and at least one Albion player admitted later, they thought all the windows would be smashed.

When the Russian Army team made a return visit, the first name the Russian coach asked about was "Kev'van". As Desmond Hackett of the *Daily Express* reported after Albion had run out 6-5 winners, "The crowd thrilled to the England-class positioning of big Derek Kevan, the man most feared by the Russians, the man who was hauled, pushed, and pulled down more than a dozen times. He scored a hat-trick. If he could only play like this for England." Predictably Kevan was then overlooked for selection.

ADDING TO KEVAN'S natural power and strength was his determination to improve by working harder as reporter Charles Harrold observed, "Albion's big, cheerful Derek Kevan has set a new fashion at the Hawthorns – voluntary afternoon practice and training. One by one he is getting all the players at it, even some of the older men, who are not always the most eager of trainers. But when you know Kevan it is understandable because his enthusiasm and keenness are infectious. Even when things are not going well for him, Kevan is still one of the most cheerful footballers I know. Ask him why he comes back most afternoons and he will tell you "I want to improve. I want to learn, and I want to get on in the game, and practice seems the way to do it."

The additional work, particularly on his ball skills, paid off. Albion opened 1957/58 in fine style, promising to be even better than the 1954 Cup winning crew. Robson, Allen and Kevan were all scoring freely and Albion boasted star names right through the team. As journalist Alan Durrant wrote "looking for a weakness in this West Bromwich side is like looking for a flaw in the koh-i-noor diamond." Alan was perhaps not taking a wide enough view for, although they remained unbeaten away from home until mid-December, too many draws at the Hawthorns saw them lagging behind eventual Champions Wolves.

Impatient supporters were considered at least partly to blame. At least their venom was no longer directed at Derek Kevan. His exploits in front of goal and his one-man battering ram act won over all the doubters. Despite his style, Derek was only six foot tall with a natural weight of just over twelve stone. Derek again. "You really have to be fit to play my type of game. It's hard work keeping down to that figure that's why I train as hard as I do."

Instead of Allen and Nicholls, Albion supporters revelled in the new partnership of Allen and Kevan. Through his "Sports Final" column, Ronnie Allen sought to sum up his main strike partner. "Churchill" as we call him. No 'tanks' for guessing why. The Number One target for our little japes. Takes some catching when he scores. Drives my barber crackers with precise instructions on how to harvest his mop. Would train all day if he was asked and he loves his football. Promises to buy me a set of golf clubs if we win the cup. That makes us all the more determined"

Ah yes, the FA Cup. Manchester City were demolished 5-1. So, too, Forest in a replay despite the Baggies only having ten men. Big Kev scored one of the five and then went one better in Round Five with a pair of goals in another demolition – 4-1 over Sheffield United, before an excited 57,000 crowd at the Hawthorns. With 18 FA Cup goals, the Albion team looked able to take on the world – which is exactly what they had to do. In the quarter-final, they drew the immediate post-Munich Manchester United. Albion couldn't overcome such raw emotion and a highly sympathetic referee, losing 1-0 in a replay.

THE TANK was in excellent form that term with 23 League and Cup goals in 38 matches, though sufficient only to finish third in the Albion goalscoring list. Two of his goals came in a 5-3 win over Birmingham, two more against Forest, but it was the impressive 4-0 demolition of Everton which put a smile on everyone's face. As reporter Bill Davies claimed "Derek Kevan, the hell-bound goal snatcher is as good any other in British football for a decade or more." But more importantly for Derek, this was World Cup year and the Ripon-born forward was now an England regular.

The Scots were his victims once again. Derek scored a hat-trick for the Football League against their Scottish counterparts and then added two more against their national side in a 4-0 thrashing at Hampden Park. The national press remained unimpressed and after England had lost 5-0 to Yugoslavia, it was again Kevan who took most of the flack. But if the cynical hacks weren't impressed, The Tank's fellow internationals certainly were. Tom Finney and Billy Wright advised the selectors they should retain Kevan up front as manager Walter Winterbottom explained, "I understand the players are convinced he is still the best man for the job. They consider he's been a victim of the sleek short passing game that has been used in the last few months." Kevan's big rival for the England shirt was Brian Clough, with 50 goals to his name for Middlesbrough. But as Big Kev pointed out "he'd been scoring in the Second Division. I'd scored all of mine in the First Division. Anyone can score goals in the Second Division."

The endorsement from his colleagues persuaded the selectors to award further caps against Wales, Ireland, Portugal, Yugoslavia, and the USSR in friendly matches, before the ultimate prize, representing England in the first ever televised World Cup, was announced. Kevan, together with fellow Albion man Bobby Robson, were the first Baggies chosen to represent their country in the 1958 Finals tournament in Sweden. Derek had a familiar face for company and apparently someone to share the stick from scribes such as Brian Glanville. "There was no-one to compensate for the staleness of Robson or the crudities of the huge centre-forward Derek Kevan." The complaint that Kevan was only a crude journeyman was a familiar, if tedious, litany. Years later, author Bob Ferrier added his own perspective. "All along, the newspaper critics obviously felt that Bobby Charlton's brilliant goal-scoring was a ready made answer to England's problem. The simplicity of this argument proved irresistible to them."

That huge centre-forward was to score half of his country's four goals in their Group Three matches in Sweden. "Playing for England was probably the highlight of my career" explained Derek. "But it was never easy. Johnny Haynes was the man alongside me in most of my games and he and I never really hit it off."

Opening with a 2-2 draw against Russia, Kevan's goal prompted less hostile prose from Glanville. "Kevan's fair head rose above the defence, even Yashin, and down into goal."

(Subsequently Kevan and Yashin forged a life-long friendship and today Derek is the proud owner of a pennant given to him by the goalkeeper). The game against Brazil finished goalless. The last group game another 2-2, this time against Austria, gave England joint second place with the Soviets. Unusually, a play-off was deemed necessary and it proved to be England's end as they were defeated by a single Soviet goal.

ANOTHER LEAGUE season and the big striker lifted the bar a little higher with a mightily impressive 28 goals from 41 games. Plus another hat-trick for the Football League against the now increasingly fearful Scots and more goals for his country. Some journeyman! Derek could play.

During the fabulous 4-3 win over League Champions Manchester United, described by reporter Alan Durrant "as some of the most breathtaking soccer it has been my privilege to see," Kevan demonstrated the full width of his repertoire, some of his cross-field passes "had the United in some awful tangles," belying his image as just "a bustler and trier." There was no better example of this than a 6-0 romp over Birmingham City. Kevan danced past three defenders for his goal. His team mates gaped.

More evidence was plentiful such as a hat-trick at Arsenal (though he still finished on the losing side) and a winner at Old Trafford. Writer David Jack still couldn't resist a dig."My old pal Derek Kevan (I criticise him, he calls me names, and we stay the best of friends) won this match for West Brom with the perfect winning goal a quarter of an hour before the end. Big Derek, who doesn't do such things when he wears an England shirt, hit his shot hard and true along the ground giving Harry Gregg no chance."

Had the England selectors considered better utilising Kevan's strengths, perhaps the big striker's scoring ratio for his country might have been higher. As it was, because of their preference for Middlesbrough's Brian Clough, Hibernain's Joe Baker and Spurs' Bobby Smith, Kevan had to wait two whole years between his last two caps, even though both matches, against the USA in May 1959 and Mexico in May 1961 resulted in England scoring eight times! Kevan ended his England career with 14 caps and eight goals. Only four Baggie men have more.

Ray Barlow regularly fed Kevan the through passes he so thrived on so logically why not call up Barlow? But the selectors weren't listening and so the much-maligned forward carried on taking the stick. "I am fighting my hardest to show the critics just what Derek Kevan can do. All the criticism of my centre-forward performance was very embarrassing but I have shrugged it off and am concentrating on my football."

In April, Albion were 2-0 down at home to Newcastle when Joe Kennedy was carried off the pitch, head pouring with blood. The defender pleaded with the club doctor to return to the action but the official refused. Fortunately, Derek Kevan was in unstoppable mood and his two goals secured the Baggies a point. "Gee, how they fought," said Joe admiringly. "Perhaps it was just as well I didn't come back on." All that effort and 26 League goals proved insufficient. Kevan was overlooked for the Scotland match and subsequently only won one more cap.

THERE'S SOMETHING ABOUT goalscoring forwards at the Albion. Think W.G., Ronnie Allen, Bomber Brown, The King, SuperBob, even Lee Hughes in his own way. All those big hitters were outgoing people, suggesting one goes with the other. Rather like a lead singer in a band, their personality is as important as the end result. Big Derek was also the life and soul of the party, gregarious and loved a drink as supporter Peter Whitehouse recalled. "I met him at the Adelphi

Dance Hall in West Bromwich and found him very pleasant. One Saturday night I was at a party in Garratt Street when he turned up along with Jock Wallace and reserve player Johnny Carvin. Derek proceeded to help himself to our beer until the smallest one of our group told him he was being unfair to us working lads who had collected hard earned money to buy the beer. He apologised and left only to return half an hour later with two crates of beer procured from the Waggon & Horses pub in West Bromwich and told us we were welcome to help ourselves."

On another occasion, Derek Kevan and Alec Jackson hired a canoe in Stratford. The boat rocked so much that Kevan dived for the bank five feet away – he missed and ended up in three feet of water. Jackson continued to paddle valiantly as the canoe sank under him, watched by thousands of amused tourists.

Like many footballers, The Tank found other sports easy. After the Baggies hierarchy boldly installed a table tennis table in the players recreation room, the Yorkshire-born forward proved to be the best exponent. He was, as Ray Barlow had it "the King of Ping." Similarly, he was the most competent darts player in the Albion squad.

KEVAN OPENED the 1959/60 season in much the same style as before with four goals in the first six games. He was now attempting to impress new manager Gordon Clark as Buckingham had resigned. The new man was often brutally frank with his players in an effort to bring out what he considered to be the best of their strengths. Clark was credited for changing Kevan's style. Sam Leitch, following a 3-2 first game victory against Manchester United, commented, "Kevan was unrecognisable from last season. He positioned brilliantly. And from his devastating, side-flicks many a snap Albion raid was set in motion. And he prodded, paraded with a new certainty and confidence. He looked a fine footballer."

Derek hit a bad patch with only three goals in the next fifteen matches. "Going through a wretched time," pronounced Eric Woodward in the Birmingham Mail. Curiously Clark didn't take the credit for that. The Tank, normally a light-hearted character, confessed, "I know because of the way I play that I've got to get goals. That's the reason I'm in the team. But I couldn't get goals. Even worse, I couldn't get into positions to miss them. I reached the point when I asked the Boss to drop me because I felt I wasn't giving the team a fair deal. But he refused to leave me out explaining I wasn't the type of player who could get my form back in the second team. It was the Boxing Day fixture against Forest that put me right and confirmed it in my mind."

Before 28,000 Baggie people, the striker scored twice, though it wasn't enough to prevent defeat. Reporter Dick Knight: "Derek Kevan, the man who reached the dizzy heights of England fame, but has been a shadow of himself this season, knew the way. Here was something of the old Kevan; the big roaring spearhead whose flashes through the middle will be one of my memories of the decade now dying."

Once he'd remembered where the net was, there was no stopping the big fella. His hat-trick knocked Plymouth out of the FA Cup in January, only his second in an Albion shirt, (an admirable feat at any time but not so according to the News Chronicle who chose to highlight the chances he missed). Only handball by a West Ham defender on the goal-line prevented another hat-trick against the Hammers just weeks later. Not that Derek had to wait long. Remarkably he topped all his previous scoring feats with five against Everton in March. His hat-trick goal was one of his classic, corkscrew headers. With just 20 minutes remaining, Albion had trailed 2-1.

Small wonder then as correspondent Rod Davies noted, "Kevan was immediately restored to his position of darling at the Hawthorns." Only a few weeks earlier, supporters had clamoured for him to be dropped. Without the goals, the ridicule of his style quickly returned. Clearly some followers of the Baggies had very short memories.

Supporter Robert Plant summed up just how maligned he was. "Surely no player in recent years has had to withstand such an avalanche of criticism, ranging from the cruel jeers of so-called Albion supporters who found the crudity of his play in his early days so highly amusing to the more refined snubs of our internal selectors who made him the scapegoat for the pathetic displays of the England team." When The Tank was unable to lead the line, the team missed his strength, such as in a 3-0 defeat at Maine Road, where their forwards were described as "lightweight in every sense of the word."

A HOME MATCH against Blackburn produced his 100th Albion goal and just three matches later; there was another hat trick to celebrate against Birmingham City. Not to be outdone, Ronnie Allen also found the net three times in a 7-1 win with the pair putting away almost every chance they had. Derek beat his personal best again; finishing with 29 goals, virtually double that of the next highest Albion scorer. His club finished fourth, a slight improvement on fifth the previous season.

Expectations of a serious crack at the Championship next time around were completely dashed by seven defeats in the first eight games. These were difficult times. Stalwart Ray Barlow had left while Ronnie Allen and Joe Kennedy were not to be far behind him. Kevan started the season not having fully recovered from an operation to straighten four toes. Even Clark admitted, "This sort of operation takes time to heal." The Baggies rallied briefly but then only secured two points from seven games in October and November.

From a fans' perspective, Albion's roller coaster form was indescribably frustrating. Covering a single goal defeat at Highbury, Bryon Butler concluded, "Albion were a geometrician's delight. They pushed the ball around all the sides of the triangles in the book. Their patterns included squares, oblongs, and diamonds. They made me dizzy. They have in Derek Kevan one of the finest bulldozers in the business. He is also intelligent. Why, therefore he spent the game pushing and prodding I cannot understand. Albion's loss was Arsenal's gain."

With Albion hovering just above the relegation zone and suffering an embarrassing 1-0 FA Cup exit at Lincoln, the Board came under heavy fire via a welter of letters to the local press. The players also received abusive correspondence. The main target was hapless Kevan, both at the Hawthorns and at his accommodation. The striker had managed 10 goals in 24 matches, not outstanding, but far more effective than any of his team mates. "All I could do was to do my best and wait for things to chang,e" said Derek, resignedly, to me.

Despite a mixed season, Albion eventually climbed to tenth in the table, Kevan's 18 League goals (in just 32 games as mumps ruled him out for four weeks) leaving him club top scorer for the third straight season.

IT WASN'T LONG before Kevan was the centre of attention once more. During a victory over Everton at the Hawthorns in August 1961, Bobby Collins was injured following a hefty challenge from The Tank. The Everton manager accused Albion of employing roughhouse tactics, hardly a diplomatic comment with the return match a week later.

These were very hard times for Kevan as he admitted himself: "I must say I've never been as surprised or hurt as in the last few days. I was booed as soon as I set foot on Goodison Park and barracked every time I got near the ball. Their manager Harry Catterick had accused us of rough play the previous week and they seemed dead set on picking on me and I was a marked man. Then I come back to the Hawthorns and the crowd were on to me almost as cruelly."

The home match was against Ipswich, in what was the Baggies fourth defeat in their opening five games. Journalist Alan Williams was shocked by the crowd's reaction. "England's most jeered and criticised centre-forward shamed the fickle fans who have made his life a misery this season. Kevan was hooted mercilessly and the Hawthorns crowd kept up a slow handclapping symphony which lasted throughout the last 15 minutes."

Quite why a side with a reputation for attractive football and including three England players in Don Howe, Bobby Robson and the Tank himself were playing so badly was indeed a cause for vexation but selecting the club top goalscorer as a scapegoat made little sense. Albion were now an unhappy ship. Burnside, Graham Williams and 'Chipper' Clark all asked for transfers. Rumours circulated that Gordon Clark was unhappy due to a personality clash with the board of Directors, intimating they refused to buy the players he recommended. Inevitably he resigned.

Enter Archie Mcaulay from Norwich City confirming, "I have all the control I want." Second game in charge and a Kevan hat-trick against Sheffield United. Despite this start, form continued to be patchy. Only a run of five wins in the last five games pushed the Baggies into the top half.

BIG KEV'S contribution was massive in those run-in games, with two each against a trio of London clubs and a remarkable four in a last-day 7-1 slaughter of Blackpool. What Kevan didn't realise at the time was that he'd spurned the chance to become an Albion record holder. Don Howe; "He'd got four, but the record demanded five. When a penalty cropped up, I offered to stand back and let him take the kick. He declined as he'd done before on the principle that the penalty kicker is the penalty kicker, no matter how badly anyone wants a hat-trick or a record." So modest Kevan finished with 34 goals after playing in every match that season, missing a club record by just one goal. Albion were heavily dependent on him. Only other one fellow Baggie managed double figures.

The club's cause was not helped by Archie Macaulay's summer decision to transfer one of England's finest players, Bobby Robson, back to Fulham, for £5,000 less than they paid for him. "I don't want to leave the Albion. I have had six happy years here and have made lots of friends. I wanted to stay. I am bitterly disappointed at the way Albion are letting me go," lamented the outgoing star. There was worse to come.

In the meantime, Kevan was still doing what he did best. There were four goals in Fulham's net with their manager Bedford Jezzard exclaiming, "Kevan must be the most dangerous player in the First Division around the goal area. He takes an awful lot of stopping." Three weeks later, Bolton certainly couldn't stop him as Derek netted three times in a 5-4 classic. Although results were improving, the team badly needed strengthening. However, the club continued to behave as if the recently abolished maximum wage was still in place and so big names looked the other way. After 13 months in charge, Macaulay made his first signing – forward Max Murray. The Scot was a complete and utter disaster. He joined the club already facing suspension and left after making just two senior appearances.

Speculation mounted that The Tank would follow Robson out of the Hawthorns. Stoke City, Manchester City, Fulham, Sheffield Wednesday, and Chelsea had all made bids. Each was refused and the Chairman's regular "No amount of money could buy Kevan" became a cliché. Albion's top man wasn't at his best but 16 goals from 28 starts told its own story. Just days after the Baggies had been beaten by Nottingham Forest in an FA Cup replay; the 173-goal man was suddenly leaving the Hawthorns.

"I didn't feel Derek had done enough this season to justify keeping him in relation to the terrific offer we had. I think it will turn out to be a wise move," said Macaulay, who was himself to depart the Hawthorns just a month later. Albion received £45,000 from Chelsea for Kevan's signature – an Albion club record figure for a departing player.

Kevan's views were rather different. "Macaulay accused me of not trying and I never let anyone say that about me, at any club. If my best wasn't good enough, I had a poor game. He accused me of not trying! He made some awful decisions. Generally, I never took it badly if a manager had a go at me but he went too far. I had to go because of his attitude. Macaulay felt I was one of the oldest players (although several were even older). When I went to see the directors they said, "We've had a bid come in for you". I was struck rigid and I didn't know what to say, or what to think, and they said, "Would you like to talk to Chelsea?" It came out of the blue, as there hadn't been any rumours, but I went. It was the worst mistake I ever made."

TONY BROWN

1961-1981

BAGGIES CAREER

Games	720
Goals	279
Caps	1

MAGIC MOMENT

His winning goal at Oldham, which secured promotion back to Division One

'BOMBER'

COMPARED with many other Hawthorns worthies featured within these pages, Tony 'Bomber' Brown poses something of an enigma. Not because of his fine goalscoring record, which features abundantly throughout this chapter, I hasten to add – more because of the fact that back then, outwardly, at least, Oldham's finest footballing export presented – and still does – a personality totally in contrast to that of many others featured within this book. The strange thing about Bomber is that when you ask older supporters for anecdotes about Tony to illustrate his persona, most will scratch their (mostly balding!) heads a little, hum and haw a bit, then, following many awe-struck testimonials as to his prodigious goalscoring abilities – never once in doubt, of course – sheepishly confess they simply don't know of any!

In short, Bomber appears to be that footballing rarity, someone supremely good at what he did, but also possessive of a remarkable ability to blend into the background when not playing for the club. Outwardly, at least, not the stuff of which cult heroes are made – and yet, when you ask those same supporters for their own list of Albion all-time greats, it's a pound to a penny the name 'Tony Brown' will feature somewhere near the top.

Quite a contradiction, that, but how come? Football isn't exactly the career of choice for those exhibiting all the hallmarks of a shrinking violet, now, is it? Self-effacement, and the beautiful game are, when played at top-level, personality traits as incompatible, seemingly, as oil and water itself. Elsewhere in these pages, you'll find 'characters' in abundance: "Good in the dressing-room," managers constantly opined when waxing lyrical on the likes of, say, Jeff Astle, John Osborne, or serial disciplinary offender Willie Johnston, even. Turning the dog-eared pages of time even further backward, there's the likes of W.G. Richardson, or little Tommy Magee, both most unremarkable people when briefly glimpsed strolling around town, say, but in total contrast to their public image, actually the very life and soul of the party, both on the field of play and off it. Even the highly talented, but ultimately doomed, Harold Bache would stand out in any crowd of footballers, if only for his undoubted academic ability, coupled with a remarkable natural talent for any other sport you'd care to name.

So, why is it Bomber is regarded with such high affection by Albion supporters when all common sense and logic would dictate that their admiration for him would always remain somewhat muted in comparison with his more outgoing peers and predecessors?

MAYBE, JUST MAYBE, I might have the answer. To understand better the dynamics that exist between players like Bomber and most Baggies supporters, it's necessary to understand just that little bit more about the area in which the Hawthorns is situated, and its chequered history. 'The Black Country', it's called around these parts, and not without good reason, either. There's a story going the rounds, possibly apocryphal, that when Queen Victoria first travelled through the area in her Royal Train, she was so disgusted by the soot-black, chemically-tainted sight that presented itself to her disbelieving eyes, she immediately ordained that forthwith, when proceeding through the region, the blinds were to be kept permanently drawn, and to remain so until further notice.

Whatever the truth of the matter, the area was pretty grim and bleak, thanks mainly to hitherto-unprecedented scientific and technological progress giving rise to the astonishingly cataclysmic degree of expansion that swept the region following the start of the Industrial Revolution. Put another way, prior to the early 1980s, when much of its manufacturing industry closed down for good, go to pretty much any British shipyard, or factory churning out widgets in quantity, and it was a pretty safe bet that you'd find there at least some components emanating straight from The Black Country.

Even the massive anchor and chains for the ill-fated Titanic were forged in nearby Netherton: go to the museum dedicated to the region's history, in Dudley, and you'll find there a classic photograph of all those workmen, hordes of them, rendered Lilliputian by the sheer size of their cargo. Hauling the thing straight from Noah Hingley's foundry to the nearby railway station saw the gang of men working themselves into a colossal sweat, one largely assuaged by the ingestion of vast quantities of beer. Not because every labouring man in the region was on the verge of alcoholism, mind – we're talking fluid replacement, pure and simple. These people drank bucketfuls, sure – but they also sweated bucketfuls, too, and it was a wise employer around these parts that incorporated the provision of beer on a daily basis into terms and conditions of employment for such men.

This astonishing toughness of both mind and body was also reflected in their choice of pets. Staffordshire Bull Terriers might well sweep all the prizes at Crufts these days, but back then, they were kept with a serious purpose indeed; as fighting dogs. Despite the best efforts of both constabulary and RSPCA to suppress such illegalities at the time, clandestine events like these were very much considered part and parcel of the local scene, and the wise person left such matters well alone. As in industry by day, so it was in the fighting ring by night: relatively small, powerfully-built, but muscular with it, hard as nails, and blessed with jaws of vice-like grip, these canines were very much forged in their owners' image. Not only could they take it, they could dish it out as well, and with 'knobs on', too. So devoted were they to these enduring little animals, it wasn't at all unusual for their owners to bring them to their place of work on a daily basis; again, it was a wise employer that 'turned a deaf 'un' to such practices.

AND THAT, if you like, is the 'missing link'. If there's one thing Black Country folk really admired back then – and still do, to a great extent – it's a 'grafter'. In other words, someone blessed with the ability to work extremely hard, irrespective of how hard the task, obnoxious the gaffer, or disgusting the working conditions, just getting their heads down and seeing the job through, no matter what. Tough work for tough people, indeed – and around the time Bomber Brown emerged from comparative youth team anonymity and into the ranks of the first team, much of the region's industrial base was still going full-blast, and with it, an awful lot of the horny-handed workforce Hawthorns regulars, still drudging without complaint through five and a half days out of the stipulated seven per week.

Remember the old saying: "It takes one to know one"? When you've spent a fair proportion of your precious half-day Saturday afternoons watching a raw-featured 16 year-old kid on the park, one seemingly blessed with talents far in advance of his chronological age, and mixing it with the very best both the Baggies and their opponents could offer, including more than a mere smattering of folk who'd represented their country at top-level, then it's only natural you end up taking a shine to the lad, isn't it? Think 'heavy manufacturing industry and the men who toiled in it', think 'hard graft', think 'Staffordshire Bull Terrier', even, and that's Bomber Brown, in a nutshell for you. No wonder his footballing skills were regarded with near-reverence by a generation with vivid memories, still, of both the Hungry Thirties and the destructive World War that followed shortly afterwards.

A convenient point, that, to make yet another comparison between Bomber and the tough world he entered as a spotty little kid some forty or so years ago: since his retirement from the game, the ravages of time have not been at all kind to the former Albion man, a situation that largely stems from the somewhat unreasonable demands that playing the game at the top level constantly makes upon the human body. It didn't help, either, that largely through ignorance, the overwhelming inclination on the part of both managers and trainers was, back then, to instruct players to rise above the pain of injury and just get back out there, no matter what. Pain being the human body's way of letting you know something's not right, and by doing so giving the sufferer the clearest indication possible it's high time they took a break.

Should someone regularly ignore such warnings, then they invariably end up with a massive price to pay in later life. In Tony's case, the constant twisting and turning demands of professional football (not to mention some more-than-unwelcome attention from defenders with DNA and general outlook on life both bordering upon the Neanderthal) placed an excessive strain upon those sorely-overworked hips and knees, resulting in the need for some extensive joint-replacement surgery over the course of the last few years or so. Pain killing cortisone injections were routinely administered in the sixties and seventies for short-term gains at the expense of long-term problems. Tony received dozens. Players endured them to maintain their first team place as half their wages were based on appearances. Manager Jimmy Hagan made his own decisions as to whether players were fit, regardless of medical advice. But there proved to be a significant price to pay in later life.

SO BAD WAS the problem at one stage, it wasn't at all unusual to see Bomber at supporter gatherings more or less unable to walk. Well, not without mobility aids such as crutches or sticks, that is. He wasn't alone. The coroner infamously noted the impact of a heavy football upon Jeff Astle's brain. In addition, John Talbot has a replacement left knee and endured a heart attack. Ian Collard has an artificial hip, while Tony has two. Yet the Bomber considered himself fortunate to have new hips – he'd seen at first hand what happened to the previous generation of players, such as Teddy Sandford. The only medical aids Teddy could use for his deteriorating hips were crutches. "They more or less ordered you to play and right throughout my career – not just me but every player – a lot of the time you'd be playing when nowhere near fit," declared Tony to the *Albion News*.

Again, it's a problem most Black Country blokes – well, those above and beyond what might be called a 'certain age', at least – can readily identify with. Amidst today's relative prosperity and advances in medical science, there's a nasty little flip-side to be encountered, and you don't have to look too far off the beaten track to see it, either. Just hang around any old-fashioned boozer in the area and some pretty debilitating and disgusting occupational conditions – pneumonocosis, silicosis, asbestosis, to name just a few – will swiftly manifest themselves, breathlessly, in the main, for your general delight and delectation. Not so much the 'living dead', these poor sods arrayed before you, but judging from all outward appearances, certainly as near to the front of the queue for the turnstiles as makes no difference.

Watch Bomber performing on the park during the sixties and seventies, and you were more or less seeing Black Country Man in all his various incarnations, good, bad and (eventually) crippled: sociability or strength of personality didn't come into it. One willing to put his future health on the line in order to get the job done that much quicker and better will always be a hero in these parts. No wonder the Hawthorns faithful took such a shine to him when they did. No wonder Bomber still suffers because of games played back when transistors, and not silicon chips, ruled the earth. No wonder we all love him to death for it now.

First and foremost, it was goals which bought Tony into the spotlight and held him there – even decades later. His popularity stems as much from the quality of his goals as their quantity. The power of his shot rivalled that of Ronnie Allen. In his salad days, Jimmy Hagan described his new first teamer as "the lad with the thunderbolt shot." His most celebrated effort was his poetry-in-motion ball-over-his-shoulder volley at Hillsborough in the 1970 FA Cup. "It was the best goal I have ever scored," agrees Tony. "It must be. It could have gone anywhere, but I happened to catch it just right. As the ball came down from Dennis Martin, I thought it was best to hit it first time rather than try to bring it under control, so I swivelled and hit it. If I live to be 100, I'll never score another goal like that." Defender John Kaye's observation summed up the moment. "There should be museums for goals like that."

Bomber's other best-known spectacular followed later the same year. His 25-yard free-kick swerved in a most banana-like fashion past Gordon Banks, with the England man not even seeing the ball. In 1970, balls just did not swerve in mid-air. Well, unless you were Jairzinho playing in that summer's World Cup at altitude in Mexico; and even if you were Pelé, Banksy tended to save 'em.

Bomber went on to score again in a highly satisfying 5-2 victory over Stoke. But there were so many other fine goals to applaud. Take Oxford in February 1976. From a loose ball after a free-kick in his own half (a free-kick he'd conceded himself), Bomber ran half the length of the pitch, holding off two determined opponents before powering the ball past keeper, Burton.

Brown had the remarkable instinct, given to few players, of running into the right spot at exactly the right time. "Taking up position is one of those things that come naturally to me," he explained to the *Albion News*. "I had to play by coming from deep because I could never play with my back to goal, because I needed to see the game in front of me. I wasn't an out-and-out striker, I did a midfield job as well."

BACK IN 1962, Albion's Manchester scout John Shore persuaded a young but talented Oldham teenager to move to the Hawthorns. Just as with Joe Kennedy, Manchester United thought they had him lined up (Tony was a regular Reds watcher), but his father told him United already had too many good young players. Young Brown agreed. "I never really wanted to sign for them. They always struck me as having too much talent."

The youngster needed to grow up quickly. As he recalled: "I used to walk to the ground with Bobby Robson, who lived just down the road from my digs. Very often, I didn't know what to say to him because he was an England international, and I was just starting out in the game." To further widen the gap, it was "Mr Robson" to the apprentices.

Tony quickly won a regular spot in the reserves with his performance against Newcastle reserves early in the 1963/64 season turned significant heads with the *Mail* correspondent declaring "Young Albion inside-right Tony Brown gave one of his most determined ever displays since he arrived at the Hawthorns. In the 75th minute, Brown – who had worked so hard through-out – was justly rewarded when he ran onto the through ball, sidestepped the keeper and then held off right-back Craig to pop the ball into the net."

Remarkably young Brown was to make his first team debut later that month, at Ipswich, just a few days shy of his 18th birthday. Hastily, he signed professional forms before the game. Although his inclusion was as a result of John Kaye failing a fitness test, manager Jimmy Hagan said of his young charge: "he has improved tremendously since last year. He deserves his chance." The debutant added timorously, "I am very thrilled." At Portman Road, Albion came from behind to win 2-1, but it was Tony Brown's equaliser that stole all the headlines. The youngster received a pass from Doug Fraser, beat off two tackles and swung a rising left footer into the roof of the net. Journalist Geoffrey Beane considered that "properly handled – and that means not rushed – he could make the grade."

Tony was not being rushed. After being rested for two games, he returned for a home match against Aston Villa. This was a barnstorming encounter in which the Baggies fought back from a two-goal deficit to win 4-3. Tony, who later confessed to "quaking in my boots", scored again, a tap-in from six yards, after a glorious run by Simpson. Even venerable Jesse Pennington was impressed with the action. "Just about the most exciting, highest scoring and cleanest derby I can remember" he enthused. By May, Brown had five goals to his name in only 13 appearances, sufficient to make him fourth top scorer. Manager Hagan was positive. "This lad works himself into so many scoring positions that if goals come from only a small percentage of them, he must finish well up the charts."

TONY WAS selected for the club's first fixture of 1965/66 – back "home" at Old Trafford. This was the United of Charlton, Law and Best in front of a full house... but the first scorer that day was young Brown, finishing smartly a cross from Kenny Foggo. Albion, watched by Tony's parents, were happy to take a 2-2 draw. Tony followed this with his first-ever hat-trick in the next match against Sunderland. "I don't feel like a hero," he protested afterwards, after his style had been compared to goal poacher extraordinaire Jimmy Greaves. "Just relieved that the ball has started going for me at last." Apparently missed chances in Holland and at Old Trafford were praying on his mind. "I worry about things like that for days." Tony was on a roll, fortunately for both himself and the club, as the main goalscorers 'Yorky' Kaye and 'Chipper' Clark wanted out. But after a run of defeats, Tony was dropped in October. Even so, "Boy Brown's" statistics looked impressive, with nine goals in 17 matches. Top scorer Jeff Astle had 10, but in 32 matches.

But the season did produce a trophy for the cabinet. Talking to the club programme, Tony claimed the team was always confident about winning the League Cup at the first time of asking. "We fancied our chances because we had started the season so well." Brown initially troubled Albion statisticians by becoming WBA's first scorer in the League Cup – against Walsall. Then he added another for good measure, explaining, "you know that Clive Clark will get crosses in, so you just have to gamble and get in the box because something would come your way." Bomber also scored in Round Three, Round Four, and every other round too. His hat-trick against Peterborough in the semi-final second leg finally squashed the determined Third Division side.

The first leg of the Final against West Ham was tightly fought, finishing 2-1 to the home side, but the second leg was not. As Tony explains "the game here was the best performance I've ever been involved in. Nobody could have stood up to us in the first half hour. They didn't know what day it was." Journalist Bryon Butler: "Albion played football of a sort that one always hopes, but rarely expects, to see in these days of safety-first thinking." Bomber contributed the third in a four-goal 35-minute blitz when he headed in Clark's lob, his tenth goal in the League Cup.

The idea of a floating forward behind a target man is commonplace these days, yet it was relatively unusual in the 1960s. The big difference in that decade was that every club played with wingers, thus maintaining a far greater emphasis on attack. "Tony used to float everywhere," agrees skipper Graham Williams. "He wouldn't play in today's game."

Tony added an new element to his game when regular spot-kick man Bobby Cram wasn't selected for the club's first foray into Europe. When the home side won an early penalty for hand-ball against DOS Utrecht, Tony's shooting power made him an obvious choice. Tony, who was on the right wing that night, was just grateful to be playing after missing 11 games through injury. He considered his second half header and carefully placed shot to complete his hat-trick, as a bonus. No other Albion man has ever scored three goals in a European game.

Fortunately, the season improved partly thanks to a new goalkeeper in Osborne, and the Bomber being switched to right-half (midfield). Albion suffered only four defeats in the rest of the season, and seven wins in the last eight secured the club's position, which had looked tenuous. Tony approved of the change. "I am thoroughly enjoying my football there. As a wing-half, I am constantly in the game and can see all of the play. There are also chances to go forward and have a crack at goal when you spot an opportunity. When I am well upfield, John Kaye drops back to cover me." As part of a 6-1 demolition of Newcastle on the last day of the season, Brown concluded his hat-trick of hat-tricks.

ALBION RESUMED proceedings in August 1967 in much the same way as the previous campaign. Too many games were lost and their first point was a fortunate one – the infamous 3-3 at Molineux with Bomber's very own prequel to the 'Hand of God.' With only minutes left and Albion a goal behind, Tony punched a cross into the Wolves net – the only part of his anatomy with which he could reach the ball. He was as startled as anyone else when the referee gave the goal. Even the away supporters were more gob-smacked than goal hungry. The Wolves goalkeeper, Phil Parkes, was so enraged that he was sent off. His manager supported him. "No wonder Parkes went mad. The ball was handled into the net." The referee required a Police escort to leave the pitch and the enraged home crowd gathered outside the main entrance to protest and who could blame them? In a quieter, less high profile team, such an occurrence would hugely uplift the profile of the individual. But in this Albion side with such an array of larger than life players like The King, Ossie and Bobby Hope, Tony merely continued his gentle ascent up the popularity ladder.

1968 was to be a special year. A life-changing goal scored by Jeff Astle with his wrong foot, secured Albion the FA Cup. As Tony recalls "I was almost in tears as I congratulated Jeff after his goal. Wow, we didn't half have a party that night." Tony regularly tells his tale about the closing minutes of the Cup Final, when both he and Graham Lovett were put clear of all bar one of Everton's defenders. "I was thinking 'we're through here'… and then I heard a voice saying, 'don't give it to me…'" Feeling disturbed by his colleague's lack of enthusiasm, Tony was obliged to ̄s to him anyway as the Everton defender was upon him. Lovett skied the ball wildly amid ̄al groans. He turned to Tony and said: "told you not to give it to me."

Tony, by his own admission, didn't make much impact on the Cup Final. His key contribution came earlier in the Cup run, such as in the Third Round at Colchester when the Baggies were in grave danger of going out. Tony scored from the penalty spot, which he later confessed was the most tense penalty of his career. The spot-kick was just enough to escape from Layer Road with a draw. The U's were flattened in the replay.

As journalist Tom Duckworth observed, "The Manchester lad has developed into a brilliant midfield player with an invaluable capacity to score goals. Not since Bobby Robson have England had a really constructive wing-half with genuine attacking skills." Rarely was that capacity more invaluable than in the following round when once again the opposition was on top. That's until the Bomber levelled from fully forty yards, with the aid of a divot. Albion beat Southampton in the replay, then their neighbours Portsmouth, before defeating Liverpool in a three-match slog. And once again in the semi-final with Albion on the receiving end of a Birmingham City onslaught, it was Bomber's low shot off the post, which ensured that the Baggies were going to Wembley.

West Bromwich Albion, FA Cup holders, were in for a busy time. In addition to defending their trophy, League matches and the League Cup, there was also the Cup Winners Cup demanding their attention. Bomber Brown was the star turn of the first round as RFC Bruges attempted to intimidate the Midlanders into submission. Reporter Gron Williams was quite clear. "The man of the match for me was Brown, who hit the first goal and came through with great verve whenever he got the chance." The midfielder scored twice in the next round against Dynamo Bucharest before the Baggies were beaten by Dunfermline in the quarter-final. By then, defending the FA Cup had become a priority. Goals by Tony Brown in the Fifth and Sixth Rounds of the Cup were the key to overcoming Arsenal and Chelsea respectively, though he did have a penalty saved at Stamford Bridge. A potentially easy passage against struggling Leicester awaited them, but not for the first time, the Baggies struggled with their favourites tag. Allan Clarke snatched their Cup away three minutes from time. It was a horrible ending to a very long season. Of Albion's 55 matches, Tony only missed one, scoring 23 times.

The late sixties followed a familiar pattern. A mixed League picture balanced by success in the Cups. The 1969/70 League Cup offered excitement and glory. Home form carried them through after some sticky away matches with the semi-final against Carlisle proving particularly tricky. Only in the second half of the second leg did the game turn in the Baggies favour. Bomber's powerful free-kick provided the key third goal in a 4-2 aggregate victory. Albion were back at Wembley! But Manchester City were too strong and the Cup went North.

LEGEND SAYS Don Howe was appointed in the summer of 1971 because Chairman Gaunt had wearied of Wembley trips and wanted his side to become League Champions. Previous incumbent Ashman was never likely to do this as his side always lacked consistency. As 1970 slid into 1971, however, Ashman's side found some consistency – they were consistently bad! The Baggies were most unfortunate with injuries that denigrated their already indifferent back division to a distinctly dodgy level. "The excuse that Albion are a very talented side who have just not clicked, is wearing a little thin," wrote exasperated reporter Tony Nash. Everyone was relying on the Bomber to maintain the club's First Division status. He did his very best.

During the close season, Tony was offered at 66/1 to finish First Division top scorer. "It seems a long shot, but I had a quid on it for fun," he admitted. The odds had shrunk to 11-4 by December and 1-2 in March. The Division's top goalscorer claimed hat-tricks against both Manchester and Spurs, scoring twice five times and even found the net on his 25th birthday, appropriately at Portman Road, the ground where he'd netted on his debut. Tony's last League goal of the season, which created a personal best (28), came in a 2-2 draw with soon-to-be-Double winners Arsenal.

His skills were finally recognised with an appearance for the Football League against the Scottish League in March 1971 (only his second selection for the League side), followed by a full cap against Wales two months later. "I was thrilled to bits when I learned I was playing," said Albion's top scorer, whose excitement would have been tempered if he had known then that he would never get another cap.

There were precious few wins to celebrate in Howe's first three months in charge. Bomber scored in each of the first four games, but after that, the entire team went on a goal fast, scoring just once (Tony again) in seven games. During several games, notably Manchester City (lost 0-2, third straight home defeat) at home, play was once again accompanied by slow handclapping. Fortunes started to turn after beating Liverpool on Boxing Day, in front of 44,000 relieved spectators. This was followed with a recovery from going two down at Ipswich to win 3-2. Bomber scored the crucial first goal and, according to newcomer John Wile, "then things started to happen." More goals against Sheffield United followed for Tony and by mid-January, he had 12 to his name, sixty per cent of the club total. Bomber was quoted as saying "since I have moved up front again and got rid of the midfield responsibility, I have been more successful." But this was the loyal clubman speaking. Brown truly considered himself to be an attacking midfielder, a Sneekes who could tackle, if you like. Still, the Bomber was flying again. As John Kaye pointed out "you can always tell when Tony is in with it. You notice it during training. In one practice session during the week, almost every shot he hit was a screamer into the net."

Not everything went to plan, with an immediate exit from the FA Cup against Coventry. Tony scored once, but was blatantly denied another when defender Bobby Parker punched his shot off the line. One supporter was so disgusted that he famously threw his pipe and apple at the myopic linesman.

A decent run of half a dozen games in March was enough to keep Albion clear of relegation danger; form sufficient for Don Howe to win Manager of the Month. Instead of keeping the whisky in house, the fiery spirit was divided up into dozens of small glass miniatures and given out to the crowd by the players... by the somewhat risky method of throwing them.

Something was clearly not right in the house of Hawthorns. A new striker, Ally Brown, arrived in March 1972, but moribund Albion needed far more strengthening. They didn't get it and the following season was even worse. The Baggies managed only nine wins in 42 games and were relegated in miserable fashion. "This is my club," Tony insisted "and going down really hurt." The Bomber found the net a dozen times, a modest total, yet considering the next highest scorer had six and his contribution was almost a third of the club total, he'd more than done his share. He didn't deserve to lose his First Division footballer status.

So just three years after a League Cup Final, Albion were more concerned with travelling to Bristol Rovers, Cardiff and Orient than Wembley. In the Second Division, Tony continued to earn "brownie points" from the Hawthorns exasperated faithful, a human beacon of hope in a depressing period. Bomber realised that as the senior professional in a struggling side. "I have to set an example to the rest of the lads". His 23 goals in Division Two, the only team member to break double figures gave hope, ultimately a false one, of a speedy return to the top League. Seven of his came in just a week, in a pair of matches against the Nottingham clubs. His hat-trick destroyed 's ambition of a FA Cup run and the following Saturday, his four goals at the City Ground did for their City rivals. "A scintillating solo performance" according to the *Argus* correspondent. "He's so fast, you can't stop him," lamented the Forest manager.

INDEED ALL WAS far from well behind the Albion scenes as Howe's promise of global domination seemed a long way off the mark. "It was drills and sessions and a lot of the time you were just standing around getting cold. I'm sure it was all clever stuff, but it just didn't work at the Albion and things went from bad to worse" said the Bomber of the former Arsenal coach, in a very rare outburst. "Without doubt, the era was the worst I played in 20 years at the Albion. The whole place had lost its spirit. The players just didn't enjoy playing." Goalkeeper John Osborne agreed "many of the older players found his intense, regimented approach very difficult to cope with. Tony Brown had to play the "numbers" game and went through probably the worst spell in his career."

Bomber Brown's Testimonial provided some light relief in May 1974. This was a curious affair of a combined Albion and Villa eleven taking on a composite Blues/Wolves XI. The idea was Don Howe's, with the two sides pre-selected by the readers of the *Sports Argus*. Twelve thousand supporters rolled up to see Tony predictably score the winner. His gross profit was said to be around the £10,000 mark.

Few would have blamed the testimonial man for wishing to leave the club after his benefit. At the age of 29 and with an impressive CV, he could have easily secured a berth with any First Division side. By not doing so, Tony was putting club before self and in the philosophical moments between the tedium of matches, his lack of selfishness served his crowd favourite status well.

There was virtually another full season of Howe to endure and Tony was losing heart in the Hawthorns Gulag. "I don't like playing in Division Two. It was a big comedown after so many years at the top." By November, he had only three goals to his name and sections of the crowd were openly showing their frustrations with his meagre tally. Home games had attendances only half of the required break-even figure. The directors finally got the message.

Willie Johnston described how they heard about the dismissal of Don Howe. "Tony and I were driving down West Brom High Street when we heard the news. Tony stopped the car and shouted 'Yessss!' That's what Tony Brown thought of Don Howe." His reaction was a common one.

The next incumbent at the Hawthorns was former Leeds midfielder Johnny Giles, who beat off strong competition from Ronnie Allen for the job. Giles knew an attacking midfielder when he saw one, and the Bomber was restored to his preferred position. "I had to form a team and do it within the context of the style we play," explained the Irishman, "and Tony in midfield is part of that plan. He's a real pro. He has worked hard at his game and fitted in well. I know that I will always get 100% from him." Bomber was back to his best, uplifted by the new spirit of belief at the club. "Some of his shooting has been tremendous," wrote John Wile, in his *Argus* column. Giles went on to fashion a promotion side for a cost of just £40,000.

Tony guaranteed his place in Albion history by scoring the goal in his birth town which secured promotion back to the First Division. "On our way to Oldham all we saw was cars and buses decked out in Albion colours. There were so many Albion fans going to the game we couldn't get off the motorway and had to have a Police escort to Boundary Park. In the dressing room before the game everyone was incredibly nervous, and then I'll always remember walking out to the pitch and seeing a mass of blue and white. It just hit you. All the players looked at each other as if to say, 'We've got to do it for them today.'" And they did, with Bomber at his best for the all-important goal – cushioning the ball with his right and volleying it into the net with his left. Cue pitch invasion with the scorer besieged by well-wishers, but that was a mere bagatelle compared to the celebrations after Ray Tinkler blew his whistle for the last time. Bomber and the Baggies were back!

The man who had tried so hard almost single handledly to keep the Baggies in the top flight three years earlier had so appropriately scored the crucial goal to take them back to Division One. A hugely appreciative support would never forget that moment and his loyalty to stick with Albion in difficult times. Fact-by-fact, the now-revered-like-never-before post-Oldham Bomber was making an awful mess of the club record books. First to go was Jesse Pennington's League appearances record, equalled against Coventry in September 1976 and then raised over 100 times to an impressive 561 starts.

Giles' possession-orientated game worked surprisingly well for Albion in the top flight and relegation was never a concern. Tony was often overshadowed by emerging talent like Bryan "Luigi" Robson (a dressing room reference to his dark hair), Derek Statham and paid-for talent like David Cross, Laurie Cunningham and later Cyrille Regis. With so many other names to worry the opposition, Tony now had a little more time and space to make an impact.

He made the most of this during the 1977/78 season, when his ability to anticipate knock-downs and half clearance gave him fifteen goals in open play. Throw in a further ten penalties in those nine months to make a remarkable total of 25 goals at the age of 33. Bomber was club top scorer for the 7th time. According to fellow veteran John Osborne, his contribution to a 3-1 early season win over Birmingham City was outstanding. "I reckon Tony gave about his best all round performance. Not only did he score a vintage goal and slam in a penalty, but he covered every inch of the pitch as if he was playing his fifth game and not his 500th or whatever."

Expectations arose that ten years after his last FA Cup Final, Bomber might be heading for another. Albion had overcome big name opposition to reach the FA Cup semi-final, but it was not to be. On a day when little went right against Ipswich Town, Bomber's spot-kick was one of the few highlights. But the Baggies did recover from that painful Highbury afternoon to claim the last League spot for the UEFA Cup.

WITH SUCH A magnificent tally from the previous season, Tony was now not far short of the club's League goals mark. "I've never been one to keep an eye out for records," he claimed, but the publicity was too powerful to ignore. The record fell in October 1978 at Elland Road with Bomber's 25-yard effort crashing home off the post. West Brom presented him with the matchball prior to the Coventry home match to mark his feat. Tony immediately broke the record again by scoring against the Sky Blues – though admittedly most of his team were finding the net that day in a 7-1 demolition.

By now, a new generation of supporters were hearing the tales of the legendary 'Bomber' Brown, but unlike most legends, he was still playing. Supporters like Richard Scarlet: "I saw my first ever match at the age of ten in February 1979, Albion v Leeds United at the Hawthorns. Scorer of my first ever live goal was the hero that is Tony Brown, edge of the box, caught on the chest and volleyed into the back of the Leeds net. I can remember it like it was yesterday. I jumped up and had my hat nicked because we were in the middle of a bunch of Leeds fans in the Rainbow Stand. For being responsible for the first goal I ever saw live, Tony Brown remains God like!"

The midfielder had only weeks earlier set a new club marker for FA Cup appearances. In March, he broke his own record for appearances in European competition. He'd already scored more goals against continental opposition than any other Albion man, but ten years on, he was able to add to the tally. Still to come was the mark for most FA Cup goals while the record for League goals was regularly re-set. Then there was 'most appearances in all competitions'. And by making a substitute appearance in a 3-1 defeat at Nottingham Forest on 12 January 1980, Albion's record breaker broke into his third decade as an Albion player.

On simple statistics alone he had become a legend, a great player, but it takes that little bit extra to turn mere legendary status into that of an iconic, Cult Hero. Of course Bomber's perm and hirsute moustache helped with that transition, almost becoming a cult all by themselves, but Brown still had more strings to his bow to reveal.

In these later years, Bomber became the club's corner taker – preferred even to such finer crosses of the ball like Willie Johnston or Laurie Cunningham. Tony's talents even extended to donning the goalkeeper's shirt. Once a very brave or very stupid John Osborne was injured in a mid-air collision with the rather large Mike Doyle of Manchester City. Despite a full five minutes of treatment, he was unable to carry on, so in between the sticks went Bomber. He stoutly kept out a fierce drive from Neil Young, but was otherwise protected by his fellow Baggies until Ossie's pain-killing injection took effect and he could return. Only seven months later, Tony had another chance to literally get his hand in. Once again, 'Aunt Sally' Osborne was on the receiving end and came off worst. Tony replaced him for the last 25 minutes and once again kept the opposition out. More by luck than judgement, though, having dropped the ball on the goal line, he was grateful that an alert Ally Robertson was on hand to hack it away.

ONCE RON ATKINSON had departed for Old Trafford in the summer of 1981, the Bomber found himself on skid row. In a shabby stunt, second time around manager Ronnie Allen wanted Brown out immediately, even refusing him leave to train with his team-mates until he found a new club. Tony subsequently turned out for Torquay, New England Tea Men and Stafford Rangers, but there was no keeping him away for long. Bomber returned to the Hawthorns first as a coach and more recently as a radio commentator and programme contributor.

Jeff Astle always felt mightily aggrieved that Tony had not received a second testimonial that Ron Atkinson promised him. He began a one-man campaign to win hearts and minds, never missing a chance to make his point to supporters or club officials. Eventually, he wore them down and the Bomber got his match against the old enemy Aston Villa. Even then, the King busied himself recruiting players, such as Bobby Gould.

"Bobby, Tony Brown's got a testimonial and I want YOU to turn out."

"Why me?"

"Because ten thousand people will turn up just to throw things at you…"

Many thousands did come, but not to pelt Gould with trash. They came to hail the man they knew as 'Bomber' for one last time.

A final thought from the man himself. "When Ron Atkinson was manager, he used to say I should have my own bed at the ground." Maybe not a bed, but there's always going to be a place for Tony Brown at the Hawthorns.

JEFF ASTLE

1964-1974

BAGGIES CAREER

Games	361
Goals	174
Caps	5

MAGIC MOMENT

Winning the 1968 FA Cup in extra-time with one sweet strike of his dodgy left peg

'THE KING'

DURING the official opening by Laraine and her grandchildren, those gates mysteriously parted a few inches, accompanied by a solitary blast of disturbingly cold air. Was that Jeff? That big, gregarious man appearing ghost-like at the Hawthorns one more time, insisting, "They're my gates. I'm going through them first." I hope so.

The Astle Gates dominate the black ironwork entrance to the Hawthorns' East Stand, a classy memorial to the one and only King Jeff. Never before have a broad base of Albion fans combined to achieve such an ambitious goal. Supporters chose the form of the memorial, raised half of the near £40,000 cost, drew up designs and directed grant aid towards the club. Fundraising was rarely easier – the urge to give was quite overpowering. One man, who played his last game over three decades ago, still touched every generation of the Albion family.

Fan Tim Joyner can still remember the King's last Albion goal in February 1974, "We were losing 2-1 to Bristol City and on came the King to rescue us with a classic header. The Brummie Roaders bellowed over and over again "Astle is our King." Some even invaded the pitch to congratulate him personally. I remember waiting anxiously for my Dad to return home from work on Monday evening, desperate to read the back page of the *Post*. There he was, in the centre of a big picture filling the sports page. Even though the memory is hazy, I'd still put it in my top 10 Albion moments." This final entry on his tally was Jeff's 171st goal for the club. Only three men had achieved more.

THE £22,400 signing from Notts County made his home debut against Wolves, almost a decade earlier, in October 1964. "Jeffrey," according to the Albion News, "led the forwards brilliantly", scoring twice as Wolverhampton were hammered 5-1 (only the crossbar's width prevented his hat-trick). A great start then, but far better was to follow.

Astle's first ever Albion goal was a header from John Kaye's chip. "It's good to be in First Division football and with the Albion" exulted one very happy striker afterwards. Photographers captured that first celebration – big grin, arms above his head, fingers outstretched – the first of many. It was one of those seminal afternoons. A new signing entered the field, but a new crowd favourite left it. Wins over Villa and Champions Liverpool (3-0) cemented his status. "A.S.T.L.E" bellowed the Brummie Road faithful. "To think I had to be asked twice to come here. I must be mad," admitted Jeff (a reference to manager Jimmy Hagan flatly refusing his request for an under the counter payment, an illegal practice rampant at the time).

Although Wolves was Jeff's first match at the Hawthorns, his first team debut had come ten days earlier at Leicester, a 'thrown-in-the-deep-end' introduction for a man who'd signed a contract barely three hours earlier. "I was so nervous, I found myself biting my nails during the match" admitted the striker later. Fortunately, his nerves were not visible off the pitch. Then *Mail* reporter

Jeff Farmer wrote "Big, strong, good in the air and forceful on the ground, the 22 year-old had a highly satisfactory debut."

In the next six years, Jeff would contribute enormously to his side reaching four Cup Finals and represent his country in the World Cup. But ever since those opening games, there was something different about Astle. Something far more significant than his hat-tricks, bravery and body strength, although all were essential. Jeff stood apart as a man.

JEFF ROLLED UP at Leicester's Filbert Street wearing a green jacket and trousers. He'd not been previously introduced to his new colleagues, so they just assumed he was the bus driver. A decade of banter and jokes, with Jeff generally leading, was underway. The Eastwood-born striker was a supreme joke teller. As Tony Brown lamented regularly, they were always the same jokes – even so Jeff was such an eloquent, convincing teller that the amusement factor never deserted him. John Osborne agreed. "I've been hearing the same jokes for 30 years and they don't get any better. He did have a new joke once. He told it on the coach five times before we got to the motorway. And another twenty times before we got to Nottingham. I'll never forget that game. Ian Storey-Moore was about to take a corner and Jeff Astle came charging back into our half. I knew something was wrong because Jeff never did any defending. "Hang on, Stories," said Jeff. And he started to tell this joke in the penalty box to six Forest players. Best of all, he told 'Stories' to "hang on while he got back to the halfway line."

If Jeff's jokes were being recycled in the mid-sixties, it's a testament to England's No. 9 that he hadn't worn them out two decades later. I can still reel them off – Steve Perryman and 'Peanuts' Astle, Graham Lovett and the bidet, the Irishman on the Golden Shot, Ossie's trousers, on tour in Blackpool – and the King reciting every one gleefully in his Eastwood accent. The delight came with the exuberant teller, not the words.

Ally Robertson: "When I was an apprentice, I was told to travel with the first team to Newcastle for the experience. In those days, we used to travel by train. And Jeff Astle said, "You sit by me, son." So there was I, feeling really nervous, sat next to the great Jeff Astle. There was a card school starting and Jeff said, "deal my cards for me…" But while I was doing that, Jeff was telling a joke… and then another and four hours later when he arrived in Newcastle, he was still telling jokes…"

Inspired by a chance remark by John Osborne, *Grorty Dick* fanzine launched its "Find Jeff a new Joke" appeal, on the basis that every Astle joke was known to every living soul. Jeff never used any of the submissions, but that was secondary to his old team mates having Astle on the receiving end for once.

Jimmy Cumbes was a fast bowler with Surrey, in addition to his goalkeeping skills. Upon his arrival from Tranmere Rovers, Jeff just couldn't wait to take the mickey. "£25,000 for a fast bowler!" he scoffed. Cumbes had been around the circuit and had his reply ready. "Aye and you could have got John Snow [England fast bowler] for £20,000." It was so like Jeff to store this exchange away for future reference. His financially amended version became a famous much used one-liner "That's typical of this club. For an extra £10,000, they could have got John Snow."

As with every joker, there's always a danger of overstepping the mark or choosing the wrong person to be on the receiving end. John Osborne again: "Jeff came into the dressing room one day, kicked the door open and bawled, 'Good morning, world. If you're not ready for me – tough luck!' Just what you wanted after a night out."

The very large John Kaye didn't take kindly to being the butt of Jeff's humour. So he grabbed Jeff, picked him up (no mean feat) and pinned him to the wall while telling him exactly what he thought of his sense of humour. In later years, Kaye gave Bobby Gould the same treatment, to popular acclaim. Nobody messed with Big John.

Inevitably, Jeff was suspected as being the cause of every wind-up, whether he was responsible or not. Tony Brown once took a phone call from a woman with a posh accent who claimed to be from the telephone exchange (this in the days when operators were needed to connect calls). According to the lady, there had been complaints in Tony's area from callers unable to get through. Although Tony protested there were no problems with his phone, the operator asked him to whistle down the line. This he did, but was then asked to repeat the whistle but louder. Tony obliged. "In the next few days, you will get a packet of bird seed," was the response and the line went dead. "Astle!" bawled Brown.

A few days later, Jeff did give him a packet of birdseed, but before any accusations could be levelled, the King was quick with his explanation. "Somebody pulled the same trick on me and I had to get my own back on somebody."

The big striker was at the centre of the coterie of Baggie players who did the rounds of social evenings at local pubs and clubs. Snooker, darts, bingo calling for old people, clothes shop modelling, pub singsongs, acting as the team's bookie, reading a lesson at a Methodist Church – Jeff would have a go at anything – except weights, as Ally Robertson explained. "Jeff hated weights. He could be good at anything he wanted to be, but he hated weights. We all had our orders for weights and regularly Jeff would say "Brian (Whitehouse, the trainer), just check what I need to do today." As soon as the trainer's back was turned, Jeff would instantly count aloud "one, two, three, four, five, six, seven, eight, nine, ten – Done!"

JEFF FINISHED HIS first season with ten goals. That this modest figure made him second top goalscorer (behind Clark with 11) said much for the Albion's need to bring in a finisher. Astle scored in the opening match of 1965/66 against West Ham, following that with another in the third game against Forest before notching his first ever hat-trick against Sheffield Wednesday. Jeff and Laraine had spent the morning in the unglamourous surroundings of Bilston market seeking a rocking horse for their daughter Dorice.

On the way home, Laraine felt absolutely ravenous, so they stopped at a chippy near West Bromwich town centre. Jeff purchased fish and chips for his missus; the trouble was, so good smelt those chips, temptation reared and Jeff succumbed, adding a fish to his purchases. Once home, not able to resist, he then nicked some chips from Laraine's plate to make the pre-match feast complete. Jeff scoffed the lot. Less than three hours later, he was lining up at the Hawthorns. Five hours later, after two deft headers and a third goal with his foot, all the press wanted to talk to him. Clearly enjoying the attention, the striker then found the net at Everton and followed that with another hat-trick the following week against Northampton.

Jeff was now the First Division's top goalscorer and was treated as such by opposing defenders. During one hard game, he picked up a knee injury and although he soldiered on for a while (managing his third hat-trick, this time against Coventry in the League Cup), a cartilage operation was required. During that era, such an operation was tricky. Jeff was out of action for two months. But even then, he was still getting noticed.

Cyril Randle worked in a radio/TV shop in West Bromwich. "Late in 1965, I was asked to put a couple of electrical sockets in a house in Springfield Crescent. When I arrived, I asked the lady her name. 'Mrs Astle,' she replied. Blimey! Sure enough, it was Jeff's wife with small baby. I was full of questions while I worked, which she answered, but she was more interested in knowing what the supporters thought of Jeff. We thought he was great, I said and, I added, if he learns that we also have to play away matches as if we could win, then he could become an England player. Just as I'd said those words, the door opened and in bounced Jeff himself. I was challenged to repeat all the comments I'd just made. So I did. Meanwhile, he'd grabbed the baby, and was lifting it high and laughing.

I considered I was a bundle of energy. But compared to him, I was a candle and Jeff was a tungsten-halogen spotlight. He heard everything I was saying, but he was everywhere at the same time. I finished, they thanked me and I left delighted!"

Fortunately, Astle was fit to take his place in the two-legged League Cup Final against West Ham. In the first leg in London, Jeff went close to scoring twice before 'Chipper' Clark set him up to despatch a low shot past Hammers' keeper Standen.

Even though the home side fought back to take a narrow 2-1 lead into the second leg, it was never going to be enough. Four Albion goals in 35 first half minutes at the Hawthorns flattened the Londoners. West Ham couldn't cope with the power and pace of Astle, Kaye, Clark and Brown. Jeff set up the final goal with a trademark header, which made life very easy in the second half. "Easy, easy, easy," bellowed Albion supporters, as they savoured each precious moment of the Baggies winning a trophy on their own ground.

Despite his Cup Final goal, Jeff hadn't properly recovered from his operation; he suffered the indignity of being dropped. Fred Bennett of the *Sports Argus* noted during the Blackpool match how "long suffering home fans showed their exasperation by chanting 'Astle, Astle' – bewailing the absence of their hero, languishing in the reserves." Jeff was immediately recalled against Leicester, claiming one goal and four assists in a 5-1 victory. His constant harassment gave City's Sjoberg an unwanted record – the only opponent to score two own goals for the Baggies in one match. After City, Jeff found the net four times in the next three matches. His season stats were impressive – 18 goals in just 27 matches.

ALBION'S CUP success continued into the following season. Fifteen goals in just four League Cup matches left a series of opponents dazed (not least Villa, crushed 6-1). Jeff found the net against both Manchester City and Swindon, but his crowning glory was reserved for the semi-final. West Ham were the déjà vu victims with four more goals conceded, three of them from Astle. Two more efforts were disallowed. The Londoners probably realised it wasn't their night when Jeff scored his first – a header from Collard's cross – after just 50 seconds. A 4-0 lead made the second leg academic.

From that high point, the season nosedived. On 1st March, the Baggies were embarrassingly beaten 3-2 by Third Division QPR in the first ever League Cup Final at Wembley, despite being 2-0 ahead at the interval. Three days later, their initial foray into Europe was also over as Bologna completed a Third Round comfortable home and away double over the flattened Albion side.

Up to then, poor League results had been alleviated by progress in Cup competitions. Jeff and his fellow forwards 'Chipper' Clark and 'Bomber' Brown scored 49 League goals between them, Jeff's contribution of 16 showed he had an eye for making something out of nothing, notably when he harassed Sheffield Wednesday's Ron Springett into dropping the ball. Astle was in swiftly, steering the ball around the keeper and into the net. And yet, despite the best efforts of the front men, the defence were conceding even more. Only a fine run of late season victories spared the Baggies from the embarrassment of relegation.

One of these key wins came at Anfield when Jeff's solitary goal was sufficient to give his team victory. Laraine Astle: "I'd gone up on the supporters' coach with Clive Clark's wife; I remember it mainly because the Kop was so quiet. I'd been told to expect a lot of shouting and chanting from them, but there was nothing. And I can see Jeff's goal as clear as day, he stood over Tommy Lawrence (aka "The Flying Pig') to put him off, Jeff managed to do that, he got the ball, rounded him, and put the ball into the back of the net! Oh – and there's one other thing I remember from that day; we went to the ladies toilets after the game, it was a brick outhouse type of thing, and it was awash in – er – something!"

A week later, Jimmy Hagan was sacked, despite his five-year contract. Jeff shared his thoughts on his first Albion manager with me years later. "Jimmy Hagan told me to stay in the opposition half of the field all the time. He came in the dressing room one Monday, with a sheet pasted with all the local Press. 'Yer on that one, that one, an' that an' that one. Well yer should, yer the leading goalscorer, aren't yer?' And then he told John Kaye off because he wasn't! But I'll nivva say anything against Jimmy Hagan because he made me a First Division footballer. He was funny in certain ways. He were the type of bloke who wouldn't speak to you one minute and worship you the next."

THE KING'S WORDS on his ex-manager to the press were typically guarded and suffered much from translation into BBC English. "I can't help thinking that, if he'd relaxed just a little and revealed just a few human touches in his dealing, he could have been a great manager." Often with Jeff's public utterances and also in his biography Striker, there was normally a stiffness, precision and formality about his words, functional phrases that gave away nothing about the real Jeff, the grinning, warm, generous, gregarious Jeff who everyone loved.

Albion's new manager was Alan Ashman, a quiet, thoughtful man whom the players took to immediately. Team spirit was instantly enhanced, with Graham Williams an imposing and popular captain. "Most of us were there for 16-17 years," he explained. "We were all part of one family. If somebody kicked one of us, they'd kicked all of us."

Jeff found the net even more regularly than before, notably in consecutive early season League matches, when he scored one against Coventry, three past Sheffield United, with two shots and a header, another at Fulham and two more against Leeds United. In the absence of regular expert Tony Brown, Jeff later managed one from the penalty spot against Stoke City. Under Ashman, Jeff was often the solitary forward, with supporting players backing him up. This system benefited the team, but Jeff of course had a very tough job.

Any hopes of a third straight League Cup Final fell at the first hurdle in another embarrassing defeat by lower Division opposition, this time a 3-1 humbling by Reading. But there was always the FA Cup. After a desperately close affair at Colchester, the Essex side was comfortably sorted out 4-0 in a replay, Jeff scoring twice. Another brace followed in a Fourth Round replay against Southampton and his crucial strike at Portsmouth helped to put the Baggies into the last eight, their first appearance in the quarter finals for a decade. And then Albion pulled out... mighty Liverpool.

The Reds had a system for the FA Cup – blanket defence to earn a draw on the road and then beat the opposition at Anfield. They got their 0-0 at the Hawthorns, so probably considered the job was done. But they'd reckoned without Jeff Astle. Albion's main man was dominant in the air and when he got on the end of a cross from Bomber Brown in the 69th minute… well that just wasn't in the script. As John Kaye eloquently said: "Have you ever heard silence? Silence is the Kop after Jeff Astle nodded that great equaliser at Anfield." The deadlock could not be broken, so the tie went to a third match at Maine Road.

This was a rough, tough, emotional encounter, watched by 56,000 people, the majority of which came from Merseyside. Goals from the King and Clive Clark were only just enough to keep the Reds at bay, who laid a late siege to the Albion goal. But this Liverpool team were big on effort, but short of class.

The semi-final against Second Division Birmingham was very different. City had nearly all the chances and missed them, whereas Albion had far fewer, but found the net. Astle, his name chanted before, during and after the game, grabbed the all-important first, pouncing on a rebound in the thirteenth minute. The goal was his 28th of the season, including at least one in every round of the Cup. When Bomber Brown added the second, Albion knew exactly where they were going.

JEFF WAS rapidly becoming a national figure, as John Kaye explained, just a few days before the Semi-Final. "Whenever Albion get on the TV, the standing joke in the dressing room is 'watch the Jeff Astle show.' Now it has come true. The 'Nottingham Flash' went through his paces at the Spring Road training ground for the television cameramen. His epic is due for showing on the commercial channel." The timing was excellent, for The King scored two hat-tricks in three days. On the Monday, just two days after the semi-final triumph, 43,000 squeezed into the Hawthorns as Albion demolished Manchester United 6-3, with Jeff getting three of them and still finding time to brawl with Nobby Stiles. Journalist Colin Malam described the evening. "Albion took Manchester United by the scruff of the neck and shook them so hard they tumbled from the top of the First Division."

Two days later, the King found the net three more times, including two splendid headers, against West Ham. The chants of "Astle for England" had new belief about them. Tom Duckworth of the Argus was supportive. "There is a new urgency and fire in Astle's play and there is no better header of a ball. But he is not just an in-the-air player. He is fast, runs into space splendidly and combines deft footwork with a splendid shot."

The King and he was definitely The King by now, was a national phenomenon. "How do you spell goal?" asked one Black Country school kid of another. "A S T L E."

Jeff duly received his England call-up, which prompted a predictable response from 'Yorky' Kaye. "We wouldn't object to Jeff being selected for England parties regularly so we can get some peace and quiet around the place."

Albion's loss was England's gain, as Francis Lee explained. "On my first England session, I met Jeff for the first time and he did nothing but tell jokes. He tells them in a voice something like Wilfred Pickles, and he has a gift of telling bad jokes with such a good delivery that you still have to laugh. The more you laugh, the more jokes he tells. I'm sure he has run out of material now, and that he is on the second time round but with a good scriptwriter he could certainly make a living out of it. "

Jeff's first cap was still a year away (v Wales at Wembley in April 1969) and only four more would follow. Five was perhaps a reasonable tally by Albion player standards, for which tradition dictates they will never earn the number of international appearances their form deserves. But perhaps there was more to the King being passed over than the usual anti-Midlands bias as Tony Brown explained. "Alan Ball told me Jeff was the only man who used to get Sir Alf wound up. Jeff was always so lively in the dressing room and he made such a row, he'd get Sir Alf steaming. The one time, it ended up with Sir Alf shouting, 'Astle! Why don't you just piss orf?' Perhaps that's why he didn't get many caps!"

It wasn't only Sir Alf that Jeff wound up. With Geoff Hurst England's first choice forward, Jeff shared reserve striker duties with another 'King', Peter Osgood of Chelsea. The King of the Brummie Road and the King of the Kings Road spent much time together, either sharing a bench or sharing a room. Jeff's musical obsession eventually brought a sharp reaction from the Londoner. Jeff relentlessly played Norman Greenbaum's *Spirit in the Sky* over and over again on the record player, driving Osgood to the point where he finally had to destroy the machine just to get some peace!

Peace was the last thing on the minds of Albion players as they prepared for their FA Cup Final appearance against Everton. At their training base in Southport, everyone wanted to talk to the King, the First Division's top scorer with 35 goals. Jeff just carried on being Jeff, with Bomber Brown regularly the Ernie Wise to Jeff's Eric Morecambe. Once the pair staged a ventriloquist act for the rest of the squad with Jeff playing the part of the dummy.

AS A SPECTACLE for neutrals, the 1968 FA Cup Final was quite dreadful. Play was constantly interrupted for free-kicks as the two sides tore into each other. Despite loud and endlessly repeated plaintive chants of "Jeff Astle" from half of Wembley, the striker saw very little of the ball. The few chances that were created all fell to Everton, including a glorious opportunity that Husband missed minutes from the end. Albion looked like pardoned men in extra time, being far more enterprising in their play.

But such occasions are made for Gods to rise above mere mortals. And, sure enough, within just a few minutes, the King made himself immortal. Astle's right foot shot rebounded back into his path off Everton central defender Brian Labone. Jeff hit it again with his far weaker left foot and the ball hit the net before Gordon West could react. "Goals like that come once in a lifetime," admitted Jeff later.

The photograph of his celebrations (silent shout, both arms above his head, fingers out-stretched to the skies) remains the most iconic of all Albion illustrations. The moment was later immortalised in the Astle Gates. Naturally, Jeff was repeatedly asked how he felt after his goal; the endless chants of "Astle, Astle", the lap of honour. He was quite candid. "I didn't feel anything. I was just numb, physically and mentally drained."

Few of the Albion players fully appreciated just what glamour was attached to the FA Cup and the team that held it. They were invited to function after function and gradually became used to people simply standing and staring at the Cup. For one function, Jeff was given custody of the Cup overnight. Securior delivered it in a big wooden box, lined with velvet, and Laraine's first thought, on removing it from said container, revolved around the overwhelming first impression that both trophy, and the blue and white ribbons still adorning it, were dirty. So she polished the Cup with metal polish and washed the ribbons.

Within minutes, there was a steady stream of local schoolchildren knocking on her door to admire the trophy, and Laraine being Laraine, she simply couldn't say 'no'. That night, concerned about the Cup's safety, the couple decided there could be only one safe repository – under their bed! Securicor took the Cup away the following morning and to this day, Laraine still holds the receipt for "one FA Cup."

THE NEXT SEASON started much as the previous one ended, with the King scoring against Manchester United, though a mere brace this time in a 3-1 win. Jeff was far more than just a fine header of the ball. He could shoot powerfully and his ball control was excellent. His long time chum 'Bomber' Brown reminded everyone that, "he was a terrific person, great to be around, a real man's man, but we shouldn't forget just what a top class striker he was." Jeff wasn't as prolific as previously because he was now literally a marked man. Yet between the maelstrom of lunging bodies and flying boots, Jeff was still being Jeff.

Supporter Rick Janowski recalled an incident in one game when an opposing player put the ball out over his own goal line, near the right corner flag at the Brummie Road End. The referee signalled for a West Brom throw-in instead of a corner. Jeff Astle nonchalantly picked up the ball where it had gone out of play and, as instructed, took a throw-in – from the goalline some three or four feet in from the corner flag. The ref laughed and made West Brom take the throw again, this time from the side touchline. I think the ref got Jeff's 'subtle' point about where the ball actually went out, even if Jeff did not get the corner he deserved. Similarly, in an otherwise hostile encounter against Bruges in the Cup Winners' Cup, Astle briefly pretended to be the referee and went through the motions of ordering a player off.

What promised to be another fine season petered out long before May. Having overcome the physical presence of two foreign sides, the Baggies were eliminated from Europe by Dunfermline. The Scots grabbed an early goal in the second leg and defended it on a sand covered pitch in sub-artic conditions.

Worse was to follow in the FA Cup semi-final. Having overcome Chelsea in the quarter-final with the winner coming from Jeff, the Baggies were strong favourites to beat struggling Leicester in the last four. In the event, City sneaked a 1-0 win, courtesy of a late Allan Clarke goal.

On the plus side, Jeff was the club's top scorer once more with 26 goals. But that wasn't enough for the King. He told everyone he'd get 30 during the 1969/70 season. And he did! As John Kaye wearily admitted, "For some time, Jeff bent our ears with his repeated vows that he would get 30 goals this season." The target was reached in the last League game of the season against Ipswich.

Along the way, he was presented with the match ball after scoring his 100th Baggies goal against Sheffield Wednesday in December. As ever, 'Yorky' Kaye got his revenge in first. "100 goals? You should have had 200 from the chances we've been making for you this season."

The following month, the Baggies twice came from behind as Crystal Palace were defeated 3-2. The King scored all three, but that day he was on a mission. Laraine had told him to score one at each end for his daughters Dawn and Dorice. Jeff obliged and put one in for his mum as well. The Sports Argus that evening declared, "Jolly Jeff hits hat-trick." The price for Jeff this time was an ankle injury that forced him to drop out of the England squad.

Increasingly, there was a price to pay for every achievement. Albion had battled their way to Wembley again in the League Cup. Goals had been shared around, but Jeff's own efforts played a main part in defeating Aston Villa, Ipswich and Leicester. The Final opponents were the formidable Manchester City. Just to play at Wembley, Jeff had intensive treatment all week for his shin and ankle injuries. The desperate state of the pitch with mud on top of frozen soil could not have helped his limbs. Nevertheless, he scored after just five minutes. But City remained strong and won 2-1 in extra time.

In the same month as the Cup Final, Jeff was selected for the Football League versus the Scottish League in the rather mundane surroundings of Highfield Road. Most of the Albion team went along to see him score twice. This was widely perceived as a great boost to his chances of playing in the World Cup in Mexico and shortly afterwards, he was indeed named in Alf Ramsey's squad. Albion supporters now had a new chant: "We all agree... Astle is better than Pelé." Jeff was at the peak of his career, scoring regularly despite heavy legal or illegal marking.

AND SO TO Mexico. And that miss. Brazilian goalkeeper Felix, who claims his performance in the England game was improved after two half-time cigarettes, was convinced that Jeff was not going to score, "because when I saw Everaldo miss it. I moved to close him down. He tried to place the ball away from me and shot it out of play." Alan Ashman put the King's contribution into perspective. "Astle's fortunes in Mexico were rather mixed. When he came on against Brazil, everything started to happen. He made two chances for Ball and missed one himself. Against Czechoslovakia, he did not receive the right service."

England lost to the eventual champions and so finished second in their group and advanced to play West Germany in the quarter-finals, where Franz Beckenbauer and his men would gain revenge for defeat in the final of '66. Astle did not feature in this game and so was able to do nothing more than watch as the Germans turned a two goal deficit into a 3-2 win in extra time.

Understandably when he returned, Jeff wasn't quite the same man who had left for South America will such high hopes. He got off the mark in the second game of the season and added five more in the next four encounters, but overall struggled to find the net. Even being made Captain made little difference. Tony Brown stuck by him loyally, "So much depends on Jeff Astle. He's my best mate off the field and we have a good understanding. He may not be scoring so many himself but he's making some for me." To mark his 300th game in February 1971, Jeff received a cake, specially made by local department store Lewis's. The King eventually managed 16 goals that term, barely half that of Tony Brown. But once again the real problem was the defence, not the attack. The Baggies finished 17th, an unacceptably low position in those days and Alan Ashman paid the price.

THE NEW MAN at the helm was Don Howe, who promised much but delivered little. He told Jeff to stop heading the ball and to become a better defensive player. Jeff's response was plain speaking at its best. "If you don't want me to head the ball, you might as well get rid of me."

Even in troubled times, Jeff was still "the man." Roger Kirkpatrick was in charge of the Manchester United versus Albion match at Stoke (Old Trafford had been closed due to crowd trouble) in August 1971. Referee Roger was something of a character at the time and players knew they could talk to him. Prior to the match, Roger was in the Albion dressing room laying down the law – not that anybody was listening – but he ended with "if you've got anything to say to me, say it now." Jeff couldn't resist. He called Roger the biggest mouthful he could possibly think of. The whole team sagged with mirth, so too did Referee Roger.

Don Howe purchased Bobby Gould in September 1971 to boost Albion's attack. Gould lasted barely a year, managing to make himself unpopular with both supporters and players. On the first day of training, he accused his new team mates of not being fit and his relationship with the squad went downhill from there. Jeff had little time for the newcomer; "He's just a runner with no talent."

Marginalised by Howe, there was only one goal for the King by December 1971, a rebound from Brown's shot at the City Ground, Nottingham.

It was no better for the team either. After a bright start, Albion won only one game in 20. Towards the end of the season, Howe dropped Astle for "not trying." The King's response, via the local press, was unusually frank. "I think I am just as well out of the side the way we are playing. I need a supply from the wing but we are not using wingers." Jeff considered he'd been rushed back to play only five weeks after an appendix operation. After a month with the stiffs, including one fixture at Bury where he reckoned, "The attendance was 28, and 23 of those came to see me," he was selected against Manchester United, and scored the winner. But there were to be no more goals that season.

One cartilage injury followed by another kept the King away from the first team until February 1973. With Albion heading for relegation, Baggies supporters craved the return of their hero. Surely Jeff could save them. When word got around that Astle would play in a third team game at Spring Road, 500 supporters turned up to cheer him on. Jeff scored twice in a 5-1 win. As team mate Joe Mayo recalled, "I used to play alongside Jeff in reserve games in the early seventies. Jeff hadn't got a cartilage left in his knees, but he was still the best player on the pitch."

Astle's messianic return to the first team in February helped his side revive with a couple of wins, but defeat in the final four matches meant relegation. The writing was on the wall for both Jeff and the Albion. He was rarely fit and the club was not the one he joined. In July 1974, Barry Fry persuaded him to join Dunstable after no offers were forthcoming from other League clubs. Jeff didn't forget his supporters. "The crowd were wonderful to me at Albion. I had my bad times, they happen to all strikers, but the fans stuck with me through thick and thin and if there is one thing I will never forget it is their complete loyalty."

Jeff returned home later for his Testimonial game – the '68 team against the current team. It was a fine opportunity for one final love-in. One supporter paid his own tribute by running onto the pitch with a bottle of Champagne. And, as befitting a King, he was carried around the pitch shoulder-high after the game. Jeff tried to get one over Jimmy Cumbes again. Handing him a box of cut-glass tankards, he added, "Don't drop them!"

"Then why pick me?" was Cumbes' instant response.

FROM DUNSTABLE, the King moved to the South Coast. Jeff himself takes up the story. "Weymouth? It were a fantastic place, but in the end the money weren't right so we come to the Midlands, to Atherstone. I had a season at Atherstone, but me knees were gerrin' worse, the injuries were cripplin', so I jacked it all in and started me own cleanin' business.

There used to be winder cleaners in the Weymouth team, their full time job, see, and once somebody said to me, Jeff, for a bit of extra money, why don't ye do a bit of winder-cleaning, with us two at dinnertime. My missus said it was a good idea... so I did. I picked up the knack of window cleanin' – not using rags, using blades and so on, and so when I moved up ter Atherstone, I'd got nothing to do in the daytime, so I thought I'd start up me own winder cleanin' round. In them days, there weren't many winder cleaners about. I put advert in the papers an' I had no end o' people on phone, so I built it up from there! I don't do just winder cleaning narh. I do carpets and suites." The tale continues thanks to a more formal interview with a PFA journalist. "I've got arthritis in both knees, now, although it doesn't affect me too badly at work. The knees couldn't stand up to football, though. It's got to the stage where I could hardly walk after a match. And I work quite a wide area. – about a 20 mile radius around where I live in Netherseal, just outside Burton."

Kevin Nolan was a Southern League linesman and thus hardened to a variety of fragile egos. Needing a carpet cleaner, he hired Jeff and was agape at the vista of "an England international on his hands and knees scrubbing my carpet." Feeling a tad guilty and wanting more of the Astle charisma, Kevin dangled an invite for a post-clean drink at his local. The King was happy to accept. "Just surreal," Kevin was heard to mutter. A week later, Kevin's wife spotted that their Mexican footstool had been overlooked. Kevin couldn't resist, "Now look here, Astle, that's twice you've missed a Mexican sitter."

Supporter Dan Fellows has only fond memories of the King. "As well as my Uncle, I'd list Jeff as one of the reasons why I love football today. I remember him as a kind, decent man who always had time for everybody who wanted to speak to him. When I was about 8 or 9, I remember having a kick about with him in our pub's beer garden. He didn't have to do that; he was there to clean windows. He also had a laugh when people would joke with him about his singing on *Fantasy Football!*

A one-off *Fantasy Football* session, a handy excuse for Frank Skinner to meet his old Albion idol, had snowballed rapidly into Friday night post-pub TV gold. Jeff was game for anything – wearing outrageous costumes and trying to sing songs he'd never heard before on live TV 150 miles from home didn't bother him. "No, it isn't degrading. It's a laugh and a joke, isn't it? You could be serious and say: 'No, I'm not going to do that,' but it's just a funny show."

Out of *Fantasy Football* sprung the *Jeff Astle Roadshow*. Supporter Tim Joyner recalled one Roadshow in the Throstle Club in the late 1990s. "An absolutely fantastic evening, during a period when Albion were absolutely dire on the pitch. Jeff's relationship with the fans in the club that evening, with all the funny stories and group singing, was a reminder that while the team, at that time, were serving up turgid dross week after week, the Albion "family" was and always will be a class act. I actually got to speak to the King that evening, in the gents toilets of all places, I'd had a few beers and was probably slurring my words but could only agree with Jeff's view that it had been a "bloody good night."

The Astle family always had time for supporters, for instance Jeff and Laraine spent their 31st wedding anniversary in the company of Kidderminster Branch of the Supporters Club. Where else would they want to be? It was always a pleasure to listen to Jeff at supporter's club meetings. He had the rare quality, through sheer warmth and strength of personality, to be quite cocky and bigheaded about his own and Albion's ability during the "golden era" without a hint of arrogance.

Jeff's health declined rapidly in 1997 and didn't recover. Bravely, Laraine soldiered on alone, concealing Jeff's rapid decline from all but family and a few trusted friends. Even though I knew his time was limited, a midnight phone call from Netherseal in January 2002 was quite devastating. The rest of Albion's support were both shocked and stunned. Flowers, scarves, shirts, photographs and other items were left at makeshift shrines all around the Hawthorns and from this public outpouring of grief came the genesis of the Albion Gates.

Jeff's family (Laraine, his three daughters and their own children), are the nearest that Albion supporters have to royalty and are treated at all times with respect and often reverence. And yet a more down to earth bunch it is hard to imagine. Grandson Matthew is with the Albion Academy. Typical of the family's modesty, young Matthew went to his club trial under his father's name and without any mention of his grandfather. The thought of another Astle leading out an Albion team brings a lump to the throat of any mature supporter.

JOHN OSBORNE

1967-1978

BAGGIES CAREER

Games	312
Caps	0

MAGIC MOMENT

His heroic goalkeeping aainst the Blues in the 1968 FA Cup semi-final was instrumental in the outplayed Baggies progressing to Wembley

'OSSIE'

> "I once read a book by Lev Yashin. He said you could wait until the penalty is actually struck because you should be fast enough to block the shot. So I thought if it's good enough for Yashin, then I'll try it. It didn't help me very much. I only saved three penalties in ten years."
>
> **John Osborne**

IN just that one self-deprecating paragraph, goalkeeper John Osborne unwittingly said so much about his own personality. These were the words of the man marked out by newspapers as the first of a new breed – an intelligent footballer. This insight was no more than the usual superficial tabloid nonsense, of course. John's much heralded six 'O' levels were not by themselves outstanding qualifications, and undoubtedly many other professionals had similar natural intelligence. But as the *Football League Review* pointed out in 1968, "people who know little about the game seem surprised that footballers can be intelligent."

What really made John stand out from the rest was his performance on a TV football-themed game show – *Quizball*.

A very youthful David Vine hosted the BBC series. The contestants were mainly from First Division clubs, plus a guest from another sport. Osborne's team consisted of himself, manager Alan Ashman, team-mate Ray Wilson plus motor-cyclist Jeff Smith. The general knowledge questions were deliberately none-too- taxing, partly because most of the contestants were perceived to have limited recall, and partly, because of its duration, the shows were highly tiring to record. Lacking sophisticated equipment, filming a half hour quiz show needed several hours of patience in a pressurised environment – on one occasion, eleven hours of patience. The Albion quartet beat Sheffield United, Fulham and Forest to win the first-series in March 1968. The trophy they triumphantly brought back to West Bromwich still resides in a club cabinet today. John's national fame was established.

JOHN OSBORNE was born on 1st December 1940 in the North Derbyshire village of Barlborough, the proud son of a fitter. In his younger days, the village was short on organised activities, and so young John amused himself roaming around the local countryside identifying local birds and animals. The twin interests of bird spotting and a thirst for knowledge remained lifelong passions. In his Albion days, he endured tedious epithets such as "The Birdman" with his usual wry smile. A different kind of bird attracted his attention as a teenager when he started going out with Jenny from the age of 15.

Although young John always played the beautiful game, in his early days he'd play either wing-half (midfield) or centre-half. His two England schoolboy caps were earned as an outfield player. Playing left-half for the Chesterfield Boys side, progression to the last eight in the English Schools Shield competition in 1956 brought welcome attention both for himself and the team's goalkeeper, a young lad called Bob Wilson. Bolton Wanderers picked up on John's talents, and signed him on amateur forms. Without an income from Bolton, John was obliged to travel daily. The distance quickly wore him down. "It meant me boarding a train every Saturday morning at 7.30 am and not arriving back home until 11.30 pm the same day. That was hopeless, and it didn't suit me at all."

Making use of his 'O' levels, John found work as a clerk with a local firm, his football itch being scratched in a tough local Miners Welfare League. As the months passed, he became resigned to office life. Fortunately at the age of 18, his local club, Chesterfield, approached Osborne and signed him for their third team. Quickly, fate presented the youngster with an opportunity. The Spireites' regular keeper failed to turn up for a match against Sheffield United's thirds at the Ball Inn ground in Sheffield. Ossie volunteered and although the ball flew past him four times, he enjoyed the new position, and continued to wear a green shirt.

At that time, the youthful Gordon Banks was Chesterfield's main keeper. When he inevitably left for Leicester, Osborne became second choice behind Ron Powell, turning out regularly for the stiffs. Even then, John's status rose only marginally from amateur to part-time professional, not becoming full-time until September 1960.

OSSIE'S FIRST TEAM debut came against Shrewsbury three months later. Patience was important though, for his first team appearances were limited over the next four years. In December 1964, a dreadful car accident injured Ron Powell so badly he never played again, while team-mate Hunt was killed. Ossie became immediate first choice keeper. Chesterfield supporters praised him for his clever positioning, and his apparent near-suicidal determination to win the ball at all costs. He was also involved in some fairly comical moments (comical, at least, from the opposing fans' point of view) that led to the club conceding bizarre goals, such as a fifty-yarder from Sammy Chapman against Mansfield in September, 1962.

John found nothing glamorous about his job. "I thought Chesterfield was it – all football's like this. It was hard. The lads working in the steelworks next door got paid more. If ever I were asked what I did for a living, I'd say Chesterfield Corporation! I wasn't going to admit I played for the football club."

The realities of lower Division football were never far away. Such was the shortage of strikers, Osborne reluctantly played up front against Crewe in a home League match. Chesterfield won 3-1, though John didn't score – probably to his quiet relief. The club coach was Oliver Thompson, an old pro himself, who always smoked while applying the rubbing oils. Occasionally, ash would drop from his fag and mix in with the oils. John often joked that most of his team-mates thought that fag ash was part of the healing process.

One of John's favourite tales was his account of an away fixture on the South Coast.

"I remember travelling to Brighton on the train. It was such a big treat for us to go on the train. When we got to Brighton, there was a big Women's Institute conference on and there weren't any taxis. So we had to go by bus. We got off by the ground and sauntered up to the players entrance. The doorman stepped out in front of us.

"Where are you off to?"

"We're the Chesterfield players."

"Yes, course you are. I've just seen you lot getting off the bus."

Anyway, Bobby Smith, the old Spurs forward was playing for Brighton, and we were 5-0 down. I was having a nightmare. Bobby was giving me hell, and they got a corner with five minutes left. "Right," I thought. "I'll sort him out." and hit him right on the side of the face. The first thing I noticed was that he didn't flinch. The second thing was that my hand was shaking. The referee came over, booked me and gave Brighton a penalty that they missed. You know those marks out of ten they give you in the *Sunday People*? Well, they gave me a nine. All the other players rang the paper up to complain, but that was the only time I hit anybody."

John's booking was one of only two he received during his entire career. The latter came two decades later in a brief return to European football with Shamrock Rovers against Banik Ostrava. "I was ever so proud of that one," he later explained. "I was booked for time wasting after 90 seconds in Czechoslovakia."

JOHN WAS AN ever-present member for Chesterfield for over two seasons. His efforts attracted the attention of Albion manager Jimmy Hagan, who had Osborne regularly watched. In January 1967, the Baggies made their move. When the Chesterfield manager inquired of him "Would you like to go to West Brom?" John's response apparently was a genuine "Why, who are they playing?"

The transfer was swiftly arranged. Ossie had a short conversation with Hagan one evening, and quickly agreed to move, with Chesterfield receiving a £10,000 cheque in exchange. Plus, if self-effacing Ossie can be believed, "double Green Shield stamps and three bags of coal". The increased salary at the Hawthorns was most welcome. John no longer needed to work part-time in the summer to make ends meet. Not only was he married to Jenny by then, he had also become a Dad to little Suzanne Denise in mid-1966.

The Albion side, intent on enhancing their reputation as a Cup team both domestically and in Europe, had rather neglected their League form. Far too many goals were flying past either Rick Sheppard or Ray Potter in the Albion goal. The club had secured only 16 points in their first 25 games (admittedly in the two points for a win era). John was handed the No. 1 shirt immediately to make his debut in a 2-1 defeat at Forest on 7 January. Within a month, he made his European debut in the Third Round of the Fairs Cup at Bologna. The Italian side ran out comfortable 3-0 winners. Ossie wasn't eligible to play for the Baggies in either their FA Cup matches or their League Cup defence that was ended in such embarrassing fashion by QPR at Wembley. At the time, improved League form seemed small consolation for followers with loftier ambitions, having to get used to Albion's fall from fifties grace. Once in between the sticks, there was no shifting Osborne, and one of his rivals for the green shirt, Ray Potter, was quickly transferred. His popularity wasn't of the instant kind, though. There wasn't any single moment, not in his early days anyway, when John suddenly became a favourite. His impact was a gradual one, combining his footballing abilities with social charm.

Supporter Gary Brookes recalls being introduced to the team's new 'keeper in a nightclub at Southampton after Albion had secured a 2-2 draw at the Dell in March.

His response was immediate, if ill considered.

"What the bloody hell have we bought a playwright for?" (John shared his name with a well-known author and playwrite from the 1950s, whose best-known work was *Look Back In Anger*)

"To see that this lot play right," responded John instantly.

Taken aback by this witty response, the best I could do in reply was to point out that 'he better be good, or he would get a lot of looking back in anger from his team-mates.'

THE NEW GOALKEEPER was now part of a very tight-knit squad of talented players. They trained together, socialised together, and even lived close together. Bonding was vital to them all. Meeting supporters was a perfectly natural and regular activity, and spotting groups of Albion's finest playing snooker in a local hall on a Thursday night was commonplace. During such regular intercourse, the natural charisma of "life and soul" Jeff Astle, combined with Ossie's ever-ready wit built bridges and created reputations.

Disciplinarian manager Hagan was quickly gone, replaced by the gentler, more player-friendly style of Alan Ashman. The initial impact was similar to that of Robson replacing Megson. Of that squad, five – Astle, Brown, Williams, Colquhoun and Hope – eventually became full internationals (although, of course, being West Midlands based, the caps were predictably few in number).

Ossie was regularly the butt of jokes, most famously when Jeff Astle was so appalled by the state of the goalkeeper's trousers – John never quite understood fashion – that he cut them up with a pair of scissors. As Ossie pointed out wearily later, a dressing room whip-round for new trousers enabled him to replace said garment and make a small profit.

The keeper was always an easy target for mickey-taking. He was notoriously reluctant to do anything in training, never quite seeing the point. Talking to reporter Ray Matts, trainer Stuart Williams observed, "Osborne would often be miserable first thing. He definitely wasn't a morning person." It was indeed fortunate for John that mild-mannered Ashman was in charge for his peak years. There was always one weekly highlight, the Friday morning 5-a-side "England" v "the scum" (Scots, Irish, Welsh etc) on the tennis courts. "Never mind losing to Arsenal on Saturday, we had to beat the scum on Friday morning. Nothing was held back – the blood used to flow," enthused Ossie.

Rarely has a career professional footballer suffered so much from pre-match nerves. As John freely admitted, "the hardest part isn't the 90 minutes – that's the easy bit. It's the mental rehearsals in the previous week – playing it out 400 times in your mind. I liken it to taking a driving test each week before 10,000 people and the examiner. I go out on Saturdays knowing that not only my livelihood, but that of ten other men, depends upon how I perform." Being physically sick in the dressing room toilets was not uncommon. Reporter Dennis Shaw recalls being awoken late at night in a Southport hotel room where the squad were enjoying a break before an important cup match. The reporter stuck his head outside his bedroom door to see Ossie with training gear and with fag bouncing the ball in the corridor, claiming to be practising his handling skills.

Long-term fan Glynis Wright has clear memories of the Albion keeper. "Just watching him in action between the sticks was a riveting experience, for Ossie was nothing but a giant bundle of nerves for the entire 90 minutes. I don't know what manner of mental torture he was going through, but just watching his act had my stomach churning fit to bust for several hours thereafter. Give the opposition time to attack, and there he would be, sweaty dark hair slicked in all directions, eyes darting everywhere, constantly checking proximity to both goal and six-yard lines, shoulders slightly hunched, knees slightly bent, slender body swaying this way and that, awaiting the latest assault upon his peace of mind. "

THE NIGHT BEFORE the 1970 League Cup Final, the players, and reporter Ray Matts, were taken to the West End to see *Fiddler On The Roof*. At the end of the first act, Ossie, a nervous wreck long before a game kicked off, decided he couldn't sit still a moment longer and had to get out of the theatre. The club couldn't let him get lost in London so near to a vital game, so Ray accompanied him on his trek around Piccadilly Circus and the naughty nightclubs of London. He just walked, and walked and walked. (As it transpired, the capital route march offered no balm. The next day Ossie proved unusually vulnerable in the air at Wembley, and he was fortunate not to be punished for a couple of glaring errors. A Mike Summerbee follow-through, kicking him in the head and the hand, which later needed five stitches, didn't help his cause either. Albion were beaten 2-1 by Manchester City.)

Being on the receiving end was commonplace. The 1968 FA Cup winning route was far longer and more painful than *Quizball's* Route 1 (the most difficult questions, but a quicker way of scoring). The hapless custodian was regularly in the wars, bravely accepting batterings from opponents to preserve his goal. His FA Cup debut came at Southampton in a Fourth Round replay, and by way of welcome, he was knocked out after just ten minutes in a collision with Frank Saul. The Southampton player caught him full on the chin. With only one substitute available from the bench in those days, for the rest of the first half, trainer Stuart Williams stood behind the goal, giving the dazed and blurred keeper a commentary "ball's on the left, Channon's moving forward, close your left hand post..." Ossie kept going until half-time on instinct, pure and simple; that, and the sheer determination and bravery under stress that renders ordinary people quite immune to pain. Albion remarkably won 3-2, with captain Graham Williams between the sticks for the second half. While his fellow players celebrated a triumph against the odds, the battered goalkeeper was en-route to hospital.Alan Ashman explained "He didn't know where he was or what time it was, and getting him off to hospital seemed the sensible thing to do."

At Portsmouth in the next round, his head got in the way of Jennings's boot. In the quarter-final, he managed to get through three fixtures against Liverpool without damaging himself. But remaining unbattered and perfectly conscious for so long created new problems as Albion supporter Keith Cotter recalls. "After the Anfield replay, there were four of us eating sandwiches as we waited in traffic on the East Lancs road. The Albion team coach pulled up alongside, John leaned out and asked if he could scrounge a sandwich, explaining they had left the ground straight after the game, and he was starving. Such were his powers of persuasion; everyone donated all their sandwiches, only to remember too late that they were hungry as well. We reminded him of this many times at the Smethwick end, and he always reckoned they were the best sandwiches he'd ever tasted. "

Birmingham City deserved to win the FA Cup semi-final, but Osborne's string of saves from Fred Pickering gave the Baggies a platform for their strikers to complete the job. In the second half, Ossie was kicked painfully intercepting a ball, but recovered quickly to crucially tip another Pickering shot onto the post. "I had a fair game that day, but I did have some good defenders around me, you know" was the goalkeeper's modest post-match response. Jeff Astle had a different opinion. "Finest game he ever played." In typical Astle style, he couldn't resist adding, "he didn't have many good ones, mind!"

And so to Wembley for the first FA Cup final ever to be televised in colour. Ossie, who was so worked up beforehand that he repeatedly bounced and missed the ball in the dressing room, didn't have a great deal to do in a brutal stalemate of a final. Almost inevitably, he received another whack for his bravery, this time across his fingers. "Everything was OK" he confided in a later interview with the club programme, "until the Everton forwards came roaring in towards me. I kept goal for 107 minutes with one hand." He also complained about the state of his left shoulder. Midway through the second half, Royle's header beat Osborne, but thankfully, John Kaye headed clear on the goal line. On such moments are cups won and lost. Perhaps in part because of his Aunt Sally characteristics, Ossie had no recollections afterwards of the big day. "Thank heavens for video," he repeatedly said later. The photographers behind his goal were happy to remind him of his urgent and repeated questions about how much time remained as the Toffees chased the game.

FROM HIS colleagues' point of view, their last line of defence seemed to always have at least one injury. One of Ossie's regular pre-match routines was to bind two of his fingers together. Perhaps his wounds were a kind of self-protection, a boost to morale along the lines of 'I'm definitely doing my bit for the team, look at all the injuries I've got.' In fact John was a born worrier, often fretting about non-existent injuries. As he was preparing for one match, he went through the ritual. Taping up his arthritic finger – later, a plastic knuckle joint was inserted – strapping up a wrist, bandaging a bruised leg, moaning about an ache in his neck. 'Don't bother any more, Ossie,' said Bobby Hope once. 'We'll call the ambulance now – and I'll go in goal.'

One of Ossie's most famous and painful interventions came during an FA Cup quarter-final. The Baggies led 2-1, with Chelsea hunting an equaliser in the last minute. Bodies were being thrown forward and when a high ball landed in the six-yard box, somehow the keeper ended up apparently sitting on the ball, though he later claimed "99% of the pace of the ball was absorbed by a much more sensitive part of my anatomy." Chelsea's Boyle tried to kick both Ossie and ball into the net, and players from both sides piled in, turning the confined area into a passable imitation of the Eton Wall game. Hard men Doug Fraser and John Kaye traded punches with Osgood and his team-mates.

In John's own words "in came the rushing Chelsea players kicking and hacking away. John Boyle was one – he lunged in and caught me somewhere. Biff, bang, wallop, and all of a sudden players were pushing and shoving each other, arms and legs were flying all over the place. As for me, I was still sitting on that darnn ball and no way was I going to let go. The referee blew for full-time, although according to most people, there were still a couple of minutes left to play. The only other thing I remember from that day was that I took the soprano lead in the sing-song on the coach on the way home."

Fans views on John's batterings were mixed. Some were indifferent; others were concerned about whether the team would be hindered. Chris Flanagan was in no doubt. "Ossie's back-from-the-dead heroics after injury were his greatest legacy. So often you'd see John stumbling around in anguish after being trampled on by a couple of cloggers only to scramble the ball away with a floundering lunge. Even when Ossie was down, he was never out. When courage was all that he'd got left, then that was what you got. John Osborne was the business."

Steve Gregory was mindful of his reaction to being hurt. "John wouldn't get shirty or downright aggressive with the perpetrator of the kick, knock or blow. You would be more than likely to see him sitting in the mud, blowing his cheeks out and shaking his crushed fingers or rubbing the bruised part of his body. After receiving a dose of the magic sponge, he would dust himself down and get ready to receive whatever else was to come his way. No whinging, moaning or play-acting. He was honest."

Manager Johnny Giles needed to take a wider view. "At the end of every pre-match talk, I made a point of asking Ossie how he was feeling. Nine times out of ten, he would reply: 'Lousy, terrible, tired, aching or fed up'. I knew then that things were going to be OK." In between mickey taking, the rest of the squad quickly learnt that to get the best out of John, they'd need to gee him up as best they could in the dressing room. The results could be startling. Occasionally, Ossie declared to all that "the opposition won't score today". Once in that frame of mind, he was nearly impossible to beat.

CORNERS WOULD HAVE him jumping around in true 'ants in the pants' fashion, all the while clinging onto one or other of the posts. 'Hyperactive' wasn't the half of it. Then would come the cross, and with it, an instantaneous transformation. Up Ossie would soar above the muck and blood of the goalmouth, attacker and defender alike, slender body breaking every law of gravity in sight to do so, skinny arms thrust skywards above his rapidly-ascending form, and, more often than not, with perfect timing. No fumbles, no indecision; once Ossie had made up his mind that ball was going to be his, that was it. 'Command of his area' they call it now, and in his own fiefdom, Ossie was Field Marshal Montgomery reincarnated. Keepers were afforded relatively little protection in those days, but no matter how desperate (or illegal!) the scramble for the ball, there weren't all that many First Division attackers around with sufficient brute strength to either bundle the lad out of it, or force him into making an error.

He might have looked outwardly frail, did Ossie, but appearances were deceptive. Having won the battle for aerial supremacy, you'd then see both upper limbs curl protectively around his newly-won prize, all the while clutching it to his chest in similar fashion to that of a baby monkey with its mother. Then those darting eyes, once more machine-gunning the opposition. During one fixture, Albion were endlessly under the cosh. Corner after corner went sailing over our goalmouth, and Ossie snuffed them all out, first time, every time. Before too long, it got to the point where you didn't need to be blessed with the gift of telepathy to realise the opposition were all mentally wondering just what they had to do to beat him. As one Black Country wag put it at the time: "It's no good yow doin' that, mate – 'ee 'as them fer cowin' breakfuss!"

And then there were John's goal-kicks – not so much a mundane duty to be performed, more a hallowed ritual. Once the ball had been placed on the correct spot, Ossie would then engage reverse gear. Slowly backing onto one or other of the posts, he'd first give the mud-encrusted studs of one boot an almighty clout on the upright, then the other. That done to his satisfaction, he'd then spit into his gloved hands, rub both together – as neither ever came into contact with the ball at those times, this could only be his eccentricity shining forth – then the run-up, after which boot would swiftly be applied to leather, said ball sent speedily on its way upstream.

ALBION SUPPORTERS have traditionally desired a rapport between themselves and the club goalkeeper. When the club's first ever custodian represents England, a feat followed by at least four more, despite the ever present bias against Midlands footballers, there's a certain standard to be maintained. In the author's initial selection of candidates for this volume, several more were considered such as Alan Miller, Brian "The Beast" Jensen, Stuart "Bruiser" Naylor and Russell Hoult. They all narrowly missed the cut, because of shortcomings in their game.

An Albion outfield crowd favourite must be a damn good player. Once elevated to that rarefied supporter-pleaser status, off-days are fine, even off-months. As Brian Glanville once notably pointed out, goalkeepers are different. Making mistakes, plural, as in more than one, is fatal. Miller was notoriously weak on crosses. "The Beast" often seemed timid for such a big man, while Bruiser Naylor was regularly dropped, additionally being perceived as "a miserable so-and-so" in his early days. The author's limited contact with Stuart actually indicated shyness, a trait he overcome in his later years to become a fine ambassador. Russell Hoult, in the words of the film, "could have been a contender". For several years, chanting his name was a normal part of matchdays. Russell was probably a victim of his time. A friendly, outgoing guy with a keen interest in the opposite sex, his copybook was soaked in later years by a series of clangers in the Baggies second promotion season. Regular mistakes are not acceptable in the modern game, and his elite status crumbled. Awful clangers dogged Tony Godden's career as well and despite an impressive 200 plus consecutive appearances, his fellow players had more confidence in him than did sections of the Albion faithful.

All Albion goalkeepers are expected as a minimum to cheerfully acknowledge the presence of the supporters. To not do so is to generate immediate ill-will, as the unfortunate Paul Whitehead discovered in the late 1990s. Although he was arguably a stronger all-round last line of defence, his refusal to acknowledge his crowd only stoked up antipathy that he was taking the place of favourite Alan Miller. Subsequently, each of Whitehead's few mistakes were loudly booed, his confidence faltered and he quickly left the club.

John Osborne took supporter interaction to a height never seen before or since. He set the gold standard that creates expectations to this day, a mark so high as to draw disbelief from recent Baggies 'keeper Russell Hoult. Russell simply refused to believe descriptions of Ossie's antics.

Turning to the crowd to ask about Villa's score, or to enquire how many minutes remained was quite low-key. Famously he'd regularly cadge fags ("Number 6" were most commonly offered) from Albion supporters, occasionally the opposition. Josie Garbett was regularly on hand to assist Albion's No.1 ease his nerves. "I'd light up a Park Drive for him, and he'd generally managed to puff through half of it before he had to dash off back to the goal." Photographers were a gentler bunch in those days, and there is only limited photographic evidence of John's smoking habit. He was snapped puffing away at Loftus Road in the mid-70s.

On other occasions, John would munch happily on Dairy Milk during the game. Other fans claim to have seen him lunching on a sandwich that he'd hidden in his cap, or even supping from a bottle of beer (widely available without restriction on the terraces until the end of the 60s). During a very one-sided game, Ossie perched himself on the wall behind the Smethwick End goal and talked to fans during the game.

Long time Baggie follower Tim Joyner recalls, "on two occasions I remember him asking the group I was standing with how the Villa were getting on. This as he took up position for the start of the second half of a game, and pulling a face if advised that they were winning. It probably seems insignificant now, but in the eyes of youngsters in their early or pre-teens, for an Albion player to actually speak to you was a major event in itself."

John didn't just charm his own supporters. In April 1970, the Baggies lost heavily, 7-0, at Old Trafford. The home following were trying to wind up the crestfallen keeper, but, game as ever, Ossie was happy to respond in like fashion. After making one save in the second half, he turned and chalked a mark on his post. The United fans loved the gesture, and chanted his name for the rest of the game. At the end of the match, he received as much applause as the home players.

Ossie impressed both sides of Manchester. During Albion's visit to Maine Road in the early 70s, a rather disturbing message was broadcast over the tannoy that the club had received a warning about a bomb in the ground. Anyone who wished to leave could do so. But the football would continue. Albion's goalkeeper theatrically picked up the ball, placed it against his ear, and then shook it.

It's impossible to confirm the veracity of some alleged incidents. Such as for instance, the unlikely exchange recounted by Everton supporter Glenn King. An Evertonian at Goodison bellowed at Ossie, "Hey Osborne, you've got a face like a pan of fried arseholes". To which the ever-jovial Osborne dropped his shorts as if to prove a similarity between his face and his posterior. This is the kind of anecdote that everyone would want to be true and would be punishable by fine and suspension in this day and age. Thankfully there were times when the sheer comedy of such moments was what mattered and this incident has become as much part of the Osborne folklore as those known to be true – another fine example of Cult Hero status, only applicable to the truly great characters.

AFTER THE remarkable high of the 1968 FA Cup Final victory came a series of lows. A long-standing injury was made worse through badly damaging his middle finger during the FA Charity Shield game. Osborne was off the pitch early again as his side were battered 6-1 by Manchester City. Arthritis in a knuckle joint led to a plastic strip being inserted into one of his fingers. The only alternative, and a brutal one, was amputation. John now had another nickname – the "bionic goalkeeper."

The Baggies' attempt to defend their Cup came to an abrupt end in the last few minutes of the 1969 Semi-Final against Leicester City as a mis-hit shot left him clutching thin air. "I think that was the goalkeeper's mistake" carefully pronounced the TV commentator. "I saw Clarkie's shot, much, much too late," confessed Ossie. "The ball flew past me, and I knew we were out." On such mistakes can careers be made or dashed. For someone so horribly aware of the responsibility for a full team of players, to make a fatal mistake in a semi-final presumably led to weeks of private self-recrimination. Yet in public, he maintained his affable persona. Nothing, as far as supporters could tell, seemed to depress him for long.

Managers have all the power over players that Roman Emperors possessed over Christians. Don Howe, appointed to the hot-seat in 1971, did not rate Ossie at all. Equally, nobody rated Don Howe, but he got to make the decisions until even the directors couldn't take any more. The Don Howe era simply wasn't the same WBA Ossie joined. Star men had either left, or were struggling with long-term injuries. Ossie wasn't enjoying participating any longer. "When you get up in the morning thinking, 'Oh, I've got to go down to that bloody place again.' When you get to that stage, it's pointless carrying on."

A brief three-match spell on loan at Walsall was a sharp reminder of the hardships of the lower Leagues. John bailed out, and in partnership with former green shirt rival Jimmy Cumbes, they ran a sports goods shop near Walsall. It seemed as if an era of fun, taciturn humour and no little achievement was over.

AND YET, Ossie continued to turn out occasionally for the Baggies Midlands Intermediate side. After six months out of the game, he decided to have another go. He did so initially on a part-time basis.

During his semi-pro period, he was quoted as saying, regarding his terms of reference, "Oh, I was being paid all right. In fact, for the time I was putting in, I was better paid then Pelé. I literally just turned up on Saturdays. I enjoyed it, though – by heck, I did. We won the Intermediate League and the Cup, and the Cup Final was one of the most fantastic matches I've ever known. We were level after extra time, and there was a right old barney about whether it should be decided on penalties. In the end, most people agreed, and we won it with the 20th penalty. It didn't matter to the other players, because they weren't old enough to drink. But I remember, by the time we'd finished, the blasted pubs were shut."

Howe would only pick Osborne for the first team games no-one could be bothered with – such as the Anglo-Italian tournament. During one game in Italy, John literally had a rude awakening. Asleep in his sixth floor room, he was abruptly awoken by a knock on the door at 2.00am. The balcony door. "Let me in," bellowed team mate Asa Hartford. "Quick! Don Howe's after me." For a serial disturber of other people's rest, the biter was being bit.

THE ARRIVAL OF Johnny Giles in the summer of 1975 gave the boy from Barlborough another go in the limelight at the unlikely age of 35. Osborne was grateful for the second chance. "Johnny Giles was the best player I ever played with or against," wrote an unusually serious Ossie, reflecting on his career in the *Albion News* prior to his testimonial. "I shall remember him for picking me up when I was almost ready to pack the game in, and giving me the opportunity to enjoy the two happiest seasons I've had in my career." Giles introduced disciplined possession football to the Hawthorns, and, as if to boost Osborne's confidence, he sold fellow keeper Latchford. After an uncertain start on his return to first team action, the Baggies just stopped conceding goals. The veteran keeper played in every match of the 1975/76 season, setting a new club record for clean sheets.

Albion had to win their last match at Oldham to pip Bolton to promotion. The Baggies' blueprint was to work furiously, concede very few goals, score just enough and be consistent. This was the same blueprint subsequently used by Gary Megson and on both occasions, a faltering Wanderers side enabled them to sprint ahead at the finish line. Twelve thousand supporters marched on Boundary Park, outnumbering the home support. Tony 'Bomber' Brown poached a vital second half goal, and a late save from the resolute keeper had the Baggies heading for the top division after three seasons away. 'Bomber' Brown and John Osborne both became members of an elite of Albion men who'd won both promotion and the FA Cup in the process.

AND IT WAS this time, even more than the preceding involvement in FA Cup triumph and regular top flight competition, which sealed Ossie's place in Albion fans' hearts.

Tim Joyner again: "in the eyes of my friends and I, starry-eyed 14 year-olds, the first impression of John Osborne was of how old he looked, he was tall and gangly and never gave the impression of being particularly quick-moving, or even match-fit which made him an unusual candidate for such a popular player, one who never seemed to fit the 1970s footballer caricature of being flash, brash and confident. I think it would be fair to say that in his mid-30s, Ossie actually could have passed for a 45 year-old."

Ossie happily admitted that he was born old, and fashion had nothing to do with him. In addition, the lack of teeth and general scruffy demeanour created some kind of empathy with supporters. If this tatty-looking individual could play football in his middle age, maybe they could as well. Of course, few could equal Ossie's deftness in plucking awkward crosses from the air and fewer still were willing to hurl themselves bodily at a striker's boot to grab a football. He might have been an absolute bundle of nerves in the dressing-room beforehand, but out there on the pitch, with the opposition chucking everything they could, legal or otherwise, in the direction of our goalmouth, and all the while gaining the upper hand, you'd see in Ossie an instantaneous transformation. Then, he was ice-cold calm itself, all pin-sharp reaction times, constantly swooping and diving for goal-bound balls in similar fashion to that of the tiny feathered creatures he came to know and love, back in those familiar Derbyshire hills of his childhood.

Former fanzine editor Glynis Wright had her own thoughts: "think of Ossie now, and immediately, a mental image of *Star Trek's* Mr. Spock comes charging into my head. Why? One reason springs readily to mind; around the time John first assumed his Albion custodial duties, BBC1 were giving the first episodes of Gene Rodenberry's sci-fi masterpiece an early-evening airing – but that's not the whole story. The thing was, take away the pointy ears, the deadpan logic, and in Leonard Nimoy, you had a dead-ringer for our keeper. I'm not sure whether it was the lined, hollow cheeks, and toothless matchday grin that did it, or the pointy facial features, but the resemblance was distinctly uncanny, to say the least. Or was it his horribly gaunt and dishevelled appearance, I wonder? Certainly, the moment my mother first clapped eyes upon him, her immediate reaction was, "Bloody 'ell, that Ossie Wossie bloke, 'ee looks 'arf clammed to jeth – needs a cowin' good feed in 'is bally, 'ee does… An a decent suit ter wear." Always had a way with words, did my mum, bless her: spot on, first time."

John retained his place for much of the first season in the top flight, despite his advancing years. Early on, league leaders Manchester United came to The Hawthorns. Giles put Albion ahead, but United were awarded a penalty and a chance to equalise. Ossie, who rarely saved penalties, was up against Irish international Gerry Daly, who was reputed never to have missed one. Daly placed his shot low to the keeper's left, but Ossie, remembering the thoughts of Lev Yashin, guessed correctly and saved. Albion went on to win 4-0.

THE BAGGIES were on the receiving end of the occasional hammering that term. Worst of these was a 7-0 mauling at Portman Road. In his later years, Ossie confessed that because he was enduring yet another injury (a bruised shoulder) and was so fed up, he didn't even try to block Whymark's long range shot for the home side's final goal. Towards the end of the season, Albion dropped only two points in nine games, prompting hopes of a UEFA Cup spot. They went to White Hart Lane with both Osborne, and understudy Bob Ward injured. Manager Giles gave a debut to a youngster called Tony Godden (Laurie Cunningham also made his debut that day). Godden made an instant impact, conceding only five goals in six matches. Yet on 9 April for the visit of Arsenal, Giles dropped Godden, giving Ossie the green shirt instead.

It was said that Godden needed to be rested due to his inexperience, but it resulted in something rarely seen at the Shrine, as the Brummie road end split into two factions, one favouring Godden, the other Osborne. "Tony, Tony Godden" bellowed one faction. "John Osborne, John Osborne" responded the other. There was some variation as "Godden – Osborne", "Godden – Osborne" echoed across the ground. And so it continued through the game until Ossie boobed, and the Gunners took the lead." Ossie is shit, Ossie is shit" roared the Godden faction, and the atmosphere became quite hostile. Osborne looked rather bemused by this, but a few minutes later, he pulled off a flying save and a unanimous chorus of "John Osborne, John Osborne" echoed around the Hawthorns. John took a bow and the hostility melted away instantly. He'd won the crowd over again, as arguably only he could, and he kept his place for the rest of the season, despite Arsenal winning that game 2-0.

Godden's elevation was inevitable. Talking to Dave Horridge of the *Daily Mirror*, John was philosophical. "I have known for some time that Albion were looking for a good, reliable goalkeeper to do a job in the reserves. Now they have got one – ME!" Ossie decided to retire at the age of 38.

His testimonial against a Johnny Giles Select XI raised £32,000, a record up to that time for a Midlands player. Over 12,000 Baggie people were keen to show their appreciation in what was the third biggest turn out for an Albion player testimonial since the war, behind only Norman Heath and Bobby Hope. Twelve thousand people plus a horse... Red Rum was paraded around the running track. Since that day, something of a myth has built up that Red Rum raced Willie Johnston the full length of the Hawthorns pitch. A lovely idea, but not true. Still, the famous racehorse did at least have a song in his honour. The Brummie Road End, in their own version of a popular chant of the time "Referee, referee, your old lady is a whore", offered

> "Red Rum,
> Red Rum,
> Your old lady is a horse
> Your old lady is a horse."

John was at his most adventurous that night. During one Albion attack, Ossie retrieved a bog roll that had been thrown onto the pitch, placed it on the penalty spot and promptly "scored". At the end of the game, there was a mass pitch invasion. Hundreds of Albion supporters performed the Dying Fly (a feature of the cult TV programme *TISWAS*) in the Brummie Road penalty area. It was a fitting end to Ossie's Baggies career.

JOHN CONTINUED to play football for anyone who would have him. He turned out for the Albion Old Stars and the Birmingham Post and Mail Rangers. Indeed, he was up for a game anywhere.

Albion supporter John Clegg recalls "He played for us once in the Warley Press team, after he'd retired, against the Warley Parks department (sorry, Sandwell Recreation And Amenities Division). We snuck him in because he was working for the *Sandwell Mail*, in the circulation department. He got through about ten tabs during the game, and blagged a Player's Number Six (plain, of course, brown packet) off me at half-time. It was men against boys. Those cheating council workers even had Dale Best from Watford in midfield. But we had Ossie, and we won 3-0."

John then moved on to Worcestershire Country Cricket Club as their Commercial Manager. He stayed there for nine years and his popularity remained undimmed. A walk around the boundary would inevitably mean stopping every few yards for an autograph or a chat.

Ossie briefly managed a non-League outfit called Colinthians 83. "My idea of management was to get 11 lads at the same ground at the same time. I was sub 18 times because we only had the 11 players. We entered the Midland Combination, but had to come out because we couldn't afford the fines. We got fined for everything. One time we kicked off with just four players and got fined £15 per player short. They were good times. Do you know that one year after I left 'em, they won the League?" Delightfully chaotic, but it worked, and it was fun. Perhaps that's a fair epithet to describe John's footballing career.

WILLIE JOHNSTON

1972-1979

BAGGIES CAREER

Games	261
Goals	28
Caps	13

MAGIC MOMENT

Wearing a bank robber's mask during a pre-match warm up, causing hilarity on the terraces and creating a legend which lives on today

'WILLIE'

HEARTWARMING pleasure comes at a price, as Albion full-back Ray Wilson pointed out: "Willie was a great entertainer, but he wasn't easy to play behind. I'd try overlapping when Willie had the ball. I had 30, 40 yards to cover while he was beating a couple of players, and when I'd got level with him, I'd say, "Willie. Now... Now... NOW!" But Willie was busy beating the opposition, and then sometimes he'd lose it, with me in front of him." Team-mate Joe Mayo was also in the queue for Willie's attention. "I'd be up front waiting for him to cross... and waiting, and waiting. He didn't know himself what he was going to do most of the time, so what chance did the rest of us have?" But Ray and Joe, and no doubt the rest of the side, were unable to vent frustration at length. How can any larger-than-life character or lovable rogue be resisted for long? Willie was life.

Willie's explanation was simple. "People want entertainment. A man taking his wife and family to the match on Saturdays pay big money, they want to be entertained – it was so easy. The manager would say, "get the ball over" and I thought I'd get it over when I'm good and ready. Besides, there were so many players in the team who would never, ever release the ball – Tony Brown, Len Cantello – if Tony Brown got the ball, he would shoot rather than pass it – and Len Cantello was the same. If I got the ball, I'd hang onto it, because I knew it would be ages before I would get it again."

Another Albion stalwart, and fellow Scot Ally Robertson did his best to support his fellow countryman. "People loved him because he was a one-off. You'll never see someone in the game like that now. Willie was a hero for me because he was a Glasgow Rangers supporter who played. I couldn't believe he was coming to West Brom. The first day he was in our dressing room, I was saying to him "You're my hero," and he was just looking at me. And I was still so excited I even offered to polish his boots... It probably took me three months to realise he was Willie Johnston, one of our players. I'd put him on a pedestal up there somewhere."

Goalkeeper John Osborne's initial memories came from a different perspective. "When we heard about the signing – it was big money for the Albion in those days – the first thing we thought of was his reputation. He'd been sent off more times than anybody else, and all that. I expected to see this huge raving lunatic at training. The following morning, there were just the normal faces. 'I thought Willie Johnston was starting today?' I said. 'He is. He's right over there.' And sitting right in the corner was this little lost lad."

Meanwhile on the terraces, supporter Steve Sant also had doubts. Big ones. "I was dumbstruck with the Willie Johnston signing. He had the kind of reputation that Lee Bowyer or Craig Bellamy have today. He was trouble. He got sent off so many times that his cumulative bans saw him sitting out huge chunks of the Scottish season. Word was he was a clever player who would rather sit in the pub than train, and had a vicious temper that got him into trouble both on and off the pitch. That strict disciplinarian Don Howe had signed him made the whole thing a bit bizarre."

The Scot came with a CV both impressive and alarming. Although born in Glasgow, Willie spent his childhood days in Fife (on the East coast of Scotland, next to Edinburgh). His father was a miner, and Willie did experience the travails of the local pit for several months before offers of an easier working life came his way. His nearest club, Raith Rovers, wanted to sign him. So too did Manchester United, who took him and his Dad to Old Trafford for a fortnight. But once the mighty Rangers indicated their interest, nothing else would do. Willie joined his boyhood club in February 1964.

Although the winger was something of a late starter, he was mightily quick in making up ground. Barely five months later, he had a League Cup winners' medal to his name, and this before he was legally old enough to drink. His status continued to rise, and by the following year, he was playing for his country against Poland.

"Bud", as he quickly became known, was a big hit. He played initially as a central striker, including being paired with one Alex Ferguson, before moving later into a wider position. His goal scoring record was highly impressive, averaging almost a goal in every three of his 200 games. Topping the list of his many achievements was scoring twice in the 1972 European Cup Winners Cup Final, when his side just held off Moscow Dynamo 3-2.

On the down side, Willie received his first dismissal in January 1969, with two more following within six months. His fourth early bath merited a three-week ban; his fifth six weeks: and then swinging a right hook at Alex Forsyth of Partick Thistle, in September 1972, earning him that infamous near ten-week final cooling off period immediately prior to his move to Albion.

THE HAWTHORNS was a culture shock for the winger. On his first day, Willie travelled down in the morning, and then trained in the afternoon. Don's first command was to insist upon 20 "quick" laps of the ground over hurdles with the rest of the players. "Anyone who finishes behind Brian Whitehouse (the trainer) will have to come back tonight." Willie had just completed another suspension, so "I'd nae trained, so I wasnae fit." Willie finished five laps behind Whitehouse, with several other first teamers also trailing in after the trainer. Protestations that this was his first day, and he'd only just arrived from Scotland, fell on deaf ears. Welcome to West Bromwich!

The transfer was a protracted one, "probably one of the longest transfer deals on record," claimed the *Albion News*. That Albion wanted the winger was clear: manager Don Howe travelled North four times to clinch the deal, although, according to the player himself, during none of those trips did Howe actually see him play. The fee agreed with Rangers was £135,000, a new club record.

Instinctively, Johnston didn't want to leave Rangers or Scotland. His reluctance to join a relegation struggle in a foreign country was understandable, but there were several very clear pointers that it was time to move. Any more sendings-off, and the Scottish Football Association would be likely to re-introduce hanging and flogging, just for him. In addition, Rangers' manager Jock Wallace had made it abundantly clear that he was no longer wanted at Ibrox. Willie had a long-standing grievance that the Gers were not paying him the same as other members of the squad. The Albion offer was an impressive increase on his current salary, so with much reluctance, he signed for the English club on 1 December 1972.

Rarely has one player's house evoked so many memories for so many people. The property, in Dunchurch Crescent, Sutton Coldfield, was always likely to stand apart from the rest, primarily because Willie bought it from the universally detested Bobby Gould. One wonders quite what state the house was in when the Johnston family (wife Margaret, plus five year-old Stephanie, and three year-old Dean) moved in. Local supporter and scout Alan Sherwood recalls calling at Gould Towers during 'Bob A Job Week', a then-annual event when scouts would do menial jobs for anyone in exchange for a shilling (5p). Gould had the young scout washing his orange and black Ford Capri – which, Alan noted, was exactly the same colour scheme as the house. Gould departed to Bristol City within a couple of weeks of the Scot's arrival, so the Johnston family's Vauxhall Viva replaced Gould's Capri, although Margaret Johnston was to do all the driving.

Albion regular Andy Jenkins recalled how he and his Dad would pass the time of day with Willie, whose major concern was that the local golf courses didn't match up to the ones he'd used in Scotland, Willie having played Troon, St. Andrew's, Gleneagles, and all the other top Scottish courses. The Johnston's neighbour was great uncle to another young West Bromwich enthusiast, Mark Hitcox. "I remember going over there in 1973, ten years-old, totally in awe of this man, who came out, knew my name, and then played 'shots-in' (with Willie as the goalie) with me and my oldest sister!"

Fred Gill worked for Sutton Council rates department, in the days of home visits. He had to call on Willie the day after Kenny Burns of Birmingham City had been sent off yet again for punching an opponent. Willie, who was not exactly renowned for turning the other cheek himself, used words to the effect of, "Oh, he's an absolute hothead!"

Willie made his debut at home to Liverpool. Sometimes, there's a collective decision made by supporters that a player will be popular before he even takes the pitch, and Willie fell into that category. The Baggies were at the wrong end of the table, the King was out injured, and so the new winger was hailed as a Messiah. His debut was a quiet one. A week later, his cross set up a late consolation goal for Bomber in his second game at Highbury. And then… not much really. Supporter Steve Sant again, "I recall his first few games as being something of an anti-climax; he just played, and not all that well as a conventional winger. He had a few tricks, but they seldom came off, and he appeared a bit bored with the whole thing."

STRUGGLING ALBION managed only two wins in Johnston's first 16 League games. These were difficult moments for both club and homesick Scot. "There were times," says Willie, "when I felt like the man who had never tasted Tartan special." The winger needed more involvement, more goals. He'd scored 60 for Rangers, and was used to roaming freely across the front line. At WBA, the wide man played 22 times without any goals at all, always wide and in a set pattern, as strictly prescribed by the manager. The one man who could really benefit from his crosses, Jeff Astle, had cartilage problems and couldn't play for three months. Even then, this wasn't the real King, and the newcomer had difficulty in building a relationship on or off the field, as the Scot explains: "When I first arrived, Jeff Astle and I used to greet one another every morning before training – but for the first month or so, I never knew exactly what Jeff said – and he never knew what I had said either."

But the real Willie surfaced occasionally. "He was warming up on the pitch a few weeks after joining Albion from Rangers," recalled Brummie Road regular Tim Joyner, then 12 years-old. "He noticed my friends and me watching, and kicked the ball high into the air towards the front of the terrace where we were standing. I can still see him laughing as we all ran for cover with expressions of terror on our faces."

With only 38 goals to their name, and an endless litany of defeats, including the crucial last four matches, Albion finished bottom of Division One. Relegation came as a terrible blow for West Bromwich supporters. The Baggies had been in the top division since 1949, and success, admittedly more in Cup competitions, was thought of as the norm.

Life started well in the Second Division, with wins in the first two games, and then errr... another victory in the thirteenth game. West Bromwich were too inconsistent to truly threaten the leaders, finishing three wins behind promoted Luton Town. Albion's Scottish winger was, however, finally making his mark. Willie added to his total of dismissals by being sent off against Swindon in September. "One defender persisted in trying to perform open surgery on my legs with his studs, and I eventually reacted by lifting my hands," wrote Willie in his biography *On the Wing*. Predictably, he was banned for three matches.

The season had few other highlights. Johnston's first Cup goal came against Exeter in October, glancing home John Wile's pass, but Albion lost in embarrassing fashion in the League Cup to their Fourth Division opposition. Two more months were to pass before Willie finally found the net in the League, one of only two goals that term. There was a double over Villa to celebrate, and a 1-0 victory, in a replay, over Everton in the FA Cup. Nearly all the healthy 27,000 crowd at the Hawthorns enjoyed the tense closing stages, even though both sides were down to ten men. Willie had been sent off again – for retaliation on Archie Styles, who also walked for the original foul. Supporters forgave him because he was, by then, firmly seated upon an untouchable pedestal, beyond criticism. Not so Don Howe.

WILLIE WAS FAST, reckless, a showman – and when he wanted to be, quite brilliant. In short, everything that Don Howe was not as a manager. With Jeff Astle forced to hang up his boots after just five more appearances, it was Willie upon whom the dreams of the Birmingham Road End rested, and they egged him on. "The King is dead – Long Live The King!"

Supporters like John Goddard loved his performances, and just wanted more. "Willie loved to take on the opposing full-back. He was a real left-winger, fast over short distances, with a tremendous left foot to put pinpoint crosses into the box. He loved getting to the goal-line before putting in a cross, or trying to beat the full-back again with close possession and tricky dribbling." One of the winger's party pieces was trying to control the goalkeeper's drop kicks on the half-volley with his behind. Always very entertaining, but rarely successful, and guaranteed to irritate the hell out of Howe – not to mention Cloughie.

At least some of his team-mates tacitly encouraged Willie The Showman. Ally Robertson again: "Being a West Brom player, we were always brought up to play football, and to me, Willie was that type – he wanted to please the crowd. We could be getting beaten 7-0, and Willie would still be Willie. He'd be doing his tricks, anything to please the crowd. That's what fans wanted to see. Pity you couldn't have ten Willies in your side. You might not win a lot, and you'd have a few sent off, but…"

As Willie said himself, "We had a great dressing room, the lads were always daring one another to do things – I was the one who was always agreeing to do the dares!" Such as the infamous mask. Prior to the last home match of the 1973/74 season, Willie accepted a £25 bet (equivalent then to two terrace season tickets) to wear a bank robber's mask during the referee's inspection and kick-about. During said inspection, he cunningly had a shirt over his head – and this being a 'nothing-on-it' end-of-season fixture against Luton, the bemasked Johnston dramatically lifted the mood on the terraces. Photographer Laurie Rampling was fortunately on hand to capture one of the iconic moments of recent Albion social history. The upbeat frame of mind also infected the players. Only Don Howe, unsurprisingly, didn't get it. He was furious with his record signing. "This is the sort of standard we've got at this club…" he bellowed, not for the first time totally misjudging where the hearts of supporters lay.

More money exchanged hands when the Scotsman accepted a bet to streak after training, along the old wooden Halfords Lane stand and onto the pitch. Once more, there was a photographer on hand to preserve one naked male body for eternity.

THESE WERE GRIM times to be a Baggie, the grimmest for several decades. Supporters generally disliked the dour Howe, with his emphasis on careful defence and the eradication of mistakes; they yearned instead for the Baggies' traditional game of attacking football and excitement. Willie was their only hope. "Willie, Willie Johnston, Willie Johnston on the wing…" was a song of praise, but also of hope. Even today, in dull times, the anthem is occasionally aired, and instantly recognised by all. There can be no greater measure of a hero's longevity at a football club than if people who were not even born when a player was in his pomp exalt his name as the saviour in times of woe.

The players had no more regard for Howe than the supporters, but they were obliged to both listen and respond to him. The credibility of the former England international was damaged by some particularly offbeat training exercises, including the notorious episode involving tethering three senior midfielders together with a length of rope in order to boost their co-ordination. Not surprisingly, maverick Johnston was one of his biggest critics. "If games were won on a blackboard, Don Howe would have won the World Cup," he sniffs.

The new 1974/75 season meandered along much like the previous one, with Albion rarely able to keep pace with the front-runners. Defeat at Villa Park in March was the final straw: apathy was setting in, with gates of only ten or eleven thousand commonplace. There were more goals for the winger this time, seven in all, sufficient to make him third top scorer behind Tony Brown (12), and Joe Mayo (8). And to no-one's great surprise, there was another early bath, at home to Bristol City, in November. Willie maintained a robust defence. "Before the match, you've got a six foot Neanderthal telling you they're going to kill you on the pitch, and when you get on there, the first tackle is just below the knee, then in comes the second – just above the knee – it's very hard not to react."

The winger was often quick to react, such as another red card in an away match at Ninian Park. But there was a curious tale behind this loss of temper. The side had travelled on Friday afternoon and were encouraged to spend the evening in a local cinema. A new film, *Emmanuelle*, was showing, so naturally, the all-male party had to go in. Their fellow watchers within the auditorium seemed to have trouble finding something in their pockets. The following day, by remarkable coincidence, the opponent who so annoyed Willie was called Emmanuel. A photographer got a picture of the incident (again!), and there was Emmanuel, down on all fours, with Willie standing over him, and it looked ever so sexual…

Albion's extrovert wide man was always up for enlivening proceedings. Supporter Peter Smith recalls a match at Craven Cottage: "The ball went into a sparsely populated area of the terrace, but no-one seemed willing to retrieve it, so Willie jumped over the fence himself. A few young kids ran over to him, so he dribbled the ball in and out of them for 20 seconds or so – they just couldn't get it off him. He then chipped the ball onto the pitch, and took the throw-in. The crowd went mad!"

With gates now down to 8,000, the Albion Board finally made a decision. They refused to extend the manager's contract, and suitably piqued, Howe resigned immediately, with four games remaining. His reign wasn't all bad. He introduced a modern physiotherapist, George Wright, who was quietly responsible for extending several players' careers. Howe also put together a squad not lacking in talent: furthermore, under his tutelage, Albion's youth set-up had blossomed. Indeed, in those four remaining games, caretaker manager Brian Whitehouse blooded an unknown youngster called Bryan Robson.

THE NEXT MANAGER, Johnny Giles, was to smoothly take the club back to where they felt they truly belonged. Giles had been there and done it as a midfielder with Matt Busby's Manchester United and Don Revie's Leeds, and was prepared to lead from the front. Every player responded to the player-manager Irishman, and, after a shaky start, an 11-game unbeaten run provided the initial momentum for a real promotion challenge. Goalscoring remained a problem for Albion (Ally Brown top scored with a paltry ten), but, significantly, it was far more of a problem for the opposition, because Albion rarely permitted them to score.

Willie contributed six goals, including one at Blackpool that *Star Soccer* (ITV's response to *Match of the Day*) chose as Goal of the Season – it was the only goal of the match, a typical darting run before beating the goalkeeper from 25 yards. "We worked with the ball nearly all the time," said Willie, many years later. "Johnny was an intelligent manager, a majestic and graceful player, and a great guy. The man was a tonic." Giles was also sent off at Luton for a hatchet job on Futcher, a former opponent, with whom he wanted to settle a score. You might say Willie and Johnny understood each other better after that, despite their different religions. Some elements of the press attempted to make capital upon the fact that one was an Irish Catholic and the other a Scottish Protestant, but neither man considered their differing faith a barrier. Willie was still Willie. His more famous antics that term included trapping the ball by sitting on it (a not unfamiliar move at Ibrox where it became known as "Doing a Bud"), and picking a fight with a linesman over a throw in.

Every Albion supporter has a favourite Willie story. Mark Pumphrey's tale occurred at home to Notts County, "who were sporting a yellow kit with a green penguin stripe down the front and back. It was an autumnal midweek match, and my Dad and I sat in the old Halfords

Lane stand — wooden benches, pipe smoke, I can see it as plain as day. Willie Johnston was giving Brian Stubbs the run around all game, and we were right on the touchline, and able to hear his "frustration". Inevitably, Stubbs scythed Willie down, and I remember my Dad and I looking at each other and expecting Johnston to be sent off any second for retaliating. Instead, our premier Scottish entertainer jumped onto the back of his assailant, and Stubbs gave him a piggy-back up and down the touchline, with Willie pretending to whip him like a horse. I remember the crowd roaring them on, and my old man's face was a picture. He's in his 70s now, and may forget a few things... but he never forgets that moment."

Years of poor gates had taken their toll on the Hawthorns coffers. The club were encouraging supporters to enter a sponsored walk in October 1975, so as to raise money for them, claiming they required 22,000 gates to break even. Until mid November, they were marooned around the 10,000 mark, and although attendances picked up steadily after this point, Giles had to boost his ranks with either home-grown youngsters or old, cheap players, inevitably Irish. Nevertheless, cut-price Albion determinedly made the most of wobbling Wanderers, of the Bolton variety, who were struggling to maintain their promotion spot. West Bromwich reeled them in game by game, amid mounting tension. In the end, it came down to a genuine 'must-win' last game at Oldham.

In a tight, tense match, with visiting hordes making up the majority of the 22,000 crowd, a second-half Tony Brown goal was just enough. A predictable pitch invasion followed, with thousands of jubilant Baggies demanding their team should re-appear. Of course they did!

Yet more extraordinary scenes followed on the way home, with the team bus royally escorted all the way along the M6 by a phalanx of 120 supporters' coaches. An obviously tired and emotional Willie gave the royal wave to all and sundry, wearing the most devilish ear splitting grin as he did it. As his wise old team-mate, John Osborne, pronounced "Willie was the softest little bugger I've met – until he had four pints of lager inside him."

BACK IN THE big time, Albion's favourite would have a far more realistic chance of playing for his country once more. He'd been ignored since November 1970, but Division One football, combined with his best form, and not being sent off since 1974, proved a powerful trio. Willie, being Willie, just had to press the self-destruct button in the League Cup. After a marvellous display against Liverpool, instrumental in defeating the Merseysiders 1-0 (some supporters swear to this day that he'd terrorised full-back Phil Neal so much that he was reduced to tears), the winger was spectacularly sent off against Brighton in the next round, because he aimed a kick at the referee's bottom. West Bromwich supporters didn't know whether to laugh or cry – so did both. Willie had varying explanations, depending upon alcohol intake. "He had me in such a rage with his cowardice..." or the far more Willy-ish, "He just wouldn't get out of the way..." Johnston picked up a £100 fine, and a five-match ban from the League, with a club punishment on top. His fourth dismissal with WBA set new club records, both numerically and for variety of competition.

Other than suspensions, Willie rarely missed games for any other reason. Remarkable, considering the treatment he regularly received from opponents he so often frustrated and teased. Even so, a break from the routine of training and playing was very welcome, which was why, come January, Albion would often treat the players to a few days in Torquay. They were encouraged to relax with the odd beer, but life was never straightforward with a certain

Scottish winger around. He carried copious quantities of farting powder, and everybody's drinks were fair game. Old hands also learned to watch out for near-empty beer glasses that mysteriously and quickly filled themselves with a liquid that was warm to the touch...

One night, the players dressed up for an evening out. Willie, predictably different, wore a kilt. He told his colleagues to watch him carefully, and soon enough, two bold girls asked, "What's under your kilt?"

"Why don't you have a look?" teased Willie.

So one of them did ...only to find a large plastic extension to Willie's willy. The girls retired giggling, and soon there was a procession, all wishing to peer under his kilt. Pure Willie.

Many years later, I asked him, if he had his Albion time over again, would he have done things differently? Willie was quite clear. "If I was playing today, I'd still have done the same things. Whether I would have got away with them is another matter! Being at the Albion was always more than just a job. My times there were the best years of my life. I was never interested in taking big cash offers from elsewhere, because West Brom were such a great club."

The Baggies adapted surprisingly well to the pressures of the top league. Their goalscoring problem was eased considerably by the arrival of Ray Treacy, David Cross, and latterly, Laurie Cunningham. Although no-one realised it at the time, the club had just signed Willie's replacement. Cunningham, in the absence of anyone else being fit, started his Albion career as a central striker, his six goals playing a significant part in Albion striving for – and only just missing out on – a UEFA Cup spot.

Willie only managed a single goal himself, but his all round contribution was mighty. Having a target man (Cross) to aim at made a difference, and his consistency was such that he received a call to join his country against Sweden, in 1977, his first cap for nearly seven years. Once back in the fold, Willie retained his place, playing in all the Home Internationals (a then popular round-robin tournament between the four home nations), and Scotland's summer tour of South America in preparation for the 1978 World Cup in Argentina.

These were exciting times for both Willie and his favourite English club. Johnny Giles had sadly departed, but led by Ronnie Allen, the Baggies carried on right from where they'd left off. Allen then introduced Cyrille Regis to the first team – and now, they were not afraid of anybody. Regis's power, allied to the trickery of Cunningham and Johnston, the emerging Bryan Robson, and the solid defence made for a powerful team. Albion lost only two of their first twelve matches.

Fan Lloyd Fletcher was among the hordes thrilled by the attacking splendours on offer. Cunningham and Johnston both featured against Manchester United in October 1977. Lloyd takes up the story: "Cunningham hadn't had that great a game, but with the score at 3-0, Johnston and Mulligan overlapped in classic fashion on the right. Paddy Mulligan put in a fierce cross from the goal line, and Laurie Cunningham volleyed it in at the near post. I have several fond and vivid memories of this. Thrashing United 4-0 for the second season in a row was a thrill in itself, but I also remember Laurie being enveloped by his colleagues (physically) and the crowd (emotionally), both for putting the icing on that cake, and redeeming his performance in great style.

And best of all, Willie celebrating near the side-line, standing still with arms aloft, was suddenly bear-hugged from behind by an old guy in a flat cap and trench coat! There was that moment of connection between the crowd, and two of our heroes; the fan on the pitch was like an emissary for those of us in the stands who just wanted to join in the jubilation of hugging those on the pitch. I think it was essential that this was an "ordinary" fan, not a youngster in baggy trousers and denim jacket - it seemed to make the moment even more poignant."

The Scot was now at his swaying, speedy best, buoyed by international recognition, having played in all the crucial qualifying matches as Scotland reached the finals of the 1978 World Cup. Willie had another new Albion record – the Baggies' most-capped Scottish player – and now he felt like he could take on the world, or even Middlesbrough defenders, as another Brummie Road-Ender, John Goddard, recalls: "I will never forget the time he terrorised a Middlesbrough full-back all match, beating him repeatedly. Willie reached the goal line at the Brummie Road End/Halfords Lane, and just stopped the ball. He put his foot on it, and gestured to the full-back with both hands to come and take it off him. It was typical Willie; he loved playing to the crowd. The full-back stood only a yard away, but refused to move, as he knew the winger would beat him again. Great theatre."

Thousands of Albion supporters were by now wearing tartan in homage to their favourite. Willie loved the attention, and played up to the crowd whenever he could, such as signing autographs in the Rainbow Stand paddock (the forerunner to the East Stand) during play.

There was a coterie of smokers in the first team squad that season. Other than Willie himself, Cyrille Regis, Ally Robertson, John Osborne, Derek Statham and Len Cantello all enjoyed the dreaded weed, but one day, Chairman Bert Millichip made a decision to ban smoking on the coach. "An' the boss said if the Chairman don't like it, we can't do it."

The players wondered what they could do. They tried placing the smokers at the front, and leaving the door open. That didn't work because the bus was going too fast, so the smoke just blew back again. Eventually, a compromise was reached: the players could have a smoke in the dressing room prior to the match, and at half-time. The result, according to the winger, was a stream of players "at quarter to three going intae the toilet for a quick drag. I even used to see players stubbin' 'em oot in the tunnel."

Despite carelessly losing another manager by not offering him a contract, Albion still managed to combine their UEFA Cup place chase with an FA Cup run. An away Fourth Round draw at Old Trafford against the Cup holders was a big ask, and yet the Baggies so nearly won at the first time of asking. United couldn't cope with their visitors' lightning counter-attacking game. It was Willie who scored, although he was quick to admit afterwards, "it was a bit of an accident. I went to nip it under Roche, but I hit it a bit too hard, and it rolled across the line. We'll murder them in the replay though – they were lucky today." (United equalised in the last minute when the ball crossed the line via the back of goalkeeper Godden's head).

United weren't murdered in the re-match, but the Baggies did triumph 3-2 after extra time in a remarkable encounter. Twice crosses from Willie set up Albion goals, and twice United retaliated, Regis scoring the crucial overtime goal. After overcoming Derby 3-2, including another goal from Willie, West Bromwich were in unchartered waters. They hadn't reached the last eight for nine years. To their horror, they pulled out domestic treble-chasers Nottingham Forest in the draw. Still, there was always Willie. He took to the field sporting a tartan bonnet. Tension, what tension? The Baggies won 2-0, with the winger showing his style by using his bottom once more to trap the ball. Not to mention a booking after an altercation with Archie Gemmill.

After such triumphs, surely West Bromwich Albion were Wembley-bound? New manager Ron Atkinson thought so, allowing the BBC to film him lifting the FA Cup. Predictably peeved, semi-final opponents Ipswich girded their loins, and hit Albion like a tornado. Nothing went right that afternoon, as their Suffolk opponents just would not let them play. Worse, Willie received a bad shoulder injury that left him little more than a passenger. Albion, 2-1 down, were chasing the game when Mick Martin was sent off for two bookable offences. Town scored a third and the FA Cup was over for the Baggies.

So, too, was the season for Willie, hampered by his shoulder complaint. He sat out the last seven games with Laurie Cunningham ominously standing in for him on the wing. Four games were won, and two drawn, sufficient for sixth spot, and a place in Europe.

AND SO TO Argentina. Famously, after their first match in the tournament (lost 3-1 to Peru), Johnston, along with Kenny Dalglish, were selected for the random drugs test. To this day, Willie maintains that the Albion club doctor, Dr Rimmer, had given him two reactivan pills to treat a cold. Because he'd been given them before, he saw no need to declare their use, but reactivan includes a stimulant called fencamsamin; it was this stimulant that would make Willie headline news all around the world. The winger was sent home in disgrace. In that era, the concept of professional sportsmen taking stimulants, either knowingly or inadvertently, was still a relatively new one. The Scottish FA banned him for life, while hostile tabloids made hay. Privately, his fellow professionals were hugely sympathetic, at least two of his team-mates admitting later that they'd also popped the same type of pills. Ally Robertson summed up the professionals' response "reactivan wasn't a drug to us, it was just a cold cure, and was blown up out of all proportion."

Willie was mentally shattered. Scorn and opprobrium poured on his head. 'Junkie' and much worse were hurled at him, both on the field and off it, his children also suffering at school. It was all too much for the unsophisticated Willie. Albion tried their best by giving him a new four-year deal, which would give him security until he was 36. Albion supporters gave their best shot too, cheering his every move, even when he was on the bench. But it wasn't enough. Laurie Cunningham had his shirt, and Willie's heart just wasn't in it any more. By Christmas, the Scot had made only eight appearances.

He requested a transfer. It was turned down. Willie asked again. It was refused once more, but in the long term, there was little value in keeping an unsettled out-of-form reserve player. Willie made one last hurrah, coming off the bench to replace Regis in a 1-0 victory over Chelsea in March, his 261st and last appearance in an Albion shirt.

ALTHOUGH OTHER English clubs had expressed an interest, it was the £100,000 offer from Vancouver Whitecaps that appealed, offering a fresh start in a different country. Playing in the North American Soccer League (NASL) did wonders for the winger, who responded favourably to admiration from supporters. With "World Cup Willie" (as he became known) featuring prominently, the Whitecaps went on to win the Soccerbowl (the NASL equivalent of the League and Cup rolled into one).

In between NASL seasons, he was permitted a five month loan spell back in the West Midlands, at Birmingham City. Although nearly all their fixtures clashed with those of the Baggies, numerous Albion supporters took in the odd game at St. Andrew's for nostalgic reasons, just to see Willie once more in full flight. Frank Worthington was in the same side, so not surprisingly; he and Willie were an entertaining double act on and off the pitch.

Among the Black Country spectating contingent was former team-mate Joe Mayo. "My mother loved Willie. I took her to see Blues play once. Willie didn't do anything all night other than one nutmeg. After the game, we went into the players' lounge and my mother asked if I could introduce her to Willie. So I did, knowing that Willie's always polite in these situations, particularly to older people. The first thing my mother said was, "Well, that was a load of rubbish, Willie!" And Willie replied, "You're just like your son…""

After another season in Canada, short spells at numerous clubs followed before retirement as a player in 1985. There then followed coaching jobs at Raith Rovers and Falkirk. Willie was now back home, with his "ain folk", in the all-embracing, insular community of the Kingdom of Fife. In 1987, he took over the Port Brae pub on the Esplanade (sea front) at Kirkcaldy. The 'Brae' is a traditional old boozer of modest appearance: half of the pub has carpet, so that's the lounge, and the other half has lino, so that's the bar.

Swearing is permitted in the bar, but not in the lounge. Regulars frequently step from one to the other, let out a string of curses – and then return to their seat.

Keen to give something back to the club, Willie recommended both Gordon Durie and Craig Levein to WBA long before other clubs spotted them. Typically, there was no response, a sad but familiar litany for both ex-players and supporters alike. Frustrated, Willie gave up offering tips, though even now it remains a source of grievance for him. One of the plus points of our currently cash rich status is that finally, there is a genuine and thorough scouting network.

TO THIS DAY, a warm welcome awaits any Albion supporter who makes the pilgrimage to Fife: dozens have done so, some several times. We're readily accepted in this Rangers-dominated pub because of Willie, and also because the Black Country is just as much a heavy drinking community as Fife. Willie is nearly 60 now, with a most unfootballer-like frame, but the twinkle in the eye and the huge grin retains the power to take any mature Baggie straight back to the 1970s.

The winger did once return to West Bromwich, as a guest of the club, appearing at the Throstle Club in late 1997 on both nights of a weekend. The evenings were full-on celebrations of the return (albeit briefly) of the great man, a whirl of noise, humour, and endless choruses of "Willie Johnston on the wing." The star guest was drinking spirits for Dutch courage (normally, he stuck to lager), and was, shall I say, rather mellow. His most memorable line was, "I scored two goals in a European Final for Rangers, yet I'm better known for taking two tablets in Argentina."

Long time supporter Steve Sant deserves the final word. "Willie was a decent player, but much more than that, he was a real bloke who lived a real life in the pubs and clubs of the area. He had weaknesses. He was too quick-tempered, and he drank too much, but in the mid-to-late 1970s, Willie was your average young bloke with a wad in his pocket. People identified with him. He was, perhaps, the last cult hero of that ilk. All since have been more aloof, harder to find. Willie earned perhaps three times what the blokes watching him earned: by the time of Super Bob it was 10 times. The players just didn't and don't mix with fans any more. You wouldn't find Kanu in the Handsworth Social Club downing mild and whisky chasers, and playing snooker. Willie was the last real star who led that sort of life. I loved him."

CYRILLE REGIS

1977-1984

BAGGIES CAREER

Games	302
Goals	112
Caps	5

MAGIC MOMENT

His extraordinary surging goal against Middlesbrough on his League debut

'SMOKIN' JOE'

"Oh, What a shot. Oh, what a Goal of the Season! Cyrille Regis!"

Commentator Alan Parry

THE Regis family are into sport. Brother Dave enjoyed a long football career. Cousin John was a damn good Olympic athlete. Half-brother Otis Robert was a Grenadian football international, niece Yasmin Regis is an exciting young triple jumper and, of course, nephew Jason Roberts is a Premier League striker. Having been dumped by Chelsea, Uncle Cyrille got Jason back on the bandwagon with a trial at Hayes, to rekindle his football career, and since then, is both agent and advisor.

To this day, Cyrille digs out the famous 5-3 win at Old Trafford for "his nephew's benefit," as Jason explains wearily. "He keeps stopping it, and saying: 'That's me!' He's great for me though, a really big influence." It was this influence that, perhaps unwittingly, caused so much friction at the Hawthorns between Jason and manager Gary Megson. Inevitably, the striker left the club, later to prove his worth at the top level with Wigan. He too has grown as a person, from the shy individual who joined the Albion from Bristol Rovers, just as his uncle developed his own personality. Around the same time, some sources suggested that other younger Albion men who also had Cyrille as their agent did not always have the rub of the green. The subsequent arrival of Cyrille's former team-mate Bryan Robson as Baggies manager greatly improved relations, and he continues to represent Albion men. Cyrille moved on from being an independent agent, joining the Stellar Group, covering the Midlands and Southern England. (Cousin John is also with the Group).

Even with a biased eye, it's possible to argue that Cyrille is the most acceptable face of modern agents. He commands respect, knows his subject intimately, and oozes honesty, charisma and charm. His eloquence is highly pervasive. Even now, at 48, superficially, he looks as fit as a butcher's dog. His paper credentials match also, with his MEBSM sports diploma; UEFA Grade A coaching licence and FA Players' Agent Licence accreditation, not to mention his City and Guilds electrician's qualification. Cyrille remains a highly popular and regular visitor to both the Hawthorns and Supporters' Club functions. He is always surrounded by people of every age seeking his autograph, testimony to the enduring nature of his celebrity amongst Baggies fans.

AS CYRILLE will himself tell you, respect has to be earned. His came the hard way. In 1963, young Cyrille was only five years-old when his parents brought him to London from French Guyana. Football was unknown to him then, an interest to be kindled initially at school. But once started, it was hard to stop in more ways than one. As his mother cheerfully observed: "If it was in front of him, he'd kick it." The enthusiastic late starter then progressed, through a series of minor clubs, to Hayes, in the Isthmian League. Cyrille was an apprentice electrician working on building sites all over London, thus he both worked and played in tough environments. Merely making training sessions on time was difficult and tiring, never mind fitting in the 60 home or away matches that comprised a single season for Hayes.

Despite his comparative youth, Cyrille competed so well that he quickly attracted interest from professional sides. Numbers vary from account to account. All were London-based, and one reputedly didn't make a move because they "didn't sign black players." It was the oft-recalled arrival of Albion's Chief Scout Ronnie Allen within Hayes' modest little stand at their Church Road ground near Heathrow airport that would change Cyrille's life. Allen watched in astonishment as the young Regis went up for a ball at a corner, despite the attention of four Ilford defenders, then put both ball and all four defenders in the net. As the then Chief Scout explained, "I went down on a cold, wintry night. In ten minutes I was convinced." This was one of 24 Regis goals that season, following 25 with his previous side Molesey.

Allen set to work to persuade the Baggies this youthful attacker was an essential buy. It wasn't easy. Such was his determination that at one point, Allen threatened to buy Regis with his own money. (Some things don't change. In 1995, Albion had the chance to buy Jason Roberts from Hayes for £250,000, but didn't take up the offer. Years later, he cost the Baggies £2 million). Allen did get his way, finally, in May 1977; one of the last acts of the Giles regime. In return, Hayes received £1,500, and later, a further £3,500, sufficient to pay for their floodlight bulbs.

Cyrille didn't arrive at the Hawthorns until July 1977, by which time Ronnie Allen had become club manager. Boldly or naively, Cyrille then negotiated his own contract, albeit taking guidance from a financial advisor before and during talks.

In the short term, Cyrille didn't even consider rapid upward mobility. As he readily admitted, "my only ambition at the start of the season was to work my way gradually into the Central League side." Albion's training regime, as much as twice daily in pre-season, was a shock to his system, both in its intensity and frequency. Endurance was never one of his strong points. He'd never been taught anything professionally, so relied on enthusiasm and raw power to get him through. In the short term, this offered something of an advantage, as professionals are routinely taught by their clubs how to respond to moves from their fellow professionals. But Cyrille had never been given an opportunity of reading the handbook, so defenders couldn't anticipate his intentions. A decade later, Lee Hughes was to enjoy the same short-term benefit.

CYRILLE STOOD six foot tall, but somehow seemed bigger. His build was a major part of the overall picture, appearing almost as wide as he was tall, not unlike the modern-day 'Big Dave', Darren Moore, incredibly strong and swift for such a big barrel-chested man. Team-mate Martyn Bennett, no midget himself, gaped, "I remember the bloody size of him when he first arrived at the club. When he took his shirt off in the dressing room, he'd got muscles on muscles. Nobody would stand next to him in the shower." Much to his consternation, Albion captain John Wile found to a mixture of delight and consternation that Cyrille could beat him comfortably in the air during training. Not just once, by luck, but repeatedly.

The new arrival was called up for Albion's third reserve match of the season against Sheffield Wednesday on 27 August 1977. Writing in the *Albion News*, Clive Leighton was impressed, "He has good ball control for a big man, shields the ball remarkably well, and can turn defenders almost at will." Cyrille scored after 22 minutes, running onto a through ball from Ally Brown, but the Baggies' second goal had far more significance. Cyrille neatly turned two markers before setting up his fellow striker. Only splendid saves from Wednesday keeper Peter Fox prevented more goals from the new boy, including tipping over a fierce drive after the striker had shaken off the attentions of no less than three Wednesday men. Other than making an early exit due to cramp, Cyrille had treated a professional side no differently to a London semi-pro outfit.

Four days after his reserve team debut, Cyrille turned out for the first team. With first choice David Cross injured, Ronnie Allen was happy to give his protégé a go against Rotherham in the League Cup.

He was fortunate to join a settled and assured side currently lacking only a regular goalscorer to move them up another level. Albion already possessed defensive solidity, exciting attacking players in Johnston and Cunningham, while a youthful Bryan Robson was key to a solid midfield featuring Tony Brown and Len Cantello. Allen's suggestion that Cyrille should "just go out and enjoy yourself" fell on nervous ears. "I was scared," admitted the soon-to-be crowd favourite. "The biggest gate I'd ever appeared in front of was about 500, and there must have been 20,000 there at the Hawthorns." The real attendance was 14,000, but the newcomer's confusion was wholly understandable.

Imagine, if you will, a youthful muscle-man, oozing pace and enthusiasm, getting by on natural instinct. The Yorkshire club's defenders were completely bamboozled by the debutant, who clearly had no clue whatsoever about the professionals' way of doing things. It was love at first sight for the Albion faithful.

The Baggies, already two goals to the good, then won a penalty. With spot-kick expert 'Bomber' Brown injured, Len Cantello somewhat reluctantly stepped up. "Give it to Cyrille" was the cry, a single voice at first from the terraces, but picked up immediately, a demand that quickly became universal. After signals between Cantello and the bench, the crowd (for once) had their way. Cyrille stepped up and gently despatched his first (and last) penalty. He was regaled with choruses of "Nice one, Cyrille", duly responding to requests for "another one" by scoring again before the end.

First choice David Cross was fit again for the next fixture against Middlesbrough, but Allen stuck with the youngster. He knew momentum when he saw it. "He wasn't fit to play, but he created such an instant success, I didn't dare leave him out." Supporter Lloyd Fletcher was among the 19,000 crowd. "There was already great expectation and excitement in his potential raw talent, you sensed a burning power waiting to be activated – and then he turned it on, beat three defenders (or five, depending on the version of the legend!) from the halfway line. The rejoicing, like the incident above, was just that notch higher, as you thrilled in something extraordinary, so exciting, that it was impossible to express it in any articulate form at all (howling, arms to the rafters). There began Regis's journey down the hero road."

The now-adoring crowd rose as one to their new striker's first League goal. The shot was scuffed past Platt in the Boro goal after a surging run: perhaps it's not surprising, though, that the debutant couldn't get a clean shot in, as he had the rather large Stuart Boam hanging onto his back at the time. Chants of "Astle is back, Astle is back..." said much about the impact of both young Cyrille and Baggies supporters' collective need for a new focal point. Actually – erm – not quite the whole crowd, as former fanzine editor Glynis Wright remembered... "In those days, I had a seat in the Rainbow Stand, the one opposite the players' tunnel. Sitting behind me was a chap whom I already knew had taken a very dim view of coloured players turning out in the sacred stripes – racist to the core and rumoured to be something to do with the National Front. Which wouldn't have mattered, really, that's the way he was, and you couldn't change bitter prejudices built up over the course of sixty years or so. And he rarely tried to impose his particular brand of poison upon others. But, that day, when Cyrille scored that wonderful goal, one of the best I've ever seen any Baggies player put away for the club, Astle included, the entire stand erupted with sheer joy. They, at least, knew raw talent bordering upon genius when they saw it. Chummy? As both sets of combatants returned to the centre-circle once more, and I was about to sit down, something made me turn around – that's when I caught a brief glimpse of him. Scowling fit to turn the entire contents of a milk-float sour, he was – and, more tellingly, amongst a stand containing thousands of people, not all of them Baggies by any means, some Boro, too, he was the only one still remaining in his seat. How sad."

He was not alone. The new recruit was aware of the disquiet from a minority of Albion people. "I think they were rebelling against me 'cause I'd taken a white guy's place."

For the sensible majority, it was one of those out-of-this-world moments when anyone can justify being a supporter; "That's why I support my team." Sadly no recording exists of this extraordinary goal. It was, after all, Middlesbrough. Who wanted to watch them? As Ronnie Allen said: "It was worth the entrance fee alone, a goal ten times better than any I scored." Cyrille himself modestly responded that he didn't think it was anything special, claiming to have scored better goals in Non-League football.

IN THEORY, Cyrille didn't fit Albion's possession style, drilled into them by the recently departed Johnny Giles. But the new boy simply didn't know how to hold the ball up, so Allen cutely decided that the team would be set up around Regis. As if to support his decision, Cyrille scored again the following week, at St. James' Park, in an impressive 3-0 demolition.

In all, Regis scored ten League goals that season, playing a significant part in helping the club qualify for Europe via a high league placing for the first time in their history. A dramatic chested-down and volleyed strike against Everton in April 1978 is still regarded by a number of supporters as Cyrille's best ever. The man himself prefers his effort at Maine Road: "I scored one against Manchester City where I was even further out than for Boro. I took the ball from ten yards inside my own half, took it all the way, and blasted it past Joe Corrigan. But the game wasn't televised, so nobody can see it now!"

There was an FA Cup run too, under, technically, Cyrille's third manager. Ron Atkinson had replaced Ronnie Allen, who'd upped sticks abruptly to Saudi Arabia. Here again, the big man's goals were crucial. Two strikes, and Dave Sexton's Manchester United were knocked out in a mud-bespattered replay. Two more at Derby and another rocket past the mighty Peter Shilton in the Forest goal in the quarter-final propelled the Baggies to their semi-final destination of Highbury against Bobby Robson's high-flying Ipswich. It was a painful, painful exit, as Cyrille recalls: "We just froze. After 15 minutes, we were losing 2-0: you looked around, we hadn't played our strongest side, Laurie was substitute, John Wile was injured. It was chaos." Ipswich eventually won 3-1.

But there was a special price for his goals that, virtually, only Cyrille had to pay. Wolves' supporters were the most noticeable, but there were many others who indulged in distasteful chanting. In their book *Samba in the Smethwick End*, Dave Bowler and Jas Bains described the 'Apocalypse Now' scene. "At the back of the Smethwick End are corrugated iron sheets. Throughout the game, Wolves supporters drum on these in a jungle rhythm, and thousands of voices chant, 'Nigger, nigger, lick my boots...'"

These were the opening bars of a disturbing symphony. Racist comments abounded from the opposition. In public, Cyrille's response was to try harder, to put a little more oomph into his shooting, to quieten the bigots by defeating their side. He didn't have to endure this alone, for team-mate Laurie Cunningham had already been there, and endured much. Only those who've truly suffered can genuinely appreciate the negative impact of such treatment. Privately, away from the need to offer the 'correct' response, what psychological effect did this insidious campaign really have upon him? I imagine we'll never know.

Shamefully, there were even racists within the club staff, as Ronnie Allen admitted, "Tony Brown had a sprained ankle, that's why I took him off at Bury (League Cup), to bring Cyrille Regis on. There was a big row on the coach on the way back from that match. One of the staff – not a player – said, 'How dare you put Cyrille Regis on for Tony Brown – we don't have black players'" Cyrille was just around the corner, and he came round in such a temper – it took four of us to stop him. It's hard to rouse Cyrille, but when he's mad, he's really mad. He shouldn't have said it, and he wouldn't apologise."

Off the field, he already had to combat his painful shyness and missing all the people he knew from London. For a time, he lived in digs near Oldbury and was a regular visitor to the Blue Ball pub, known locally as 'Alice's Palace'. The formidable Alice ran this traditional old boozer. Remarkably, despite her normal antipathy towards all people she considered not to be British (i.e. white), she took a shine to Cyrille, even maintaining a stock of Mars bars behind the bar just for his consumption. His shyness would persist. As late as 1982, the striker attended a Supporters Club function in Halesowen, but felt completely unable to say anything to the assembled few dozen faithful. A surprised, but diplomatic Branch Chairman hastily came to his rescue. Two and a half decades later, Cyrille would become Freeman of the Borough.

Gradually over the years, Regis found ways to overcome his somewhat reticent nature. The premature demise of a friend had a dramatic impact, as Cyrille himself explains: "I became a Christian after the death of Laurie Cunningham in a road accident in 1989. We were good friends, very close. We'd had a few beers in Madrid one day… we had a crash. The car rolled over two or three times, but we managed to get out. Two years later, it was the same circum-stances, but Laurie's dead. His life was like mine, he had everything as far as material wealth, and when he died, it made me realise that wealth isn't everything, and I needed answers." His new faith had a profound impact on the striker. His whole persona changed, and for a time, he resembled an American evangelical speaker, his presence a little overwhelming. Perhaps fortunately, his psychological metamorphosis continued further.

ALBION COULD have lost Regis almost as quickly as they found him. St.-Etienne were dangling £750,000 in the summer of 1978. He could have taken the money and broken away from the abuse, but he saw a football club on a roll, and decided to stay. This was the first of several temptations put in front of "Big C", some official approaches, others definitely not.

Cyrille started the 1978/79 season as the leader of the attack, yet it was all too easily forgotten that he'd played barely 30 League games, and was still only 20 years-old. He was a year younger than Bryan Robson, and two years behind Laurie Cunningham: indeed Albion's Number 9 was the youngest member of that delightful side. Alistair Brown was a clever foil for the youngster, scoring 18 times, but the weight of expectation was always with Cyrille. He was our leader, our figurehead, and our inspiration. The big goalscoring centre-forward thing is always a factor with Baggie people.

Laurie Cunningham was hugely respected, but the thought constantly persisted that he came across as somewhat aloof, and a bit of a 'loner'. Not true for those who really knew him, but that was an opportunity denied to nearly all supporters. The feeling was commonplace that Cyrille could do anything, that his solid frame was unstoppable: the only thing perceived to be holding him back was Cyrille himself. Even his great chum, Cunningham, used to call him "Pussyfoot."

It was always 'Cyrille', never 'Regis'. The media freely used both names and certain other artificial nicknames, too, but for the supporters, 'Cyrille' was identification enough and remains so to this day. That season, nearly all the senior players had their own chant. It was a pre-match ritual to go through the card. "Laurie, Laurie Cunningham". "One Bryan Robson", "Wile, Wile, Wile" and so on, but the most familiar refrain was "Cee-rul, Cee-rul" or the slightly-less-often: "We'll drink a drink a drink to Cyrille the King, the King…"

The trouble with great teams like the 1978/79 side is that they're not appreciated fully until their demise. At the time, supporters simply take high quality for granted, and ask for more. With three wins and two draws in the first five games, the pace was set. Drawing 1-1 with Liverpool was a disappointment, and so too was a single goal defeat by Spurs. Supporters wanted more. A remarkable 19-match unbeaten run followed, including back-to-back wins at Highbury, and Old Trafford; "The 5-3", as awestruck contemporary Baggies supporters refer to it. Every subsequent generation has seen and admired the recording of the 5-3, including commentator Gerald Sinstadt's adulatory shriek of "Oh, what a goal!" as Cyrille buried the Baggies' final strike, courtesy of his chum Laurie Cunningham, who was at his very best on that brass-monkey December afternoon.

Cyrille wasn't a terribly regular scorer – but he didn't need to be. Most of the 16 first-teamers (and of those, three only managed five games between them) knew where the net was, so the big striker was just as invaluable creating holes for others to run into.

On New Year's Day, the Baggies beat Bristol City 3-1 on a distinctly ice-bound Hawthorns pitch. A week later, a draw at Norwich was sufficient to give them top spot. Having got to the top of the mountain, they then proceeded to slide, very gently at first, down again. A big freeze concertinaed their fixtures, and painful defeats by main rivals Liverpool, and then Leeds, knocked them back. Even losing only one of their next 16 League matches wasn't quite sufficient to keep them in contention with The Reds. A weary WBA team often scored once, and were then obliged to hang onto their advantage like grim death. Still, a 1-0 defeat of Everton in April seemed significant insofar as at least this surely ensured second spot. The Scousers' top striker was regaled throughout with chants of "Bob Latchford, Cyrille wants your England shirt." but even the consolation of runners-up spot was removed by a goal from Nottingham Forest's Trevor Francis in the 81st minute of the last game. Albion finished third, not second. The dismay was intense.

Cyrille was then badly injured in a pre-season friendly against China, and without him, plus the now-departed Cunningham and Cantello, the following season was mightily frustrating. By the time he returned in November, the priority was pulling away from the bottom end of the Division. As a measure of their paucity of attacking ideas, Albion had no less than ten goalless League draws, and 19 draws in all, in 42 League games. Twelve more followed in 1980/81, with half of those without goals. Albion qualified for Europe, but it seemed such small beer, compared to Aston Villa winning the Championship.

ALBION MANAGER Ron Atkinson's oft-repeated comment: "To see the best of Cyrille, it's necessary to give him a sharp kick up the backside…" was accepted as common wisdom. The manager would thump his charge in the stomach, or rub Vicks (an over-the-counter embrocation) all over him, anything to give the striker "motivation." On another occasion, the forward was summoned into Atkinson's office to be told, "I want more aggression and more goals from you."

It's undoubtedly true that "Big C" often looked languid, lacked sufficient belligerence, even, but a more productive approach for such a shrinking violet may have been an arm around the shoulder. As Coventry manager John Sillett so pertinently commented much later: "He couldn't stand a rollicking that well."

Cyrille claimed, "I don't get angry. I don't need to." Yet everybody loses it sometimes, Albion's No. 9 included. He was sent off against Aston Villa in May 1982, after an incident with Ken McNaught. "Just a niggling thing," Cyrille later explained. Some niggle, with the defender receiving a retaliatory punch. There's something primeval buried inside most Albion supporters, quietly whispering: "Punched a Villa player? Good for him!" But more sensible council prevails. Not only did his dismissal play a part in giving the Birmingham side a late winner, his subsequent suspension damaged Albion's chances of staying up. Regis tried to excuse his actions: "I can take all the kickings, and all the elbows. I always have. But when someone does you off the ball, that's beyond the mark." Big C didn't have a distinguished record against the neighbours. As he said himself, the following season: "I have never scored against Aston Villa", adding: "Derby games against Villa are always more like a war."

His first goal against the Brummies from B6 finally came on the opening day of the 1983/84 season, in a 4-3 spectacular, sadly at Albion's expense. In the return game, the claret and blue side had their noses in front with only six minutes left. Dramatically, Garry Thompson scored twice in three minutes, and while the alleged fish-lovers were still reeling, big Cyrille took the ball off Des Bremner on the halfway line, and ran half the length of the pitch to defeat Nigel Spink. The only pity was that the goal blitz came so late; it was hard to take in, let alone enjoy reminding the visitors of the score.

Cyrille scored more goals under the returned Ronnie Allen in the 1981/82 season than in any of the Atkinson years, and this despite a seemingly random rotation of five different partners that term. Allen had the advantage of being the man who gave Cyrille his chance, but, more importantly, being a great forward himself, he had a better understanding of the job requirements. He listened. He encouraged. As Ronnie said: "I was disappointed he has not got any better during my absence. He needs help and understanding, and then you'll see something really special." More prosaically, he told Cyrille not to defend. Said the striker: "Ronnie said I was an explosive player, and he wanted me to do all my work in one half." Mutual respect was the key, for few of Cyrille's team-mates enjoyed the same rapport, or even understanding, with Ronnie Allen.

Ah yes, respect. As much as goals, skills and endeavour matter on the football field, it's often positive human contact that elevates a footballer to new levels of respect and admiration. 'Crumbs from the rich man's table' syndrome creates a dining out experience for many, but sometimes, there's more to be had. Take, for example, the experience of long-time Baggie Steve Sant: "I walked back from a training session at the Albion School in Halfords Lane with a very muddied Cyrille and Laurie Cunningham. They asked me if I shouldn't be at school. That brassed me off no end, as I was 19, actually on strike at the time, and told them so. They joked around, throwing snowballs at the other players. Len Cantello responded by chucking a bucket of icy water over them (and me!) They disappeared into the changing rooms in the Halfords Lane stand, and that was that.

I went into the Woodman pub, more to dry out and get warm than anything else, and ten minutes later Cyrille came in, wearing just a shirt and jeans. He asked the barmaid if some-body was about, the answer was negative and he made to walk out when he spotted me. He then banged some change down on the counter, then nodded at me, saying to the barmaid: 'His next one's on me'. He smiled a huge smile, and disappeared. I sat up, and saw a sports car speed off toward Handsworth. I didn't get the chance to say anything, but in magical days of my life that's up there, top ten no question!"

Long time supporter Keith Cotter witnessed another 'Cyrille meets the public' incident, albeit one with a less positive outcome. "Half a dozen building workers entered the West Bromwich Conservative Club, and spotted Len Cantello and Cyrille were playing snooker. The workmen loudly questioned the footballers' fitness, claiming that their proper job made them fitter and stronger. They were persistent, refusing to be ignored.

Finally Len grew weary of the taunts, and set a challenge to one of the workers, asking him to do one press-up, and then jump and touch a mark he set on the wall, repeating the exercise with an extra press-up each time. The local tittered, saying he could do press-ups all night. Unfortunately for him, Len was astute. The jump in between the press-ups is a killer, and he only managed six before collapsing breathlessly, completing 21 in total. Len did 55 without breathing hard. Cyrille's competitor was asked to lift one of the heavy easy chairs upright by one leg. He couldn't get it off the ground. Cyrille simply grasped the leg of the chair and raised it to waist height before replacing it. Len and Cyrille returned to their snooker, as their red-faced challengers exited stage right. "

RONNIE ALLEN'S Albion was in transition that term, using 28 players. After England interna-tional Bryan Robson had been lured away by medals, fame and fortune at Old Trafford, the Baggies needed at least a month to recover. Another third of the regular midfield, Remi Moses, went with him. The previous season's top scorer, Peter Barnes, had already departed, Mills, Deehan, Owen, Batson, Cowdrill and Godden all indicated they would rather like to follow them out. The ship was not a terribly happy one.

Albion relied heavily on the attacking impetus of two men – the overlapping talents of Derek Statham, and the goals and acceleration of Cyrille. Initially, his form varied from hat-tricks against Swansea (his power with the gas pedal the catalyst for all three), and Blues (City manager Jim Smith: "The lad is incredible. When he wants to play, he can be terrifying"), to rather lethargic showings. In November, everything clicked for Cyrille, and his 13 goals in the next 11 games made him the First Division's top goalscorer. He'd never previously been this consistent, nor would he be so again. "I've never scored so well for so long in one season."

The manager readily offered his explanation. "The problem was to find ways to use Cyrille's power. All the good players I've ever known have gone to meet the ball, always attacked the ball. Cyrille would come so far, and then stop, so that he was getting clobbered by the centre-back and losing control."

Regis particularly got up West Ham's nose, scoring in all three of Albion's League Cup matches against the Londoners, ignoring abuse from the supporters he'd identified as being the most racist. As reporter Ray Matts wrote: "As an exercise in perception, pace and powerful running, it was sheer perfection."

Two goals from the striker saw off Wolverhampton Wanderers, though his marker, Joe Gallagher, remained unimpressed. "Cyrille Regis for England? Don't make me laugh. Cyrille is a very good pal of mine, and we have a drink together, but I have never rated him as a centre-forward." With friends like these…

Fortunately, Gallagher wasn't picking the national side. Ron Greenwood chose him for the bench against Northern Ireland, and so it came to be that with 20 minutes left, Cyrille Regis became a full England international. He didn't find the net, but enjoyed the experience. "The crowd singing "Nice One, Cyrille" gave me a little more confidence." Bit-part roles followed against Wales and Iceland, as 'Big C' nurtured hopes of joining the World Cup squad for Spain that year, but a thigh muscle injury then made the question academic.

SIX GOALS FROM Cyrille made the difference in a hard fought League Cup campaign. However, the two legged semi-final tie against Spurs, who were to finish fourth in the League that season, was always a big ask. The Londoners' defence paid special attention to Albion's only real goalscorer (the next highest scorer that season, midfielder Steve Mackenzie, managed just five), and they pinched the tie 1-0 on aggregate.

A trio of lower Division clubs were uncomfortably overcome in the FA Cup, including Norwich in the Fifth Round. The Canaries' defence could only look helpless as Cyrille famously controlled the ball, steamed forward, then beat the goalkeeper with an archetypal shot. *Match of the Day's* Alan Parry's memorable commentary ran thus: "Regis takes it well on the chest, and that's a lovely piece of control by Regis, and – OH WHAT A SHOT, OH WHAT A GOAL OF THE SEASON! CYRILLE REGIS!" The quarter-final draw was kind, with perennially-wet Coventry rolling up at the Hawthorns for a comfortable 2-0 defeat, with goals by Owen and Cyrille again, who hit the ball with such force that the goalkeeper, only a yard distant as it entered the net, could only watch.

After losing against Spurs, everyone connected with Albion was frantic to win the FA Cup semi-final to get to Wembley. Second Division QPR were their opponents, which didn't sound daunting, however the Baggies' form was wretched, with only one win in the previous nine League games. Rangers knew exactly what to do. Man-mark Regis with big Bob Hazell, make sure that full-back Statham couldn't get forward, and then just wait for a chance. The plan worked perfectly. QPR won 1-0, leaving the Black Country's finest bereft. As the Rangers defender explained, "I was told to follow him everywhere. I just knew he wouldn't score, man, I just knew it. I had so much adrenalin pumping inside me."

Morale wrecked, the League slump continued, with even Coventry managing to beat the Baggies. Albion lost seven in a row. During the last of these, a solitary supporter staged a sit-down protest on the centre-circle at half time. His efforts were warmly appreciated.

Perhaps buoyed by his second international appearance (ten minutes against Wales), Cyrille's first goal in almost two months, and his late assist for Monaghan, helped immensely in defeating Wolves 2-1 in a horribly tense affair. Surely sufficient to relegate Wanderers, and keep Albion up? But three more defeats followed, and in the end, the Baggies had to win two of their three remaining games to stay up. In another sweat-filled encounter, goals from Regis "the most important one I've scored all season" and Owen were enough to beat Notts County 2-1, leaving

WBA to beat either Leeds or Stoke to send one of them down in their place. The Leeds game will be forever remembered for the actions of the Leeds United supporters pulling down the Smethwick End fencing, in an extremely hostile fashion. In an evil atmosphere, the Baggies were the better of two nervous sides. Big Cyrille came to the rescue again with a goal in a 2-0 win. The Baggies were safe, which is more than could be said of both the ground and its Black Country occupants after the game.

HAVING COME so close to the drop, Ronnie Allen stood aside as manager. A replacement was urgently required to get WBA back to the right end of the table. With home matches often drawing only eleven or twelve thousand, somebody with bags of both presence and charisma was needed to bring back the crowds.

Ron Wylie was a mighty curious choice being a former Villa man, possessing no Albion link, and no great pedigree for the position either. With four preferred candidates having declined the job, there was an element of desperation, of having to get anybody as manager. Cyrille scored his first goal at the Victoria Ground, Stoke, in a 3-0 win, in only The Baggies' fourth game of the season (an incredibly fortuitous result, for which, ever since, West Brom have had to pay with endless defeats in the Potteries).

The Baggies were briefly second in the League table, but this was not to last. Form came and went, but patience for poor results was in short supply. Two 6-1 defeats in the space of a month didn't help the mood either. As did being 3-0 up at home to Swansea, where the "defenders were scared out of their wits with worry every time Cyrille Regis charged at them", only to concede three in 16 minutes. In an attempt to steady the ship, Wylie opted for three central defenders, thereby grinding out a series of goalless draws, but now he was being accused of boring football. Dissatisfaction continued, with gates at only half the number required to meet the club's 23,000 break-even target as poor football conspired with the recession, and the ever-present fear of hooliganism, to keep supporters away.

There were some highlights, ample to keep current-day Albion followers happy, but expectations were higher at this time. Beating Ipswich at Portman Road 4-3, after being 3-2 behind, with three minutes to play, was remarkable in itself. Even more unusual was the fact that all the goalscorers – Regis, Thompson, Perry and Zondervan – had all previously endured abuse in their career because of the colour of their skin. And beating Villa 3-1 in a snowstorm is always worth savouring.

To be fair, Wylie's team suffered a horrendous run of injuries just at the time he was under orders to cut the wage bill. His downfall, though, was his loyalty: his Number 2, Mike Kelly, was deeply unpopular. With the League position deteriorating, patience ran out at home to Nottingham Forest. When the manager can hear supporters of his own club urging the opposition to score more, it's time to go. Within a week he had done precisely that, resigning in protest after the Directors asked searching questions about the future of Mike Kelly.

Johnny Giles was brought back – and the excitement was tangible, almost. As Cyrille said himself, "There's a real buzz about the place, and a new challenge for all the players. I never had the chance to work with Mr Giles because he left so soon, but I can't wait to work with him now."

But he had to wait because yet another injury put him out for five weeks. His presence was missed. Giles had a rocky start, including losing a FA Cup Fifth Round match to Third Division Plymouth. Thankfully, the arrival of two new midfielders, Hunt and Grealish, produced three superb results on the bounce – a 1-0 win at Spurs (Cyrille's header won the day against the club he supported as a boy), a 3-0 slaughter of Stoke City (a purists' treat, including one sequence of 38 passes) and, best of all, beating Manchester United 2-0, Atkinson, Robson and all. Cyrille notched the clinching second goal. After that, a series of hard luck stories and missed opportunities meant the Baggies weren't safe until the last but one game. These were uncomfortable times all round.

Regis found the net in a 4-0 defeat of Luton in September 1984, with what turned out to be his final Albion goal. The following month, Cyrille signed for Coventry for £300,000, with the Baggies basically taking the first offer that came along. Perhaps the absence of an agent to advise caution was significant. After all, local media had implied interest from a series of big name clubs over the previous six months. But Coventry, the only local-ish club that Albion supporters cannot take too seriously? Regis freely admitted to being off his game and furthermore thought that the manager didn't rate him alongside Thompson. Giles, in effect, agreed, saying, "I did not feel Cyrille and Thompson complemented each other."

At the time the big striker's departure was not greatly mourned. Loss of form over an extended period, including endless missed chances, regular injuries (playing only 26 and 30 League games in the previous two seasons), and the presence of the even bigger and never-shirked-a-challenge Garry Thompson, who scored a hat-trick against Forest just a week later, all provided reasons to look the other way. His Cult Hero light bulb had dimmed slowly, albeit perceptibly, over two exasperating years.

BUT CYRILLE always maintained a semi-presence at the Hawthorns and in Baggies fans' hearts while he was away.

For a long time, the Highfield Road move looked a hasty, ill-thought-out one. City manager Gould was sacked within two months, thus maintaining the pattern that whenever an Albion icon moved in, Gould moved out (quite literally, in the case of Willie Johnston).

City struggled badly for two years, until a fortunate coming-together of John Sillett and George Curtis gradually created a marvellous dressing room. Cyrille had a new role. He held the ball, and his team-mates played off him. As he explained later, "It made me a better person to go through those tough times." The Sky Blues then had an unlikely FA Cup run, beating one fancied opponent after another. Coventry did battle with then-Second Division Leeds United in a semi-final at the same time WBA played a League game at St. Andrews. Respect now restored, "Cyrille's going to Wembley" was chant of the day in Small Heath. Coventry duly overcame Leeds, and went on to beat Spurs in the Cup Final. Many Albion supporters had eyes only for Cyrille, and were so pleased that a member of the excellent 78/79 side had won a medal – something, anything! This feeling extended to all of the team, with some fans even willing to accept Wolves lifting the Freight Rover trophy, purely because of the benefits it bestowed on Ally Robertson.

Cyrille's form not only won him an FA Cup winners medal, but, some five years after winning an appearance against West Germany, he also managed to earn another England cap by making a cameo appearance in England's 8-0 shoot of Turkey in October 1987.

Two years later, when City manager Sillett left in 1990, his replacement Terry Butcher gave Cyrille a free. Ron Atkinson, now running Aston Villa, was quick to recruit him as his first signing, even though the former Albion man was 32. Cyrille was heading home, but in easy stages. "I know Cyrille has found God. Now I want him to find the devil," said Ron Atkinson. It was a typical Atkinson one-liner, showing his knowledge of how to make friends in the press, but perhaps not really understanding those people whose careers were in his hands.

Two years later, the striker wasn't quite ready to return to his favourite football ground, so made do by signing for Wolverhampton instead. During his time with Villa, Albion were enduring a dismal time in the lower Divisions, so their paths did not cross. Not so with Wolves, who found themselves quickly up against a revitalised Albion team back in the old Second Division, and quite desperate to get one over the old-gold gang. The clubs literally clashed at the Hawthorns. With the home side 3-2 up and all fingernails gone, the visitors made a substitution. Baggies man Stew Jeens remembered the moment. "When Cyrille stepped out to replace an injured Bully in the 3-2 game, the ovation he received from both sets of supporters that day is still a cherished memory. If he'd scored an equaliser, I can't imagine what my reaction would have been." It was a big dilemma, fortunately not one to be faced.

After Wolves, Cyrille played for Wycombe Wanderers and then Chester City before being forced into hanging up his boots after 740 appearances, suffering from calcification of his leg muscles. After trying for managerial posts elsewhere, Cyrille was welcomed back to the Hawthorns in a coaching capacity in February 1997, admitting, "it's about who you know, not what you know." He worked under Ray Harford initially, whose coaching brilliance contrasted with his dour public image. After Harford, came Denis Smith. Cyrille wanted to progress, but although his job was secure for as long as he wanted, he couldn't improve his status at the Hawthorns. He did however wear an Albion shirt again.

In August 1999, a 41-year-old Cyrille made a four-minute cameo appearance in the Bass Charity Vase. A scratch Albion side beat Gresley Rovers reserves (an unfortunate double booking for Gresley) to finally win the ancient trophy after twelve years of trying. To the one hundred or so spectators present, the moment of the Baggies coach entering the field one final time somehow seemed highly significant.

Once Smith had departed, replaced by Mogadon-man Brian Little, Cyrille's frustration grew. He wanted more than simply working with reserves and youngsters, and resigned, shortly after Brian Little had himself left, to look after his new flock.

DON GOODMAN

1987-1991

BAGGIES CAREER

Games	181
Goals	63
Caps	0

MAGIC MOMENT

His hat-trick against Crystal Palace in 1988 capped a fine run by the club, lifting everyone's spirits in dark times

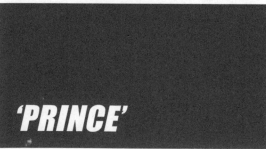

'PRINCE'

ODSAL was a visible symbol of how the once proud had fallen. A Friday evening in December 1986 saw a crowd of 4,500 in a huge, but uncovered and rutted rugby ground. Welcome to the Second Division, Albion! The only shelter for visitors was in the toilets and the only 'food' in a hot-dog van. Stair-rod rain descended all evening. Modest and cheap though the Albion side appeared that night, they were far too fluent for City. The Baggies won 3-1, including a spectacular strike from Robert Hopkins (a prime example of the Baggies' desperation).

It's worth recalling the twelve sodden Albion men that night. The team comprised Naylor, Whitehead, Cowdrill, Palmer, Dyson, Dickinson, Hopkins, Anderson, Mackenzie, Williamson, Crooks and sub Burrows. It's all too easy to label this Baggies XI as being a desperately dull and talentless bunch, yet four of the side were later transferred to top division clubs. One of them won England B caps, while another secured 18 full caps. In truth, this negative perception was brought about by the culture shock of the Second Division after a decade at the top level, and the grim tactics imposed by manager Ron Saunders, who only ever seemed happy when he was miserable.

CITY PLAYED AT the vast desolate stadium at the other end of Bradford due to the Valley Parade fire in May 1985. Most of their players from that horrific day were still with the club and each bore searing memories. None more so than young forward Don Goodman. His girlfriend had been among the victims. As he explained many years later, "It's not something I like to dwell on... but you can imagine. Every time there's a disaster around the world, whether it's an earthquake, crash or whatever, it brings it all back to you." He wasn't alone. City favourite Stuart McCall dashed to hospital to see his badly burned father, while skipper Peter Jackson broke a window in the players' lounge to get his family clear.

Despite their defeat by the Albion, Ron Saunders was impressed by two of the younger City players. He immediately approached Bradford to buy Martin Singleton, who duly made his Albion debut the following week. And there was another he fancied, who wasn't immediately available – 20-year-old Don Goodman, a striker who boasted oodles of pace, but only a one in four strike rate. Three months later, the deal was done.

Don explained to me how the transfer had come about. "The Bradford manager Trevor Cherry had been sacked. His replacement, Terry Dolan, then dropped me without any explanation, even though I was the club's top scorer. I was very angry. I went on the transfer list and after that I was only a substitute most of the time. I kept plodding away and banged in lots of goals for the reserves, yet he kept selecting other people in my place in the first team. I had heard through unofficial channels that Barnsley definitely wanted me and they'd offered £50,000, yet City turned that down.

I was training on transfer deadline day on 26th March 1987, thinking, 'That's me stuck here to the end of the season,' when all of a sudden these cameras from BBC Nationwide turned up. They seemed to be zooming in on me. I thought 'great'. Somebody said it must be a big club that had come in for me, but then I heard that the attnetion was all due to some Elland Road racial taunts.

So I went back after training and a couple of players had heard whispers about plastic. 'Somebody with a plastic pitch is in for you,' they said. City had got Ron Futcher from Oldham, who wanted to swap him for me. Bradford wanted Futcher plus £10,000 and Oldham didn't have the money. Then I got a call, so I thought, 'There's no harm in having a chat with Oldham.' I went into the office and the manager asked if I still wanted to go and I said, 'Yes.' He said, 'Well, it's West Brom.' Funnily enough, as a young lad, I'd supported West Brom. Heroes such as Cyrille. For no reason other than I liked the way they played when Atkinson was in charge the first time. It was mainly my Dad. He's a big West Brom fan. He follows attractive football."

His official version for the press and Albion supporters struck a different tone, though it's to his credit that he didn't play on his tenuous Albion links.

"I was out training at 11 o'clock on the Thursday morning. By 4 o'clock, I'd signed the transfer forms after a car dash down the M6." Don added, hopefully, for the benefit of his new employers, "I needed to get away and I couldn't have landed at a better set-up. It's like a different planet here. The club are geared to First Division football, they belong there and I want to help them to promotion."

Don's £50,000 recruitment was just part of a busy day for the Baggies. They'd sold two forwards that day – Garth Crooks and Stewart Evans – and bought in Steve Lynex and Don, at a small profit, naturally. Deals had to be done that way because those were the orders Saunders operated under. It's undeniable that the former Villa manager took on this role with enthusiasm, mercilessly rooting out all the big earners/names at the club since he'd taken over Albion's sinking top Division ship. Having spent limited time in his company, it was easy to argue that he frankly disliked all big name players. But as the talent went out of the door, the positive results went with them.

Goodman arrived at a severely depressed club, with sagging gates and, after only one win in twelve matches, one nervously eying relegation places only three points distant. The previous Saturday had seen a 1-0 defeat by Blackburn Rovers, with the 8,500 supporters bellowing "Saunders out" and "what a load of rubbish."

DONALD RALPH GOODMAN was to become the main reason to stick with the Albion in these desperate times. He was born in Leeds in May 1966. At an early age, football was his passion. To achieve this goal he needed some extra assistance, as he explains, "When I was a youngster, I was quite a puny kid and my Dad decided I needed building up quite a bit. He was a champion weight-lifter on his island over in the West Indies before coming to this country, so he knew what he was doing. He kitted me out with a set of weights up in the bedroom and put me through a series of weight-training exercises that did the trick. Without that little bit of extra strength and power, I doubt whether I would have ever got into the pro game in the first place."

His chance came after a recommendation by Ken Parkin, manager of his Leeds-based junior club Collingham FC. City were impressed and agreed a flexible arrangement whereby Don signed non-contract terms for them in July 1983, but continued his apprenticeship as an electrician. Don passed both part 1 and part 2 of his City and Guilds qualifications, but then put any idea of becoming a sparks to one side by signing professional forms on his 18th birthday. His debut came against Newport County. He later went on to score five times as part of the powerful City side that won the Third Division Championship in 1985. His biggest impact on a single game to date had been a seven-minute FA Cup hat-trick against Tow Law Town.

Goodman went straight into the Albion side to face rampant Oldham Athletic at Boundary Park. His contribution is best described as "low-key", though he did set up one opportunity for striking partner Bobby Williamson. The visitors led for most of the game, but two Athletic goals in the last three minutes flattened them.

The reality of West Brom's situation sunk in a week later for Don when barely 6,000 turned out for Sunderland at the Hawthorns. When the Mackems took a two-goal lead, "Saunders out" again did the rounds. Every mistake by a Baggies player was booed, and, possibly affected by the situation, Goodman could never quite reach the passes directed at him. Unexpectedly, Albion recovered to draw 2-2.

Results improved slightly – they simply had to. Don notched his first goal at Selhurst Park on 18 April, sufficient to earn the Black Country outfit a vital point. A slick four-man move led to Hopkins crossing to Goodman, who mercifully was completely unmarked and gleefully thumped in his debut goal. There was nearly a second as Don made use of his best asset – his pace – to steam past three Palace men. Keeper George Wood was equal to his shot. Unfortunately for Don, the *Sports Argus* waxed lyrical about Albion's new goalscorer – John Goodman!

Albion ground out a couple of functional 1-0 wins to ensure their safety. Thus there was nothing riding on the last day of the season when Goodman lined up against his old side Bradford City at the Hawthorns – and on his 21st birthday too. The birthday boy scored when he finished off Anderson's cross with a comfortable header. The Baggies went 2-0 up while City proceeded to have two players sent off. Don was embarrassed, "sending someone off a quarter of an hour before the end of the season? There's no need for it, I told the ref. One of them – Evans – just caught me, no big deal. The funny thing is that Evans' father and father-in-law are a couple of my biggest fans. His own father was saying after the game, "he deserved to go for that." With the aid of a dubious late penalty and an overhead kick, the nine-men Yorkshire side scrambled a draw. The outcome somehow summed up the frustrations of the gritted teeth season.

RON SAUNDERS continued his remoulding of the squad in the close season. England B cap Steve Mackenzie left for Charlton and full international Derek Statham followed him out shortly afterwards to Southampton. Saunders signed Tony "the Belly" Kelly from Stoke for £60,000, so there was no need for alarm. "He's a tremendous player," insisted Ron. "Some West Brom supporters always seem to have something to moan about. They are only interested in knocking us." Presumably the few remaining loyal contributors to the club coffers were cheered by those kind words. "Kelly is twenty light years ahead of Mackenzie," insisted the manager, clearly by now inhabiting his own planet.

By the end of August, Albion sat on the bottom of Division Two, also hurting from a two-legged defeat in the League Cup by Walsall. These were simply desperate times. Supporters made a big effort to have Saunders sacked at Elland Road including some who discreetly entered the home end to cheer on Leeds. The Board finally agreed and Saunders was out of a job. Goodman was generous in his praise of the outgoing gaffer at the time. "I liked him. I owe him a lot; he brought me here. He taught me a few tricks. I'm 21 and I've got a lot to learn. He liked the odd joke, and he was a joker, it's just that occasionally we didn't know whether he was joking or not."

Much to everyone's relief, Ron Atkinson was chosen as the new manager. The Hawthorns badly needed a lift and Ron, on his second coming, talked a great job. One of Mr Bojangles' numerous early proclamations was, "I have a feeling that Don Goodman has a lot going for him."

Don scored in his first game for the new incumbent, a route one effort in a vital 2-1 win over Shrewsbury. Subsequently he played second fiddle to new signing Andy Gray. Goodman looked more enthusiastic under Atkinson, but his co-ordination remained a problem. Put simply, he fell over at key moments. Were it ever thus. City supporters described their former striker as "spending more time on his arse than his feet." Don, as ever, was candid in his response to my obvious question. "Yeah, It's weird. I think I've got flat feet, but I do think I'm getting over it now. You couldn't have believed it at one time."

Prince, as he was often known due to his resemblance to the pop star of the same name, next found the net in Portugal. Atkinson had used his contacts to set up a relaxing break on the Algarve, with a token match against a Portuguese Second Division side. The relaxing break turned out to be anything but, as Goodman played a bit part in Tony Kelly punching a local fireman through a plate glass window. Both players were fined two weeks wages and "twenty light years" Kelly was transfer listed.

'Prince' Goodman featured only rarely as a goalscorer during these times – certainly not enough to bring him any kind of hero status. He certainly contributed to the team, setting up Andy Gray for his debut goal at Plymouth and winning a penalty at Middlesbrough. Don was a genuinely nice guy with a ready grin, but 7 goals in 34 starts plus six more from the bench wasn't what Albion needed. A hat-trick in a Testimonial match in February against Spurs raised everyone's hopes, producing a supportive quote from Andy Gray.

"Don gets into good positions, but he has missed a few chances this season and to knock three past Tottenham will have done his confidence no harm at all." Sadly, this proved to be a false dawn.

Every match report included variants of 'Goodman glaring misses' or 'had Goodman's finishing matched his tenacity…' "I'm not a natural goalscorer," admitted Don. "I like to think I cause a lot of problems and take a lot of weight off other people – maybe I wear their defence out a bit. Mind, it got to the point against Bournemouth where I'm through for the third time and I thought 'Bloody hell, here I am again.'" Don wasn't alone in his thoughts and with top scorer Andy Gray only managing ten, the Baggies had to work desperately hard to retain their Second Division status, which they eventually did with only one game to spare.

FORTUNATELY HELP was on the way in the shape of one-to-one tuition with new coach Stuart Pearson. "Stuart transformed my game – he made me unrecognisable to the player I was. He had tremendous knowledge of how strikers should play. I learned, for example, to be more relaxed in front of goal, not to panic or snatch at chances and also to be a bit greedier than I was. Ninety nine per cent of the credit for my game goes to Stuart."

Naturally such an improvement needed time. Fortunately careful (and cheap) teambuilding by Atkinson gave the Baggies new confidence. Centre-half Chris Whyte's arrival gave the defence a new solidity and a new striker, South African John Paskin, made an early positive impact. Carlton Palmer's influence was increasing and so too was that of midfield anchor Brian Talbot. Results were much improved.

'Donno' was finding the net once more, though being sent off at Home Park, Plymouth didn't help his cause. He retaliated after Plymouth keeper Cherry barged into him. The referee missed the incident, but the linesman didn't and so the striker walked. Team-mate Brian Talbot was not impressed, "I didn't see exactly what happened myself, but listening to Don, it seems he did retaliate with his elbow. There can be no excuse, and speaking as chairman of the PFA as well as a player, this type of incident, which has been creeping more and more into the game, does concern me."

Unwisely, in the very next game, Goodman again reacted angrily to a challenge from Ipswich's Forrest. Fortunately, the referee let the incident go. Had the official reached a different conclusion to make a pair of dismissals, Goodman's career path may have been different.

Ron Atkinson's career path was definitely different – he was lured away to Spain. Brian Talbot was given temporary charge and under him the Baggies blossomed, winning five straight League games. This was manna from heaven for success-starved supporters who told the Board very loudly and repeatedly, "Talbot is our man." The Board were obliged to agree. Because of his suspension, the Leeds-born man only appeared in the fifth of those wins, an exciting come-from-behind triumph over Oxford. The feel good factor was every-where, except possibly from Albion's underscoring striker. The new manager expected more effort and more goals from him.

Suddenly he got them.

At the end of November, Albion lined up against Palace in their most exciting league position for years. In a terrific 5-3 spectacular, Don hit his first League hat-trick. The *Argus* described his final goal thus, "Palmer released Anderson down the left. The winger measured his centre to perfection enabling Goodman to complete his hat-trick with a downward header at the far post." He also found time and space to set up Hopkins for the killer fifth, a tap-in, which the ex-Blues man seemingly did his best to miss... and failed.

Brian Talbot was a relieved man – though cautious, "Don knows that one performance doesn't suddenly make him a good player. I will be expecting many more goals from him this season." Talbot had a limited amount of money to spend to improve the team and if Goodman could find the net more regularly, the money could be better invested elsewhere.

"I wouldn't call myself a natural goalscorer like Tommy Tynan at Plymouth," bizarrely confessed the hat-trick man. "Or even my own hero, Mark Hughes at Man United. I like to get involved in all aspects of the game and to make opportunities for other players. In the Palace game I had three chances and put them all away. Before that, I could have six in a match and miss the lot." He added, in best football speak "hopefully, this is the turning point." It was.

Albion defeated Hull City 2-0 in their next home game. Goodman scored both, one of them set up by his manager. Eight days on, the Baggies slaughtered Stoke City 6-0 in one of the most comprehensive stuffings anyone might wish for. This was personal, as Talbot bitterly felt that Stoke, as his previous club, had pushed him out unfairly. The whole side responded to the gaffer's frenzied urgings and Don added two more to his personal tally.

Prince had seven goals to his name in just three home matches – previously that would have been equivalent to a whole season's worth. He was elevated from his 'just another forward' status, his name was repeatedly chanted "Donno, Donno". Goodman was now the main man, a source of hope and inspiration in these difficult times. He knew where the net was – at last. He was Albion supporters' much needed response to the up-the-road running sore that was Steve Bull, who was well en route to 37 goals and a second straight promotion. Wolves' fans never missed an opportunity to remind their neighbours just how cheaply Albion had sold the Tipton born striker to them. Now there could be a retort, genuine ammunition to hurl back.

With his Charlie George-esque long hair, Don looked the part too; a freewheeling, quick turning, imaginative, youthful and good-looking striker. Then regular attendee Ian Thomas remembers Don, "He gave us hope. In a team of old men and plodders, he was young, dynamic and fast. Don deserves recognition for single handledly trying to re-introduce moustaches to the football scene." Goodman had far more hair than most – at times enough for three men. His 'tache was broad and lavish.

Ron Saunders, roundly blamed evermore for selling Bull so cheaply, was quick to chip in. "People thought I'd made a mistake, but I always reckoned he would go up in value. All that is happening now is that his potential is coming to fruition. With Don, it's very much a matter of confidence." The reborn striker went to to find the net against Oldham and Shrewsbury as Albion overtook Chelsea to go top of the Division in the New Year.

His mentor Stuart Pearson also pitched into the Goodman vocal love-in. "He is a good learner and listener, and prepared to work hard at his game to get still better. What impresses me is his close control and the effectiveness of the runs he now makes. He has always been as quick as any striker in the league, but now he puts that to better use. He has got self-belief now and bags of confidence. The world is his oyster." In yet another of those curious links that always seem to tie one Albion cult hero with another, Clare Astle, youngest daughter of the King called her new rabbit "Goodman".

BUT SUCH ELEVATED status brings with it plenty of attention of all kinds – much of it the unwanted variety. In an act both ruthless and cynical, FA Cup opponents Everton singled out Goodman and Colin Anderson as the Baggies' main men. Anderson was taken out in the first match with a quite appalling lunge. Goodman followed in the replay. As the Argus had it, "A team who underlined their fear of Goodman by dragging him down whenever he threatened them." Everton eventually secured their Fourth Round place 1-0 in extra time, despite all the backing that 5,000 travelling supporters could offer. "It's all very well having a mean defence," said Martin Lewis, one of the travelling throng, "but without Donno, it was only going to be a matter of time before they scored." Gary Robson agreed. "Losing Don was the worst thing that could have happened to us. I'm convinced we would have beaten Everton if Don had stayed on the pitch." It was a victory for brute force over footballing skill.

The Baggies' season was wrecked. Their squad, already painfully thin on numbers, couldn't cope without their key men. Goodman was out for a month and invaluable wide man 'Diego' Anderson even longer. The one-time League leaders went seven games without a victory.

As Goodman himself pondered, "I wonder how many goals I might have scored but for that injury? That completely threw me. I was never the same again – never 100 per cent when I returned." Goodman's brace sparked a 2-1 win over Leeds in March (the first one volleyed in after 21 seconds). Following that win, his team collected a further 11 points out of the next 15. The play-off dream was back on. But those were the last goals from the club's top striker.

Brian Talbot had one more chance to turn the season around. Club bad boys Hopkins and Palmer were sent off at Bradford City. Both had previously caused the club embarrasment off the field and so Talbot acted – transferring them. The sale of Palmer to Sheffield Wednesday for £850,000 funded the purchase of new forwards Colin West and Gary Bannister, plus Ian Banks, Paul Raven and Ronnie Robinson. West scored reasonably frequently and "Raves" stayed for ten years. However the perception remained that Talbot had not bought well and the side were poorer for it.

The arrival of targetman West changed Albion's game to a more predictable physical pattern. April came and went without any League victories. "It is a fact that Don Goodman's goals, so important to us at one stage, have dried up for seven games," admitted the once more stressed Brian Talbot. "Of course, all strikers go through lean periods like this, but maybe Don will have to give way to the challenge of others if he can't get it back." Empty words for Albion didn't have a replacement for a fit and scoring Goodman.

A 0-0 draw against Sunderland in the last but one game in early May finally killed off any promotion hopes. The Baggies finished 9th, four points short of a play-off place. After so many years of struggling at the wrong end of the table, Albion supporters regarded ninth spot as highly positive. Many hundreds, dressed in beachware and carrying surfboards, refused to leave Boothferry Park, Hull until the team returned to take a bow at the end of a generally positive campaign, sparked by top scorer Goodman's goals.

SEASON 1989/90, then, was obviously going to build on the achievement of the previous one. Classy Bernard McNally was added to the team's engine room, while the now fully fit Don had a new partner in Kevin Bartlett, a young Goodman Mark II – incredibly fast, but with only a limited knowledge of where he was going and why. Albion supporters expected… and in classic Albion style were let down. Sheffield United in dayglo yellow were the Baggies' first opponents and dazzled their hosts in a comfortable 3-0 victory. Neither Brian Talbot or Albion ever fully recovered from this shock. Goodman was in decent form, though, with three goals in the next four games and in addition forced Greenall of Oxford United into conceding an own goal. Reporter Dennis Sunley summed up the resurgence after a victory at Filbert Street in September. "Goodman's goal was his third in four games and on this sort of form, he is going to cause defences up and down the country quite a few headaches."

Three straight away wins followed at West Ham, Bradford City in the League Cup (6-6 on away goals after being 3-1 down from the home leg) and Watford. Kevin Bartlett was quick to praise his striking partner. "Don holds things up and wins a lot in the air," not realising just how new these attributes really were, the results of so many hours training with 'Pancho' Pearson.

The hat-trick of wins on the road boosted everyone's morale. A boost was necessary as the arrival of Wolves in the Division and the resumption of local derby hostilities had upped the stakes. It was so typical of Albion that there were no victories in any of the next six League matches. These were grim afternoons for their brittle defence – particularly a painful home defeat by Wolves not to mention the shocking 5-1 defeat at home to Newcastle, in which Sam Allardyce made his only appearance in an Albion shirt. Goodman's 50th senior goal was no comfort at all.

There was some consolation in the Cups when the team showed something of their best form. After the remarkable comeback against Bradford City, WBA travelled to Newcastle in the next round and pulled off a backs-to-the-wall 1-0 victory. The run ended at Derby in Round Four. In the FA Cup, Albion beat two First Division sides at home before pulling out the plum – home to Aston Villa. The Villains were too strong in the end, but had to work very hard and notably adjusted their rearguard line-up to stop Goodman running at them. The Cup victories were sufficient to ward off some criticism of Brian Talbot, despite his side slipping down the table.

Blameless too was Goodman, enjoying his most prolific season ever. His final tally was 21 League goals, easily sufficient to top the club goalscoring charts for the second time (no-one else could muster double figures), indeed it was the highest League tally since Bomber Brown in 1970. Most noticeably, there was a hat-trick against Barnsley in a 7-0 slaughter, through a header and by twice breaking the Tykes' offside trap. There was also Don's one and only succesful penalty conversion to note, against Swindon Town, which was born out of desperation. Regular penalty taker Bernie McNally had already missed one. So had Graham Harbey. When the Baggies remarkably secured a third spot-kick, it was the striker who stepped up. Despite such largesse from the referee, Albion still contrived to lose 2-1.

Goodman managed to score both home and away against Leeds United, helping Albion to take four points from the eventual champions. At Elland Road, Leeds were 2-0 up after 54 minutes. The home-town boy takes up the tale: "they must have caught us offside 20 times, but we beat the trap three times and scored twice." Goodman was rugby-tackled by Chris Fairclough the first time he broke free. "I think he would have done it the second time – but he knew he would have been sent off." Set free by Hodson, Don sped off to score Albion's first and later he teamed up with Bartlett for an unexpected equaliser. "I now approach every game believing I can score," exulted Don afterwards. And Baggies fans felt likewise. Not since the advent of Cyrille Regis had they imbued so much confidence in a regular supply of goals from one source.

DON FREQUENTED bars in and around Broad Street, Birmingham and all who met him were struck by his charm and ready wit. He was frank too, perhaps dangerously so for an off-duty footballer. Such was his new found respect that all his confidences appeared to be respected. Perversely these attributes only properly came to the fore after his departure. With Albion's manager imposing a ban on players attending fans functions, supporters of other age groups didn't have an opportunity to meet Don socially. The easy-going sixties with regular supporter-player interaction as the norm was long gone.

Subsequent extended interviews allowed his perception and easy going style to show through, a style which later would give him numerous media opportunities. Such was his positive influence that, when he returned to the Hawthorns wearing a Wolves shirt, barracking was at best half-hearted and largely confined to his increasing rampant hair which frankly did invite ridicule. The style, if that's the word, resembled a black sprouting bush. Albion supporters did stop short of applauding him as they did with Cyrille. After all, there are pecking orders to observe, even with cult heroes. Supporter Ian Thomas remembers seeing Don with his family, "His two lads has wild afros – just like their Dad."

The Baggies only secured their 1990 League safety in the 45th match with a nervous 2-2 draw at Oakwell. Albion's main striker came close to securing a stress-relieving win when his shot was kicked off the line. Relegation fears hampered his morale during the run-in with much poor ball control and according to one correspondent to the *Argus* "needing a field to turn around in." With only six home wins all season, the faithful following were despondent once more. Manager Talbot was asked for explanations and his observations included, "We didn't have anybody alongside Don Goodman to score goals." Bartlett ultimately wasn't the answer. Neither were Thomas, West, Bannister, Foster or Robson. Meanwhile Everton, Oldham and Nottingham Forest had all enquired about Prince's availability.

The answer was never found. The question was removed instead. In a particularly grim pre-season friendly at Swansea, Albion lost 5-0 with Goodman sent off for violent conduct. The referee claimed the Albion man headbutted his opponent (accounts vary as to whether this was Andy Legg or Chris Coleman). Don was adamant: "I did not strike or even lay a finger on the Swansea player" a view shared in the away end. Curiously, although the Football League indicated the referee had made a mistake, the official refused to confirm his error in writing, so the three-match ban remained.

Don's post-ban return was brief – lasting only a couple of games, thanks to a torn hamstring at Hull City. "It was as if a bullet had exploded in my leg," he lamented, through gritted teeth. "I can't find the words to describe how depressed I feel." His manager probably felt the same way. His top striker was out of action for a further seven weeks. As Andy Colquhoun of the *Birmingham Post* put it, "Goodman has been a source of frustration as well as hope for Albion supporters."

Even though West and Bannister had bought Talbot some credibility with eight goals each, a succession of late goals conceded made the Hawthorns natives quite hostile. Six goals hit Albion's net inside the last seven minutes in just four games, four of them in the 89th minute. When this was followed by Wolves scoring an equaliser in injury time, Albion supporters were incandescent. "We've lost our best striker for half a season," wailed the beleaguered manager.

As if to prove his talismanic status, Goodman returned with a big bang. As a substitute against Blackburn he set up a goal for Colin West. He won a penalty against Swindon and scored his first of the season on Boxing Day – but then he was out again, this time with a calf strain.

The Baggies – top striker out, leaking defence, only six wins all season, manager under pressure, supporters militant – were drawn against hitherto unknown non-league side Woking in the FA Cup Third round. Woking were not even a Conference club yet, but a team on a roll and full of confidence. In Albion's often glorious history, they had never previously lost to non-League opposition, home or away. The fear was palpable that afternoon. Although Colin West scored first, by the time Darren Bradley had added Albion's second, Woking had four to their name – three of them notched by a man whose name still grates – Tim Buzaglo.

Such was the bitterness and depression that Bradley's goal was barracked. Goodman himself offered a fair summary of the club's most depressing Cup exit. "We were humiliated, embarrassed. A part-time side trounced us and, even though I wasn't playing, it didn't make the weekend pass any easier. I was in a foul mood and never forgot the experience."

Neither did Brian Talbot. Within days, he left the building, P45 in hand. With Stuart 'Pancho' Pearson in temporary charge, the technical quality of the play improved greatly, but the results remained mixed. The highlight was a comprehensive and classy stuffing of Blackburn Rovers, 3-0 at Ewood Park, with Don trebling his contribution for the season.

The question of who should be the next manager divided supporters, but the nearest to any kind of consensus held that long ball merchant Bobby Gould was not welcome at the Hawthorns. There was plentiful evidence to support this, such as a fanzine survey and regular chants of "We don't want you, Bobby Gould." The Directors chose Bobby Gould. Years later, certain directors privately admitted that Gould had sweet-talked them into giving him the job.

The new manager's first game finished 0-0 against eventually promoted West Ham, but six wretched defeats followed, destroying the club's safety margin.

The football was grim. The results were grim and so was the mood. But amidst all the grime there was still Don Goodman, who resumed his one man scoring spree. Hardly anyone else could find the net as Gould tinkered vainly with one useless signing after another. Draws were not really good enough, but that's all the team could manage. In the 44th game, they drew with Port Vale after missing two penalties – Goodman was the culprit for one of them. Infamously, much-maligned Club Chairman John Silk tried to defend his position later with the words, "I didn't miss the penalties against Port Vale." The 45th game was yet another 1-1 draw, this time against Newcastle United. The good news was, it was just enough if Albion could win their final match at Bristol Rovers' Twerton Park in Bath. The bad news was they'd have to do it without Goodman, who was injured once again. Certain club officials to this day hint that Goodman could have played at Bath, a claim denied by the player.

Displaying the eccentricity which later became his trademark, Gould paired two forwards at Bristol Rovers who'd never previously played together, introduced a rookie forward in errr... midfield, while the top goalscorer (Bannister) sat on the bench. The result was yet another draw, even after Rovers had a man sent off. The Bristol side, urged on by fanatical support, fought tigerishly to relegate their former highly unpopular manager. Unbelievably the famous West Bromwich Albion were in the Third Division for the first time in their long history. No day since or probably before was quite this black for Albion supporters.

FOOTBALL LIFE must go on – even though the Baggies' next League fixture was against Exeter City. Albion swept the Devon side away 6-3 with Goodman twice outpacing his opponents. When Donno notched the winner in the next game at Darlington, everyone felt more confident.

But although results were OK, the performances were poor, not helped by another seven game absence from Goodman. He returned to score against Shrewsbury and League leaders Brentford, also achieving a personal milestone – finally scoring in a Cup match for Albion. With the exception of a solitary effort in the much-derided Simod Cup, Don had not found the net in either FA Cup or League Cup. His goal against Swindon in the League Cup was matched by another, during the indignity of a First Round FA Cup match against Marlow. His presence during a 6-0 win was later to cost him dearly.

For he was clearly better than the Third Division and Albion were struggling to hold on to him. His days at the Hawthorns were numbered. The player himself admitted he wanted out. Talking to the *Albion News* in October 1991, he said, "Whether I'm still here in May remains to be seen. I am very ambitious and I want to play in the First Division." His comments were remarkably candid for an official publication.

Actually, Don had already privately agreed with Albion's Board that if the right offer came in, he could go. The Board anticipated £1 million, possibly from West Ham and so rejected outright the initial £750,000 preferred by Sunderland, who needed a replacement for their hero, 'Magic' Marco Gabbiadini, recently departed for Crystal Palace. The North East side were aware of the Baggies' financial difficulties, so let them sweat for six weeks before returning to offer £900,000. By December 1991, Albion's overdraft was in excess of £1 million, and their bank threatened to foreclose. They had to accept the Mackems' offer. Sunderland's manager Denis Smith was confident with his new purchase: "He's quick, strong, brave, and above all, he scores goals."

"I had no wish to play Third Division football for a second longer than was necessary," explained Goodman. Neither did Albion's supporters, but they were stuck with it. From their perspective, the players who'd got this famous old club into this sorry state should be busting a gut to retrieve the position. The prospect of their talisman jumping ship was not well received.

After what turned out to be his final game against Stoke in November 1991, supporters hurled abuse at Goodman, even though his 63rd Albion goal contributed to a 2-2 draw. As supporter David Norman concluded at the time, "WBA are effluent rather than affluent following the sale of Don Goodman."

Without Goodman, the already grey season took on all the attraction of Torquay in January. Albion even managed to lose there as well – 1-0.

Just who would score the goals? The answer was but another month away, though no-one knew that at the time. Goodman offered a departing olive branch, "Albion supporters put me on the pedestal, they were absolutely wonderful towards me and I'll never ever forget that nor be able to thank them enough for that. They were great, and they gave me confidence and they helped me become a better player."

There was a silver lining in the cloud of their hero's sale. Goodman's departure presented a handy stick to beat Gould with (even though it wasn't his fault) and as the results worsened, even the Board realised he just had to go. With his departure in May 1992, the rebuilding could properly start.

Sunderland went all the way to the FA Cup Final that season, but the Leeds-born striker remained a frustrated watcher, after his appearance against Marlow for Albion. Neither did he ever reach the Premiership, getting no nearer than defeat in the Play-off semi-final. Meanwhile, proceeds from his sale enabled Bobby Gould to purchase one Bob Taylor.

BOB TAYLOR

1992-1998
2000-2003

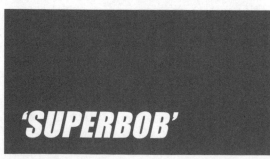

BAGGIES CAREER

Games	377
Goals	131
Caps	0

MAGIC MOMENT

Scoring the Premiership promotion clincher in 2002 against Crystal Palace

'SUPERBOB'

IN 1991 Albion were slumped at their lowest point in their history in status terms, if not financially, though pennies were far from abundant. The highly unpopular Bobby Gould took over a club in disarray following the FA defeat by Woking and arguably made the situation worse with his odd signings and even odder tactics. Albion were relegated into the old Third Division, on the last day of the season at Twerton Park, unable to beat a ten-man Bristol Rovers.

Albion's first ever third tier season started brightly, but progress became staccato. With the club guaranteed to finish in their lowest position ever, nothing but full involvement in chasing automatic promotion would satisfy supporters. A fixture at Bolton saw the infamous forward line of rookies in Adrian Foster and Les Piggott, a pairing once selected in a fanzine poll as the "worst pair of strikers ever played in an Albion match." Their combined tally of goals after their eventual departure was three, with one of those really an OG. Albion lost 3-0 at Burnden Park and Gould invited several embarrassed pressmen into the dressing room to put their questions directly to the players.

Don 'Donno' Goodman was the big hope to get us out of this mess, with nine goals to his name, but a combination of the club's financial shortcomings and Goodman's frustrations at operating at such a low level, meant a swift parting of the ways was inevitable. He left in December, and with him went the remaining hopes of the frustrated following. The remaining forwards were frankly quite wretched – hardly worthy of being of the lineage of WG, Allen, Astle, Brown and Regis and it says something that the most effective attacker was the diminutive Gary Robson, normally a midfielder, but pressed into service up front. The football was poor, but the results were about acceptable until Donno's departure. Subsequently, there was only one win in five games in January, culminating in a 3-2 defeat at home to Swansea, after being two goals ahead. This was one poke in the eye too many for the remaining faithful, who staged a protest sit-in at the Brummie Road End.

Gould, ever the eccentric, volunteered to take a microphone into the bawling masses to answer their questions. In response to one shouted enquiry, he promised that a new forward would be signed very soon. He kept his word. That forward was Bob Taylor.

BOB WAS BORN in Easington, County Durham on 3 February 1967. He was the latest addition to a mining family. His father went down the pit. So did his brother and their father before them. Inevitably, Bob was earmarked for the same job – what else was there in Horden? The prospect didn't appeal. "I didn't want to be stuck down a pit in the dark or have to do that kind of back-breaking work." In the end, he didn't have the choice to make because the mine closed shortly before he left school. Little Horden was never the same again. His Dad and the rest of the workforce were all out of work.

But there was always sport. Sporting versatility is in the blood of many of the Taylor clan. Bob's sister Glenda played golf, tennis, hockey and football in her younger days before joining the army. Much later, Bob's daughter Chantelle followed her aunt, also playing netball, basketball and hockey. Bob himself was a decent cricketer as schoolmate Dave Clayton recalls, "I was at Dene House School in Peterlee with Bob Taylor. He and I made a stand to spank Easington School at cricket. Result!" Latterly, Bob both batted and bowled powerfully in a testimonial cricket match for team-mate Daryl Burgess. In addition, during his own benefit season, he knocked spots off experienced bowls players despite claiming never to have played before.

Leeds was his first club. He played alongside David Batty in the juniors, but took better penalties. Known then as "Bobby Box", (presumably after a TV character) his first team debut arrived in April 1986. He played around 40 games for the Whites and was part of the Leeds squad that came so close to defeating Charlton in the first modern day Play-off Final in 1986/87.

Then came a move to the West Country and a highly successful spell with Bristol as City fan Chris Smith recalls, "The 1989/90 season was the most enjoyable that I can remember and SuperBob was largely responsible for that. There was a feeling of invincibility that season, that however many the opposition scored, we would score at least one more, with Bob at the heart of it. His partnership with Robbie Turner was fantastic. He was a strong target man, the perfect foil for Taylor, who made the most of Turner's flick-ons and held up play. Not that Bob didn't create a fair few of his own goals, he was the all round striker with both tap-ins in the six-yard area or powerful shots from outside the box.

The other memorable moments included his hat-tricks, the professionalism that he displayed on and off the pitch, the injury that caused him to miss four or five games at the end of the season, a massive factor in the Gas (Rovers) pipping us to the title, and his habit of wearing sweatbands and throwing them into the crowd at the end of the game. My mate still has one and treasures it to this day."

Famously, legend has it that 'Bob, Bob, SuperBob' (as he was serenaded at Ashton Gate) was once carried off in pain on a stretcher in a match against Crewe. He insisted on the bearers carrying him around three sides of the ground so he could sign autographs from his prone position. It's a great story, but almost certainly a myth.

A change of management at Ashton Gate had the new manager, Jimmy Lumsden, in need of cash for new signings. Dangling was £300,000 on offer from Albion for Taylor. By then, City had a number of decent strikers and Bob was far from an automatic choice. They took the money. Bob was happy with the chance of a new start. He'd recently lost his Mother and living in the West Country now seemed just too far away from home.

ALBION'S NEW MAN started in fine style as author and supporter Richard Brentnall recalls, "In his first 142 minutes, Taylor cut a dream coat figure. The touch, perception, elusiveness and finishing has been evident against Brentford, and against Blues, he displayed with his first goal, two other qualities that we've been sorely lacking; alertness and agility inside the box."

Brentford were the League leaders and fancied their chances against the misfiring Albion side. However, Gary Robson's through ball gave the debutant a chance in the 11th minute. The new boy buried his opportunity, witht the ball rebounding off the body of the charging goal-keeper. A second goal by Fereday completed a highly satisfactory win.

A week later came the local derby at St. Andrew's and another win – this time by an impressive 3-0 margin – and Albion were top of the Division, all thanks to SuperBob. Taylor scored two of the three, the first a diving header. There was belief that day, new hope and the difference was put down to the new striker. Albion supporters had a new focus, a new favourite. The slim, almost gangly figure with a mass of black hair and Dirk Bogarde thighs was quick to add reality to an unreal situation. "It's not always going to be this good," he warned on local radio. He was correct. A narrow defeat four days later to perennial pests Stoke City lost the momentum and the side went backwards rapidly.

Bob was originally dubbed 'Trigger' Taylor, because of his resemblance to the dim character in *Only Fools and Horses*. This was a short-lived moniker. Prefixing suitable Christian names with "Super" was quite fashionable at that time; indeed the new signing had already been SuperBob at Ashton Gate.

His arrival and early achievements gave everyone a reason to keep going, to stick with the under performing outfit rather than shrug the shoulders, and walk away, never to return. That and the opportunity to tell Gould exactly what you thought of him. "Back Bob, Barrack Bobby," if you will. Most did. At least, the referees were grateful. With Gould's infamous player choices and increasingly bizarre 'motivation tactics', he simply had to go.

But Gould wouldn't be pushed, even after a comfortable 3-0 home win over Preston, when he was advised loudly "We still hate you, Bobby Gould," followed by a rousing chorus from home and away supporters of "Gould Out." The Board didn't respond until the season ended at Shrewsbury, when supporters revealed the true depth of their feelings by touting a coffin around the ground, plus more vitriol aimed at the hapless manager culminating in a pitch invasion in the 88th minute. SuperBob already had seven goals to his name in a limited number of matches, but even they couldn't save Gould.

WITH THE BENEFIT of sepia-tinged and brightly-hued spectacles, it's possible to make a strong case that the second season in the Third Division was the most enjoyable for the post-1978 generation. New manager Osvaldo Ardiles had an attacking policy, aided by nervous opponents, who regularly felt an urge to defend and hardly anybody could stop the Baggies – or Bob in particular – from finding the net. "They were such nail-biting games to play in," revealed Bob. "Even if we were in front, you could never be sure we'd hold on it because all we ever did was push further and further forwards."

The memories of dreadful games, such as losing 1-0 at Springfield Park in heavy rain, on open terrace and a muddy grassy bank, are hard to retain. Albion's manager Ardiles wasn't terribly concerned, remaining typically laid-back. "My players are human and have problems like everybody else. They may have rowed with their partners, not had much sleep or be feeling a little under the weather." The frustrations of only finishing fourth, behind three other strong sides, also faded quickly after promotion was secured the hard way.

What does lodge in the memory about 1992/93 are matches when we strutted like Kings on and off the pitch at places like Chester, Mansfield and Rotherham – taking over the ground (or even the town), while the players took over the pitch. These are powerful, positive memories. Bob Taylor found the net 37 times that season. This despite being lumbered with an assortment of ill-fitting partners including Garner, Speedie, Blissett and Robson. Not to mention the Play-offs. It's completely impossible to describe what going to Wembley means to supporters, after being deprived of visiting the Twin Towers for almost a quarter of a century.

The business end of that season saw the arrival of a young forward from Newcastle – Andy Hunt. The pair were an immediate success. "Me and Hunty hit it off straight away. Andy was a bit like me, the fans liked him and he was level headed, but he never got above his status. If one of us wasn't scoring, then the other one was. We also read each others game really well, which helped a lot. Andy was good in the air, won a few flick-ons for me, and I used to hold up the ball and bring Andy into the game. We never worked on it either, we just clicked, the only time I can remember us working on our game was when we used to do shooting practice in training."

Although, the Taylor and Hunt partnership blossomed, West Brom found progress hard to maintain in the higher Division and struggled for the next few seasons. As a result, both Hunt and Taylor left the First Division for the Premiership. Bob genuinely didn't want to leave. "There were a lot of issues within the club. The manager wanted me to go on loan and I didn't want to go at first. It was a major wrench to leave, but, in the end, I went out on loan to the Premiership to Bolton. I loved it; I scored against Manchester United at Old Trafford, and against the Villa at their place. I was living out my dreams."

Albion's manager by this time was Denis Smith, who by coincidence, bought Goodman while at Sunderland and who, shortly after Bob left Bristol, took over the manager's hot seat at Ashton Gate. The striker always maintains he got on well with all Albion managers, even the irascible Alan Buckley. "When I went in for training with Alan Buckley, I'd say 'Morning, Gaffer' and he would go down on his knees to me, you know, and do the 'I'm not worthy' thing – 'I'm not worthy, SuperBob'". Bob would make an exception for Denis Smith. Bob privately seethed at the treatment meted out to him. He was adamant that Denis had it in for him from the day he started, claiming that Bob was overweight and liked a drink. After the spell on loan, Bob returned briefly to the Hawthorns before leaving permanently for Bolton.

Denis Smith assured everyone that SuperBob was offered a new deal. He "implored him to stay" prior to the final home game – yet according to him, Bob didn't give him the courtesy of responding to his offer. "What more could I do – short of going down on my knees and licking his boots?" It was true that a new deal was offered – a non-negotiable one-year deal. Bob wanted three years to take him to a testimonial. As the 12-month offer was non-negotiable, the response could be only 'yes' or 'no'.

Director John Wile backed Smith; "The manager couldn't agree a contract with him at the level the player wanted and that was it. He was just another player that had come to the end of his contract and he was allowed to leave to Bolton, the same as anybody else." But SuperBob was never just another player like everybody else, and such ill-considered management-speak did little for Wile's standing amongst supporters.

Smith left. Wile left. The Chairman left. The resident mice left, weary of such thin pickings. A new manager arrived… and then left. Situation normal. In came another manager, a hungry one this time in Gary Megson, but Albion continued to flounder, relegation back among the dead men of the newly rechristened Division Two beckoned. He needed inspiration, the kind that can only come from a goalscorer, a talisman, a legend. But Megson had to find a cheap one. Someone who lived locally and better still, knew at least some of the current players. There could only be one.

"I got a phone call asking me if I'd like to go back to West Brom," says Bob, "and I jumped at the chance. I didn't even think about it, my heart ruled my head really!" This time the deal was for two and half years, plus a testimonial. Less money than at Bolton, but a longer deal and a welcome opportunity to spend more time at the family home in Lichfield.

Martin Lewis, plus daughter Carly and Bethany are Newcastle (Staffs) based Albion supporters. "I'll never forget that day," explains Martin. "When I picked up Carly from school, I said to her 'we're staying up.'

'How do you know?' asks my daughter.

'Because we've got Bob Taylor back.'"

IT WAS a shrewd move. The return of the great man restored belief to mentally battered supporters, while his charisma boosted his team-mates, including Lee Hughes, who'd always looked up to the elder statesman. Lee was to play only two more games that season, due to injury and so goalscoring was down to Bob. His first came at promotion-chasing Barnsley in April, a looping header from a free-kick. Relief and belief flowed in equal measure. Four more precious strikes that term did just enough to maintain First Division status. SuperBob was the saviour.

From this modest position, Albion moved forward rapidly, propelled by maximum velocity by Megson and a string of new, more talented arrivals. The signing of £2 million striker Jason Roberts meant Bob was relegated to a bit-part role. He was on hand to score vital goals against Tranmere and Burnley, the latter effectively knocking the Lancastrians out of the play-off picture. The place went to the Baggies instead, who had their chances to beat Bolton, but didn't take them and went out. The 2001/02 season had explored exciting new ground, but the one after would far exceed it.

In the early matches, little went right. Losing at Bescot 4-1 in blazing opening day heat, was grim. In the first home game, an infuriating 0-1 to bloody Grimsby, Bob not only missed a penalty, Jimmy Quinn replaced him. It's hard to say which was more embarrassing. Was the King dead?

Watford away, after two home wins, felt significant. "Bobby on the spot" followed up to tuck home a penalty rebound. The Baggies took a two-goal lead, and hung onto the three points, despite being down to ten men and defending their penalty area in Alamo-like fashion. Goalkeeper Russell Hoult even saved an injury time penalty. The result lifted everybody, and the chase was on at the right end of table.

The high at Watford contrasted with the low of Preston in February. Not only did Albion lose to a promotion rival, far worse was the season-ending injury to top striker Jason Roberts. This combination of defeat and the loss of JR, felt like a turning point. Worse still, Wolves were disappearing over the horizon, believing their job was done to secure the second automatic promotion spot. Just reaching the Play-offs that night felt an impossible target. Gaining 28 points from the remaining 30 on offer sounded as likely as striking matches on soap.

And yet…

ARISE SIR BOB. His superb positional sense had him right time, right place, to score a late winner at Nottingham Forest. With nerves overcoming everyone, Bob polishing off a corner at Highfield Road was sufficient to push the Baggies alongside a now brown-shorted Wolverhampton. Despite a dislocated finger, the rejuvenated striker's volley then earned a point against Rotherham to put the Baggies clear in second place. Then came Bradford City.

Tales to tell your Grandchildren No. 73. In a match that Albion had to win, there was no score as time added on arrived. Super Bob, on the left hand touchline of the penalty box, attempted to twist round Andy Myers, who made contact with his knee. Down went Bob. The referee gave a penalty and Igor Balis did the business. Those are the bare facts, but these are words that do no justice to the occasion, that can reflect the nerves, the tension, the screaming frustration of the 6,000 strong away support. City were saying goodbye to Stuart McCall and didn't want his farewell spoilt. Albion had pounded away in the latter stages, with every forward possible on the field.

The penalty merely twisted the elastic band of tension further. The Baggies had missed penalties all season long and this was Igor's first for WBA. Life, as we knew it, stopped for several minutes. Myers protested about the decision. Bob needed treatment. Apparently McCall just had to be substituted, very slowly, at that moment. City's keeper Coombe dallied as long as he dared. Igor wasn't worried. Bang – top corner, no problem. Players and supporters rushed together in a mass hugging session. Others sat down sharply, legs suddenly wobbly. Others wept with relief. Rarely has life as an Albion supporter felt so good.

After such drama, the final match of the season against Palace seemed quite tame really – even though it was truly shit or bust. The Londoners knew their place as "also rans" and only threatened the Albion goal once. Strikes from Darren 'Big Dave' Moore and, inevitably, SuperBob lit the touch paper for the biggest celebrations in the town for a decade or more – all the bigger for having denied the Wolves.

BOB ONLY played parts of six games for the Baggies in the Premier League. "I'd have liked to have played more. I've played in the Premiership before with Bolton, but to play there with West Brom was special. I'd worked hard for ten years of my life to get there and to come on in the first game against Man United was special for me. My only wish was if I could have got a goal for West Brom, which really would have been the icing on the cake for me."

The end of Bob's Albion career was terribly sad and so unnecessary. For a reason that remains unclear to Bob and was never explained in public by the manager, he was completely frozen out for the last five months of his contract. Bob trained with the kids and played for the reserve side. Young Albion men like Simon Brown and Tam Mkandawire, who went on to continue their careers at other clubs, were grateful to have him around, but this was no way to treat such a fine clubman. After the last reserve game of the season, he was told not to bother training any more, with the clear inference that his career was over.

THAT LEFT BOB ample time to work on his Testimonial projects. Various fund-raising activities had already taken place throughout the year, such as a casino night. Supporter John Groarke, in the mistaken belief that an evening with Bob as a drinking buddy was up for grabs rather than just his shirt, invested literally hundreds of pounds in casino chips. It was an inadvertent gesture that said much about the popularity of the man. On the day of Albion's final Premier League game against Newcastle, Bob was booked into the Club Shop for a pre-match autograph signing session of his tribute video/ DVD. Imagine his surprise when he discovered he was playing!

Having not trained for a week or having met his first team colleagues professionally that year was not great preparation. Bob was predictably out-of-sorts. He only lasted fifteen minutes before limping off with tears in his eyes.

Both sets of supporters gave him a standing ovation, many with moist eyes of their own.

Despite the rather bold £15 admission charge for what was a scratch match against an assortment of former team-mates and anyone else whose arm could be twisted, Bob's testimonial was attended by 12,000 people, which tells its own story. It was genuinely fun too, unlike many moribund benefits. Despite his injury, Bob made a token appearance up front. He returned again in the second half in goal, playing at every opportunity to the crowd. Finally, he grabbed a microphone and gave an impromptu speech over the PA to tumultuous enthusiasm. Such poignancy. It felt to everyone present like the end of an era.

WHY DOES HE remain a crowd hero even now? Initially goals. Finding the net gets you noticed at the Hawthorns and regular scorers are always most popular. Bob boasts 131 Albion goals to his name, and only seven men in Albion's long and glorious history can claim more.

His goals were rarely spectacular – with a few exceptions. In the infamous "paddy field" match at Luton in May 1994, Bob took on and beat several defenders, who just couldn't keep their feet, before sliding the ball past the keeper. Also, in 1995, he dived between two Wolves defenders to reach a perfect centre from Lee Ashcroft to finish off the Staffordshire side. His qualities revolved more around timing, being in the right place at the right moment, and holding the ball up to bring others into play. He was all effort and never shrank from the physical side of the game.

Long-time fan Ian Thomson recalls another match at Kenilworth Road. "There was the slightly comical sight of Bob Taylor squaring up to Luton's yellow-shirted giant goalkeeper Feuer. The keeper was chatting away to Bob and doing a lot of finger wagging. Bob pulled himself up to his greatest height in this standoff and put on a brave face. Try as he did, poor Bob was made to look like a small school-kid being confronted by the school bully. The unfortunate ending to the incident was a booking for the striker."

Similarly, in a much celebrated comeback at Exeter City (2-0 down to 3-2 up), Bob was undeterred by goalkeeper Kevin Miller charging out at him, hands at neck height and ran straight into a boot in his ribs. While Bob was off the field receiving treatment, team-mate Ian Hamilton put away the winner from the spot past the substitute keeper – Miller having been sent-off.

Years later, Miller got his revenge. Albion had just scored at Barnsley to reduce a deficit to 3-2. Miller refused to release the ball to Bob for a quick kick-off. Worse, he acted as though the Albion man had punched him. Bob denied any wrongdoing, but was still dismissed, one of only two red cards whilst with the Baggies. The other early bath came at Southend, for two tackles, neither of which was particularly vicious.

Bob was never quick, so asking him to chase long balls was rather futile. Because the North-Easterner became a favourite so quickly, at fault for losing possession was never Bob, but the passing player. "Give him a ball" was the more polite of comments, but indicates how supporters confer a certain elevated status to a favourite.

Typically as a striker, his confidence dipped when he wasn't scoring. Explains Bob, "I hate going on a long spell without scoring. I'm a goalscorer, that's what I do, I know I can score goals, but the more games go on, the more frustrated you get and the more you suffer and the more your game suffers. Goals are what you're judged on." Suffering such as the Huddersfield home match in 1997/98 when Bob played 45 minutes where he couldn't win the ball, couldn't hold it, couldn't pass it. Each mistake drew another curse and another agonised expression from a man painfully at war with himself. The half-time substitution was a mercy.

Bob went from November 1994 to March 1995 without a goal, eventually finding the net at Fratton Park. Typically, the match had significance. The Baggies were slipping worryingly towards the bottom three with only one win in seven. The first was a gift from 25 yards that keeper Knight fumbled. Thus rejuvenated, and with the small midweek travelling crowd urging him on, Bob then hit the bar and had another cleared off the line before winning the game in the 87th minute, running onto a perfect Agnew cross. Bob was back. A week later, came his previously mentioned diving header to secure a win against Wolverhampton.

A MEASURE of any Albion player's popularity is the supporter's reaction to them when they return with their new club. Comparatively few, if any, these days have affections maintained once they depart for footballing pastures new. Bob Taylor was an exception, as author and supporter Ian Thomson recalled on a visit to the Reebok Stadium in February 1999. "I can't imagine that any player can ever have received a more rousing ovation from the fans of a former club than that which we heard when the announcer read Bob's name out before the game. If Bolton fans didn't realise what an absolute diamond they have got their hands on before that wonderfully spontaneous show of appreciation, they should have been left in no doubt thereafter."

Bob scored his 12th goal of his season that day – for Bolton. This was the game where, in an emotional and utterly genuine moment, he swapped shirts with Lee Hughes post-match and ran to the away supporters kissing the Baggies' badge. He explained later that his departure to Bolton had been hasty and there was no time to say goodbye to Albion people. This was his belated thank-you.

Bob still remembers his first visit to the Hawthorns as a Bolton player. When he came on as a substitute, "the whole ground stood up for me, a standing ovation all the way round. The press guys at Bolton said they'd never seen anything like it, I had the Chairman come down to say he'd never seen such a response for a single player. People talk about the hair standing up on the back of your neck and it does, you get a tingle and that's what does it for me. I do love the club and the bond I have with the people, the fans and that's special for me."

SuperBob is far more than the sum of his goals and the significance behind them. There's both gratitude and relief that for a decade, it was Bob who was there when we needed him to keep us in the Division or propel us into the Division above.

Despite all those goals in the 1992/93 Play-off Season, he surprisingly didn't score in the Play-offs. But he did set up Andy Hunt for the aggregate equaliser in the semi-final against Swansea and he was through on goal at Wembley before Swan brought him down and was sent off. A year later, he started the move for Ashcroft's goal at Fratton Park, which kept the Baggies up. In May 2000, Bob scored the key first goal against Champions Charlton that again preserved our status. Two years after that came the goal of dreams – the clincher against Palace, which put Albion into the Premier League. Promotion and what it meant to players and supporters alike are captured in that iconic picture of Bob celebrating that goal. There are variants on the background, depending on the photographer, but all centre on the popular striker – mouth open in a bellow of triumph, eyes alight and arms seeking the skies in which it was written that the veteran striker would score that day. Captain Derek McInnes picked up on the vibe and dreamt the previous night that Bob would find the net. Bob was modest enough to laugh at that prophecy.

Ah yes, modesty. One of his major endearing qualities is that he doesn't seek to exploit his status, wage negotiations excepted. He's always got time for supporters. "For me, the club is the fans. They welcomed me with open arms, they gave me a chance and still to this day, they give me a chance. I missed a penalty against Grimsby, a chance against Swindon and many others and still they support me and chant my name." Fine words, almost a cliché for modern players, but Bob backs the words with deeds, attending supporter's functions, weddings, birthdays – often low key, refusing all expenses in a throwback to Jeff Astle's day. Presumably his modest background helps maintains his popularity and his 'man of the people' status – son of a miner, who endured an YTS scheme with Age Concern for a year, and later worked as a bin man. Bob understands hard times and those in need of a hand.

SuperBob was one of a tiny handful of Albion people who visited Ronnie Allen in his care home. When Lee Hughes needed a friend, Taylor was there for him, offering what support he could. Once the press stopped looking, he visited the prison. In addition; he was a one-man boost for sick children in Sandwell Hospital.

BOB DOES FIND being a supporter quite difficult. To quote him literally, "I dunnoor how yees stond it". The then Tamworth forward was at the famous 'Great Escape' fixture against Portsmouth in May 2005. During the second half, it all became too much for him and, stricken with nervous tension, our hero had to retreat to the bar downstairs. "I was up and down like a yo-yo!" After the tension was over, he was spotted capering around on the turf with several thousand others.

The Bob Taylor sense of humour is never far away. In May 2003, the end of season theme at Blackburn was 'referees at Rovers' to reflect the influence the men in black had had on our season. Although technically still on Albion's books, Bob travelled on the Supporters coaches and wore referee's gear.

There's a legendary Albion supporter known universally as "long-haired Mick" for obvious reasons. Mick Hamblett was one of 14 Baggies followers who travelled to Cosenza for a point-less Anglo-Italian League fixture (neither side could qualify) just before one Christmas. As the numbers were so small, fans and players mixed the previous night. Mick had just bought a round of drinks and was carrying them on a tray across the bar, when he was seized around the waist from behind. Before he could protest too much, his belt was swiftly undone and his trousers sank to his ankles. The contents of the tray capsized in all directions. Mick swivelled angrily to meet his assailant only to find a grinning Bob Taylor. And yes, Bob did get another round in.

Albion supporter Simon Cotter has only embarrassing memories of his contact with the Great Man. He confessed, "I crashed into the back of Super Bob's car at the Scott Arms (a road junction in Great Barr, Birmingham). "This was during his first spell with us and just after an operation on his ankle, so his wife was driving. I didn't care that I'd dented my own car. I was thinking about his, but thankfully it was fine."

TAYLOR'S FOOTBALL ODYSSEY continued elsewhere post Albion – firstly at Cheltenham, where he scored a few goals though recurring injuries proved his downfall. Followers of the Robins became accustomed to the regular presence of Albion supporters at their games as Bob admitted. "I don't want to sound wrong about this, but at Cheltenham, the number of Albion supporters turning up was embarrassing. They'd come in cars, minibuses, coaches sometimes, all be wearing the blue and white stripes and the Cheltenham people got used to having them about – like part of the scenery." It was this author's misfortune that when he went to Whaddon Road for a League match with Hull City, Bob was on the sub's bench. He left the bench as a second half substitute, only to return it a minute later after a sickening but totally accidental collision with the opposition goalkeeper. Another injury and several more games missed meant that Cheltenham didn't renew his deal and so, as no more full-time offers came his way. Bob settled for the less stressful life of a part-time professional with Tamworth in the Nationwide Conference.

The difference in standard was noticeable; according to Bob, "It is a different scenario to what I am used to. I've always had full-time training and so on. When you get to my age, many people would be happy to go part-time, but I miss the day-to-day involvement. In saying that, we have a good craic with the lads training twice a week here. And I have lost all the pressure that goes with the full-time game. So I am now back to enjoying playing football for the sake of it, like when I was 17 to 18 years-old. Football is a business now, so you get stress day-in, day-out with managers pushing you for results. I am not one who likes that. I used to take football home with me and my family suffered from it. I was miserable after a defeat. But I am more relaxed now. Tamworth is a tidy little club and I love it here. But if we get beat then I accept it and have a pint after the game."

For all of Tamworth's League matches in the South-East, a group of London-based Albion supporters inevitably turned up to cheer on their hero and barrack anyone who tackles him unfairly. Being the Conference, they have the opportunity to join their favourite number nine in the club bar after the game.

THE NEWS OF his drinking and driving offence in November 2005 was dreadfully flattening. The story was reported in neutral, almost hushed tones in the press and unusually, few people chose the "serve him right" line. There was precious little debate on the subject, as if to mention Bob's court appearance would somehow make the problem worse. Something died that day, one of the hero worship bulbs expired, never to be replaced. I surmised at the time that Bob was having difficulty adjusting to the real world, missing the day-to-day involvement of the full-time game. He didn't miss "the bollockings", he was quite clear on that subject, but perhaps like demobbed soldiers, what he missed, possibly without even realising, was the discipline.

"Playing football is the only thing I know... I've always said I'm as thick as two short planks," are familiar sentiments from the North-Easterner over the years. Bob is anything but thick. As an orator, he's erudite, passionate and eminently believable. He was both fortunate and unfortunate to realise at a very early age that all he wanted to do was play football. Fortunate that his schoolboy realisation gave him complete focus to chase his dream. He was fortunate to have the talent to back his imagination. Unfortunate that his dream affected his schooling. "I sometimes wish I'd put more into other things at school."

In the meantime, SuperBob continues to pull on his boots even now at the age of 39, on a non-contract basis with Kidderminster Harriers under manager and admirer Mark Yates. "I remember Bernie McNally telling me, "Whatever you do, don't retire... keep playing as long as you can." I was already 35, going on 36 and since then, hanging up my boots has never really been in my thoughts. Besides, playing football is the only thing I know... I will play even if it's for the Dog & Duck. While I can keep myself fit, I will carry on. It's a challenge to push myself. That's why I haven't really been tempted to go for coaching qualifications because it could just affect my focus on playing. I would like to start at the bottom of the coaching ladder and work my way up. Coaches need respect and you only get that by working your way up. Maybe I could begin by coaching youngsters. I need to learn man-management and how to talk to people. I'd love to half believe that one day I'd return to West Brom. It would be difficult though, the fans hold me up there with the likes of Jeff Astle."

Ah yes, those coaching qualifications. As long ago as 1995, Bob was talking of obtaining said qualifications. He did secure the first part of the UEFA badge at Bolton, but almost a decade later it's fair to wonder whether Bob is serious about this career path. It's hard to imagine such an essentially decent person taking on the sometimes-dictatorial nature of football coaching.

Final word as ever from Bob: "I'd like to think I've always given value for money, whatever the results. I don't think I've ever gone on the pitch and not given 100% for whichever club I've played for. I always try and work hard even when things are not going well for me, and mebbe that's why the fans have always been behind me so much, even when things haven't been so good, because they can see how hard I'm trying."

LEE HUGHES

1997-2001
2002-2004

BAGGIES CAREER

Games	237
Goals	98
Caps	0

MAGIC MOMENT

Scoring twice at Crewe in his second Albion match to turn the game around

'HUGHESIE'

> "Lee isn't a bad lad. On the few occasions I've talked with him at any length, I've invariably found him to be a typical Black Country bloke, the sort you'll find propping up bars in any pub from here to Tipton, and with an accent you could fry faggots on. No airs or graces whatsoever. Had he still been employed as a roofer, you wouldn't have looked at him twice."
>
> Glynis's Diary on Baggies.com

LEE Hughes had it all – fame, family, wealth, dream job and respect. He lost it all and everyone was a loser. Try to imagine the feelgood football film *When Saturday Comes* running remorselessly backwards, the good times sliding away in a hedonistic orgy. An orgy with a fatal outcome.

It's not easy to pinpoint when exactly his career moved from upward mobility onto the slippery slope. Rumours about Lee's nocturnal activities (late nights, drink, drugs, women etc) were always part of his Hawthorns baggage, as were consequent tales of the football club's alleged level of 'smoothing'. In December 1998, for instance, Lee sported a fat lip, the result of a 'fall', a 'fight' or a 'slip on ice', depending on which account you believed. Clearly though, Lee's departure to Coventry was a watershed, the end of an era. The 'local boy made good' image was exchanged for cold hard cash.

Lee had a clause in his contract that enabled him to go if Albion were offered over £5 million; one agreed by then Chairman Paul Thompson. Manager Gary Megson didn't want the "best goalscorer outside the Premier League" to leave. Certainly he fitted the manager's mould of an ideal footballer – enthusiastic with a maniacal work rate. The Smethwick goalscorer played for Megson either as a central striker or occasionally wide, and willingly tackled back enthusiastically.

Coventry was a bad choice for so many reasons, but the Sky Blues were the only bidders. They were not a Premiership side, so the transfer was easy to perceive as greed rather than ambition. As an Albion man, Lee should have known that Coventry are never taken seriously, much to do with a 7-1 thrashing in their chocolate mud strip in 1978/79, followed by numerous stuffings ever since. His insistence that "Coventry were a more ambitious club" or the even more unrealistic claim that Albion were trying to sell him to Wolves sounded simply pathetic.

No, he'd gone for the money, head turned by an agent. The move increased Lee's salary spectacularly – probably by 60%. However, he wasn't exactly on the breadline at the Hawthorns. His numerous critics wondered just how much money he really needed. A five-figure weekly cheque seemed decent enough remuneration for someone in his or her dream job.

The Sky Blues' comparative nearness didn't help either because there were too many reminders via local newspapers and television. City frankly couldn't afford a £5,001,000 transfer.

Their debts were not quite of Leeds United's Third World proportions, but what possessed the club's bank to authorise such a massive outgoing without the Premier League financial bulwark is not recorded. With Highfield Road already sold, not even the traditional land security was available. And with City being in the same Division as the Baggies, there was a day of reckoning in store.

While Coventry struggled to come to terms with the in your face nature of the second tier of football, Albion managed very nicely without Hughes. The meeting of the two clubs at the Hawthorns brought down much opprobrium upon the exile's head. "One greedy roofer" was a loud, popular, but not universal refrain. A goodly proportion of the home support refused to join in, silently preferring to remember the happier times. So-called 'big club' Coventry could only half-fill the away end and predictably lost to Albion again, 1-0. Lee salvaged some brownie points by applauding his former supporters after the game.

By the time of the return match in Easter, Lee Hughes was but a mere sideshow. 'Dingle Chasing' was occupying all supporters' waking hours, including some when they'd rather be asleep. Albion sat in third spot, just behind a wilting Wolverhampton. The Staffordshire side were left wandering after a lunchtime defeat by Manchester City. An Albion win would leave the Baggies just a point short of second place. Could 16 years of hurt be at an end?

Whipped up by a frantic, bulging-eyed support, the Albion team acted like a threshing machine on their Coventry opponents. Hughes was left isolated, receiving only high balls from his rattled colleagues. It quickly became clear anyway from his body language that he had no intention of scoring that afternoon. He was subbed quite early in the second half, leaving the field to mocking choruses of "you should have stayed with a big club." More magnanimously, later cries of "Hughesie, Hughesie, give us a wave" from the Albion following brought an enthu-siastic response. After the match, which WBA won 1-0 to continue their march on the Premier League, prodigal Lee was spotted leaning out of a window in the main stand, punching the air in triumph at any Albion supporters passing by. He later left Highfield Road in the company of his former team-mates.

THE SCENE WAS set for the prodigal's return to the Hawthorns in the summer, an inevitable one, given that Coventry were flat broke, while the Baggies needed to boost their Premier League ranks. Furthermore, Hughes' goalscoring record for City was modest and twice he'd been sent off (despite his regular disputes with referees, he was never dismissed in Albion colours).

City tried for more cash, but Albion kept their nerve and agreed that the second half of the original transfer fee would not be paid. Lee bounced around the Hawthorns excitedly as if nothing had changed. "It felt like I'd come back home," he said. "It was just such a great feeling pulling the shirt on. Playing in the Premiership was always a dream for me."

But the player-supporter relationship would never be the same again. He was now just another forward. Scoring goals changes moods, but Lee was to manage just one all season – and that in the League Cup against a Wigan Athletic side then two Divisions lower. Lack of goals dogged the Baggies all season, as did ill luck and they were all too soon relegated. A match report in the Albion fanzine *Grorty Dick* summed up the striker's showing, "All our best chances fell to the former roofer, (yes, it was a good match in that respect as we had more than one) and typically these days, the opposition keeper swallowed the lot. It was both heartening and disheartening at the same time. Heartening that he was getting in the right positions and shooting and disheartening because our Rooney prototype is, right now, a football jaffa."

Ah yes, Rooney. The similarities between Wayne Rooney and Lee Hughes in their early days are obvious. Both street footballers, angry, unpredictable, grateful young men, and so marvellous to watch. They were spontaneous. But Albion's Rooney was no more. The season at Highfield Road seemed to put more thought into Lee's life. His interviews were now at least semi-lucid, now that he was familiar with the footballers' lexicon of clichés. The thought process changed his game too. His ball control was tighter, but only at the expense of his instinct. That inner sixth sense, which lay behind his extraordinary goalscoring, was no more, replaced by traditional moves learnt on the training ground. His performance was poorer for it.

Post Coventry, the quiet whispers that surrounded his non-playing activities rose to a new shrillness. The delights of playing for the Baggies seemed to take second place to earthier pleasures as the striker hinted, when asked about the downside of playing on a Sunday. "All yer mates gooing aert Sat'day night and yow cor goo aert."

A FEW STORIES were just too far-fetched to have any credence, such as "He's staying at Megson's house because it's the only way he can keep Hughes off drugs." The rest were not so easily dismissed, such was their volume and wide provenance. His driving record was not good. After one earlier incident, he'd taken the option of a two day driving improvement course at Oldbury, in a class with several Wolves supporters in it. But Hughes failed to benefit from the experience. A later potential drink driving charge was headed off by means of a large cheque to the victim. He became even more notoriously unreliable, regularly failing to show for a variety of pre-arranged PR-type functions. While Albion were winning matches back in Division One and Hughes scoring reasonably regularly, the emperor's clothes syndrome prevailed. Nobody seriously wanted that boat rocked. There was undoubtedly a degree of management blind eyes. However, Lee was a natural athlete, and regardless of whatever he'd allegedly done or not done the previous night, full-on training was never a problem.

In October 2003, Lee scored a surprise winner in extra-time at St. James' Park to knock Premiership Newcastle out of the Carling Cup. He ran off to the left side of the stadium to celebrate, curious as the away support was in the opposite direction. Another winning goal followed just a few days later in a quite extraordinary victory at West Ham. Neil Clement recalled: "I remember warming up with Lee Hughes, and he was getting a lot of stick from their fans. He just said to me he fancied himself to score if he came on." Albion battled back from 3-0 down to win 4-3, with substitute Hughes taking advantage of a David James error to find the net via a defender's leg. Off the back of such memorable moments are crowd favourites made. The former roofer was well on the way to rebuilding affections.

But barely a fortnight later on 22nd November, Lee Hughes was at the wheel of his Mercedes when it struck a Renault Megane driven by 56-year-old Douglas Graham. Graham was killed instantly, while his wife Maureen was badly injured. Lee left the scene. Unbeknown to the author (fortunately, to avoid a personal dilemma), the fugitive reportedly hid from Police in a small terraced house, just two streets away from my own home. Two days later, Lee turned himself in and the legal wheels started to move.

Once bailed, he was available again for selection. Because Hughes was on the receiving end from opposition supporters, the instinctive desire to defend your club and all who sailed in her took over. During Lee's return to first team football as a substitute at Bradford City, a mixed reception from the sparse away following was countered with overwhelming hostility from the Yorkshiremen. The instinct of "My club – right or wrong" kicked in immediately. The striker, who looked well off the pace, looked grateful for any kind of support, and expansively showed his appreciation after the end of the game. Slowly, after a few matches, the opposition abuse faded away and with it the need to support the Smethwick striker. Hughes completed the season with a reasonable, if not outstanding goalscoring record.

But at the trial in August 2004, all those grapevine-whispered mitigating circumstances melted away and the bald facts were that an Albion player drove recklessly and killed Douglas Graham. Hughes had absconded, with the judge deciding that he'd done so because he had exceeded the alcohol limit. What was quickly apparent was that Lee had no real defence. His hugely expensive legal team had nothing to work with. Hughes was sentenced to six years in prison. There was no doubt about his guilt, but the length of the sentence was surprisingly punitive.

With a legal bill probably in excess of £500,000, the lavish Solihull house was sold, to another footballer with a far cleaner nose – Emile Heskey. Anna Hughes and her two young siblings moved to a small terraced property in Smethwick to be nearer the in-laws, but even this support was not enough for the under-pressure young mum. She sought comfort from another man. Unfortunately for her, the Hughes family remain newsworthy and her affair was listed in detail in a Sunday newspaper. More pressure and more recriminations naturally followed. Lee is already in his fifth different prison and appears to have lost his chances of parole after three years following an apparent find of illicit contraband in his open nick cell. Stupid just isn't the word any longer. The setback has probably finished off his last hope of restarting his career in a lower Division. The mighty has fallen.

BUT IT WASN'T always so. Lee Brett Hughes was born on 22 May 1976 in Dudley Road Hospital in Birmingham. In line with his brothers, Clint and Brett, parents Bill and Gail chose names from cowboy films. Lee was what might be perceived as a traditional Black Country child. He was never considered to have any academic tendencies. When put on the spot, one of his primary school teachers diplomatically said, "Put it this way, he wasn't in my top group." Sport has always been his passion – football, cricket, golf (though all water obstacles continued to defeat him) – it all came so naturally. He was friendly and amiable, and only really knew Smethwick. He once described his favourite smell as 'curry'.

After turning out for a number of well-known boys football teams at the age of 13, he signed for Albion as a full-back. As Lee himself put it, "the organisation wasn't very good, though." There's a cute picture in *Grorty Dick* fanzine of a training session with guest Stanley Matthews next to a wide-eyed 14-year-old Lee Hughes, wearing full WBA gear. Eventually, coach Cyril Lea broke the news that the Baggies weren't going to offer him an YTS deal. "That was horrible. It killed me really. I thought that was my chance at West Brom over and done with," admitted Lee, years later.

The Smethwick youngster tried out unsuccessfully for Walsall, where in his two games, he played once in goal and the other up front, where he scored a hat-trick. According to Hughes, Walsall reneged on a promise to offer him an apprenticeship. Then "I played a few games for Swansea and things were going well, but I played the last game with flu and didn't do myself justice. I thought I'd blown my chance of ever becoming a footballer then." Oldbury United were also similarly unimpressed before Kidderminster Harriers Youth gave him a go.

The young forward hoped to get a YTS place at the Harriers, but in the end there was no decision for management to make – the Conference side felt they couldn't justify the attendant costs and cut the programme. Lee continued to play for the Youth side until he was 18, in between working for a living with his uncle in his long-established roofing business. Not always with the greatest of success. Wendy Maxfield observed Lee and two other workers re-roofing her neighbour's garage. One of the three subsequently put his foot through the roof, and the hole was patched with a refuse sack.

Lee made his Harriers first team debut against Northwich Victoria in September 1994. His impact wasn't immediate, and there were numerous substitute appearances, but there was no doubt the young lad with bright red hair was very quick and direct.

Lee's Dad travelled to every game. Bill Hughes is a genuine Albion fan, but put his son first and followed him home and away with the Harriers. Lee always wanted to turn professional, and had trials with Sheffield Wednesday, "I got injured on the second day there," and Wolves, "I wouldn't have been that keen on signing for them."

Hughes played at Wembley in the 1995 FA Trophy Final (lost 2-1 to Woking after extra time) "I was nervous. When I was getting changed, I kept thinking about all the other people who'd got changed in that changing room. And the pitch was like a carpet." The experience remained one of his all-time favourite football moments. The other came later – scoring from the penalty spot against Wolves.

With Lee pushing their attack forward, Kidderminster improved. Their 11th place in the Conference in 1994/95 became 7th a year later and then, with Hughes leading the Conference scoring charts, they finished in second place, five points behind Champions Macclesfield. The redhead was setting new records, becoming the youngest player to turn out for the England semi-pro team (v Ireland in 1996) and the youngest to score a hat-trick in the Conference (v Bath). It was obvious that even if Harriers weren't joining the Football League, their top goalscorer would be. Bristol City made the first pitch, offering £200,000. Harriers declined the offer.

Albion coach John Trewick first watched Lee Hughes, and recommended him to WBA in 1995. Albion manager Buckley, of course, always knew best, and considered he didn't need any advice from anybody. Howard Martin was one of a number of supporters who gently tried to persuade irascible Eastwood-born Bucko that a certain ginger-haired Albion-loving wide player at Kiddy Harriers was worth purchasing. Although Howard's enquiry was gently put using all of his experience as a business consultant, the response was not. "I pick the team, not you."

The departure of the irascible Buckley late in the 1996/97 season led to the arrival of Ray Harford, a progressive manager keen to embrace new ideas. Trewick's suggestion was well received. Albion approached Harriers in the summer and Kidderminster listened. The Baggies offered more than the £200,000 dangled by Bristol City, and could add the carrot of regular lucrative pre-season friendlies. Furthermore, Harriers knew that Hughes's dream was to play for 'his' club. "I never wanted to play anywhere else," he would later claim, and to block his path would be counterproductive. A fee of £250,000 was agreed.

HUGHES' FIRST appearances in the famous blue and white came in pre-season friendlies in July 1997. Lee worked hard, even frantically. Sometimes a player is a Cult Hero before he kicks a ball, purely because of his reputation, such as Michael Owen's arrival at Newcastle. Lee was willed to succeed, 'our representative on the pitch', the ultimate player – 'lived local, supported local', a kid who kissed the club badge and meant it.

The programme of warm-up games concluded with a Hawthorns match against Premier League Chelsea. The Londoners were strolling, with an experienced, albeit second-string defence, dominating the huffing lower division opposition. At half-time, on came a slim player with fiery red hair who didn't know or care about the conventions of the professional game. He was going to run at Chelsea, and they could try to stop him.

Within minutes, the Londoners' back four were looking at each other anxiously. This unknown kid could embarrass them. They double-marked him, sometimes with a third man behind. Lee loved it. He just ran at them with the ball. Chelsea were just happy to get the ball away anywhere… for a corner, free-kick, whatever. "Hughesie, Hughesie" bellowed the Hawthorns faithful for the first time. Lee didn't manage to score that day, though he had nine shots.

His competitive debut followed in a brief showing as a substitute in the first home League game against Tranmere. Albion's next fixture was at Gresty Road. Two late goals from Lee turned the 2-1 deficit into a late 3-2 win. His first, from a Kilbane pass, saw him arc the ball with his right foot past the keeper. The winner saw him twist free inside the box before lashing the ball into the roof of the net. As supporter Richard Brentnall put it, "the 90th minute strike provoked the visitors' enclosure into a passable impression of Rampton hit by a mortar shell."

The Alex had been outwitting Albion for years, so this victory was particularly sweet, not least because the Baggies were second in the table after three games. During those difficult times, desperate supporters would milk every positive dry. Lee was interviewed on BBC Radio Two afterwards where he sounded every inch the naïve Black Country lad. Comparisons were quickly drawn with Cyrille Regis's dramatic debut against Rotherham. Even Sean Bean in *When Saturday Comes* would be impressed with such a start.

Hughes only played 30 minutes at Crewe. This was often the case under Harford, who wanted to "introduce him gently." From his perspective, there wasn't any hurry. His chosen formation was 4-5-1 with the clever Andy Hunt as the preferred front-runner. Should he need to chase the game or rest Hunt, he had Bob Taylor and Paul Peschisolido to call upon.

Only when Harford resigned, to be replaced by Denis Smith, could Lee remove the splinters from his bottom. Denis realised straightaway that he'd got a natural goalscorer in the squad, and made full use of his talents. He was wise enough not to impose rigid training methods on his protégé. Lee succeeded through pure instinct. Nature simply took over, and guided the youngster at high speed towards the net. His philosophy was simple. "Other than one or two like Steve Bruce, I dunno their nairmes. Never bovva to look at the programme. I just stond on their shoulder and do 'em for pairce."

LEE HUGHES was born to score goals. His natural speed was allied to an instinctive ability to defeat goalkeepers. Give him time to think about options, such as one-on-ones and he'd struggle, but try "hit this ball" and he'd hit it. Throw in aggression, a genuine love of a football club, and unpredictable play, and the combination made him mightily difficult to subdue.

"There's nothing to match playing for Albion at the Hawthorns. You run through the tunnel and look at where you used to stand as a lad. It's just the biggest buzz." Sounds as though a benevolent journalist added a little polish to the original expression, but the enthusiasm was genuine.

One prominent Albion supporter stopped outside Barclays Bank in Soho Road, Birmingham to use the cash point. Lee arrived shortly after and, as they knew each other slightly, easily fell into conversation. Albion's new signing was bubbling over with excitement, and couldn't help himself. The conversation became a monologue as the ginger-haired one rattled on like a busted flush about WBA, oblivious of subtle and not so subtle hints that the supporter wanted to move on. The fan finally resorted to direct action. "Lee... f*** off!"

Lee demonstrated his genuine passion for the club when he missed a match at Gigg Lane due to suspension. Being booked was an occupational hazard for Lee; nearly all were for kicking the ball away or dissent. He was invited to appear on cult Saturday morning Sky TV show *Soccer AM* to demonstrate his arm-swinging goal celebration. Afterwards, he chose to fly from London to Manchester, then onward to Bury to sit with the Albion supporters. He was famously received. By then, he even had an Albion tattoo to show off. Following a dismal team performance, he was ironically voted as Man of the Match by supporters, just for turning up.

Before he became a regular, Lee was happy to join his Dad on the terracing. The author witnessed the youngster being searched by a steward at Kenilworth Road and couldn't resist adding "be careful what you're doing. That's a million pound striker you're handling." The official looked suitably embarrassed: "I'm sorry – I didn't know." Months later at a fans' function, Lee admitted, "I still see myself as a supporter."

Even in his later, more cynical days, he still remembered his roots. The Balti Kid attended Jeff Astle's funeral at Netherseal in Derbyshire. As a Coventry player, he could easily consider that the occasion was nothing to do with him. But the prodigal son made the effort, and Laraine Astle was pleased to see him. Perhaps his appearance was not so much of a surprise. When Albion were at home and Coventry gameless, he'd still be spotted at the Hawthorns, celebrating goals as lustily as any supporter.

His obvious dislike of Wolves only added to his popularity. Through fair means or sometimes foul, as in Kevin Muscat's sly elbow, he was never permitted a goal in open play against the Wanderers, though he did once score from a penalty that he'd won himself. When Albion defeated their Staffordshire rivals 2-0 in November 1998, Lee celebrated as if he'd scored the Baggies second goal, rather than Shaun Murphy. He later admitted that he knew he hadn't scored, but just wanted to wind the Wolves fans up.

INTO HIS second season in 1998/99, with a lucrative new four-year contract, there was an expectation that Lee would score in every game. Those expectations were close to being met with 28 goals by January (only one in Cup competitions as Albion didn't really do cups at that time). Had he not missed six one-on-ones with the goalkeeper in the first three games, the tally would have been even higher. Still, as the *Sunday Mirror* put it, "Hughes doesn't just score goals, he scores quality goals – the brace against Stockport were world class."

Lee scored numerous pairs plus three hat-tricks, just one short of the club record tally for a single season. His first triple came in twenty second-half minutes at Port Vale, even if the linesman was the only person to spot the ball having crossed the line for his third. "His fresh faced enthusiasm was positively anachronistic in today's cynical game," offered the *Stoke Sentinel*. After his third hat-trick, against Huddersfield Town in November, "Hughesie for England" was the chant of the day.

The Ginger Ninja achieved all this with intermittent support from a mediocre team. He was expected to win high balls and chase anything. As supporter Kevin Candon opined at the time, "The obsession with belting the ball towards the bobbing red head of the pale goal-magician may be understandable, but it asks too much of Hughes, as it would any striker given accuracy on the scale of custard pie throwing." Hughes was now the "hottest striker in the country" according to the *Birmingham Post*. Sister publication the *Sunday Mercury* produced a life-size poster of a young-looking Lee.

BUT SIGNS OF burn-out were quickly evident. While the team depended upon him for goals, Lee became a marked man – literally sometimes in the case of Oxford's goalkeeper Gerrard, who "chased Hughes like a schoolboy in the playground, before knocking him to the floor." Lee was substituted quickly, but still missed the next two games. Gerrard remained on the field.

As the festive season rolled round, the press concentrated on Lee's efforts to score 28 goals before Christmas, a feat that would win him a Mazda sports car. In the end, he needed a hat-trick against Tranmere and couldn't even manage one against very determined opposition. The striker found the extra pressure uncomfortable. "I'm just glad it's all over now" being his post-match comment. The car was later lent to him anyway, though it was probably rather pedestrian for Lee, who, toyshop-like, seemingly bought a new BMW or Mercedes every three months. But the high expectation of scoring goals, plus dealing with fans, agents, the press and so on was becoming generally too much of a burden for such a callow youth. As manager Denis Smith noted, "He's constantly being pestered by people and he's too nice a lad to say 'no' and everybody wants him.."

Lee bought his first house, literally around the corner from his parents' home, in modest Smethwick. The advantages of staying close to both his family, and his favourite local balti restaurants were obvious, but this was not a wise move. Apart from being a BMW insurer's nightmare location (Lee's annual insurance bill was thought to be £8,000), over-enthusiastic Albion supporters, the local drunks and Wolves followers all considered Chez Hughes fair game. Newspaper speculation that he was moving to Middlesbrough didn't help either… or a written transfer request, code for an agent-inspired "I want more money."

After so long in the lower Division footballing wilderness, the need for a prophet for supporters to pin their hopes upon became increasingly important to them. In the end, an abrasive, yet eloquent Mancunian, who lived in Yorkshire but worked in the Black Country took that role. But years before the arrival of Megson, Lee was discovering just how hard it was to please everybody all of the time. His very naiveté at first was his protection. But as he grew used to the lucrative football life and paradise became a workplace, his attitude slowly hardened. So did his moods. He learnt to say 'no'. He learnt rudeness quite easily in his quest for self.

Another season meant another pay rise for Lee, and another manager. Mogadon man Brian Little dampened everyone's enthusiasm, including his own. His insistence of regularly playing Lee as a sole striker, a role he was ill-equipped to carry out, had a major impact on the forward's goal tally being cut by half.

This was a dreadful, couldn't-care-less time, with the manager so wrapped up in his own personal problems the team were able to do what they wished. Dwindling supporter interest increased the pressure at the bank, which insisted on the sale of Kevin Kilbane to Sunderland in

December, or they would foreclose on the overdraft. For the bare 200 supporters who travelled to sub-zero Grimsby the same day, the club had rarely such hit a low. For months, Chairman Tony Hale insisted there was money to spend, when clearly there was not. The gallant few were more interested in inquests than action that night, though Lee did find the net as Albion secured a 1-1 draw. After a further three months of awful performances, Brian Little invited the Board to sack him. They took him up on his kind offer. In came the whirling hurricane Gary Megson to retain the club's second tier status – just. A Lee Hughes hat-trick against Tranmere helped, so did his brave effort against Ipswich, but it came at a price. He damaged his knee so badly in a full-on collision with visiting keeper Richard Wright that he missed Albion's last six games. There was arguably a long-term impact as, to this day, his family are convinced that he never regained his top speed after the injury. In the short term however, his re-focussed team mates did enough without him. The Throstles, and Lee, were about to fly again.

BUT BEFORE THAT, the Smethwick striker made a major commitment. He'd previously had a very public and embarrassing relationship with a lap dancer, but this was the real deal. He travelled to Croatia to marry air stewardess Anna Kuzmanic in June 2000. When baby Mia arrived at the end of the year, fervent hopes were widely expressed that the former roofer would change his ways. He was a husband, a father, his mentor and inspiration Bob Taylor was back at the Hawthorns, and he had a dream lucrative job… what more could anybody want?

But still the accusations and tittle-tattle persisted. Now they had a harder edge, with drugs mentioned most often.

Buoyed by a better team, including costly strike partner Jason Roberts, and the urgings of manager Megson, Lee returned to form in 2000/01. In a brilliant purple patch, he scored back-to-back hat-tricks against Gillingham and Preston in November. Neither opposition played poorly, it was just their misfortune to come up against a marksman who was in devastating form.

Chance, goal. Chance, goal – metronome like. The sense of inevitability was palpable, with the roar of triumph seeming to start before he made contact with the ball. The striker was also in remarkable form in training.

Said manager Megson, "Lee has had a marvellous few days and he deserves all his success. His three goals against Gillingham all came from inside the box. This week, they were all long-range efforts. His all-round game at the moment is magnificent and he has a real appetite for goals. He is working his socks off." Or even his boots, because the pair of threes were both scored in borrowed boots, those of injured skipper Derek McInnes.

The consecutive hat-tricks coincided with the birth of his first child. Everything seemed to be going right for Lee – almost too much happiness in one go. At the time, questions were asked that if Lee was in such good form without having sex, just what was own goal-king centre-half Tony Butler doing off the field? By the end of the season, Lee had an impressive 23 goals in all competitions. Albion reached the Play-offs, the club's highest finishing position for 15 years. This was real excitement for Baggies everywhere. And then Lee sent himself to Coventry.

AFTER THE Court pronouncements, most Albion supporters were quick to instantly condemn. They felt betrayed, and took the words of the tabloid press as their opinion. Only a minority, such as long-time fan Stuart Russell, tried to understand or look beyond the superficial facts: "How the old adages "Judge not lest ye be judged" and "There but for the grace of God…" apply!

Us older members of the community remember a time before breathalysers and the like when we frequently got behind the wheel knowing ourselves to be well over any sensible limit. In Africa, party after party saw cars roar off after the driver had to be virtually carried to his vehicle. A small percentage didn't get away with it, killing themselves or someone else and in the process ruining several lives. I and many others were the lucky ones – Lee Hughes was part of that unlucky "small percentage.'

None of this is to excuse him or to try to reduce the impact his behaviour has had on the Graham family, or the passenger who now has to spend the rest of her life in a wheelchair. For her there is no reprieve. Lee can be free after three years and will be able to rebuild his life. Even so, Lee has lost his career, his income, his reputation, and his future. Mr Graham has lost his life.

But Lee has to live with something worse than loss. It is the fact that he himself caused the loss. How he must wish he could go back to the moment just before the crash and phoned for a taxi. Even worse than loss is the corrosive effect of guilt and irreversibility. Lee is now suffering far more than a six-year gaol sentence; every day he has to live with the guilt that is surely eating into his soul – and so he should. But then, so should a lot of the rest of us – and we've got off scot free.

In some small technical way, all Albion supporters have a cameo role in Lee Hughes' downfall. Accidentally of course, but to hero-worship Lee was a burden for him in many ways. (To develop the analogy to even more uncomfortable heights, there were terrace encouragements for The King to head the ball more often and supporters offering John Osborne cigarettes. Both were detrimental to the individuals' health. Neither the players nor their families would ever point fingers, more likely the opposite. The risks in that era were not always obvious.)

Many of the current England squad came from modest, inner-city council estate backgrounds. They've all had the benefit of media training and lifestyle guidance from Premier League clubs anxious to protect their investment. Lee didn't even have the benefit of an YTS apprenticeship. The Albion were not strong financially or, arguably, even in common sense terms, when the Ginger One arrived in exchange for a big cheque. New arrivals, irrespective of cost or country of origin, had to fend for themselves as best they could. One bank official of the author's acquaintance who remains anonymous, told me a sad tale of one of the club's foreign players who barely spoke a word of English, trying vainly to open an account with a West Bromwich bank. Had my acquaintance not been an Albion supporter who went out of his way to resolve the issue, the outcome for said player might have been a frustrating one.

But that doesn't matter. This lad was local, lived with his family, and was scoring goals, so everything must be OK. 'He'll be fine,' such was the club view.

LEE HUGHES once had much in common with Robbie Fowler. Both lived near to their club. Both came from a family of genuine football supporters. Both were natural goalscorers and both hit the big-time at an early and unprepared age. In his recent frank autobiography, Fowler readily admitted to a "lot of mistakes". He wised up quickly through his own efforts with the full support of a huge club. Fowler is now the richest sportsman in the country, while Lee Hughes is At Her Majesty's Pleasure.

Few supporters appear to have any sympathy with Hughes. For sure, he's been incredibly stupid, and the Graham family will have to live with the tragic consequences. The hurt he's inflicted on his family cannot easily be dismissed either. Yet for me, at heart he remains a naïve Black Country kid who was easily led.

In some ways, we've never replaced Lee. No goalscorer since has been anywhere near as effective. Albion started season 2006/07 with the top club scorer amongst the squad being a central defender. I suspect, in this money-driven age, that this chapter may never have a sequel.

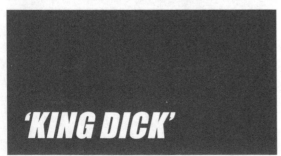

RICHARD SNEEKES

1996-2001

BAGGIES CAREER

Games	253
Goals	34
Caps	0

MAGIC MOMENT

The gas bill-paying 30 yard effort at Leicester City, which stuck in the stanchion of the goal

WEST BROMWICH BUILDING SOCIETY

'KING DICK'

THE Leicester City goalkeeper grimaced at the ball wedged in the supportive metal triangle between post and bar. He'd barely seen it coming at him from 30 yards out. A visiting Albion player with spectacular long hair was accepting congratulations from team-mates while hundreds of exuberant supporters in the elongated bus shelter that formed the visitors' accommodation at Filbert Street bellowed his name. "Sneekes… Sneekes." There were other cries too from a jolly contingent waving their betting slips "that's my gas bill paid." Midfielder Richard Sneekes, the Black Country's answer to Rapunzel, was in the middle of an extraordinary purple patch for the Baggies. The news clearly hadn't reached the bookmakers of Leicester who offered odds on 12/1 on the visitors' new signing scoring the first goal. The little betting kiosk had never dealt with such a long queue.

RICHARD SNEEKES' first club was his local side Ajax of Amsterdam, a pedigree both unhelpful and helpful at the same time. He'd joined their famous academy straight from school, learning what he wanted to learn. Even at that early age, he was showing signs of wanting to go his own way, to make up his own mind up – difficult in the essentially dictatorial world of football. Initially, his talent took centre stage and he made his first team debut at the age of 16 in 1985 against Haarlem, playing alongside Marco van Basten and Frank Rijkaard. He became the club's youngest ever debutant (even though the record was subsequently beaten by Clarence Seedorf, Richard's picture still hangs in the club museum).

A combination of his ego and stiff competition meant that, although he was playing regular Dutch schoolboy internationals, even a couple of Under 21 matches, his club appearances were limited to just three. Shouting something very uncomplimentary at the Ajax reserve manager during a game was not a great career move, particularly as club boss Johann Cruyff was in earshot.

He was transferred to FC Volendam for the 1988/89 season, where he scored his first senior goals, 7 in 31 matches. From there, he moved on to play 127 games for Fortuna Sittard where he took on a more defensive role. After three seasons' experience, he took the chance of a season-long loan to Lugano in Switzerland. Richard found the football easy, a lower standard than he was used to. Most of the players spoke German, so he could communicate well enough until he learned Italian. Languages have never been a problem for the midfielder – he's fluent in four and can get by in several others. For Lugano Richard had a scoring ratio of one in two, which attracted attention elsewhere which was fortunate because there was no contract on offer with the hard-up Swiss.

Bolton Wanderers offered him a trial and Richard was tempted by the passion of English football. "In England, the dressing room is noisy with lots of nice music. In Holland, it is very different, very tactical, the dressing room is very quiet and you must concentrate all the time." The triallist was made part of Bruce Rioch's summer tour of Scotland in 1994. He had a stinker in the first game at Dunfermline, startled by the speed and physical presence of the British style. "Thankfully, I played well and scored four goals in the next two games (at Ross County and Caledonian Thistle) and everything took off from there." Bolton gave Fortuna Sittard £160,000 for his services in August 1994. It was a bold move all round as there were at that time few foreign players in the English game.

"I knew a lot of people back home thought that I wouldn't stay at Bolton very long, that I wouldn't last six months," admitted Richard. Fortunately Wanderers were a passing side, which suited his style. He regularly played alongside Jason McAteer in the centre of the Wanderers team, though it was generally Jason who had the license to roam forward. There were other plus points as the man himself explains, "It was a family club, something I didn't find at other clubs and Bruce Rioch was a fantastic manager. He could be firm, but he was a lovely man and I think he was the beginning of what Bolton is today, a top Premiership team." Even today, Rioch remains Richard's favourite gaffer, in what is a very short list. Off the pitch, the Dutchman lived in a hotel only for a month, thanks to the Bolton chairman, using his property business interests to find the newcomer a house. (Richard was later to follow in the Chairman's footsteps and invest in property himself). In his time with Bolton, Richard was part of the side that reached the League Cup Final and also won the Play-offs (mainly thanks to two goals from Fabian de Freitas) to enter the Premiership. "Playing at Wembley for Bolton was the pinnacle of my career," said Sneekes a decade later. Promotion brought with it new players and Richard was increasingly overlooked. Rioch had departed and his replacement Colin Todd gave him only fourteen games (one goal). With Bolton lying bottom of the Premiership and more new players arriving, Richard couldn't see much future at Burnden Park.

MEANWHILE BACK in the real Second Division in 1995/96, West Bromwich Albion were once again struggling to retain their status. The previous year, manager Alan Buckley kept a floundering Albion side up, but a record-breaking run of one point in 14 matches saw them in grave danger once again. Through dint of much shouting, the diminutive gaffer steadied the ship to a degree, but linkage between deafened midfield and punch-drunk forwards was poor in an essentially rigid defensive line-up.

Richard sat in the Halfords Lane directors box for the Albion versus Port Vale match in March 1996. As a selling tool, a dismal 1-1 draw didn't overly help. "A lack of cerebral function," wrote the Birmingham Post reporter of his would-be team mates. At least it was the fifth game unbeaten and there was clearly a first team place up for grabs. After almost a fortnight of agonising, consultation with former Albion man Romeo Zondervan and backroom negotiations, the Dutchman signed for his second English club on 11th March. The fee was £400,000, so the Wanderers had doubled their money. Equally it was a big spend for the Baggies, their biggest single outgoing for fifteen years, a transaction only made possible by a cash injection by new director Paul Thompson. It was to be the biggest ever transfer in Alan Buckley's long managerial career.

Naturally Richard was pounced upon for his thoughts and, as was to become the norm, he was always willing to express them. "Albion have the quality players and skill to keep us in this Division," he offered as his token PR gesture before adding, "the manager is very enthusiastic and he likes to play passing football. That is my kind of game and the reason I finally decided to come here."

Cynical supporters questioned why a Premier League player should wish to move to the ailing Baggies. Their suspicions were heightened with the revelation that, although Sneekes had signed a two and a half year deal, the package included an escape clause should West Bromwich be relegated.

As ever, the acid test came on the Hawthorns pitch. Sneekes' debut was against bottom of the table Watford. Although he barely knew the rest of the side, he just got on with his trademark runs through the middle. One such run earned him his debut goal, a feat overshadowed by Bob Taylor's solitary Albion hat-trick and the home side somehow conspiring to lose a 3-0 lead. The eventual 4-4 draw felt a big let-down, but manager Alan Buckley praised the debutant, "he was brilliant on the ball and the movement leading up to the goal was something else." But he couldn't resist adding a barb: "after spending two weeks talking to his agent, the least he could do was give us a goal or two."

His new signing obliged, scoring the winner in his second game, a 2-1 defeat of Barnsley and followed that with another, a close-range effort in a morale-boosting 1-1 draw at St. Andrew's. Local sports writer Leon Hickman was impressed, "Sneekes has provided West Brom with definition, as well as three goals in three games, speeding through midfield into positions of such menace they were possibly even less appreciated by his team mates than by Blues defenders. He is exactly what Albion have been missing for years, a player of pace and accuracy around whom to make the passing patterns that are only pretty embroidery unless they also have needle." Cyrille Regis in 1977 was the last Albion man to score in his first three games, but there was more at stake in 1996 as every point was precious.

RICHARD'S STYLE and panache enlivened a functional team playing carefully to orders. Most supporters took to the new arrival immediately. Supporter David Norman wrote in the pages of *Grorty Dick* fanzine, "On his first couple of performances, Sneekes looks a different class to the typical run of the mill players we have signed in the past. He made an immediate impact and he's the only player in the side who can make a one to one chance look so simple. That said, he tends to drift out of games in the later stages and he hasn't added a great deal of bulk to an already light midfield." Sneekes himself explained, "It's my natural game. In Holland, they call it the Bergkamp position, but I was playing that way for Ajax before Bergkamp ever played for the club."

But not everyone was won over or indeed ever would be. In this more cynical modern age, more is expected in return for big salaries. Supporter and author Ian Thomson offered a different perspective, "Everybody tried, even hardened shirkers like Richard Sneekes. He even arrived in time for some physical confrontations, though I don't know whether this was deliberate on his part. Richard does remind me of the battleground stretcher-bearer, forever arriving at the scene of the action just after it has moved off somewhere else." Both comments retained a measure of validity throughout Sneekes' Albion days.

Scoring in four consecutive games (Watford away 1-1) was too much to ask, however Sneekes immediately made up for it by scoring both goals in a 2-0 win at Portsmouth. Both were trademark dashes, accompanied by absolute belief that he'd score. After another blank against Luton, Richard's last minute six-yard tap-in winner against Millwall gave him six from seven matches – from midfield. And it was with this exciting background that Albion supporters multiplied their money twelve fold by loaning it temporarily to a bookmaker in Leicester.

The Dutchman's goal wasn't sufficient to win the Filbert Street encounter as the play-off hopefuls battered away frantically at Albion's defence. They equalised and threatened to win it until, in injury time, Sneekes' corner found Raven's head presenting Albion with an unlikely win. Leicester supporters were furious and bombarded their local radio station that night with criticism, mainly aimed at new manager Martin O'Neill. The Irishman kept a tape of the phone-in that night and barely a month later after his side won promotion to the Premier League, reminded sections of his now huge personal fan club just what a fickle bunch they were.

With such a run of results, relegation for the Baggies was unthinkable. Richard scored his eighth in a 3-1 defeat of Grimsby. Local radio commentator Tom Ross tried to sum up the moment, "The delightful Dutchman does it again. A saviour, a hero and the fans and stewards are bowing to this long haired man from Holland. Michael Bolton in shorts has done it again." There was another goal to celebrate in a 2-2 draw at Norwich. So many Albion supporters were thrilled by the revival that 500 were locked out, despite City having 10,000 empty seats.

On the plus side, relegation was no longer a threat and Albion could ease off a little. Sunderland needed a point for promotion, so we let them have it, the last away game was a 1-1 stroll at Barnsley before the Baggies finished with a flourish in a 3-2 defeat of promoted Derby. The three top scorers Hunt, Taylor and Sneekes all found the net to make a round 50 goals for the three of them in League and Cup. The newcomer had chipped in with ten in just 13 games. The Baggies finished 11th, ahead of both Blues and Wolves.

Sneekes swept the boards at the Player of the Year award, although it was difficult to spot him because everyone seemed to be wearing long blonde Sneekes wigs. As Supporters Club Chairman Clive Stapleton pointed out during the presentations, "he has to go down as one of the best bits of business this club has ever done." The man himself was genuinely embarrassed, uncomfortable with the hero-worshipping rituals and trying to dampen down expectations in what was perfect English, but with then Molby-esque Scouse overtones (a Brummie twang was to quickly replace the Liverpudlian). Only a decade later could he bring himself to admit, "I had a great time."

SUCH FORM couldn't last and indeed it didn't. Opposition got the message about the running man from Holland. Although the side remained unbeaten away until November 1997, too many draws and home defeats left everyone frustrated. Each loss was followed by Buckley screaming at his charges for a minimum of 45 minutes. In addition, Buckley had returned yet again to former club Grimsby to buy another attacking midfielder, Paul Groves. Playing the two together didn't work. The hapless Groves received a lot of stick partly because he was from Grimsby and because there was a perception he was literally getting in Richard's way.

There were some glimpses of the Dutchman at his best, such as setting up all three goals against Tranmere in September. In his remarkably honest and self-written column in the *Sports Argus*, he insisted, "I want to be known as a team player. To me, assisting in a goal is just as important. It is the result that matters, not who scores." His thoughts were always bold and brave, providing a fascinating read, but, by not towing the party line, there were so many recriminations that he eventually felt obliged to give it up. "Playing football is a privilege and it also carries with it a responsibility," he sadly noted.

Alan Buckley was the first of several Albion gaffers who wanted Sneekes to play his part in defending. But Richard didn't really do tackling. Neither did he respond well to Buckley's rants. Although in public, he tried, albeit half-heartedly, to maintain the status quo, in private he considered his Boss lacked constructive ideas. Defeats were punished by endless sessions of running.

Furthermore, Richard found Buckley's disciplinarian attitude stifling. When he and another midfielder Stacey Coldicott were told to cut their hair, Stacey immediately complied. Richard ignored the instruction. By November, he could contain his frustrations no longer and talked to the press, "I've had no chance to run onto the ball. All I have been able to do is play the ball back that is negative. I am being asked to get back and cover." His PR timing was spot on because disillusionment with Buckley was increasing all round the Hawthorns.

Richard had just four goals by Christmas, including one on his 28th birthday at Swindon Town. He ran with the ball from 35 yards out into the penalty box and volleyed home with aplomb. There was also a 25-yard spectacular against QPR in a 4-1 triumph. Reporter Leon Hickman: "Sneekes set the tone of the game with a whiplash fifth minute shot of the kind he delivered with the dependability of the milkman last season. The Dutchman then proceeded to probe tellingly, now more like a dentist."

A second defeat by Wolves in embarrassing fashion (the infamous Crichton "dodgy keeper" match) saw the wolves gathering outside manager Buckley's door. Restraining his true feelings, Richard's line to the local press was a party line cry. "We need to show we are mentally tough and we can do that by getting harder into challenges." He hastily felt obliged to add, "I know that I am not the best in that area, but I will have to start working harder." After a limp showing in the next home game against Oldham, Buckley was sacked.

HIS REPLACEMENT was Ray Harford, better known as a coach than a manager, but what a coach! Sneekes and the rest of the side took to him immediately, recording a memorable 3-2 win at St. Andrew's before Harford's appointment was made official. Suitably encouraged, Richard scored against Norwich and Southend, the latter a spectacular effort when, with back to goal, he turned and volleyed home from 25 yards. The gallant few in Sneekes wigs in the Brummie End were suitably impressed.

The Dutchman now felt he could come clean on his Buckley frustrations. "I reached the stage where I hated getting up in the morning to go training. I was played out of position and I was lucky if I got one chance every five games. I was frustrated, angry and very unhappy. I seriously thought of asking for a transfer. But the new manager has totally transformed the atmosphere in our dressing room and on the pitch. He doesn't need to shout at players or belittle them."

Albion finished the season in 16th place, with Sneekes scoring eight times. But his goals weren't so important in a squad that now boasted Hunt, Taylor and Peschisolido. That summer, Harford added the attacking talents of Kevin Kilbane and the youthful Lee Hughes to his ranks. There was no shortage of goalscorers, but could Albion stop the goals going in? Harford's solution was to strengthen the midfield in a 4-5-1 formation. The tactically astute Hunt was the lone striker, with Sneekes given free rein in support. Two powerful ball winners sat behind him. Such an arrangement was perfect for the Dutchman. "As long as I've got the freedom to express myself, to do what I do best, I'm happy." His game was at an exuberant peak – passing with panache, running, jinking; even a bit of tackling. Richard was so impressed with Harford both as a coach and as an intelligent man. "Brilliant coach: he kept players inter-ested and involved, even when they weren't in the side, and he was a lovely guy to talk to. You might have thought by looking at him he was a grumpy sort of guy but he wasn't like that at all. He knew the game, and knew what he was talking about..." The respect was mutual. "Sneekes makes some great runs," said Harford. "He allows others to get chances because he takes the eye of the defenders."

West Brom began to string results together. The first three games were won, opponents caught unawares by the Baggies' new formation. But they learnt and results became harder to achieve. Oxford United were one of the beneficiaries and their manager Denis Smith later admitted that Sneekes was quite easy to mark. "You could see him charging forward as soon as Albion had the ball. 'Here he comes again.' Our defenders at Oxford used to laugh at him."

A week later, Portsmouth defenders weren't laughing as Richard showed the full width of his vision. His corner set up Mardon for the first goal, his free-kick set up Hunt for the second, while his deflected volley gave Hunt the third. Urged on by some inspirational coaching, Albion actually won four games in a row, to reach the startling heights of second place. The last victory came courtesy of a winning goal by Sneekes against a bewildered Birmingham City, bewildered because they'd dominated the entire game. Sneekes had one chance late in the game and took it. It was his fourth successive goal in this hotly contested local derby and showcased Sneekes at his imperial best. He picked up the ball ten yards outside his own box before laying it off, kept on running and received the return pass just inside the Blues' box and fired in Muller-like from a low angle. Cue fantastic scenes and a spontaneous chant of "One chance, we only need one chance!" – a cry still used to this day.

Paul Franks on *BBC Radio WM* spoke of "daylight robbery." He asked, "Did you see anything? It happened between 1.00pm and 2.50pm in the Hawthorns area of West Bromwich. A wealthy former England international footballer [Trevor Francis] and his team were robbed. It was pleasant. The assailant had long blond hair and spoke with a foreign accent, believed to be Dutch. Do you know him? He left his victims with nothing. Battered, bruised and cursing their luck, were you in the area at the time. Did you see what happened?"

Sadly, this was to be the pinnacle for Ray Harford and Sneekes too. The following week, promotion certainties Middlesbrough beat their visitors 1-0. The Dutchman missed a good chance and gave the ball away for their winner. And then... Harford announced he was leaving. His argument that his regular travelling from his London base was damaging his marriage sounded dubious, considering his previous club was Blackburn and that his Hawthorns training sessions were regularly only twice weekly, leaving the other days to his coach John Trewick. But, despite much begging and pleading, exit stage left Harford. He was to admit later it was the biggest mistake he'd ever made, but that was no consolation at the time.

THEIR CONFIDENCE dented, the Baggies managed only one win (a close run 3-2 victory over Stockport with Sneekes scoring) in the next nine games. In the tenth game, they travelled to Molineux. The home side singled out the Dutchman for special treatment. After various wild hacks at his person, the infamous Kevin Muscat finished off the job in only the 14th minute with a lunge that Rob Bishop of the *Mail* described as "crude beyond belief." Sneekes, under-standably, was furious, complaining he was the "victim of a hatchet job". He feared his leg was broken. Thankfully it wasn't.

Perversely the loss of their stretchered-off creative midfielder only aided Albion, who brought on hard running Stacey Coldicott to join the simply hard Butler in the middle. The pair of them steamed into Wolves and took over midfield. Once on top, Andy Hunt's 72nd minute goal completed a memorable double.

But only two more wins that season left the Baggies in tenth spot. There were no more League goals for the Dutchman, though he did score twice in an enjoyable 3-1 FA Cup defeat of bogey side Stoke. This prompted the *Birmingham Mail* to comment "there is a small piece of land, front right of the penalty area at the Brummie Road end of the Hawthorns that is forever Richard Sneekes."

Through his column in the *Argus*, Richard dropped repeated heavy hints that the 1997/98 season was to be his last in England. "I love the club, but I have been thinking about this for some time." As befits a man who polarised opinions between fans who loved him one minute for scoring a wonderful goal and loathed him the next for not racing back forty yards to tackle, some supporters were offended by his words, considering him to be selfish and greedy, sentiments that in reality made little sense. Ray Harford had offered him a three-year contract and with just one forward, Sneekes' support runs were fundamental to the whole team plan. Any return to Holland would be to a poorer League and far poorer wages. Richard simply missed his family. His *Argus* notes also revealed his social conscience – rare even then for footballers; a genuine awareness of those less fortunate than himself. For instance in the last pain-racked, confused months of Ronnie Allen's life, Richard did his best to comfort Ronnie's wife Cynthia. He understood much of the turmoil they endured because his own grandfather was also suffering from Alzheimer's.

But Richard didn't move his family from Sutton that summer or any other, though there were to be many more occasions when he spoke longingly of moving home. His problem was simple, as he explained years later. "The kids have grown up here. Three of them were born in England and they've all lived as English kids. They like going to Holland to visit relatives, but we go back less and less." Richard and his wife Shirley have five children aged between 4 and 21. In Richard's latter Albion days, his eldest daughter was dating one of his team-mates. The mickey taking was no doubt unrelenting.

AFTER HARFORD, the next Albion managers were Denis Smith and Brian Little. Smith was passionate and honest, but couldn't stop Albion leaking goals, whereas Little gave the worrying appearance of heading towards a breakdown. Neither could bring Albion any success and neither really got the best from Sneekes. As webmaster Sid Collins from wbaunofficial.com had it, "Under Brian Little, Sneekes was a bit more like his old self, but started running around like a man possessed. His workrate seemed to double for many of the games, but only to the detriment of his attacking play." One outcome of this manic behaviour was Sneekes rapidly picking up seven bookings for tackling the man rather than the ball. Comically for one so regularly criticised for not getting 'stuck in', he was briefly one of the most booked players in the Division.

It was highly noticeable how Smith was now singing from a diplomatic team sheet about the Dutch midfielder, "Richard's been a big part of us all season. I have more conversations with Richard than anybody else. He is tremendously intelligent, super as far as his football is concerned. He's first class, and he can play. What I want to do is blend him into a team pattern, at times he wants to do it his way, and I want him to do it my way, but you know, fair play to him, he's a good trainer, he might not always like it. It's taken time for Richard to decide, whether we like one another off the field or about what we do on the field, we might agree to differ, but when he comes in here, he's been super for me for the foreign players with the language."

How carefully and finely tuned those words were and from a gaffer not really noted for eloquent prose. One major coup for Smith was the signing of a young Italian player in Enzo Maresca (together with two other Italians) and Sneekes' fluency in Italian was vital to prevent the young genius from being isolated. In theory, the pair competed for the "centro campista" position, but Richard was always going to put the man ahead of the football. His translation/ mentor duties became quite familiar as more and more foreign players joined the Hawthorns.

RICHARD WAS always a bit different, as Glynis Wright recalled after one encounter. "The strange thing about Richard is the fact that should you ever pass him in the street, it wouldn't immediately hit you that he was a former player. Take tonight for example; when we first clapped eyes on him wearing his trademark baseball cap, rounded off with hooded top, T-shirt, well-worn jeans and white trainers, he looked for all the world more like an off-duty brickie than someone who had graced both Premiership and First Division stages. Add to that those well-remembered long blonde locks of his, and what you have left is an image far removed indeed from the normal media stereotype of a top-rank player."

Richard befriended some rank and file supporters and met them regularly socially. He made the effort to learn the names of many others and always acknowledged their presence with unfailing politeness. On away trips, as Lee Hughes wrestled with the bigger words in the *Sun*, Sneekes was studying the *Financial Times*. He's a highly intelligent, articulate and inde-pendent man – all qualities that many managers regard as some kind of a threat.

Truthfully, it's quite easy to imagine the former Ajax man (in itself another source of division) would not be straightforward to manage. Being a complex character, there were so many people and policies he wasn't keen on. He often appeared moody. All shades of Cantona, though Richard would resent the comparison. Echoes of Ruud Gullit too, with his understated laidback cool image. "Who gives a shit?" was his view on many minor football matters. Also, "There are more important things than football." Such as his family. Always first for him to the degree that he always resented overnight stays or foreign tours.

There were only a few highlights for Richard as the year 2000 approached. His comically elevated position in the bookings chart (which earned him a new sobriquet "Dick Van Clog"); a fine strike in an unexpected 2-0 win at play-off hopefuls Watford briefly (and falsely) raised everyone's hopes; and a rare headed goal in an otherwise awful 5-1 rout by Crewe. That rare bright spot had to last a long time as Richard suffered more than most during the torpor of Brian Little's reign. One win in 16 matches told its own story. Little was finally led away, but not before Albion's League status was again in danger. The team were horrible to watch, low on confidence and generally only playing one forward. As the end approached, the gallows humour surfaced: "we'll score before I die" was a popular refrain.

The turnstile entrance of the managers' office clicked again. Little was replaced by the relative unknown Gary Megson. The newcomer was a man in a hurry – having been turfed out of Stoke City by the incoming Icelandic consortium, recently ensconced at the Britannia Stadium – to get more from the players, get disillusioned supporters back on board and make the most of his opportunity at a club with potential. His handpicked cavalry arrived in the shape of five new players, including the inspirational return of SuperBob Taylor. Bob is to an extent, everybody's mate, but he is a particularly good friend of Richard's.

Seemingly, everybody was now pulling for the club in their hour of need. Results improved and 'King Dick' finally found the net at promotion-chasing Barnsley in April 2000, his first goal in 12 months. It was a penalty, Sneekes' first go from the spot, but the regular marksman was injured and he was a senior player who needed a goal... a week later he scored again from the same position, in an extraordinary 4-4 draw against his old club Bolton Wanderers. The great escape was now most definitely on.

Urged on by passionate supporters, the Albion side sweated through the last few games and did just enough to keep their fate in their own hands for the last match – home to Champions Charlton. Fortunately Athletic weren't overly concerned, particularly one Andy Hunt, who showed no inclination to inflict grief on his old team mates. Cometh the hour, cometh the man – Richard Sneekes tucked away the first goal, sweeping in a left wing centre. Taylor added a second and the job was done. At the time, the overwhelming feeling of relief felt like promotion, probably because Albion supporters had forgotten what promotion felt like.

FROM THAT POSITION, Albion moved forward, buoyed by six more signings and driven forward by their manager. This was a novelty, an exciting one and nobody wanted to rock the boat. But independent Richard was hinting subtlety, and then not so subtlety, that the emperor wore no clothes. These were brave suggestions at a time when Gary Megson walked on water. Few frankly wanted to hear that there was another side to the manager – a domineering bully, a Ferguson without the silverware, if you like. His observations were dismissed and Sneekes was derided as "lazy", "do him good" etc. But Richard was used to walking alone. Years would pass before other players dared to come out of the cupboard with similar grievances. Only then did understanding and appreciation of the issue widen, even if it is a truth still not accepted universally. Some supporters consider poor man-management as being of no great consequence.

It's entirely appropriate that Sneekes' most spectacular contribution to the season came against the manager's wishes. Albion were drawing 1-1 at Premier League Derby County in the first leg of the League Cup – a respectable situation given, at that time, the Baggies had been unable to beat a side from a higher Division for at least a decade. When Sneekes received the ball thirty yards from goal, he ignored his manager's bawled command to pass and instead found the net in spectacular fashion. Albion had a hugely enjoyable first leg win to savour while Richard later secured 'Goal of the Season' from supporters.

As Richard said later "I played a certain way to stay in the team and be part of a team that looked as if it might get promoted, which every player wants to be associated with. You can either turn against it like some of my colleagues did only to rot in the reserves or you get on with it." His manager demanded that all his midfielders had to play like he did in his playing days, ultra high tempo, endless tackling and running. So Richard ran... and ran and even tackled occasionally too – which always drew a half-ironic cheer. He kept his place in the team, in fact only three players made more starts that season.

But as Richard, the purveyor of the Beautiful Game, explained, "I wasn't looking forward to games. I wasn't playing how I was brought up. That year with Megson destroyed my love for football." Playing an unnatural game was only part of the problem, because after all he'd grafted immensely under Ray Harford. It was more carrying out the orders of a man he didn't respect, despised even. He was particularly critical that Megson bore a grudge for evermore, citing examples of players ten years down the line who were still suffering from negative references from Megson. His private opinion on his last Albion manager isn't printable. Gifted people in any walk of life have choices.

Richard didn't score many goals, but then again finding the net was not really his job. In the Megson team, the forwards scored the goals and the central midfield provided the graft and some inspiration. Albion did have a strong team spirit and guts. After so many years of limp passionless showings, this was great news indeed. Being a goal down or even two goals down was no longer "game over" as Crystal Palace discovered in February. They were 2-0 up very quickly, but found themselves under siege. It was the Dutchman who led the fight-back. The BBC's Adrian Goldberg described the goal, "His brilliant drive after 43 minutes brought Albion back into the match at 2-1. A free-kick 25 yards out was tapped short by Clement to Sneekes, who skipped past the lunging Ruddock (a very blunt razor) and his vicious shot skimmed all the way home." Albion drew 2-2, yet had created so many chances they could easily have taken all three points. Sneekes' strike was his 30th Albion goal. It was also his last.

Amid huge excitement, the Baggies made the play-offs with a game to spare. This was heady stuff indeed, that reached its zenith with a 2-0 lead over Bolton in the first leg. Sadly Wanderers took advantage of defensive nervousness to escape with a 2-2 draw, took the lead early in the second leg and there was no way back. To an extent, defeat almost didn't matter such was the pride in achieving something, anything and the last few pointless minutes were played out amid a cacophony of noise from the away end. The victorious Bolton fans were embarrassingly drowned out. Few realised that the weary Sneekes saluting the now all-standing, saluting Albion support was the last glimpse we'd have of him in an Albion shirt after 200 plus starts.

Sneekes was released on a free transfer in June 2001 amid a bitter exchange of words. "Everyone expected that I would be offered a new contract, but it just didn't happen. I was disappointed with that." Such was the rancour between manager and player that a parting of the ways had become inevitable. Had Albion finished mid-table or skipper McInnes been fit; Richard may have left even sooner. The manager's view was that Sneekes hadn't worked hard enough and hadn't followed his instructions.

SNEEKES TOOK the first local-ish offer that came along – from Stockport County. He'd had offers from clubs in other countries, but now had no wish to move his family. As he later admitted, "I made the wrong choice in going to Stockport. I was too impatient and made a bad decision." County had hung on grimly to their First Division place for so long through organisation and workrate. Now they were on the slippery slope from whence they came. It's hard to imagine a sharper contrast between Stockport's long ball game and Richard's free thinking subtlety and intelligence. "They're a Conference side," he told friends later.

Albion visited Stockport in October. Curious how this largely routine away win had so much significance for so many people – Gary Megson and Derek McInnes (return to former club), SuperBob Taylor (first goals of the season), Darren Moore (gained a new nickname) and Jason Van Blerk (another recent ex-Albion recruit from the Cheshire side).

Bottom placed County could do no more than hump long balls from defence, a fatal tactic against a side as big and strong defensively as Albion. The Dutchman ran around helplessly in the middle, harassed by Derek McInnes, craving the ball, but seeing none of it. His name was chanted repeatedly by the Albion support mostly filling two sides of the ground. Mercifully, Sneekes was substituted midway through the second half with County two down. The visiting contingent once again chanted his name and demanded "Sneekes, Sneekes, give us a wave" (a huge and rare honour for an opposition player). Richard obliged with a wave and a rueful grin. In the opposite dugout, Megson wore his 'death stare' expression.

Sneekes got out of Stockport quickly and tried Fourth Division Hull City. This suited him more, but decided to leave when a new manager insisted he move to the area. He then played briefly in Denmark, commuting each weekend, but his heart was no longer in it. These days, he co-owns the well-known classic Italian restaurant Angelos in Sutton, while building up his property portfolio of 20 plus houses, mainly in Bolton. Richard regularly turns out in charity matches and annually stars in the Midland Masters tournament, a format for which his skills are ideally suited. Nowadays, he's mellowed somewhat and is far more comfortable without the restrictions of a footballer's life.

Post-Megson ("When I heard Megson had gone, I drank champagne for three days solid, then went onto beer!"), he's felt able to return to the Hawthorns, but appropriately purely as one of us – a supporter.

DARREN MOORE

'BIG DAVE'

2001-2006

BAGGIES CAREER

Games	116
Goals	6
Caps	4

MAGIC MOMENT

Scoring the first goal in the win against Crystal Palace to secure promotion to the Premier League. Many Baggies fans never thought we'd see the day

THE extended training period for professions such as medicine and the law is both accepted and respected. It's necessary and essential. Yet, little consideration or appreciation is accorded to the lengthy apprenticeship undergone by would-be professional footballers. Nowadays, this starts at eight years old. It's sport, its fun; it's not meant to be taken seriously. All correct, of course, but lurking beneath the surface is the need to learn, to progress, and to catch the coach's eye. As the lad grows, so too must his commitment.

There will be more training, more learning, more sacrifices and more games. Teenage footballers have social and school activities limited and cannot enjoy the monetary benefits of weekend shop work. For those still hanging on grimly to the programme at 16, there's more pressure. Always, individuals must be better, quicker and fitter than their team-mates. The attrition rate is quite horrendous. A few, a tiny few, are destined for the very top. The rest have to slog on in the hope of a lucky break, catching someone's eye or notebook. This after what is arguably an eight-to-ten year learning programme, longer than that of a nurse, an engineer...

Darren Moore was in the "slog" category. He'd always wanted to be a footballer. Nothing else would do. Yet at the ridiculously early age of 16, the Handsworth-born teenager was already in the last chance career saloon having been released by Walsall. He was reduced to being panned by lower division prospectors seeking out something bright and shiny among the left-overs.

Torquay United were furiously prospecting in Birmingham in the summer of 1990, offering trials to anyone looking remotely likely. Young Darren already stood out as a big lad and being big at Torquay's level is literally half the battle. After a week's trial, the Gulls offered him an apprenticeship and the teenager took the opportunity, though with some reluctance. Leaving behind his close family at just 16 was tough for him.

Torquay programme contributor Jon Aroussi takes up the story. "I got an early insight into Darren as I was a regular at Torquay's reserve games in the early nineties. He was a raw (and very hefty!) talent then, but you could see he would go far – he was the clichéd defensive rock, and scared forwards with his bulk. So it was quite a surprise to discover what a gentle soul he was off the pitch.

You get used to seeing Gulls players around the pubs and clubs, but I only once saw Darren out on the town. Otherwise, I used to live just around the corner from his future wife Angie in Paignton, and would often see them very traditionally 'courting', walking in the nearby gardens and the like. Never saw Lee Sharpe doing that! There's no denying Darren was a very popular player at Torquay. He looked a bit iffy in his early first team appearances, but I think the fans warmed to him so much (as they usually do) because he was such a trier.

Once, when we were attacking the family stand, Bruno (as he was inevitably nicknamed) went up for a corner and met the cross perfectly. From the edge of the area, he headed the ball right over the family stand and towards Ellacombe Baths. To this day, I can count on the fingers of one hand the other players who have managed to head the ball out of the ground.

One of Moore's most notable days was being sent off in the Play-offs. Torquay were at Preston on 18 May 1994 with a two-goal lead to defend. The second leg score was 1-1 and Wembley was in sight... but then the sending off of Bruno changed the game completely. Torquay's ten men eventually lost 4-1 after extra time. Bruno was on the ground, being held down by North End's Raynor, who had hold of his shirt and, in an effort to free himself, he put downward pressure on Raynor's forearm... you could hardly call it a punch. However, Raynor immediately threw his hands up to his face and rolled around dramatically. The 17,000 strong PNE crowd bayed for Bruno to be sent off and the official duly obliged.

Darren was also known for attempting the odd 'sprint' down the wing, most of which usually ended somewhere past the halfway line. I remember one particular end to end run which saw Bruno puffing like a steam train, thighs wobbling, ground shaking (possibly), evading tackle after tackle. Naturally, he got to the edge of the box and scuffed his shot miles wide, but he got a massive ovation and cheers."

Exactly the stuff that over 120 years of Baggies heroes have been made of.

AFTER JUST OVER 100 games for Torquay, Doncaster made an offer for the 19 year-old. Rovers were in a higher Division, so this was a step up and the fee of £62,500 became a new club record for Rovers. Darren or 'Bruno', as he was still called, was as popular at Belle Vue as he was in Devon and was chosen as Supporters Club Player of the Year in each of the next two years.

In the summer of 1997, First Division Bradford City made an approach. Rovers asked for £750,000 for his signature, over ten times the fee they'd paid Torquay. Manager Kerry Dixon defended the club position. "Some people might think that figure is a little over the top for a Division Three player, but it is how highly we rate Darren. He is only a young man and we consider him to be the best centre-half in the lower divisions. He is unbeatable in the air and he is very quick for such a big man. I am sorry to see Darren go." The final fee was £90,000.

The big defender was keen to properly say goodbye. "I am sorry to be leaving Doncaster because I have been happy here... I always gave 100 per cent for Doncaster Rovers every time I went out and I think that the fans respected me for that... Hopefully, the money the club will get for me will help it to survive."

At City, Darren quickly found a travelling companion in defender Wayne Jacobs. They both lived in Rotherham. Wayne was a born-again Christian, a source of great fascination for Darren, who'd been brought up in a strongly Christian family, but decided that faith and football weren't compatible. He'd put football first, "I didn't think I could serve God and football at the same time," but always a nagging doubt remained. Jacobs brought the issue to the fore. Darren accompanied Wayne when he addressed Christians in Sport meetings and felt both inspired and uplifted.

Within twelve months of his arrival, Bradford City had a serious go at promotion to the Premier League. That season, WBA were just Play-off hopefuls, reliant on Lee Hughes' goals. They needed points from a February visit to Valley Parade, but never looked like getting any because Hughes was completely marked out of the game by one Darren Moore. In desperation, Hughes resorted to some pretty feeble diving. It was the first time that Albion supporters became aware of the existence of the huge defender, and his efforts earned some grudging respect, mainly along the lines of "look at the size of him!"

On the last day of the season, Bradford City had to win at Molineux for promotion, whereas the home side had to win to get into the play-offs. Thus it was at Prenton Park, that a huge away following gave up backing Albion's feeble, lifeless efforts and listened excitedly as City recorded a 3-2 victory.

Darren had his dream shot at the Premiership, but the dream didn't last long. He thought he was worth almost double the weekly wage City were offering him, but Bradford Chairman Geoffrey Richmond disagreed strongly. The player made just three appearances from the first team bench, as the defender explained. "I trained with the first team, but I was told I wouldn't be considered. It meant I was training all week, but there was nothing at the end of it."

BUT SOMETHING ELSE was happening in Moore's life, something more significant than mere football. "That autumn, Wayne was facing a potentially career-ending injury, but I witnessed him making a remarkable recovery after attending a prayer meeting. Wayne went along to a church where people prayed and prayed for him, and, that night, he felt things begin to happen in his knee. Within three or four weeks he was back playing again." Darren knew what he must do next. "I invited Him into my life to be my Lord and Saviour"

When the chance to move to Portsmouth for £550,000 on a four year deal came up in November, the Yorkshire side, fearful of a free transfer at the end of the season, were eager to take the money. Darren didn't share this sense of certainty. He didn't know anybody in Hampshire. He prayed for guidance and his faith led him to the South Coast. Darren and his wife Angie joined a Baptist church in Portsmouth and quickly found themselves amongst friends.

Comically, a month after the big stopper had departed; City posted their annual Christmas card, featuring a team photograph from the start of the season. Somebody else's head was 'photoshopped' onto Darren's body. They might have got away with it, had it been another black player. A year later, Bradford were offering players twice as much money as Darren was seeking.

The big defender's indecision about moving to Portsmouth was inconsequential compared to his moving to Albion 66 games later. This was a drama, a long-winded, confusing and tedious soap opera with claims and counter claims. As Baggie people saw it, Darren had an opportunity to move out of Pompey's reserves to Albion's up-and-coming first team and return home to boot. Naturally, fans assumed money was at the root of the impasse. It was only much later that it slowly dawned that Darren's reasons were not financial, it was far more about leaving his chum Linvoy Primus and his Faith and Football charity project work in which he was heavily involved.

The transfer saga began shortly after pre-season training started and wasn't finalised until several weeks into the season. Most managers would have moved on by then. But Megson wanted Moore and nobody else would do. It was only later that Albion supporters understood just why this man mountain was worth waiting for. Throughout the Great Wait for his services, the man at the centre was unfazed. He knew exactly what was to happen and when, as Darren explained to the Faith and Football website. "One night a still voice told me that I would move to West Brom, but that there were still things which needed to be done at Portsmouth before it would be completed." Things that needed to be done included supporting his chum Linvoy Primus through the process of becoming a Christian. Unfortunately, none of these secular needs were communicated through the press.

Darren finally put pen to paper in mid-September with Pompey receiving £750,000 in exchange. Then fanzine editor Glynis Wright, who happened to be inside the club offices the following day after an interview, was the first fan to meet the new signing. "When I clapped eyes on him, I thought it was an eclipse walking down the stairs, such is the sheer size and bulk of the bloke." With no-one at the club apparently looking after the new boy, it was beholden on Glynis to direct Darren to the Players' Lounge.

The Moores bought a new house in Solihull, sensibly situated next to an Albion supporter. At first glance, it was all too easy to do a double take as Angie was as short and small as her husband is tall and wide. Albion supporters seem to like their players large. A modicum of skill to go with their build will give them a decent chance of becoming a crowd favourite. Other than the obvious successes like The King, Cyrille and The Tank, Garry Thompson was a mightily big lad, who earned admiration for his suicidal approach to the game. Brian 'the Beast' Jensen was another and so too John 'Yorky' Kaye.

Megson, too, liked big men, introducing Sean Gregan and Geoff Horsfield, both of whom were well liked. But if they're big and can't play, then there's no hiding place is there, 'Rambo' George Reilly? Not many had a good word for Kevin Campbell. Few appeared larger than Big Dave at six foot two and fifteen stone. His talents dovetailed perfectly with the job that Gary Megson had in mind – a bloody big stopper that nobody was going to get past.

Moore made his debut at Watford, an ideal substitute as Albion were hanging onto a slender lead with only ten men. A seriously big defender was just what the wagon-circled Baggies back-line needed. The large away following cheered him on enthusiastically, while it was all too easy to imagine the Watford players muttering, "Oh shit, look at the size of him." The Baggies managed to hold onto their 2-1 score. It felt like a key result, a big victory against the odds, not least because of Russell Hoult's penalty save in injury time. Previously stuttering West Bromwich now had an away win to their name. Moore's first start was at home to Burnley in a trademark Albion 1-0 victory and he quickly became a regular. His height and power added so much to the Megson workrate and effort ethos. As skipper Derek McInnes put it, "You look at Darren and you feel like it's going to take something to get past him."

AS ALL ALBION supporters know, Darren Moore's nickname stems from a character in a Pot Noodle advert. Not for us the obvious 'Mooro' from the players or 'Bruno' from all his previous clubs. The new name just popped up spontaneously during an evening match at Stockport County. There are at least two supporters claiming to be the originator, so diplomacy dictates credit to both Fab Tracanna of Wednesbury and Mark Dixon from the London Branch for their inspiration. Here's Mark's version "It dawned on me that the increasingly impressive monster at the heart of our defence looked like the big-haired invisible friend from the Pot Noodle advert. I relayed this information to the lads around me and they agreed the surprising similarity. Thereafter, every full-blooded defensive header was cheered with a 'Go on, Big Dave' and other similar shouts. It generated much mirth around us and soon after, the chant of 'Big Dave, there's only Big Dave' seemed to spread into general usage at all the subsequent matches."

Darren was comfortable with his new monicker, fortunately, as within a matter of months, 'Big Dave' was his proper name as far as supporters were concerned. Children would regularly ask "Dave, can I have your autograph?" and all too many adults would also forget when encountering the big man. "I like to think I'm approachable off the field, that I give time to help people when I can, and that takes strength. The 'Big Dave' shouts are great. It's nice to hear all that." The ever-increasing volume of Pot Noodle always in and around his dressing room locker didn't perturb him as his team-mates exercised the usual standard of players' humour. When he heard about a group of Big Dave impersonators attending games, Darren was eager to get a picture of them. When the club fanzine tracked one down for him, Big Dave made sure it was pinned to the players' notice board.

Even though he'd only been at the club a few months and was unlikely to have ever met any of the family, Darren attended Jeff Astle's funeral, along with Captain Derek McInnes and management Gary Megson and Frank Burrows. His thoughts were so typical of the man. "It was a real honour to be there and it was important for us all to do the right thing for him in his memory."

Ian Thomson is an author and an Albion supporter of some vintage. "Other than Matt Elliott, I haven't seen a First Division centre-half snuff out West Brom's attacking threat with such consummate command. He has this ability, scarcely attributable to Albion defenders of recent times, to position himself correctly for dealing with crosses and dispatching them upfield with some power. Curiously, he seems to struggle with what you would imagine is the easier skill of positioning himself on the end of goalkeeper's punts."

Moore's first goal came in November 2001. Not from a set piece as you might imagine, but an unlikely shot from 40 yards. The goal came too late to salvage a point in an irritating 2-1 defeat by Rotherham United. No-one was more irritated than Big Dave, who thought he was the victim of a racist slur that afternoon. He made a complaint. Rotherham duly investigated and discovered a simple misunderstanding. Exhortations from the crowd of "Come on, Monkey" were not aimed at Big Dave, rather they were words of encouragement for the Millers' wide player Andy Monkhouse.

A month later and the Baggies had some business to sort out at Molineux. Just like the previous season, Albion were competing for the play-offs. Yet their comparative success was being eclipsed by a Wolverhampton mob confident of automatic promotion. That lunchtime, numerous Black Country folks of (normally) sober habit and demeanour screamed like madmen and whirled like Dervishes on acid.

WBA got their noses in front thanks to a Jordao goal and would not give it up. Tempers flared and players piled into a scrimmage. Shaun Newton was late for the party. He charged into the fray, straight into Big Dave and rebounded like a table-tennis ball. After that, he kept his distance. Wolves were trying to mix it, but mix it with a Megson team? They've never been very bright.

Of course, Sheffield United were the ultimate mixers in the infamous 'Battle of Bramall Lane'. The Blades' three dismissals are too fresh in the memory to need repeating. Other incidents, such as the racial abuse of one of Albion's substitutes, the Sheffield player who just ran off the field never to return and attempts by Santos to enter the away dressing room to have another go at Andy Johnson, received less coverage. One of the counter accusations thrown by United supporters to lessen their guilt was that Big Dave punched a Sheffield player in one of the rucks. Frankly, it's impossible to imagine Darren hitting anybody. Ever. The Baggies accepted the belated awarding of the three points for 83 minutes of work and tried to put everything else behind them.

After Sheffield, just seven games remained. Manchester City were certain Champions, but just behind them Wolves were wobbling. To have any hope of overhauling them, Albion needed nearly all of those 21 remaining points. They grabbed 19 and it would have been 21 had the referee joined the rest of the world in seeing the infamous shot over the line against Rotherham.

It's hard several years on to fully do justice to how desperately, gut-wrenchingly tense those remaining games really were. Only three goals were conceded as Big Dave & Co formed an impenetrable barrier in front of Russell Hoult's deckchair (Hoult kept a clean sheet in 27 League and Cup games). But scoring themselves was hard without key forward Jason Roberts. Old warhorse Bob Taylor's ability to be in the right place at the right time proved crucial.

The Baggies' 93rd minute penalty at Bradford in the 45th game, put away by a hitherto unknown spot-kick specialist, is one classic tale for the grandchildren. Wolves were so nearly back in pole position with one game left, claws outstretched for the prize… and then Igor Balis snatched it back. The celebration was primeval.

The final game at home to Palace was a moist-eyed one. I never ever thought I'd see the day that the Baggies would re-join the top Division of the English League. Did Frank Skinner really only have thoughts for England with his famous line "thirty years of hurt?" And our man mountain was there at the right place at the right time at both ends of the field. Big Dave's first half close-in effort killed the growing tension dead. The Baggies were 1-0 up and everyone knew what that meant.

Wolves' pre-match grasping at straw contention that Palace striker Morrison would score a hat-trick, merely demonstrated that their nerve (or another part of their anatomy), had gone. Morrison, barracked throughout, barely had a kick. Perhaps, just perhaps, Big Dave had a word in his ear. SuperBob Taylor (who else?) added Albion's second. Job done, it was party time. I doubt being an Albion supporter will ever feel so good again.

BIG DAVE had no time to rest that summer. His charity, Faith in Football, aims to break down myths about Christianity and help underprivileged children through football. He and Linvoy Primus, together with others, spent nine days in India in May, running football workshops and visiting churches and orphanages during the rest of the day. "It hits you in the face wherever you go, the poverty is frightening, and yet the people out there are so warm, so welcoming, so generous with their time and with what little they have. It's very humbling, and it was one of the best things I've ever done in my life." Though he's understandably reticent on the subject, stories abound that Darren donated his entire promotion bonus to the charity.

Just what constitutes a Cult Hero is an ever-evolving concept over the decades. Around the birth of our football club, they were invariably local lads who made good. Later, a goal-scoring centre-forward was always likely to be favourite. That the players lived in and were part of the community was taken as the norm, remaining true into the sixties and slightly beyond. In the days of the King and the Bomber, supporters knew their team would regularly visit the Throstles Club en bloc and be genuinely pleased to do so, smoking, drinking, playing snooker, darts etc with fans were perfectly normal activities. To see Mrs Astle or Mrs Bomber in the queue in the butcher's shop was routine. The local press were considered part of the Albion family, where the Baggies went so did they and if the players ended up having too many drinks so did Ray Matts etc.

In the modern era supporters and players rarely, if ever, meet. So a modern equivalent of cult status is largely defined by hand signals and body language. An upraised thumb, acknowledgement of the support or just looking committed is normally as good as it gets at the top level. Big Dave's charity and church work was possibly the last exception remaining to the current 'no fraternisation' rule, though even here, anecdotal evidence strongly indicates club officials 'had a word' to limit his interaction with outsiders.

The Baggies' first attempt at running up the Premier League mountain ultimately flopped. Everything conspired against them – a change of Chairman, the introduction of a transfer window and a quite awful run of opening fixtures against all the best clubs.

The season opened proudly at the Theatre of Slumbers in Manchester. That day, Albion supporters gave their side terrific support and the team responded. There were some reasonable chances created before United won the day with a late goal. But for the supporters and Darren, just being there would do for a start. "When I went out at Manchester United on the opening day, it brought a dream that I've had since I was eight or nine to reality."

And yet after six games, Albion had three wins to their name (one of them thanks to a rare Big Dave goal against Fulham,, which the man himself revealed was one of the highlights of his Albion career) and looked confident. When myopic referees were added to the burden, the tipping point was reached and the club sunk. After 38 matches, the total of victories had only risen to a miserable six. The seemingly endless succession of defeats took its toll on every-body, even though supporters made a stupendous effort to back the team. That their efforts met with so little response on the field or off it, was least a contributory factor in the silence of the Hawthorns ever since.

The swift forwards of the top Division regularly showed up Moore's lack of pace yet his popularity remained undiminished. To his credit, another headed goal from the centre-half at Maine Road was important in a morale-boosting, but ultimately futile, 2-1 win in February. In addition, his presence was very handy against the bigger strikers, notably Everton's Ferguson.

On the debit side, his short backpass was directly responsible for Russell Hoult bringing down Michael Owen at Anfield. Hoult was sent off and another defeat was imminent. At Goodison Park, Wayne Rooney teased him by standing off the big defender with the ball and inviting him to come and get it. The subsequent backlash says much about the changing nature of the game. His peers deemed Young Wayne's party trick 'unprofessional". Whither now Willie Johnston at his best?

Big Dave's season finished two months early with a cruciate knee problem. Even though the League position was hopeless, his reassuringly large presence and charisma was instantly missed. Missed for nine months in total before a joyful roar greeted his late appearance from the bench in Albion's 3-0 win at the City Ground, Nottingham in November 2003. Most foot-ballers would be depressed by such a lengthy absence. Not so Big Dave. "I believe that such experiences mould you as a person, and I turned this one into a positive. We are taught to count such a test and trial as a joy and my time in physiotherapy was a joyous period."

Once relegated, Megson set out to secure a second straight promotion, using exactly the same tactics as before. Spend big money on big physical players and squeeze the life out of the opposition. The tactics worked again, but with a different response from many supporters. The first time around, being at the right end of the table was such a novel concept that any method of securing victory was considered fair game. But the second time, with better players and far greater resources than nearly all of the real Second Division, enthusiasm for grinding out 1-0 results was far less.

Home matches were horribly familiar. An hour of sterility before bringing on young Lloyd Dyer to use his pace to set up the winning goal. Promotion was curiously inevitable. Every time Albion wobbled, so did their promotion chasing opponents. Of course, there were some high-lights such as a return visit to Bramall Lane. In a predictably bone-shuddering encounter, the

Baggies pinched a 2-1 victory, with Big Dave managing to score at both ends. Albions' crucial equaliser came from a corner. As Neil Clement lined up in his appointed attacking position, Darren told him "to get out of the way" and took his place. Seconds later, Big Dave's head was making Mr Warnock very cross indeed.

Those who had doubts about the inevitability of promotion were silenced in a genuinely thrilling 3-2 win at Ipswich, the first win at Portman Road since 1984. A Sunday evening victory at Sunderland, the last opposition still standing, effectively wrapped promotion up with four games remaining. Albion defended with 11 men for the full game and pinched a 1-0 win in the last minute. Satisfying, but faintly embarrassing at the same time. Once safely over the line, the players basically gave up, losing the last three matches and further flattening the mood of celebration.

In an attempt to stay in the Premier League the second time around, new players were brought in, including several expensive defenders. Big Dave was out of the picture as new boys like Purse and Albrechtsen were preferred. Big Dave was completely unabashed at being overlooked and kept his belief in himself and the team as Glynis Wright discovered. "Let me pass on a helpful hint; when talking to our ginormous defender, never, never let it slip that you lack faith in the ability of the lads to come up trumps, because if you do, you'll get not a bunch of fives, but a five or ten-minute lecture on the power of positive thought! And that's what I got in heaps and Darren being the charismatic guy that he is, I came away thinking we could conquer the Universe tomorrow, never mind bloody Man City the following day! If that's a small sample of his preaching style, I reckon the greater part of the population in these parts will be converted unto the ways of righteousness by the time Mr. Moore hangs up his boots."

After eight games without a win, Big Dave got his chance against Bolton. He was an ideal choice to deal with the Wanderers' muscle men and the Baggies finally got their first win. But it was too little, too late for the manager. His Premier League players rebelled against his abrasive manner and the dismal 3-0 defeat at Crystal Palace a fortnight later was Megson's last in charge. Big Dave kept his place for a few games under new manager Bryan Robson, but the former England international needed more than Darren could give and he was out of the first team once more. Full-back Neil Clement was converted to centre-half and performed so effectively that Big Dave's days as a Premier League player were numbered.

He played little direct part in the tense later stages of the so-called 'Great Escape', other than a superb display as a fifth defender as the Baggies tried and failed to extract a point from a weakened Arsenal. Otherwise, Big Dave did his best to encourage from the bench or the sidelines as the Baggies famously became the first, and so far only, club who were bottom at Christmas to retain their Premier League place.

BIG DAVE had his own challenge – a five day sponsored walk of the Great Wall of China for his charity. This was no tourist stroll. The group of walkers were tackling uncultivated parts of the wall as the man himself explained "I think we covered something like 80,000 steps up on the Wall according to the guys who had pedometers – I didn't need to go into pre-season after that! In the five days we covered about 50 miles, which doesn't sound that much, but when you think about the terrain, the fact that about 80% of it was uphill, that was pretty fierce. The walk raised at least £50,000 to support orphanages in India."

Why did he go? Because he cared. "We want people to understand our vision of what we're trying to do and to buy into it. I've been very lucky in my life and it's important to me that I can help out people less fortunate than me, to give them a head start, or shed some light on their lives."

Darren's Albion days ended abruptly and painfully at Wigan early in 2006 where a pair of challenges, the first possibly excusable, the second definitely not, forced the referee to send him off. Poor Big Dave. He was so keen to make the most of a rare first team appearance, but his crude lunge at Jason Roberts took some swallowing. Running off the pitch prematurely amid a chorus of angry cries from the frustrated away support was a rotten curtain call. That Darren couldn't handle the pace of the Premiership had become more and more evident; witness him being at fault for all three Newcastle goals earlier in the season. Even the recent tradition of immediately bringing him on as soon as Everton introduced Ferguson was ended. Curtis Davies, or 'Small Dave' as he was briefly known, was deemed able to keep a grip on the Scottish striker.

It was clear that, barring emergencies, Big Dave wasn't going to be playing any more for the first team. He was still under contract for a further 18 months and no-one resented his continued inspiring presence around the Hawthorns. Indeed, the club's media department would wheel him out every time they had a difficult message to sell. But Darren just wanted to play and honourably accepted a bid from Derby for his services in the January 2006 transfer window, just days after Wigan. Ironically, just a few weeks later, Albion had a defensive emergency at Fulham and without the big defender, felt obliged to field another, clearly unfit centre-back. Albion were hammered 6-1.

Manager Bryan Robson commented, "he's been a great servant to West Brom and we wish him all the best." Though truthful enough, his words didn't seem to quite do justice to the man, though, of course, Robson hadn't been around for the promotion seasons. Thankfully, the man with the money, Chief Executive Jeremy Peace had a fuller picture. "Darren has been a tremendous ambassador for the club both on and off the pitch since he joined us four years ago. He has been unstinting in his support of the club in its dealings with the local community and on that front he leaves a big hole to fill."

One regular fan, known universally as Des Baggie (nicknames are commonplace around the Hawthorns), had his own personal recollection. "My best memory of Big Dave was at the famous 'it was in the 93rd minute' Bradford game. Hundreds of otherwise ticket-less Baggies bought corporate tickets in desperation. Such were their numbers, they swamped the posh seats and someone was even bold enough to take a flag. Naturally, they had to travel to the game in suits and ties, but there was compensation in the form of access to the club lounge after the game. The atmosphere resembled a drug high without any drugs after the last minute penalty winner. Big Dave was the only player to come into the lounge and meet the supporters to a roar of 'Big Dave. There's only one Big Dave.' He stayed and signed autographs for everyone that wanted one, standing head and shoulders above all the Baggie supporters. I'm looking at his autograph on my Bradford programme and feeling very sad that he has left us. He was a giant amongst so many pygmies at the Albion and if only our hierarchy had a fraction of the honesty and passion for the club that he did we would be in so much better shape."

His departure was immediate, as the Rams' needs were great. There wasn't much time to say goodbye to his playing colleagues, never mind supporters. Just like Bob Taylor, that wasn't sufficient. Big Dave cheered everyone up during the interval of a moribund home defeat by Middlesbrough by the simple act of stepping onto the pitch.

Boldly, he took the microphone. "I'd like to thank everyone for their support. The amount of letters and emails I have received from fans since I left has been truly tremendous. That's why I wanted to come back and say my farewells properly." The chorus of 'Big Dave, there's only one Big Dave' was predictable, its volume and scale with all four sides of the ground joining in was not. It was also noticeable how warmly all the bending and stretching Albion substitutes greeted their former team-mate. He had a word for all of them individually.

And then Albion's last footballer with a heart and a real understanding of supporters was gone. For now.

Bibliography

It might be quicker to list where my fellow researchers or I haven't looked! All of the following corroborated facts, produced new lines of pursuit and/or useful quotes

Albion News
The Athlete
The Baggies
Birmingham Post
Birmingham Mail
Birmingham Gazette
Daily Express
Daily Mail
The Express and Star
Fingerpost fanzine
Grorty Dick fanzine
Sporting Mail
The Sports Argus
West Bromwich Chronicle/Midland Chronicle
West Bromwich Free Press
The private archives of Terry Wills, Norman Bartlam and the Bache family
Glynis's Diary on *www.baggies.com* and earlier *www.wbaunofficial.com*

The Who's Who of West Bromwich Albion
Tony Matthews

The Essential History of West Bromwich Albion
Gavin Mcowan

King of the Hawthorns – Jeff Astle story
John Homer, Glen Wilmore

Striker
Jeff Astle

The History of the Birmingham Senior Cup – 1876-1905
Steve Carr

Official History of WBA
W. Ellery Jephcott

It's Goals That Count
Ronnie Allen

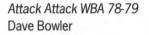

Attack Attack WBA 78-79
Dave Bowler

Samba at the Smethwick End
Dave Bowler and Jas Bains

SuperBob – the Bob Taylor Story
John Homer, Glen Willmore

On the Wing
Willie Johnston

Bomber Brown – the Tony Brown Story
John Homer, Glen Willmore

West Bromwich Albion – One Hundred Great Matches
Glen Willmore

West Bromwich Albion: Soccer in the Black Country, 1879 to 1965
Peter Morris

Dreaming of the Greed League
Glynis Wright

Brum's the Word
Malcolm Boyden

My father and other working class heroes
Gary Imlach

Gas Masks and Goalposts
Anton Rippon

West Bromwich Albion Football Book
Ray Matts

Bob Wilson: My Autobiography
Bob Wilson

What Price the Treble?
Chris Hartle

Subscribers

Rob Aldridge	Cyrille Regis	Steve Long	Bobby Hope
Bob Amey	Bobby Hope	Robert Loughran	Joe Kennedy
Ray Andrews	Ronnie Allen	Winston Lunn	Tony Brown
Dave & Peter Baxendale	Willie Johnston	Helen Moore	Tony Brown
Michelle Bennett	Bob Taylor	Jan Moore	Bob Taylor
Mervyn Bishop	Ronnie Allen	Stephen Murray	John Osbourne
Steven Bishop	Willie Johnston	David Neale	
Stian Bøe	Bob Taylor	Phil Peacock	Willie Johnston
Clive Blake	Derek Kevan	Brian Pearce	Willie Johnston
Dennis Brennan	Ronnie Allen	Jon Peters	Tony Brown
P Brinton	Clive Clark	Mark Pumphrey	Willie Johnston
Mick Bryan	Willie Johnston	Andrew Roberts	Tony Brown
Martyn Butt	Bob Taylor	Mike Rotchell	Ronnie Allen
Roger Cassingham	Willie Johnston	Jonathan Clive Round	Len Millard
Ian Cole	Jeff Astle	Julian Rowe	Willie Johnston
Paul Collins	Derek Kevan	John Grant Rowley	Bob Taylor
Nigel Colmer	Cyrille Regis	Colin Simpson	Ronnie Allen
Mrs V Compton	Jeff Astle	Reg Stephens	Tony Brown
Jim Curry	Bobby Hope	Ian Stroud	Bob Taylor
Tony Darby	Tony Brown	Paul Sutton	Derek Kevan
Rosemarie Davids	Ronnie Allen	David Taylor	Willie Johnston
Jonathan & Verity Eden	Darren Moore	Jeff Taylor	Jeff Astle
Steve Finn	Bob Taylor	M Tully	Richard Sneekes
Mr A Fisher	Ray Barlow	Fred Usher	Derek Kevan
Chris Flanagan	Derek Kevan	David Valder	John Osborne
Mrs Foster	Tony Brown	Matthew Walker	Don Goodman
D Fryer	Bob Taylor	Dean Walton	Jeff Astle
Peter George	Ray Barlow	Malcolm Warrilow	Bob Taylor
John Goddard	Willie Johnston	Nick Westcott	Clive Clark
Mike Griffin	Derek Kevan	Jenny & Peter White	Cyrille Regis
Dave Halfpenny	Bobby Hope	Sean Whitlock	Derek Kevan
Barry Hammerton	Bob Taylor	JW Derek Wilkes	Len Millard
Moyra Hampson	Ronnie Allen	Graham Willetts	Cyrille Regis
Simon Handy	Cyrille Regis	Tony Wilson	Bobby Hope
David Heal	Chuck Drury	Paul Woolgar	Jeff Astle
Andy & Callum Heselgrove	Bob Taylor	Karen Wright	Jeff Astle
Malcolm Hicks	Bobby Hope		
James Hickson	Bob Taylor		
Lise Holmes	Bob Taylor		
John Honick	Tony Brown		
Stephen Horne	Willie Johnston		
Ian Hoult	Bob Taylor		
Dave Howard	Derek Kevan		
David Howe	Cyrille Regis		
AG Howells	Tony Brown		
Bryn Johnson	Zoltan Gera		
David Johnson	Tony Brown		
David Jones	Gary Strodder		
V Jones	Willie Johnston		
Tim Joyner	Willie Johnston		
Gordon Kendrick	Bobby Robson		
Stuart King	Willie Johnston		
Derek Lewis	Jeff Astle		

Top Eight Voted For Players

Willie Johnston	15
Bob Taylor	15
Tony Brown	10
Derek Kevan	8
Ronnie Allen	7
Jeff Astle	7
Bobby Hope	6
Cyrille Regis	6